Radicalism & Reform

Published for the
Organization of
American Historians

Ross E. Paulson

Radicalism & Reform

The Vrooman Family and American
Social Thought, 1837–1937

UNIVERSITY OF KENTUCKY PRESS · 1968

Preface

The story of this book begins at Harvard University in the spring of 1958 in Professor Frank Freidel's graduate seminar in American history. With Professor Freidel's encouragement I began to examine the activities of the Vrooman brothers from 1893 to 1903. I had first noticed a reference to them in Benjamin Orange Flower's book on the reformers and radicals of the 1890's. A preliminary bibliographical survey indicated a rich field of material in their writings. My original intention was to study the reform techniques favored by the brothers to isolate "preprogressive" influences in their activities. My preliminary investigation uncovered so many intriguing questions, riddles, and problems that I could scarcely contain the Vrooman story within the original outline. It soon became apparent that there was something more than a question of techniques and influences involved in the family's story. The whole history of the reform movement from the Civil War to the New Deal was enacted in miniature within the family's experience, the abstract positions of various philosophies were represented by brothers arguing within a common tradition, and the whole cycle of change and accommodation was encompassed within the bounds of their activities. The Vrooman brothers and the American reform tradition became, therefore, the subject of my doctoral dissertation.

While I was a Research Fellow at Yale University Divinity School in 1964-1965 I was intrigued by the similarities between events in the Vrooman story and certain contemporary events: the social action theology of the seminarians, the "free university" movement among the undergraduates, the academic freedom controversies surrounding the dismissal of a popular professor, the coalition attempts among the young socialists of the May 2nd movement, the urban renewal efforts of Mayor Richard Lee's administration, the institutionalization of equality of opportunity in the Office of Economic Opportunity, the reform versus reaction rhetoric of the 1964 presidential election. After discussing the matter with Professor Freidel, I decided to take another look at the Vrooman story from a broader perspective.

Teaching and researching the field of American intellectual history provided the key that unlocked the mystery of the Vrooman family's place in American history. I now saw that I had utilized too narrow an approach methodologically, that two traditions— reform *and* radical—were intertwined in the Vrooman story, and that techniques of agitation are secondary to ultimate goals. In short, in shifting from a pragmatic to a general semantic approach to methodology, I began to see more clearly the role of ideas in shaping the behavior of the Vroomans.

During my preliminary investigations I read with interest Dr. Harlan B. Phillips' remarkable study of Walter Vrooman. The events discussed by Phillips took on a new meaning and relevance when seen in the context of the Vrooman brothers' common endeavors. In the present study, I have attempted to show the meaning of Walter's activities within the family and within the reform and radical movements in America. In particular, I have indicated what he borrowed from his brothers, what they borrowed from him, and how his erratic tactics affected his brothers' efforts. In general, I concur with Phillips' analysis of Walter's personality, but I demur on his estimate of Walter's influence on Charles A. Beard and on his general estimate of Walter's significance in American history. In brief, Phillips sees him as a "restless child of progress" whose passionate activities can be considered constructive "only in the sense of adding to the atmosphere of concern."[1] My own conclusions are given in the following study.

Some of my obligations to other scholars, librarians, and friends for encouragement, assistance, and hospitality in preparing the Vrooman story were acknowledged in detail in my dissertation and are too numerous to be repeated here. However, I cannot allow the following work to appear without recording the continuing interest and help of the following individuals. Mr. and Mrs. Carl S. Vrooman of Bloomington, Illinois, opened not only their papers and

---

[1] Harlan Buddington Phillips, "Walter Vrooman: Restless Child of Progress" (unpublished Ph.D. dissertation, Dept. of History, Columbia University, 1954), 280.

memories for me but their hearts as well. The William Denslow family of Trenton, Missouri, have maintained an interest in the Vrooman story that transcends the local implications of the Ruskin College incident. Dr. Ernest Bader of Washburn University in Topeka, Kansas, has selflessly devoted much effort to digging additional information out of Kansas newspapers; Dr. Harold Sponberg, formerly president of Washburn and now president of Eastern Michigan University, opened the Washburn College Archives and the Congregational Historical Collection for our use. Dr. C. W. Sorensen, president of Augustana College, Rock Island, Illinois, and the Faculty Research Committee provided funds for additional research, assistance in preparation of the manuscript, and reduction in teaching load to support the Vrooman project. Mrs. Allan Bogue of Madison, Wisconsin, provided judicious criticism of the manuscript. Finally, without the encouragement and advice of Frank Freidel and the sustaining love of my wife, Avis, this work would never have been completed. Responsibility for any errors and shortcomings, of course, rests with me.

During the writing of this book, Carl Vrooman, the last of the brothers discussed in this study, died as a result of complications following an accident in Bloomington, Illinois. It is in respect to his memory and in honor of his contribution to American history that I present the following work to the scholarly community.

I am indebted to the following institutions for use of copyrighted or controlled manuscript material: The Macmillan Company for permission to quote extensively from William Allen White's *Autobiography;* the State Historical Society of Wisconsin for permission to quote or cite material from the Richard T. Ely and Henry Demarest Lloyd papers; Yale University Library for permission to quote from letters in the Colonel House papers; and the Nebraska State Historical Society for unrestricted use of the C. A. Sorensen papers. I am especially grateful to the Organization of American Historians for conferring upon this manuscript the Frederick Jackson Turner Award for 1967. It should be mentioned that the concluding section of the manuscript was added after the manuscript was read by the Frederick Jackson Turner Committee.

Contents

Of Radicalism & Reform

William Allen White's classic description of the attitude of the "proper people" of Emporia, Kansas, toward the "hayseed reformers" of 1890 illustrates the continuity within the American reform tradition since the Civil War:

> Then out of the nowhere into the here came trouble. We laughed at it, of course. I remember one day in the midst of spring, when Senator Murdock came home from one of his predatory excursions to Topeka and Kansas City, I told him with glee about a meeting in the Courthouse of the county committee of the Farmers' Alliance. They were arranging to call a mass convention to put out a county ticket. It was funny. I listed the leaders of the meeting. Among them were all the town and county malcontents who had been blowing off since the days of the Grangers and the Greenbackers, and who had supported Ben Butler in '84 and the Union Labor party in '88, which polled less than 10 per cent of the vote. We knew that the Farmers' Alliance had been organizing in the county, and presumed it was just another of those farmer cooperatives which would start a store and maybe build an elevator, last two or three years, and then dry up and blow away—such things had been happening since the beginning of the settlement of the county.[1]

White's subsequent career as a Progressive reformer raises some questions about the nature of this continuity.

Why are ideas and proposals that are denounced as dangerous heresies in one period of our history regarded as commonsense measures in a later period, even by those who formerly opposed them? Why, after violent debate on reform measures, dire forecasts of disaster, and repeated changes in the law have reforms had so little real impact on the fundamental institutions of our society? Why has our society denounced the reformer, embraced the reform, and given the credit for the changes either to the instinctively conservative legislators who passed the law or to the inherently radical agitators who denounced it as an inadequate palliative or a patent sham?[1]

Similar questions can be raised about continuity in the radical tradition in American history. The rise of the "new radicals" in the 1960's in England and the United States after the proclaimed "end of ideology" in the 1950's seemed to imply a break in continuity. Even a brief survey of the writings of the new radicals showed, however, that their intellectual roots ran deep into the history of the radical tradition of the nineteenth and early twentieth centuries. The Young Socialist Alliance appealed to Trotsky, the Young People's Socialist League could not forget the Communist betrayals of Socialism in the past, and the New-Left radicals rejected the "democratic centralism" of the authoritarian Communists in the 1930's in favor of the democratic decentralization of the Socialist party of Eugene Debs.[2] New-Left Socialists of all varieties still looked to Marx, although their interest had shifted from his economic predictions and theory of history to the Socialist humanism of the young Marx and his concepts of alienation, dehumanization, and class consciousness.[3] Even the radical elements of the Negro protest movement and antiwar groups found strength in Thoreau's essay "On Civil Disobedience," in W. E. DuBois' writings on Negro history, and in Marcus Garvey's black nationalism.[4]

Certain questions can be raised, then, about continuity in the

[1] *The Autobiography of William Allen White* (New York: Macmillan, 1946), 181–82.

[2] See Daniel Bell, *The End of Ideology: On the Exhaustion of Political Ideology in the Fifties,* rev. ed. (New York: Collier Books, 1961). On the new radicalism, see Paul Jacobs and Saul Landau, *The New Radicals: A Report with Documents* (New York: Random House, 1966); Irving Howe, ed., *The Radical Papers: Essays in Democratic Socialism* (New York: Doubleday, 1966); and Bryan Magee, *The New Radicalism* (New York: St. Martins Press, 1963). The illustrations cited above are from the New Left; the same point is illustrated by the growth of the New Right. See Daniel Bell, ed., *The Radical Right* (New York: Doubleday, 1963).

[3] Eric Fromm, ed., *Socialist Humanism: An International Symposium* (New York: Doubleday, 1965) is a useful introduction to this trend. C. Wright Mills, *The Marxist* (New York: Delta Books, 1962) is another.

[4] Francis L. Broderick and August Meier, eds., *Negro Protest Thought in the Twentieth Century* (Indianapolis: Bobbs-Merrill, 1965); C. Eric Lincoln, *The Black Muslims in America* (Boston: Beacon Press, 1961), Chap. 3; and Staughton Lynd, *Nonviolence in America: A Documentary History* (Indianapolis: Bobbs-Merrill, 1965).

radical as well as in the reform tradition. The first question that needs to be raised is simply, "Why has radicalism continued to exist and to draw new recruits in America?" The history of Socialism and Communism in America is the story of repeated failures. The careful student of history, regardless of his opinion on the contemporary status of American society—whether it is creeping, running, or sliding toward or away from Socialism or Communism—cannot lightly dismiss the evidence that in the number of their adherents, the votes they attract, and their ability to win converts Socialism and Communism in America have always been distinctly minority phenomena. Why then have young people continued to join? A small library on this question alone is now available.[5]

More important, perhaps, than the questions of personal psychology is the question of historical influence. Has a continuing radical tradition forced American society to correct its more glaring defects? Have radical proposals been taken over by reformers and modified to fit the American temper? Or have reformers acted to prevent radical programs from gaining in popularity? Has a left-oriented radical tradition run its course in American history; has a right-oriented radical tradition arisen in contemporary times to take its place?

To broach such questions about continuity in the reform and radical traditions—indeed even to use the terms—raises a host of allied questions. What is reform? Who is a reformer? Is the radical the same as the reformer? Are radicalism and reform synonymous? Does the use of the terms commit the historian to a particular historical value standard in evaluating the period; is he taking sides and losing objectivity? Do both terms carry such favorable emotional overtones for the current generation of historians that they judge all reform or radical activity as implicitly good, regardless of the means employed? Does commitment to the classic values of liberalism preclude a critical approach to the study of reform and radical activity in history? Such questions require explanations and working definitions before they can be answered.

[5] The treatment ranges from the personal-confessional, such as Richard Crossman, ed., *The God That Failed* (New York: Harper, 1949), to the sociological-analytical, such as Nathan Glazer, *The Social Basis of American Communism* (New York: Harcourt, Brace & World, 1961).

From the point of view of intellectual history radicalism may be defined as the rejection of the basic assumptions of a society or culture. Reform, on the other hand, is the acceptance of the basic assumptions coupled with a critical assessment of the failure of the society to live up to the standards implied in these assumptions. Reformers call for change in order to fulfill the promise of the assumptions. The reformer, therefore, objects primarily to the performance of his society, not its professions. In fact, he seeks to heal the breach between the two and to achieve the professed goals. The radical, on the other hand, carries his rejection of the performance to the point where he also rejects the professions of his society. In a sense, the reformer ultimately loves that which he tries to change; the radical hates it and rejects it totally.

The definition of reform and radicalism in terms of intellectual positions avoids some of the ambiguities of the traditional use of means alone as the criterion for the distinction between reform and radicalism. Reformers are said to favor slow, moderate, evolutionary means; radicals the violent, sudden, or revolutionary. However, since "radicals" have frequently used gradual, "reformist," and evolutionary means and "reformers" have sometimes advocated violent, sudden, and revolutionary ones, the distinction is not always useful in historical analysis. By using the intellectual criterion the Socialist in America who rejects the private ownership of the means of production and advocates public or collective ownership can be designated a radical, regardless of the means advocated or used to achieve his proclaimed goal. By the same token, the Progressive who accepted the private ownership of property and sought to extend the opportunity to enjoy ownership or to preserve the right of ownership by changes in the law can be designated a reformer, regardless of the rhetoric he used to achieve it. Strategies of action, or means, are more frequently a function of the immediate situation than of long-term goals. It is a man's ultimate goal, not his immediate means, that determines whether he is a radical or a reformer.

Philosophically, reform can be described as the attempt to achieve the ideals or values of a society; radicalism as the attempt to change them. The problem here is not to confuse a belief in ideals with philosophical idealism or the practical idealism of orators who ignore unpleasant realities to proclaim romantic visions. If ideals are viewed not as projections of absolute standards or as the ultimate components of reality, but as the ground rules of civilized behavior derived from the history of a culture, then the relation of ideals to reform and radicalism becomes clearer. Thus, trial by jury or the presumption of innocence are the ideals or values of segments of western culture not because they were derived from a contemplation of the prerequisites of justice by a philosopher or because they were found to reflect the nature of the creator in creation by a theologian, but because ordinary men learned from experience that they were minimal guarantees for their self-protection.[6]

Methodologically, therefore, the historian does not have to enter into the controversies over whether ideals "pull" men through history or whether social or economic conditions "push" them, whether ideals are but reflections of material interests or transcendent victories over them, or whether intellectuals "proclaim" or common people "embody" ideals. Since ideals, as defined above, emerge from the history of a people and are subject to change, the reformer and radical can play their respective roles in the total process along with everyone else. The historian, by following particular men in the unique context of their times, can describe their intellectual positions and patterns of behavior and help to clarify their ideals at various points in history. Such definitions can also account for the changing content of the reform and radical traditions in American history. Since both are functions of the intellectual orthodoxy, they are inherently dynamic in content in a society where the democratic process includes the slowly changing formation of an intellectual consensus as part of the political process.[7]

Psychologically, reform and radicalism are part of the process of self-identification. Or, more broadly stated, protest is a process of self-identification and neither proves nor disproves the truth of the matter under controversy. Reform and radicalism involve an ele-

[6] From this definition it should be clear that an ideal is born in a cry of despair. It is an assertion of an "ought" against the realities of the given situation. Once it becomes institutionalized through settlement of the controversy that gave rise to its articulation, the ideal becomes a cultural norm for future behavior.

[7] The attempt of some recent historians to draw a distinction between a conflict approach to American history and a consensus approach is a false dichotomy. Consensus emerges out of conflict in a democratic society as part of the process of compromise and adjustment.

ment of judgment of one's society. When a man is convinced that his society has failed in some respect to live up to its goals or ideals, how can he live with this fact? The man who accepts the basic premises of his society, but who cannot identify himself with his own pattern of behavior within the current context of his society, may seek to overcome the tensions by attempting to redefine the nature of the world around him. He may "idealize" his society at the same time that he criticizes it. In the name of the "true" and perfect America he condemns the present imperfect America. The result may be pure catharsis for the individual, but the historian should avoid the temptation to dissolve the history of reform into the psychology, or psychosis, of the reformer. Real problems in the concrete world of social, political, economic, and personal relations may have led the reformer to his initial judgment.

The radical seeks self-identification by a process of negation. Whatever the initial facts that created his critical evaluation of his society, he is unable simply to idealize it. Rather, he seeks to amend all of its failings by projecting their opposites into his vision of the "perfect" society. If the private ownership of property leads to unemployment or poverty, then the only solution in his mind is to reject the assumption and to leap over to its opposite: common ownership. But, as the sociologists of knowledge are fond of pointing out, since the category of affirmation is determined by the category of negation, the radical is still a mental prisoner of his society. While this process sounds like Hegelian logic, the historian must be careful not to impose it mechanically upon the data of history.

Such a conception of reform and radicalism as aspects of self-identification opens the possibility that not all reforms are beneficial. Functionally, there is no necessary equation between reform and liberal value. The peculiar coexistence of reform and reaction, of anti-intellectualism and idealism, of "populistic" demagoguery and elitist *noblesse oblige* that has intrigued historians lately is entirely understandable.[8] Since the reformer is trying to bend reality to fit

---

[8] The extensive controversy over these points that followed the publishing of Richard Hofstadter's *The Age of Reform: From Bryan to F.D.R.; Anti-Intellectualism in American Life;* and *The Paranoid Style in American Politics* can be followed in the *American Historical Review* and other journals, from 1956 to the present.

the dimensions of his idealized, abstract world, the nobility of his ideals need have little connection with the baseness of his means. Or, to look at it from another perspective, the violence and paranoid style of his rhetoric may be an expression of the need for catharsis. He symbolically slays his enemies in his oratory and establishes his own identity in reference to the ideal world postulated in his rhetoric. Reform is one way of accommodating ourselves to that to which we are alien by nature.

In a similar fashion the radical would seldom fit into the society that he projects in his rhetoric because it is a compensatory imposition of order on the chaos of fact beyond his control. The libertarian prophet of the regimented society would be the first to perish if his dream world were realized.

The possibility that reform and radicalism may take either liberal or illiberal form is a useful insight for the historian, but is essentially a disconcerting one. It means that he cannot avoid making moral judgments in studying history. He cannot pin the label of reform or radical upon a historical character and act as if that label gave the actor *carte blanche* for his actions or a plenary indulgence for historical "sins."

What makes a man a reformer or a radical? When does he begin to cast a critical eye on his society and begin to call for its reformation or reconstruction? Social scientists say that one of the prerequisites is a disruption of expectations, the creation of psychological discomfort, and the presence of doubt about the certainty of the future course of one's life. The term "alienation" is much bandied about, more often to the confusion than to the clarification of the issue. Two kinds of alienation are frequently confused in recent literature: estrangement from society (self-exile or aloneness) and estrangement from self through society (depersonalization).[9] But neither concept adequately describes the phenomena of the social and political reformer who finds his "true self" by participating in society and who loathes the isolation of social ostracism. Similarly, the radical is alienated from the current realities of his society but

[9] Harold Rosenberg, "It Can Happen to Anyone," *New York Times Book Review,* Dec. 20, 1964, p. 1, a review of Gerald Sykes, ed., *Alienation: The Cultural Climate of Our Times* (New York: Braziller, 1964).

at the same time embraces the abstract perfection of his projected future society. In a sense, the reformer is "of" but not "in" his world; the radical is "in" it, but not "of" it.[10]

The definition offered above shifts the historian's attention from the means of action to the motives. Admittedly, this is a risky procedure. While means are historically objective, motives are subjective. The historical assessment of motives is at best an exercise in reasonable inference from available data and at the least a risky venture in value judgment. The attention to motive is essential, however, in solving a peculiar methodological problem in the history of reform. Crudely stated, the question is, "Does the support of a third-party ticket in politics *per se* distinguish the reformer from the nonreformer?" Insurgency or independent political action can be a shrewd political maneuver to achieve the ordinary goals of political action: public office or power, legislative preferment, or public esteem. It is when political action is pursued not for its own sake but for another controlling purpose that the candidate moves closer to the category of reformer. To pursue a campaign that is doomed to failure in order to educate the public or to call one's country to achieve an ideal is one of the hallmarks of the reformer.

The assessment of motives also raises the issue of self-interest versus idealism. The definitions offered here do not imply that the reformer seeks only the common public good or interest while the nonreformer seeks only his own good or interest. There is an element of self-interest in every human action. Man is so constituted that he can throw the cloak of idealism over any action, whether or not it springs from self-interest. What has distinguished the reformer from his contemporaries in our history is that he has held a different conception of the common interest. In the early nineteenth century the prevailing intellectual orthodoxy, inherited from the eighteenth century, held that the common interest was something other than, apart from, and greater than the sum of the individual interests of the members of the society. It was an objective reality perceived by the dispassionate exercise of reason by enlightened men. The new democratic reformers proclaimed that the common interest was

---

[10] See the perceptive article by Daniel Bell on the Socialist ethical dilemmas in *End of Ideology,* Chap. 12.

simply the sum of individual interests; the prevailing outlines of the common interest could be determined by majority vote. Each man by pursuing his own good contributed to the common good. They solved the problem of self-interest and common interest by postulating their identities.

In the last half of the nineteenth century, when this view had itself hardened into a new orthodoxy, there arose a new breed of reformers. As shall be shown in this book, the new reformers regarded self-interest as a source of evil and postulated a common interest that was greater than the sum of "for each his own." To describe these changing conceptions of the common interest is one of the tasks of the historian, but he must, in all fairness, point out the inevitable element of self-interest in all systems.

To return, then, to the question of continuity in the reform and radical traditions, the historian needs to keep three factors constantly before him: ideas, individuals, and institutions.

If the reformer and radical are to be identified by their positions in reference to the intellectual assumptions of their societies, then the historian of necessity must show the climate of ideas in which they acted. The tracing of the history of ideas or of lines of intellectual influence in American history is one of the favorite techniques of modern historians; however, one must be careful not to assume that ideas have had a constant meaning in history. General semanticists remind us that meaning is dependent upon intention, context, and emotional screening by the receivers. For example, to assume that the use of Jacksonian antimonopoly slogans by the Populists implied a shared meaning is to obscure crucial differences. The antimonopoly sentiment of the 1830's was designed to prevent governments from granting privileges through public charter. The antimonopoly sentiment of the 1880's was designed to cause government to overcome privileges already granted by public charter. The solution advocated by the first school of thought was government negation; the solution advocated by the second was government regulation.[11]

[11] See Lee Benson, *The Concept of Jacksonian Democracy: New York as a Test Case* (Princeton: Princeton University Press, 1961), 62–63, 86, for further discussion of the methodological point that similarity does not prove continuity.

If the historian is to assess motives in history, then he must see the individual not only as a person with a unique personality but also as an actor playing functional roles within social institutions. Particularly in the history of reform and radicalism it is important to ask: Who were these "labor leaders without organizations, politicians without parties, women without husbands, and cranks, visionaries, and agitators without jobs" who sought to change America? [12] What was the background of these self-appointed architects of the future? Where did they intend to lead the reform and radical movements? While some individuals were thrown into them by changes in their economic or social status and others were drawn into it by intellectual predilections, a few individuals were born into the traditions, nourished on agitation, and raised on third-party politics. These birthright reformers and radicals formed the hard core that sustained the movements through depression and prosperity, success and failure, and dissolution and reorganization. Continuity within a family is but a microcosm of continuity within the larger traditions of American history.

If the historian is to illustrate continuity in all its manifestations, he must be concerned, then, not only with the individual, his motives, and his intellectual positions, but also with the institutions through which he worked: political parties, labor unions, churches, civic unions, and experimental communities.

The multiplicity of reform and radical organizations in the late nineteenth and the early twentieth centuries appears, at first glance, to indicate a certain vitality within the two traditions. But it also reveals a fundamental weakness in them. Far from representing mass movements, many of these reform and radical ventures represented only temporary alliances between diehard reformers and lifelong radicals whose differences prevented effective, large-scale cooperation. Behind the facade of widespread enthusiasm for reform and persistent vitality in radicalism the historian finds a pattern of multiple loyalties—"interlocking directorates," strategic alliances, and sudden schisms.

To trace how ideas interact with the aspirations of men, to see the individual in his context, to reconstruct his involvement in insti-

[12] Norman J. Ware, *The Labor Movement in the United States, 1860–1895: A Study in Democracy* (New York: D. Appleton, 1929), 11.

tutions—these are all tasks that can best be accomplished within a restricted compass. What follows in this book is a case study of one family that spans a century of American history, from 1837 to 1937. It begins with the story of Hiram Perkins Vrooman, a farmboy in northwest Ohio in the 1840's. It follows his career into the 1880's in an attempt to determine how, when, and why he became a reformer. The focus then shifts to Hiram Vrooman's sons, who joined the reform and radical movements in Kansas in the turbulent 1880's. The story of the Vrooman brothers is followed in detail until the 1930's, when the last of the Vrooman brothers, Carl, broke with the New Deal.

Throughout this book, one basic question is posed: Why did this small group of lifelong reformers and radicals have to work so hard, scheme so long, and suffer so much in their attempts to change American society?

Part of the answer lies, of course, in the nature of the American political system. Politics is the art of the possible—so runs the familiar aphorism. By the same token, agitation can be defined as the art of making the impossible seem possible, whether the impossible be the reformer's call for the fulfillment of a society's ideals or the radical's call for a totally new society. In this sense much of the reform and radical activity of the last quarter of the nineteenth century can be considered simply as an attempt to educate the public, to convince segments of it that changes were necessary and possible. Some of these proposed changes were incorporated into the legislative programs of the major political parties during the first quarter of the twentieth century.

Part of the answer, on the other hand, lies in the nature of the changes in social structure that accompanied the continuing industrialization of American society. In the economic sphere, radicals and reformers saw that large, complex economic units had replaced a multitude of smaller, competitive units. Some denounced these trusts and combines and framed their reform programs to destroy, circumvent, or control them. Others welcomed them as inevitable and sought to harness them for the benefit of all. Only a few fully understood that this same process of consolidation, of creating nationwide social institutions, was proceeding apace in all fields of American life, including the reform and radical movements.

The significance of this correlation between social structure and social organizations becomes apparent when the characteristic organizations of the 1870's and 1880's are contrasted with those of today. The characteristic organizations of the post-Civil War era, such as the Patrons of Husbandry and the Knights of Labor, were composed of lodges similar to those of the Masonic order, complete with secret oaths and rituals. These lodges engaged in independent political campaigns, cooperative economic ventures, and educational programs. They participated in national affairs through a loosely organized federation. The characteristic social organizations of today are national associations, open to all, nonsectarian, and ostensibly nonpartisan. They are tightly organized and controlled by national executive bodies. They engage in public relations projects, lobbying, and pressure politics.

To conclude simply that there has been a historical shift from a grassroots, egalitarian approach to public affairs in the 1870's and 1880's to an elite, "organization man" approach in the twentieth century is an oversimplification. The point is, rather, that such changes reflect basic changes in social structure. In the relatively egalitarian setting of the 1870's and 1880's, in which the milltown, county seat, and junction city characterized the social and political life of much of the nation, the scale of social distance was correspondingly restricted. Men dealt with one another face to face. The representatives of various functional groups could speak directly to the public on current topics. When there were only six ministers in town, each could speak through the pulpit or press and be accorded some deference. But when the size of the cities had increased so that there were sixty, or six hundred, or six thousand clergymen in one area, then the need for an organization to consolidate and coordinate the views of the clergy became apparent. Such groups fulfill an important role in modern society. Who speaks for labor? For the church? For the poor? For the reformers? As our social structure has become more elaborate, complicated, and national in scope, so has the need for spokesmanship organizations.

Some of the intermediate steps in the process of creating new social organizations are illustrated by the experience of the Vrooman brothers. In the labor movement of the 1880's, the social gospel movement of the 1890's, the educational ferment of the late 1890's, the cooperative movement of the 1900's, and the political campaigns of the Progressive era, they participated in many experiments in agitational technique and organization designed to accommodate their efforts to the unique problems presented by an increasingly complex society. A careful examination of some of these experiments will help to explain more than the course of the Vrooman brothers' efforts. It will also reveal some of the peculiar characteristics of the American political tradition, such as the simultaneous emphasis in the Progressive era on both direct democracy and government by experts.

The Vrooman family chronicle is a case study in the story of continuity within the reform and radical traditions. Here are mirrored the conflicts between ideals and individual aspirations, the battles within social organizations, and the changes in social structure, that helped to shape the two traditions.[13]

[13] The theory offered here is not to be construed as limiting individual responses to breaks in expectations of the fulfillment of social goals to only two patterns, radicalism and reform. Robert K. Merton, *Social Theory and Social Structure* (Glencoe, Ill.: The Free Press, 1957), 131–60, offers a typology of five modes for individual adaptation in such situations. An approximate parallel between Merton's system and mine would be as follows:

Modes of Adaptation	Intellectual Positions
Conformity	Instinctual conservatism
Innovation	Reform
Ritualism	Ideological conservatism
Retreatism	Apolitical apathy
Rebellion	Radicalism

Merton is interested in the social factors that condition such responses; I am interested in the consequences that flow from them. He is using a sociology of knowledge approach that is deterministic; I am using a general semantic approach that is voluntaristic.

Christopher Lasch, *The New Radicalism in America, 1889–1963* (New York: Knopf, 1965) also uses a sociology of knowledge methodology. He defines the radical in terms of social status, views radicalism as an aspect of the social history of the intellectuals, and portrays intellectuals as a social type. I define radical in terms of intellectual positions, view radicalism as an aspect of intellectual history, and expand the concept of intellectual to include representative thinkers as well as formal thinkers. In short, Lasch is interested in the intellectual as a social type; I am interested in the radical as an intellectual type.

Furthermore, Lasch emphasizes the act of rebellion from class values, particularly middle-class values; I emphasize the reaffirmation of cultural values in reform and the rejection of them in radicalism. Not every one who revolts against middle-class values is a radical; only those who assert an alternate pattern of values should be so named.

Chapter One

The Entrepreneurial Dream, *1837-1870*

THE LADDERS OF MOBILITY, 1837–1866

The citizens of Eureka, Kansas, were startled, and amused, one night in July, 1880, when a crowd of boys built a bonfire at the corner of Second and Main streets and hauled Judge Vrooman down to the festivities on a wagon. With a great hurrah and some pleading they persuaded him to give a speech. Passersby edged in closer to the circle of light, nudged each other, and inquired about the proceedings. Hadn't they heard? Judge Vrooman had been nominated for governor by the Greenback-Labor convention at Topeka. Some smiled, some scoffed, and some just looked at the five dark-eyed Vrooman boys prancing around their father and shook their heads. Yes, the Vroomans were at it again.

The editor of the Eureka *Herald* printed an appropriate note in the next issue. "We congratulate Judge Vrooman on the distinction conferred upon him by his party," he wrote. "If the Greenback party should elect a Governor, we know of no member of that party in the state we would prefer to Judge Vrooman." [1] Voters who wanted to know about Judge Vrooman's background could read the campaign biography printed in the Topeka *Living Age.* There they would read that he had been born in Johnstown, Montgomery County, New York, in 1828, that he had been an abolitionist in Ohio in 1843, a Free Soiler in Michigan in 1854, and a reconstruction Republican in Missouri in 1865. "He is a temperance man in theory and practice; exceedingly tolerant in his opinions, though," the biography hastened to reassure the reader, "a consistent member of a religious organization which believes in a Christian democracy and a democratic Christianity." [2]

What paths had led Hiram Perkins Vrooman from his birthplace in New York to this precipitous moment in his career? Why had he ended up on a minor third-party ticket, a subject of friendly criticism and abuse? When the ballots were counted in November, 1880, he received only 19,477 votes, compared to 115,204 for the Republican and 65,557 for the Democratic candidate.[3] But does a reformer lose simply because he has not won an election? The answers to these questions emerge from the story of Hiram's boyhood. The story begins in Toledo, Ohio, in 1836.

Toledo and surrounding Lucas County were booming in 1836. The county had been formally organized in 1835; the "boundary war" with Michigan had been settled peacefully in June of 1836, giving the ten-mile "Toledo strip" to Ohio, while Michigan received the upper peninsula in compensation; the Wabash and Erie Canal had been started; and a charter had been secured from the state legislature for a railroad to be built between Toledo and Adrian, Michigan. "During the 'flush times' of 1835 and 1836, paper money ruled all values, and everybody was rich in 'rags and lampblack,' and 'water' or 'corner' lots," a pioneering citizen recalled. "A spirit, adverse to making money by the old methods, was rife throughout the land." [4] In 1837 the county commissioners received the county's share of the federal surplus under the state distribution act and began lending it at 6 percent on good real estate security.[5] Although "the whole Maumee valley was filled with eastern fortune hunters," another pioneer wrote, "Jackson's specie circular soon brought their airy fabric into ruin." [6]

The collapse of the land boom, followed by the Panic of 1837,

[1] Aug. 5, 1880, p. 4, cols. 1–2.

[2] Topeka (Kans.) *Living Age,* Oct. 15, 1880, clipping in Kansas State Historical Society Biographical Collections, V, I, 341.

[3] Daniel Webster Wilder, *The Annals of Kansas,* new ed. (Topeka: Kansas Publishing House, 1886), 907.

[4] H. S. Knapp, *History of the Maumee Valley* (Toledo: Blade Mammouth Printing Company, 1872), 629.

[5] Clark Waggoner, ed., *History of the City of Toledo and Lucas County, Ohio* (Toledo: Blade Printing Company, 1888), 314, 325.

[6] Knapp, *Maumee Valley,* 542.

brought hard times to the Toledo area. Many of the problems that would plague American life for the next century could be seen in miniature in this obscure corner of Ohio: the instability of the banking system, the cycles of land speculation and collapse, the craze for internal improvements—both railroads and canals—that saddled the local governments with debts, the shortages of credit that hampered equality of entrepreneurial opportunity, the inexplicable shifts in the patterns of migration and transportation that bypassed certain areas and left the map plotted with unbuilt towns and the land dotted with abandoned homesteads. Debt, poverty, and hopelessness piled up as the delinquent tax lists appeared in the papers. "Many a suffering farmer then wished the money had remained a surplus in the National Treasury." [7]

In June, 1837, John A. Vrooman, a farmer from the Mohawk Valley, New York, arrived in Toledo with his wife and eight children.[8] He moved northwest of Toledo, near the newly plotted village of Sylvania, and started to farm. With the times hard, crops poor, and credit scarce, it was not an easy life. The credit and currency shortage particularly hampered farmers in their land transactions. When John Vrooman helped his eldest son, Garrett, in setting up farming on his own in 1839, the mortgage transaction had to be completed with promissory notes. Part of the land was secured on a two-year lease.[9]

Hard times, hard work, and hard luck have been the lot of many young farmboys in American history, and John Vrooman's sons were no exceptions. In later years Hiram Perkins Vrooman could recall how roots snagged in the plow and snapped back to whip his legs black and blue with bruises. Education traditionally has been one

[7] Waggoner, *History,* 325.

[8] Knapp, *Maumee Valley,* 657; Grace Vrooman Wickersham and Ernest B. Comstock, *The Vrooman Family in America: The Descendants of Hendrick Meese Vrooman Who Came from Holland to America in 1664* (Dallas: privately printed in 1949), 142–46, 214–16. John A. Vrooman, born Sept. 24, 1791, married Elizabeth Bingham in 1814 in Johnstown, N.Y. The following children are of particular importance for this study: Garrett, born Jan. 17, 1818; Hiram Perkins, born July 24, 1828; and Jacob Alexander, born Jan. 17, 1831.

[9] Lucas County, Ohio, *Record of Deeds,* Book 5, pp. 532, 533; Lucas County, Ohio, *Record of Mortgages,* Book 3, p. 190. For the census records of 1840 on John A. Vrooman see population schedules, Richfield Township, Lucas County, Ohio, microfilm in Toledo Public Library.

of the ladders of advancement from the farm to a better career, and when their chance came, Hiram and his younger brother Jacob seized it eagerly. In 1844 four enterprising men secured a charter from the state for the Sylvania High School Company. John Vrooman was one of the forty interested citizens who bought stock in the corporation and sent his children to the school. After high school Hiram and Jacob studied at an academy in Maumee, Ohio, and for a brief period Hiram taught school.[10]

Hiram Vrooman's campaign biography of 1880 claimed that he was an abolitionist in Ohio in 1843. Abolitionist, or at least anti-slavery, sentiment was evident in Lucas County as early as 1838. Anti-slavery meetings were held at the Presbyterian church in Maumee, and the formation of an antislavery society was discussed.[11] The *Youth's Emancipator,* an abolitionist paper published by the Oberlin Youth's Anti-Slavery Society, was circulated throughout northwest Ohio in the 1840's with appeals such as the following:

To Youth

The present is an age of reform. For evidence of this we have only to look at the temperance reformation.... Yes, you who read this, though youth, may exert an influence in favor of truth. Look at the cold water army of America, numbering its tens of thousands, and tell me if they exert no influence. And why can not an *anti-slavery* army be raised of American youth? [12]

There is no evidence in the available records to prove that fifteen-year-old Hiram Vrooman was an abolitionist in 1843. Perhaps the 1880 claim was simply political oratory. On the other hand, abolitionism was present in Lucas County at the time, and he may well have responded to it.

In 1849 personal misfortune caught up with John Vrooman. Land

---

[10] Conversation with Carl Vrooman, Nov. 28, 1960; Charles Sumner Van Tassel, *Story of the Maumee Valley, Toledo, and the Sandusky Region* (Chicago: S. J. Clarke, 1929), II, 1669–70; Citizens Historical Association, "Carl Schurz Vrooman," type-written report in the Illinois State Historical Library, Springfield, Ill.; Topeka (Kans.) *Journal,* March 12, 1908, clipping in Kansas State Historical Society Biographical Collections, V, I, 343.

[11] Maumee (Ohio) *Express,* Jan. 20, 1838, p. 2, col. 4; Jan. 23, 1838, p. 4, col. 3.

[12] *Youth's Emancipator* (Oberlin, Ohio), Sept., 1842, p. 3, col. 3; Wilbur H. Siebert, *The Underground Railroad from Slavery to Freedom* (New York: Macmillan, 1898), 92, 112, 425, discusses antislavery activity in Toledo and Lucas County.

that he had taken on mortgage with his eldest son, Garrett, was foreclosed and returned to the owner by the sheriff. In May, 1850, the Bank of Worcester failed, and its circulating notes were repudiated. Rumors spread that the Bank of Toledo was implicated in the crash, and a run on the bank began. The bank, in an attempt to prevent disaster, put the squeeze on its own debtors, and one of those who felt the pinch was John Vrooman. Unable to meet his notes, he had to stand by and watch a sheriff's sale dispose of a horse, a sled, a sleigh, a lumber wagon, and ten acres of growing wheat to satisfy the debt.[13]

John Vrooman's misfortune may have been one of the factors that turned Hiram's life into a different path. The census records for 1850 list Hiram and Jacob as students but indicate that they had not attended school within the year. In May, 1850, Hiram began to study law. Perhaps he was seeking a way to help his father with his legal difficulties, or perhaps he was seeking escape from the cycle of rural indebtedness that encumbered his family.[14]

Hiram moved across the state boundary into Monroe County, Michigan, where he taught school and continued to read law. Monroe County seemed the ideal location for a fresh start on a new career. Halfway between Toledo and Detroit, it was experiencing a railroad boom in 1851 and 1852. In February, 1853, Hiram was admitted as an attorney before the Michigan Supreme Court. He immediately plunged into a career of law and local politics, along with his brother Jacob. In March, 1854, Jacob was nominated for school inspector on the Democratic ticket and was elected the following month. At the same time Hiram was appointed solicitor for the newly elected Common Council in Monroe.[15]

The Vrooman brothers blazed across the social horizon of Monroe

[13] Lucas County, Ohio, *Record of Deeds,* Book 19, p. 160; *Daily Toledo Blade,* June 13, 1850, p. 2, col. 4; June 18, 1850, p. 2, col. 1.

[14] [Alfred Theodore Andreas, ed.], *History of the State of Kansas* (Chicago: A. T. Andreas, 1883), 581; Population Schedules, Census of 1850, Sylvania Township, Lucas County, Ohio, 110, microfilm in Toledo Public Library. In April, 1850, Hiram lent $250 to his older brother Garrett for the purchase of a farm. Perhaps he regretted this a month later when he was unable to help his father. See Lucas County, Ohio, *Record of Mortgages,* Book 6, p. 309.

[15] Talcott E. Wing, ed., *History of Monroe County, Michigan* (New York: Munsell, 1890), 231; Western Historical Company, *History of St. Clair County, Michigan* (Chicago: A. T. Andreas, 1883), 406; Monroe (Mich.) *Commercial,* March 23, 1854, p. 2, col. 1; April 6, 1854, p. 3, col. 2; April 13, 1854, p. 3, col. 3.

County like two new comets. Hiram had the characteristic Vrooman features of dark hair, dark and piercing eyes, sharp nose, and sensitive mouth. In later years he grew a full beard and loved to parade as General Grant at masquerade parties. Jacob, the younger brother, was much in demand as an orator, particularly with the Young Ladies' Literary Society.[16]

The Vrooman brothers had entered politics at a crucial point in American history. The Kansas-Nebraska Act, still pending in the House of Representatives in April, 1854, was splintering the old political alliances and destroying the Whig party.

For almost a quarter of a century the Democratic party had dominated American life, both politically and ideologically. Its particular version of the negative liberal state, of government reduced to its nominal functions, had inspired a whole generation of Americans. Allan Nevins has written of this period, "The history of the time is incomprehensible unless its pervasive belief in the evils of strong government, its regard for local and state autonomy, and its faith in unfettered individualism as the mainsprings of progress are clearly grasped."[17] The heart of the Democratic creed could be summed up in a phrase from the 1856 platform: "that every citizen and every section of the country has a right to demand and insist upon an equality of rights and privileges."[18]

The central issue in the political struggles of the nineteenth century was the meaning of equality. The eighteenth-century revolutionaries had fought to establish the primary political and legal meaning of equality; the nineteenth-century inheritors of their tradition read an economic content into the older concepts. Equality to them meant primarily equality of opportunity, the right to exploit the resources of the vast continent before them. Even the slavery issue became pertinent to many of them only in so far as the specter of slave labor in the territories threatened their hopes for economic opportunity in those areas. The battle between the Whigs and Democrats had been over the means to achieve equality of opportunity, not

[16] Monroe *Commercial*, July 6, 1854, p. 3, col. 1; Feb. 22, 1855, p. 3, col. 1.
[17] Allan Nevins, *Ordeal of the Union*, I, *Fruits of Manifest Destiny, 1847–1852* (New York: Scribner's, 1947), 159.
[18] Kirk H. Porter and Donald Bruce Johnson, *National Party Platforms, 1840–1964* (Urbana: University of Illinois Press, 1966), 24.

over the goal itself. The Democrats would reduce the role of the central government in favor of individual and state action; the Whigs—and later the new Republicans—would expand the role of the central government in the areas of transportation, banking, and public land disposal. A whole new era of American politics was dawning.[19]

The Vrooman brothers were prepared to cast their lot with the Democrats and to dance a symbolic jig on the coffin of the Whigs. When a group of Free Soil Democrats, radical Whigs, and dissident Democrats announced plans to hold a convention at Jackson, Michigan, to form a new political coalition, Hiram taunted the new Republicans with a Fourth of July toast: "Our Glorious Union: May she ever be preserved from the baneful influence of demagogues, fanatics, and sectional parties." [20]

When Hiram was nominated for prosecuting attorney by the Monroe County Democratic convention in the fall, the editor of the local paper noted: "Mr. Vrooman, for Prosecuting Attorney, is also a new candidate, but a young man that has lived in the county for many years. By his industry, perseverance and correct habits, he has acquired a standing which inspires confidence." [21] Hiram's victory in the November elections increased his stature within the party. In May, 1856, he was elected a delegate to the Democratic state convention that endorsed Lewis Cass for senator, James Buchanan for president, and "squatter sovereignty" for Kansas. Contrary to the campaign biography of 1880, Hiram had started his career not as a supporter of the Free Soil party, but as a loyal member of the squatter-sovereignty wing of the Democratic party.[22]

[19] On the ideology of the two parties in the 1840's, see Lee Benson, *The Concept of Jacksonian Democracy: New York as a Test Case* (Princeton: Princeton University Press, 1961), Chaps. 11, 13.

[20] Monroe *Commercial*, July 6, 1854, p. 3, col. 2. The term radical Whig is used here in its contemporary meaning and not in the special sense established in the introduction.

[21] *Ibid.*, Oct. 12, 1854, p. 2, col. 3.

[22] Wing, ed., *Monroe County*, 278; Monroe *Commercial*, May 29, 1856, p. 1, col. 5. An index of the increasing status of the Vrooman brothers is found in their land transactions. In May, 1854, Hiram, Jacob and another brother cosigned a mortgage with their father for eighty acres in Sylvania township, Lucas County, Ohio. The money, $750, was borrowed from Coast Craft of Monroe, Mich., for two years on terms of 10 percent per year. The note was paid in full and on time. Lucas County, Ohio, *Record of Mortgages*, Book 8, p. 572.

The winds of political change were blowing hard in 1856, and the Vrooman brothers tacked in the wrong direction. The new Republican party was increasing in strength throughout southern Michigan. In the fall elections Hiram Vrooman, the Democratic nominee for circuit court commissioner in Monroe County, was defeated as the Republicans won most of the county offices and carried the county for their electoral slate. Although Hiram's social status continued to rise—he was elected to the Masonic lodge in January, 1857—his political and economic future was jeopardized by the onslaught in August of the Panic of 1857. The railroad boom in the county collapsed, and the economy became stagnant. There seemed to be no future for the Vrooman brothers in Monroe County.[23]

Faced with a bleak outlook in 1858 from the continuing depression, Hiram and Jacob Vrooman looked around for a new location to advance their fortunes, both political and economic. They selected Port Huron, Michigan, north of Detroit, where the St. Clair River formed a natural transportation link between Lake Huron and Lake Erie. Port Huron had received a state charter for a city government in 1857, the lumber industry gave promise of a great potential for the area, and a federal customs district indicated the possibility of political favoritism.

The Vrooman brothers established themselves in Port Huron in May, 1858, as lawyers and real estate speculators. The next September, Jacob, aged twenty-six, married Mary Lucretia Carl, aged nineteen, in Port Huron with Hiram and his younger sister Della as witnesses.[24]

The onslaught of the Civil War did not seem to disturb the pattern of Hiram's and Jacob's careers. Neither served in the military. On February 20, 1862, Hiram, then thirty-four years old, married Sarah Jane Buffington, the daughter of Henry C. Buffington, a Republican

[23] Monroe *Commercial,* Nov. 13, 1856, p. 3, col. 1; Wing, *Monroe County,* 232, 332. An indication of Hiram's economic position in early 1857 can be found in his lending activities in Lucas County. In January, Hiram and his father lent $1,200 on a mortgage to a resident of Lucas County. *Record of Mortgages,* Book 11, p. 97. The last activity by Hiram in Lucas County was a land sale in July, 1857. *Record of Deeds,* Book 29, p. 551.

[24] Western Historical Company, *St. Clair County,* 449, 503, 511; Works Projects Administration, *Michigan: A Guide to the Wolverine State* (New York: Oxford University Press, 1941), 361; St. Clair County, Mich., *Record of Deeds,* Book 3, p. 599; St. Clair County, Mich., *Marriage Records,* 87.

newspaper editor, in Kalamazoo, Michigan. In July, Hiram's father-in-law moved to Port Huron and became the editor of the influential Port Huron *Press*. With the war disrupting normal political patterns Hiram moved back into politics as a Unionist and won a seat on the Port Huron Common Council in April, 1863.[25]

The Unionist movement of 1863 in Michigan was a coalition of conservative Republicans with prowar Democrats. Popular discontent with the progress of the war was manifest in widespread victories by this fusion ticket in 1863.[26]

When the issue of bounties for enlistments arose in the Port Huron Common Council, Hiram supported resolutions to raise five thousand dollars by taxes and to pay a bounty of one hundred dollars for each enlistment. When this proved insufficient, he moved that the council raise an additional seven thousand dollars and increase the bonus to two hundred dollars. His brother, Jacob, offered to fill the city's quota of enlistments for two hundred dollars per man by buying certificates from the commanding officers of men who had voluntarily reenlisted and applying these certificates against the city's quota.[27]

In April, 1864, the Vrooman-Buffington clique began to lose power within the local Unionist movement. The Common Council switched its printing patronage from the Port Huron *Press* to the rival *Commercial*.[28] In July, Hiram Vrooman and Henry Buffington attended the county Unionist convention as delegates from Port Huron. The convention endorsed the Lincoln-Johnson ticket and tried to maintain solidarity by avoiding issues. "We deem it not only

[25] Kalamazoo (Mich.) *Gazette*, Feb. 21, 1862, p. 3, col. 3; City of Port Huron, Mich., *Minutes of the Common Council, 1857–1864*, pp. 302–307. Henry C. Buffington had been an editor of the Grundy County *Herald* (Morris, Ill.), during 1854–1855, then a Republican editor in Ottawa, Ill., from 1857 to 1859. In 1860 he became the editor of the Kalamazoo (Mich.) *Telegraph*. See Franklin W. Scott, *Newspapers and Periodicals of Illinois, 1814–1879*, vol. VI of *Illinois Historical Collections* (Springfield: Illinois State Historical Society, 1910), 247, 270; Samuel W. Durant, ed., *History of Kalamazoo County, Michigan* (Philadelphia: Everts and Abbott, 1880), 264.

[26] Harriette M. Dilla, *The Politics of Michigan, 1865–1878* (New York: Columbia University Press, 1912), 26-30.

[27] City of Port Huron, Mich., *Minutes of the Common Council, 1857–1864*, pp. 324-25, 327, 332-33; Port Huron (Mich.) *Press*, Jan. 4, 1864, p. 1, col. 1; Aug. 17, 1864, p. 3, col. 1.

[28] Port Huron *Press*, April 6, 1864, p. 2, col. 2; May 11, 1864, p. 3, col. 1.

impolitic but positively injurious to the national cause to present any party issue to the people," their resolutions declared, "but deem it our sacred duty to declare that the great object of this campaign should be the election of such men to the offices...as are pledged to the cordial support of the government in its efforts to crush out the rebellion and resolve its authority over every foot of national territory." [29] By August, 1864, Jacob Vrooman had to defend publicly his action in promising to fulfill the city's enlistment quota. He complained that other towns had raised the bounty to three and four hundred dollars and that he could not pay money out of his own pocket to compete. In the November elections the final blow fell upon the Vrooman-Buffington cause as the Peace Democrats carried Port Huron for McClellan. [30] Had the political tide turned against them?

THE MEANING OF EQUALITY, 1866–1870

Once again Hiram Vrooman had to weigh the prospects for his future. He was thirty-six years old, his family was increasing, and his identification with the Unionist movement was jeopardizing his political future, as the Peace Democrats seemed to be gaining control of Port Huron. In February, 1865, he offered his house and lot for sale or exchange and looked around for a new location. A year later he had moved his family to an entirely new area of the country—Macon City, Missouri. [31]

Macon City, at the junction of the St. Joseph and North Missouri railroads in northern Missouri, in 1866, was an ideal location for ambitious young men. In 1863 the county seat had been forcibly moved to Macon City from the pro-Confederate town of Bloomington. The agricultural and mineral resources of the area, coupled with adequate transportation facilities, made it attractive for speculators. The radi-

[29] *Ibid.*, July 6, 1864, p. 3, col. 2.

[30] *Ibid.*, Aug. 17, 1864, p. 3, col. 1; Nov. 16, 1864, p. 3, col. 2.

[31] *Ibid.*, Feb. 25, 1865, p. 2, col. 4; Nov. 22, 1865, p. 2, col. 5; Feb. 7, 1866, p. 3, col. 2. Two children were born in Port Huron: Frank Buffington, Nov. 20, 1862, and Harry Chase, April 13, 1864. The first evidence of Hiram's activity in Macon City is a deed signed on March 6, 1866. See Macon County, Missouri, *Record of Mortgages*, Book V, p. 541.

cal Republicans had secured control of the state government in 1864, forced through a new constitution with a test oath that disqualified all former Confederate sympathizers, and ousted the hostile state supreme court judges. Their program of encouraging state and county aid to railroads and of creating a favorable climate for business enterprises made Missouri an attractive haven for radical Republicans from the North.[32]

In Macon City Hiram made a fresh start on his career and entered a new line of endeavor. He had been lending money on agricultural mortgages and speculating in real estate since 1850. The returns, combined with income from legal fees and compensation from public office, had proved insufficient to his needs. Now he became a full-fledged entrepreneur. In July, 1867, he joined a group of investors in taking over and reorganizing the Missouri Central Insurance Company. Hiram was designated vice-president of the firm, while one of his law partners, Jacob Gilstrap, was placed on the board of directors. His other partner, Abner L. Gilstrap, editor of the Macon *Republican* and a director of the North Missouri Insurance Company, was deeply involved in a plan to have Macon County buy stock in the projected Missouri and Mississippi Railroad line from Macon City to Keokuk, Iowa.[33]

In joining the ranks of the entrepreneurs Hiram Vrooman and the Gilstraps were responding to the stepped-up tempo of economic activity that accompanied the Civil War and extended into the postwar period. The entrepreneurial dream of success through investment in enterprise was part of the nineteenth-century belief in equality of opportunity. But entrepreneurial ventures required capital beyond the capacity of the ordinary businessman to accumulate through thrift and personal savings. How was he to secure adequate

---

[32] Wilson Nicely, *The Great Southwest: Guide for Emigrants and Capitalists* (St. Louis: R. P. Studley, 1867), 7–10; Floyd C. Shoemaker "Macon," *Missouri Historical Review*, LI (Oct., 1956), 362–72; William E. Smith, *The Francis Preston Blair Family in Politics* (New York: Macmillan, 1933), II, 347. The term radical Republican is used here in its contemporary meaning and not in the special sense established in the introduction.

[33] Macon (Mo.) *Argus*, July 3, 1867, p. 3, col. 4; Aug. 7, 1867, p. 2, col. 1; Oct. 16, 1867, p. 2, col. 6; Oct. 30, 1867, p. 2, col. 2. For the complete story of the M. and M. Railroad, see E. M. Violette, "The Missouri and Mississippi Railroad Debt," *Missouri Historical Review*, XV (April, 1921), 487–518, 617–47.

capital for his venture? Sale of stock to the public offered one avenue, but it was full of risks for the unwary and was not generally used except by railroads. Borrowing from a bank offered another route, but bankers wanted sound collateral and personal knowledge of the integrity of the recipient in addition to a generous rate of interest on their loan. Realizing a high rate of profit on prices through inflation seemed to be an easier route to quick capital, but the price level, according to the economic thought of the day, was determined by the quantity of currency in circulation, not by the desires of the seller. Government subsidy of an enterprise, through either direct grants or indirect support by purchase of stock to be paid for from future tax revenues, offered another attractive road to quick capital for those with political influence.

The post-Civil War entrepreneur was inevitably drawn into the arena of politics in his search for capital. Sale of stock to the public or enjoyment of the safeguards of limited liability depended upon securing a charter of incorporation from the state legislature. Borrowing from a bank brought the entrepreneur face-to-face with the wartime laws that had taxed state bank notes out of existence and turned national bank notes, printed by the United States, over to privately owned national banks for distribution. Realizing an excess profit from inflation depended upon favorable action by the national government in maintaining the quantity of wartime Treasury notes (or greenbacks) in circulation. Securing a government subsidy or a stock purchase by a government unit required political skill in a day when the spoils system was rampant in American politics. Reconstruction of the South, the status of the Negro, and relations with the rest of the world might occupy the attention of national political leaders, but the rank-and-file voter was more deeply concerned with entrepreneurial issues related to the meaning of equality for his hopes and dreams.

Did equality of opportunity exist if one man or group of men secured a charter of incorporation through political influence while another, lacking this influence, did not? Did equality of opportunity exist if the national banks preferred to lend their notes to established, large-scale entrepreneurs and not to newcomers? Did it exist if the national bank preferred its political allies to the friends of the state banks? Was equality of opportunity meaningful if the United States

Treasury, catering to the wishes of the holders of government bonds, withdrew greenbacks from circulation and paid the bond holders in hard-to-acquire gold coins? Was equality of opportunity effective if one group of citizens was taxed to provide capital for another through subsidies or stock purchases? These were the kinds of questions that troubled the political debates of post-Civil War America.

Some of the ways in which the men of the 1860's and 1870's attempted to bend their inherited ideologies to answer these questions can be found in the activities of the radical Republicans of Macon County. They managed somehow to combine the individualism of Herbert Spencer's "law of equal freedom" with the Republican principles of positive government action to aid the entrepreneur. An editorial in the Macon *Argus* explained:

But we do not propose to measure our duty by democratic or conservative standards. The radical party is in favor of the broadest liberty for all men, and its aim should be to respect and protect the rights of all. It is a progressive party, and should keep pace with the developments of the times, the march of events. The war has ended, slavery has passed away, and we believe we are moving forward to a higher and holier destiny than we have hitherto aspired to; that we have been rising higher in the scale of civilization, until we have reached the point of making a practical recognition of the sublime doctrine taught in the Declaration of Independence— the equal rights of all men to liberty and a voice in forming and administering the laws by which they are to be governed.[34]

Liberty to pursue the entrepreneurial dream, participation in forming the law, protection for property rights by a unified national government—this was the ideology of the radical Republicans.

When Henry C. Buffington visited his son-in-law in April, 1866, he wrote back to friends in Port Huron that Hiram's office was "the headquarters of the radicals," among whom he occupied "a prominent and leading position." Whether Hiram could apply the ideology of the Macon County radicals to the credit crisis of the postwar depression and still retain his leadership in the Republican party became the crucial test of his new career.[35]

[34] Macon (Mo.) *Argus*, Sept. 11, 1867, p. 1, col. 4.
[35] Port Huron *Press*, May 2, 1866, p. 2, col. 1.

The radical Republicans of Macon County were divided into two factions in 1867. The Gilstrap or city faction, including Hiram Vrooman, drew its major support from the Macon City wards. The rival county faction, headed by J. T. Clements and John M. London, controlled the county Republican committee. When the county faction issued a call for ward conventions, the city faction issued a blistering rejoinder: "The undersigned Republicans and Taxpayers of Macon City, detesting all cliques and wire-pulling, and denying the right or the policy of a portion or all of the County committee to call Ward and City meetings, respectfully ask the tax payers of the Republican party in said city, *and all others believing in retrenchment,* [italics added] and a change in the civil policy in our city government [to meet on December 20, 1867, to nominate candidates for city elections]." [36] Hiram signed the city faction's statement, and acted as the temporary chairman for the meeting. The city faction nominated its own slate of candidates for the coming elections.[37]

The city faction carried the Macon City elections in January, 1868. The new council offered Hiram the position of city attorney, but he declined. He aspired to a more important post. The state legislature passed a law creating a common pleas court for Macon County, with complete probate jurisdiction and a salary of at least six hundred dollars a year. Through political influence in the state capital Hiram was appointed to preside over the newly created court until the next regular election. He quickly dissolved his partnership with the Gilstraps, appointed his wife's brother-in-law, Major Samuel J. Wilson, as his clerk, and began holding term sessions. The appointment was praised in the Macon City papers by the city faction and in the St. Louis papers by friendly editors.[38]

The creation of the new common pleas court turned out to be another bone of contention between the city and county factions. The county faction, through the Macon *Journal,* raised a howl about "peculiar features" in the bill. The abolition of the probate court slighted Judge D. E. Wilson, a county man. The provision that the

[36] Macon (Mo.) *Argus,* Dec. 18, 1867, p. 3, col. 2; Dec. 25, 1867, p. 2, col. 4.

[37] *Ibid.,* Dec. 25, 1867, p. 2, col. 4.

[38] *Ibid.,* Jan. 15, 1868, p. 2, col. 1; Jan. 29, 1868, p. 3, col. 2; March 4, 1868, p. 2, col. 7; April 4, 1868, p. 3, col. 2; April 15, 1868, p. 3, cols. 2, 4; April 22, 1868, p. 2, col. 2; p. 3, col. 2.

new common pleas judge be over thirty years old was viewed as an attempt "to exclude certain young lawyers of the city of known merit and popularity." [39]

More important than Hiram's role in setting up the new court was his service to the city faction as chairman of the resolutions committee of a special meeting called in late December, 1867, to consider the financial condition of the county in the light of the continuing depression. The resolutions went far beyond the immediate problems to take up the whole question of national monetary policy since the beginning of the Civil War. The sale of government bonds to the public during the war had laid the base for a postwar political conflict. The National Banking Act allowed national banks to issue bank notes on the face value of 90 percent of the government bonds that they held as reserves. Any move by Congress or the Treasury that threatened the stability of these bonds would jeopardize the entire credit structure of the country. Any move by Congress or the Treasury, on the other hand, to contract the volume of Treasury notes, or greenbacks, in circulation would challenge the schemes of small entrepreneurs to accumulate capital through inflation of the price level. The issue was brought to the fore by the introduction of the Sherman bill in December, 1867, calling for the refunding of the federal debt in new government bonds payable in gold and exempt from the wartime federal taxes still on the books. [40]

The resolutions brought forth by Hiram's committee clearly expressed the attitudes of the small entrepreneurs toward the issues in the controversy.

Whereas: The great and increasing prostration of business in the Great West is the subject of most grave concern to our laboring men and business classes, as well as to the success of our internal improvements; and whereas, this prostration and consequent increase of the burden of taxation is mostly attributable to the deficiency, in quantity, of our circulating

[39] Macon (Mo.) *Journal*, April 9, 1869, p. 2, col. 1.

[40] Irwin Unger, *The Greenback Era: A Social and Political History of American Finance, 1865–1879* (Princeton: Princeton University Press, 1964) Chap. 1 and pp. 87–88. The Sherman bill came before the Senate in Dec., 1867, for first reading, but was withdrawn for changes and reintroduced in Feb., 1868. Unger, *Greenback Era*, p. 88, n. 78. This sequence of events is important in considering the narrative of Hiram Vrooman's activities in 1867 and 1868.

medium called *legal tender notes,* and the mismanagement of the financial affairs of the nation by the Secretary of the Treasury, under the Retiring Act of Congress, and by assuming that the liabilities contracted to be paid in *legal tender notes* shall be paid in gold; wherefore:—

Resolved, 1st ... we are fully convinced that the Government may, honorably to itself and with justice to its creditors, discharge, at least, $1,600,-000,000 of its liabilities in *legal tender notes* from time to time, as the time for redemption may arrive.

2d. That, as the Congress in 1862, asserted the power to declare United States Treasury Notes a legal tender in payment of all debts, public and private, except duties on imports, not withstanding the contract may have been for a specified payment in gold, as has been decided by the Courts under said laws, Congress has the same power now, and it is a duty they owe to the people to provide by law, for the payment of the outstanding national debt contained in [government bonds commonly called] "five twenties" and "seven thirties," where not payable in coin on their face, by the issue of legal tender notes as required....

4th. That to pay this debt in gold, principal and interest, and exempt the debt from taxation for all that time, as is proposed by the Sherman bill [now pending in the Senate], is a proposition the most monstrous, and if it shall be successfully fastened upon the country, will bankrupt the nation, and establish a monied aristocracy more powerful, overbearing and domineering than the aristocracy of slavery, from which we have just escaped, and end in repudiation....

6th. That gold and silver, as well as paper money, obtain their chief value from the force of law, and therefore, legal tender notes of the United States can no more depreciate than can gold and silver.... The more lawful money we have in circulation the higher will be the prices which labor and property will command, and to the same extent will it be easier, *and possible* to pay off the national debt....

8th. [The Sherman bill] offers a premium to capital to retire from business, discriminates in favor of capital and against labor, will sell the poor man's last cow and homestead to pay those golden taxes for the benefit of the holders of the golden bonds, while his wife and children will be turned out into the woods and prairies to listen to the golden songs of poverty.[41]

Hiram discussed the resolutions and moved their adoption. The city faction endorsed them wholeheartedly.

[41] Macon (Mo.) *Argus,* Jan. 1, 1868, p. 2, col. 5.

In July, 1868, Hiram chaired the resolutions committee for the county Republican convention and brought before the convention soft-money resolutions stronger in language and more sweeping in terms than those of the December meeting. The resolutions called for payment of the federal debt in legal tender notes fundable at the option of the holder into forty-year bonds with 4 percent interest, abolition of the National Banking Act, replacement of national bank notes with legal tender notes, abolition of the Freedmen's Bureau on the establishment of loyal reconstruction governments, and adherence to rigid economy in government. The ideology behind the resolutions was spelled out in sharp tones:

That a discrimination between capital and labor, making the non-producer's claims payable in gold, and the producer's and tax payer's claims payable in another and less valuable currency, is an injustice and iniquity unworthy of a liberal government, and should not be submitted to by a free people any longer than a remedy can be found at the ballot box....

Resolved, that the Republican party is opposed alike to monopolies and class legislation; that its chief end has been to secure equality of rights to all before the law, to protect the poor, to remove the shackles of slavery from the oppressed, and to elevate the masses of the people....

Resolved, that recognizing equality of rights as one of the cardinal principles of Republican government, we declare ourselves in favor of restoring all men now disenfranchised by the Constitution of Missouri, to the right of suffrage as soon as it can be done in a legal and constitutional manner.[42]

The county faction, which supported the hard-money position within the Republican party, complained that the resolutions ignored the Chicago platform on which Grant and Colfax had been nominated. They also accused the resolutions committee of acting in a high-handed manner in declaring verbal war on the "Wall Street sharks and speculators who lie safely ensconced behind their breastworks of untaxed golden bonds."[43]

When the Republican state convention met a few weeks later, the county faction allied with some dissident members of the convention

[42] *Ibid.,* July 8, 1868, p. 2, cols. 2-3.
[43] *Ibid.,* July 9, 1868, p. 2, col. 2.

in an attempt to have the Macon County delegates ousted on the grounds that their resolutions on finance did not represent "sound Republicanism." Ignoring the fact that important national leaders in the Republican party supported similar greenback proposals, they tried to convict the Macon County delegates of heresy on the currency issue. The delegation was seated in spite of the protest, and a motion to condemn the Macon County resolutions was ruled out of order. The convention attempted to paper over the differences by endorsing the national platform and calling for payment of the national debt in good faith.[44]

In September, 1868, the balance of power within the Republican party in Macon County seemed to be shifting toward the county faction. They controlled the county convention that nominated the fall slate and endorsed D. E. Wilson for judge of the common pleas court. Hiram Vrooman countered by announcing that he would run for the position as an independent candidate. The Democratic party, which had been slowly reorganizing in the county, resolved not to place a candidate in opposition to him, thereby giving him their tacit endorsement. The city faction, realizing the weakness of the independent label and the liability of the Democratic label, created an ostensibly nonpartisan Peoples ticket to support Hiram and other independent candidates. The county faction attempted to scare loyal Republicans away from the new ticket by charging that fusion with the Democrats was equivalent to treason; however, the Peoples ticket carried the county in the November elections.[45]

Hiram and the city faction had weathered the November battles, but other troubles began to pile up against them. In December, 1868, Hiram, Abner Gilstrap, and other local entrepreneurs held a meeting to discuss the possibility of promoting a railroad connecting Macon City to Omaha, Nebraska. Articles of incorporation were drawn up, and Hiram Vrooman and Abner Gilstrap were appointed to a committee to present the proposal to the St. Louis Board of Trade. When the St. Louis, Macon, and Omaha Air Line Railroad

[44] *Ibid.,* July 22, 1868, p. 2, cols. 1, 4–5; Sept. 16, 1868, p. 2, col. 2.

[45] *Ibid.,* Sept. 9, 1868, p. 2, col. 1; p. 2, col. 3; Sept. 30, 1868, p. 2, col. 4; Oct. 7, 1868, p. 2, col. 4; Oct. 14, 1868, p. 2, col. 3; Nov. 4, 1868, p. 2, col. 1. Hiram defeated D. E. Wilson by a majority of 431 votes. Hiram's third son, Walter Watkins Vrooman, was born on Jan. 8, 1869.

Company was formally organized, however, they were both defeated in the elections for board members from Macon County.[46]

By November, 1869, Hiram again confronted dual challenges to his position in the courts and in local politics. In legal matters a suit before the state supreme court challenged the jurisdiction of his common pleas court over misdemeanors. Hiram won the suit, but the issue antagonized the friends of the district court judge. In politics the relative strength of the hard-money forces in the Republican party had been growing during 1869 after the passage of the Public Credit Act in March. This act pledged the federal government to redeem the "five twenty" bonds in gold, both principal and interest. Thus, hard-money advocates, such as the county faction in Macon County, could stigmatize their greenback opponents, among them the city faction, as being unfaithful to the Republican administration's stand. In January, 1870, the county faction ticket won the Macon City elections, defeating the *ad hoc* Peoples ticket supported by the city faction Republicans and fusionist Democrats.[47]

By 1870 Hiram Vrooman could look back over twenty years of public life. The outlines of that life fell into the classic pattern of advancement for nineteenth-century society. From rural poverty he had climbed the ladder of social mobility to become an entrepreneur. Now at the peak of his career, at age forty-two, he was a moderately wealthy man, a respected judge, an influential politician, an insurance executive, and a successful land speculator.

It had not been easy to achieve such success in the middle of the nineteenth century. There was a cyclical pattern to his life that had been repeated in Monroe, Port Huron, and Macon City. Combining politics with the law, he would enter politics under the banner of the predominant party—Democratic in Monroe, Unionist-Republican in Port Huron, radical Republican in Macon City. When changes in political fortune coincided with changes in his economic prospects, as they did in 1857 and 1865, he would pack up, move to another location, and begin again. The new locations had a similarity, too.

---

[46] *Ibid.*, Dec. 23, 1868, p. 2, cols. 2–3.

[47] *Ibid.*, Nov. 10, 1869, p. 2, col. 2; Dec. 22, 1869, p. 2, cols. 2–3; Jan. 12, 1870, p. 2, col. 1. For growth of hard-money factions in the Republican party see Unger, *Greenback Era,* 43, 93–94.

They were all railroad or transportation centers, county seats, and booming communities. If his campaign biography of 1880 did not accurately reflect the realities of his past, this was not conscious mendacity; it was just the *modus vivendi* of American politics. The truth was colored slightly to fit the current tastes.

Hiram Vrooman's espousal of greenback ideas in the years 1868 through 1869 did not automatically make him a reformer. As Professor Unger has shown, there were many varieties of greenbackism in 1869, and not all of them reflected a utopian or reformist sentiment.[48] Since there was no prevailing consensus within the Republican party on monetary policy, all options were equally orthodox and acceptable. It was the action of the Republican party in March, 1869, in adopting the gold bond plan and in linking itself to the interests of the large entrepreneurs that established the orthodoxy of the next decade and, by the same token, raised the possibility of radical and reformist positions on the issue.

The entrepreneurial greenbackism advocated by Hiram Vrooman in 1868 and 1869 was clothed in appeals to the doctrine of equal rights, but it reflected the credit needs of the small entrepreneurs of the western boomtowns. It was self-interest, not idealism, that prompted their greenbackism; it was the vehicle of regular political action, not reform. The primary motive of their greenbackism was to enhance their own positions at the expense of others, not to call American society to task for its failure to achieve an ideal.

Reform involves an element of judgment upon one's society. Only when a man is convinced that his society has failed to live up to a goal or an ideal can he take a reform position. When a man has achieved his fondest aims, does he judge his society as failing? Hiram Vrooman had achieved his goals; American society had been good to him.

[48] *Greenback Era*, Chaps. 2, 3.

Chapter Two

The Making of a Reformer,
1871-1884

TURN TO REFORM, 1871–1876

What are the steps that turn a man from the role of an ordinary politician to that of a reform politician? The break in expectations of the future, a critical attitude toward contemporary events, the idealization of society's values, the transformation of politics from a means of achieving immediate goals into an end in itself—these are some of the steps that have been described by social scientists.[1]

The context within which Judge Hiram Vrooman found himself making the turn toward reform was the creation of the liberal Republican movement in Missouri in 1871 and 1872. An editorial in the Macon *Republican* in May, 1871, noted: "We warn the Democracy of the county that there is a movement on foot, in high political circles, which has for its object the selling out of the party, body and soul, to the Republicans. The plot is to so manipulate the wires that the Democratic organization shall be withdrawn from the contest in 1872, and what is known as a 'Liberal Republican' shall be nominated by the disaffected wing of the Radicals with the understanding that Democrats are pledged to support him." [2] In its broad outline, this prediction was essentially correct. But the results were not those expected by the creators of the liberal Republican movement.

The liberal Republican movement in Missouri was largely the creation of one man—Carl Schurz. Schurz, a German "forty-eighter" refugee, had moved to Missouri from Detroit in the spring of 1867 to become editor of the St. Louis *Westliche Post*. He quickly moved into a position of strength within the Republican party in Missouri. When Republican Senator John B. Henderson of Missouri voted against impeachment of Johnson and forfeited his political future, Schurz stepped into the breach to challenge Charles D. Drake for control of the party. Schurz's election to the Senate in 1869 "revealed a rising group of moderates among the Radicals who were loath to continue the policy of proscription and insistent that recognition be given to newer economic and social problems." [3]

The initial issues that sparked the liberal Republican movement were related to Reconstruction and disenfranchisement of former Confederates. Economic and moral issues such as free trade and civil service reform also occupied Schurz's attention. In his analysis of the situation the Civil War had created a "new order of things" based upon abolition of slavery and the establishment of a free labor society. The essence of the new order was equality of rights. The corruptions of the Grant era were challenging this new order. "New issues will create new parties," he warned his colleagues in the Senate in December, 1870, and "the only way to preserve the vitality of the Republican party is to make it the party of progressive reforms; in other words, the new party, which is bound to come in one form or another." He hastened to assure his fellow senators that he did not mean "that as a party of reforms it should lightly catch up every new 'ism' hatched by heated brains; but it should resolutely address itself to the reformation of the abuses and the solution of the problems" which were becoming more evident daily. Schurz's ideal was a great moral uprising of the people to sweep away the existing party machinery along with its corruptions and abuses. [4]

Schurz's call for a reformation of the Republican party or for the formation of a new party found a sympathetic follower in Hiram Vrooman. The continuing credit problem and the intraparty struggle in Macon County left him vulnerable and in need of new allies and new avenues to political power. He made a trip to Michigan and Ohio in September, 1871, and found those areas just as hard up for

[1] Stanley M. Elkins, *Slavery: A Problem in American Institutional and Intellectual Life* (New York: The Universal Library, 1959), 157–64; David Brion Davis, ed., *Ante-Bellum Reform* (New York: Harper and Row, 1967).

[2] Macon (Mo.) *Republican*, May 16, 1871, p. 1, col. 4.

[3] Thomas S. Barclay, *The Liberal Republican Movement in Missouri: 1865–1921* (Columbia: State Historical Society of Missouri, 1926), 162.

[4] Frederic Bancroft, ed., *Speeches, Correspondence and Political Papers of Carl Schurz* (New York: Putnam, 1913), II, 60, 64; Carl Schurz, *The Reminiscences of Carl Schurz* (New York: McClures, 1908), III, 340.

cash and credit and just as drought-stricken as Macon County. When he returned to Macon City, he also found that the county faction in the Republican party had acquired firm control over the county convention. When the state Republican convention fell under the control of the Drake group and repudiated the Schurz group's platform, the liberal Republicans under Schurz bolted the convention and issued a call for a new convention. Hiram Vrooman, the Gilstraps, and all the supporters of the old Peoples ticket in Macon City signed the call. "Judge Vrooman will adjourn the Common Pleas court for the Bummers dance," the opposition Macon *Republican* chided in a slur on the liberals; "the judge's machine seldom runs down. His court is as near perpetual motion as human ingenuity can invent." [5]

The manifesto of the bolters was a curious document that appealed more to Democrats than to erstwhile Republicans. After recounting the reasons why the Democratic party could not hope to regain national power the address moved to its central point:

The war, and the exercise of despotic power, absolutely necessary to the conduct of civil war, put in motion influences, which threaten the destruction of the State Governments, and to centralize all power in the Government at Washington. Unless this centralizing tendency be checked, and the State Governments be preserved, our country must become a centralized despotism, and the liberties of the people lost.... We do not know, nor do we charge, that President Grant wants his country a centralized despotism, but it is not in his power, nor in the power of any mortal man, to stem the current. Who can stem it? No man, no faction, no party can. But, THE PEOPLE CAN DO IT. The remedy is alone with the masses. Arouse them to a true sense of the perils of the hour; and, upheaving from the great heart of the Nation will come a mighty power, that will stay this despotic tendency, and save the liberties of the people. We must therefore have a bold, independent movement of the people, responsible not at all for the miserable blunders of Democracy, and sharing not at all in the sins of Radicalism. [6]

The only specific issues mentioned in the address were those closely related to Reconstruction: preservation of state governments, su-

[5] Macon (Mo.) *Republican*, Oct. 25, 1871, p. 3, col. 5; Jan. 31, 1872, p. 2, col. 4; April 3, 1872, p. 2, col. 1. The quote is from April 3, 1872, p. 2, col. 3.

[6] *Ibid.*, April 10, 1872, p. 1, col. 6. The address was signed by H. P. Vrooman and both of the Gilstraps.

premacy of civil over military authority, freedom of the press, right of habeas corpus, and trial by jury. For the moment it urged the Democrats not to waste time on "ordinary political issues" or to try to resurrect the old Democracy for the sake of second-rate office-holders.[7]

Politics makes strange bedfellows. The liberal Republican movement in Missouri was no exception. Carl Schurz, a Republican, a free trader, civil service advocate, and hard-money resumptionist, presided over an uneasy coalition that included former free soil Democrats, greenback Republicans, and office-hungry politicians of all sorts. His rival for leadership in the liberal Republican movement, B. Gratz Brown, was a former free soil Democrat who had been elected governor in 1870 with moderate Republican support. The Missouri liberal Republican convention in April, 1872, adopted a platform that endorsed the war amendments, called for universal amnesty for disenfranchised citizens, and expressed gratitude to the veterans of the war. On the newer issues, it advocated civil service laws, a single term for the president, adjustment of federal taxes, a speedy return to a hard-money policy, and it opposed land grants to railroads or corporations. Despite the hard-money provision, Hiram Vrooman agreed to attend the national liberal Republican convention at Cincinnati as a delegate for Missouri. Opposition papers sneered that the liberal delegates were all oldtime Democrats, except for Hiram and one other, "and they were never Republicans to hurt any." [8]

The story of the Cincinnati convention has been told in detail elsewhere. The split in the Missouri delegation between the Schurz and Brown factions, the support of Horace Greeley by the Brown faction in a bid for the vice-presidential nomination for Brown, and the equivocation of the platform on the tariff issue damaged the cause of the liberal Republican movement, both nationally and in Missouri. When Hiram returned from the convention, he was subjected to satirical attacks in the local papers. "As Vrooman was so prominent in the convention," one wrote, "I thought he would be satisfied, but

[7] *Ibid.*, p. 1, col. 7.
[8] Earle Dudley Ross, *The Liberal Republican Movement* (New York: H. Holt, 1919), 61, 95–96; Macon (Mo.) *Republican,* May 1, 1872, p. 2, cols. 2–3.

who ever saw one of our party that *was* satisfied. Vrooman demands
an office. A very small office will do, so I recommend him to be sent
on a mission to Queen Emma." In fact, Hiram had declined to consider nomination for lieutenant governor in 1870 and apparently had
no plans for political office in 1872.[9]

The satirical attacks on Hiram continued as the fall elections approached. The Macon *Republican* scolded the Democratic *Times*
and informed them in mock seriousness: "When Vrooman smiles,
every democrat in the county grins, when he frowns they tremble,
when he strokes his beard, they pray. He knocked your primary elections to smithereens, and when his program is prepared, the democrats must toe the scratch." The Democrats were not about to play
possum any longer. They refused to abandon their separate organization and carried the county by three hundred votes in the fall elections. The liberals had been squeezed out by both parties.[10]

Hiram Vrooman's enthusiasm for reformers such as Horace Greeley and Carl Schurz had helped to carry him into the liberal Republican movement. When his fourth and fifth sons were born, he
named them Hiram Greeley and Carl Schurz Vrooman to show his
compatriots that he was "working hand in glove" with Greeley and
Schurz.[11]

While the liberal Republican movement was unsuccessful as a
political stratagem, it served a useful function in American history.
It helped to consolidate southern opposition to the excesses of carpet-
bagger rule and, at the same time, committed the rejuvenated Democracy to the acceptance of the suffrage amendments. In the same
way, the liberal Republican campaign fostered cooperation among
the civil service advocates, free traders, and genteel liberals of the

[9] Macon (Mo.) *Republican,* May 15, 1872, p. 2, col. 2; Topeka (Kans.) *Journal,*
March 12, 1908, clipping in Kansas State Historical Society Biographical Collections,
V, I, 343. For the Cincinnati convention see Eric F. Goldman, *Rendezvous with
Destiny* (New York: Vintage Books, 1958); Ross, *Liberal Republican Movement;*
and Norma L. Peterson, *Freedom and Franchise: The Political Career of B. Gratz
Brown* (Columbia: University of Missouri Press, 1965).

[10] Macon (Mo.) *Republican,* Sept. 4, 1872, p. 2, col. 2; Nov. 6, 1872, p. 2, col. 1;
Ross, *Liberal Republican Movement,* 237.

[11] "The Foremost Democratic Dirt Farmer," mimeographed document prepared
for the 1924 Democratic National Convention, p. 11, Vrooman papers. Hiram Greeley
Vrooman was born on March 1, 1871, and Carl Schurz Vrooman on Oct. 25, 1872.
A sixth son, Roy, died at an early age and is not included in this study.

urban centers and promoted independent political movements in the West. While concerned with the problems left over from the Civil War, the movement of 1872 had sounded a note of warning against the new problems that accompanied the industrialism, commercialism, and corruption of the age of the spoilsmen. The election of 1872 thus marked the transition between two eras of American history.[12]

Hiram Vrooman's political difficulties in the 1872 elections were but a prelude to the economic disaster that accompanied the onset of the Panic of 1873. Hiram was deeply involved with the Gilstraps in the insurance business, particularly in the North Missouri Insurance Company. Hiram's father-in-law, H. C. Buffington, had been appointed Michigan state agent for the company in 1872, and offices had been opened in Ohio the same year. The disastrous fires of 1871 in Chicago and Boston had placed a severe drain on the entire insurance system and had ruined numerous companies. The North Missouri Insurance Company was not involved, but public confidence in the reliability of insurance firms was severely shaken. In January, 1873, some residents of Macon City suggested an ordinance to tax insurance company assets as the personal property of the directors and stockholders. In June, 1873, the Ohio insurance commissioner withdrew the license of the North Missouri Insurance Company because of rumors and local opposition, and a severe drain was placed on its assets. A group of St. Louis businessmen replenished the stock, took control, and moved the offices of the firm to St. Louis.[13]

As Hiram Vrooman's political and economic position began to decline, so did his position in public affairs. In April, 1873, an editorial in the Macon *Republican* pointed out that, as the only Republican judicial district in the county, Macon City needed a candidate for judge who was a businessman and a faithful Republican, an obvious slur on Hiram. In August, 1873, a group of citizens gathered to discuss the possibility of securing a subscription loan to entice a manufacturer to build a plant in Macon City. Hiram was appointed to the committee of canvassers. He called upon members of an earlier manufacturing association to disband their old organization and to

---

[12] Ross, *Liberal Republican Movement*, 237–39.
[13] Macon (Mo.) *Republican*, Jan. 31, 1872, p. 3, col. 1; Nov. 13, 1872, p. 2, col. 2; Jan. 29, 1873, p. 2, cols. 3–4; June 11, 1873, p. 2, col. 2; June 25, 1873, p. 2, col. 1.

join the new one. When the new association elected its board of directors, however, Hiram was not one of those considered.[14]

The hopes of the Macon County entrepreneurs for the future of their area had always rested ultimately on its prospects as a major railroad junction for northern Missouri. The projected M. & M. Railroad to Keokuk and the "airline" route to Omaha had involved the taking of stock by the county government, the city government, and numerous individual investors in Macon and surrounding counties. The M. & M. Railroad entered into a contract for construction of the line with the Iowa Railroad Contracting Company, an interest of J. Edgar Thompson, Thomas A. Scott, Jewett A. Stone, and Andrew Carnegie, and the prospects for Macon County seemed bright.

The M. & M. promised to pay for the construction at the rate of forty thousand dollars a mile, half in first mortgage bonds and half in common stock, and to turn over all assets to the construction company. Local pundits remarked: "Railroads have now three gauges— a broad gauge, a narrow gauge, and a mortgage." Since all the men backing the construction company were "well known capitalists and railroad men," local boosters felt confident that the value of M. & M. stock would rise as construction began. But the county commissioners grew suspicious, and in April, 1873, they sought a writ of mandamus in the court to force the M. & M. Railroad Company to open its books. Then, on September 18, 1873, Jay Cooke and Company failed in New York. The ensuing fall in security prices destroyed all hope of completing the road and of turning Macon City into a major railroad center.[15]

The Panic of 1873 dealt a death blow to Hiram Vrooman's sagging fortunes. Since January, 1873, he had been selling his real estate holdings in an attempt to raise capital and conveying some of his property to his brother, Jacob, who acted as his trustee. After the full force of the panic hit Macon County in October, 1873, Hiram was so desperate that he sold his furniture to his partner. In March, 1874, he set out for the state capital to see what he could do to rescue his court

[14] *Ibid.,* April 9, 1873, p. 2, col. 1; Aug. 21, 1873, p. 2, col. 4; Sept. 11, 1873, p. 3, col. 4.
[15] *Ibid.,* Jan. 31, 1872, p. 2, col. 1; Feb. 19, 1873, p. 2, col. 4; April 9, 1873, p. 2, col. 2. See E. M. Violette, "The Missouri and Mississippi Railroad Debt," *Missouri Historical Review,* XV (April, 1921), 495.

position from encroachment by a new common pleas court in neighboring Cambria. The legislature changed the name of the Macon County common pleas court to probate court and fixed new terms that began immediately. But even this maneuver was not enough to save Hiram. The North Missouri Insurance Company failed in April, 1874. On April 13, 1874, Hiram sold all his interests in the fees of office due as judge and clerk of the new probate court and moved to Washington, Missouri, in Franklin County on the Missouri River.[16]

The collapse of the liberal Republican movement and of his personal fortune left Hiram Vrooman politically stranded. He abandoned the Republican party in 1875 and had nowhere to go. The Grange had been organizing in Macon County during 1873 and began to complain about paying personal property taxes to support railroad bonds held by the county. A letter to the editor of the Macon *Republican* noted:

Farmers clubs similar to those of Illinois are springing up all over our state.... Farmers are swiftly becoming a confirmed set of grumblers. They grumble at the merchant because he endeavors to make a reasonable per cent upon the money he invests. They grumble at the mechanic because he demands but reasonable wages for his hard earned skill. They grumble at the local and general government because they are under obligations to pay a paltry per cent of their effects to sustain the government that protects themselves and their property; and some, if the whole truth were known, grumble at God Almighty because we have so much rain.[17]

Hiram's father, who had moved from Ohio to Missouri in 1872, helped to organize Farmers Clubs in Macon County. But Hiram had little in common with the Grangers. When the Macon County Granger newspaper surveyed the occupations of former county

[16] Macon County, Mo., *Record of Deeds,* Book 19, p. 126 (Hiram sold a piano, a sofa, an armchair, five spring-bottom horsehair chairs, and two oil paintings, one of George Washington and one of Daniel Webster, to his partner Samuel J. Wilson); Macon (Mo.) *Republican,* March 12, 1874, p. 2, cols. 3-4; p. 3, col. 2; April 2, 1874, p. 3, col. 4; April 16, 1874, p. 2, col. 5; April 30, 1874, p. 3, col. 2. For the sale of office fees, see *Record of Deeds,* Book 19, p. 254. Conclusions on Hiram's financial status in 1873 are based on an analysis of land deeds in the office of Macon County recorder of deeds. Jacob Vrooman came to Macon in 1870 and engaged in law and real estate transactions. *Record of Deeds,* Book 17, p. 442.

[17] May 28, 1873, p. 2, col. 3.

officeholders to substantiate its claim that the farmers were the back-
bone of the county's political system, they listed Hiram as a lawyer.[18]

Without the badge of a virtuous yeoman farmer Hiram had little
political future with the Grangers. Independents, former liberal
Republicans, and Grangers ran an *ad hoc* Peoples ticket in the 1874
Missouri state elections with a platform calling for railroad regulation, reduction in taxes, civil service reform, and resumption of specie
payments, but the Democrats swept the election with ease.[19]

Hiram Vrooman spent the next two years in fruitless wandering.
Jacob Vrooman, who had also encountered hard times, sold his holdings in Macon City and moved to St. Louis, where he formed a law
partnership with Abner Gilstrap. But Missouri no longer held any
promise for Hiram. In September, 1875, he sold his remaining property in Macon City for fifteen hundred dollars and moved to Decatur, Illinois. In settlement of an old debt Hiram secured a 160-acre
farm on payment of the nominal fee of one dollar. He opened a law
office, but he was not successful. Although Decatur was the center of
the Independent Reform party agitation for Illinois, Hiram took
little part in local politics. In April, 1876, he gave up the farm, closed
his law office, and moved his family to Kansas.[20]

GREENBACKISM IN KANSAS, 1876–1884

Council Grove, Kansas, Hiram's new location, was typical of the
towns that he selected whenever he relocated to promote his career.
Situated on the Missouri, Kansas, and Texas Railroad halfway between Junction City, on the Kansas Pacific, and Emporia, on the
Atchison, Topeka and Santa Fe, Council Grove was the Morris
County seat and the commercial center for the fertile Neosho River
valley. The population was only 712 in 1876, making it easy for new-

---

[18] *Ibid.*, April 30, 1873, p. 3, col. 2; *Missouri Granger* (Macon City), July 12, 1872,
p. 2, col. 2.

[19] Walter B. Stevens, "The Political Turmoil of 1874 in Missouri," *Missouri Historical Review*, XXXI (Oct., 1936), 3–9; Solon J. Buck, *The Granger Movement*, Harvard Historical Studies, XIX (Cambridge: Harvard University Press, 1913), 100–101;
Ross, *Liberal Republican Movement*, 213.

[20] Macon County, Mo., *Record of Deeds*, Book 22, p. 338; Decatur (Ill.) *Republican*,
Nov. 16, 1875, p. 3, col. 1; Dec. 3, 1875, p. 3, col. 3; Dec. 31, 1875, p. 3, col. 2;
June 2, 1876, p. 3, col. 3; Macon County, Ill., *Record of Deeds*, Book 35, p. 556;
Book 61, p. 225.

comers to establish themselves. Hiram's activities in Council Grove showed a marked departure from his previous pattern of behavior in Monroe, Port Huron, and Macon City. No sooner had he established a law office than he plunged into reform politics as a backer of the diminutive Greenback party. The local Greenback supporters met in Hiram's office and designated him as one of the three delegates to attend the Greenback congressional convention at Emporia. Hiram Vrooman was back in politics as a full-fledged reformer.[21]

The Greenback movement of 1876 had all the trappings of a holy crusade. The veto by Grant of the bill to increase the greenbacks in circulation to four hundred million and the passage of the Specie Resumption Act by Congress had given the Greenback movement a focus, a center of opposition, and a new sense of urgency. The country had a deadline with disaster if specie payments were resumed in January, 1879, as the law provided—or at least this is what the Greenbackers believed.

In May, 1876, entrepreneurial Greenbackers, utopian labor Greenbackers, and newly converted agrarian Greenbackers from the Grange united in a convention at Indianapolis to form the Independent Reform—or National Greenback—party. "At bottom it consisted of True Believers—greenback ideologues who had converged on the movement from many directions." Whatever their previous allegiances, "they all shared a common vision that transcended their origins and their day-to-day occupations. From the beginning, Greenbackism had the quality of a transfiguring faith, but its quasi-religious nature had never emerged so clearly as it did at Indianapolis." [22]

Hiram Vrooman plunged into the Greenback campaign of 1876 like a man possessed and worked within both the Greenback and Democratic parties to support the cause. When the Morris County Democrats met in convention, Hiram gave "a ringing speech" and was elected a delegate to the senatorial convention. The results of the campaign were meager, and in Morris County only thirty votes were cast for the Greenback party's presidential candidate, Peter

[21] Dale E. Morgan, ed., *Rand McNally's Pioneer Atlas of the American West* (Chicago: Rand McNally, 1956), 16; Council Grove (Kans.) *Democrat*, May 25, 1876, p. 3, col. 1; Aug. 17, 1876, p. 3, col. 2; Aug. 24, 1876, p. 3, col. 1.

[22] Irwin Unger, *The Greenback Era: A Social and Political History of American Finance, 1865–1879* (Princeton: Princeton University Press, 1964), 306.

Cooper. The statewide election results showed that Greenback sentiment could claim between five and six thousand voters, only 5 to 6 percent of the electorate. Greenback sentiment in the Democratic party could carry an additional twenty thousand votes, about 18 percent of the electorate. Even in Kansas, the prospects for the new party were not too bright.[23]

The Greenback campaign of 1876 had coincided with the continuing and deepening depression started by the Panic of 1873. In 1877 the depression hit rock bottom with successive wage cuts on some of the major railroads. The Great Strike of 1877, which began on July 14, soon turned into a violent confrontation between labor and government as state militia and federal troops clashed with strikers and their angry sympathizers. When the conflict collapsed into anarchy with mob violence and rioting in Pittsburgh, Baltimore, Chicago, and St. Louis, two new forces were injected into American political life. The first was a great Communist scare. The second was a renewed sense of the need for political action among trade union leaders.[24]

Since the bloody uprising of the Paris Commune in 1871, the epithets "Communist" or "Internationalist" had been used against any disturbers of the public equilibrium in the United States. A few refugees from the Commune found their way to America along with other members of the First International, but the epithet was not reserved for members of these organizations. The Grange, for example, had been attacked in 1873 for being Communistic. One reporter attended a Grange convention in New York and wrote:

The majority of the delegation was composed of a conglomeration of Presidents of N.Y. leagues of Internationalists, Free Love Societies, Social reformers of the Victoria Woodhull School, and politicians of the lowest

[23] June G. Cabe and Charles A. Sullivant, *Kansas Votes: National Elections, 1859–1956* (Lawrence: University of Kansas, 1957), 12–13, 104–105; Clarence J. Hein and Charles A. Sullivant, *Kansas Votes: Gubernatorial Elections, 1859–1956* (Lawrence: University of Kansas, 1958). Since these studies combine the totals of all third parties, the exact figures for the Greenbackers were established from other sources. See Daniel Webster Wilder, *Annals of Kansas,* new ed. (Topeka: Kansas Publishing House, 1886); William F. Zornow, *Kansas: A History of the Jayhawk State* (Norman: University of Oklahoma Press, 1957), 131–32.

[24] Robert Bruce, *1877: Year of Violence* (Indianapolis: Bobbs-Merrill, 1959); Dennis Tilden Lynch, *The Wild Seventies* (New York: D. Appleton-Century, 1941), Chaps. 45–50.

class. We listened to all the speakers, and must say that the worst principles of the Paris Commune were unblushingly advocated. It was charged by several speakers ... that the members of all corporations and joint stock companies were thieves and scoundrels, that the drones in life's busy hives should receive as much as the busy workers, that there should be a forcible division and equalization of property.[25]

The Internationalists, or Communists, did not start the riots of the Great Strike of 1877, but they did try to exploit them for their own advantage.

When the labor leaders who had been aroused by government action in the strike moved into politics in 1877, they sought an alliance with the reformist Greenbackers rather than with the radical Internationalists in order not to be condemned by the public's anti-Communist mood. In Kansas and Missouri some labor unions joined with Greenback clubs and Granges to form Greenback-Labor parties. The 1878 platform of the Kansas Greenback-Labor party specifically condemned Communism: "That equivalent for equivalent is the natural law of exchange, and we are equally hostile to any form of Communism which seeks to appropriate the wealth of others without giving an equivalent, whether it be at once, and with violence, or gradually at the rate of ten to twenty percent a year—both modes are violations of natural and moral law, and should be abolished." [26] The Democratic party had a unique answer to the problem. They blamed "the rising spirit of Communism" on the financial policies of the Republican administration.[27]

The merger of the labor groups with the Greenbackers also brought a new note of militancy to the Greenback-Labor platform. The Greenback platform of 1877 had contained a simple clause designed to appeal to the labor vote: "Labor should receive its just reward, and we believe the same may be brought about through the

[25] Reprinted in Macon (Mo.) *Republican,* June 18, 1873, p. 2, col. 2. Victoria Claffin Woodhull ran for President in 1872 on the Equal Rights ticket. She was a free-love advocate and a Communist of sorts.

[26] Wilder, *Annals of Kansas,* 793.

[27] *Ibid.,* 806. For details of the Missouri Greenback-Labor alliance see *Proceedings of the Missouri State Greenback Convention, October 4, 1877,* document in Widener Library, Harvard; Russell M. Nolen, "The Labor Movement in St. Louis from 1860 to 1870," *Missouri Historical Review,* XXXIV (Jan., 1940), 160–74.

adoption by Congress of the principles of the Independent Greenback party, which will restore confidence in all business circles, and
thereby unlock and put to work the dormant capital which has so
long lain idle." [28]

The Greenback-Labor platform of 1878, on the other hand, declared "that the claims of humanity should be considered first, and
the claims of mere property second; that labor is the active and productive capital of the country, and should be protected and fostered
rather than idle money." [29] The 1878 platform also condemned
usury, denounced "the unfair discrimination made between the
wages paid to laboring men and the fees and salaries of office-
holders and professional men," and advocated government control
of "all channels of domestic commerce."

Hiram Vrooman favored the fusion of the Greenbackers with the
laboring groups in Kansas. In September, 1877, he presided over the
Morris County committee of Greenback, independent reform, and
workingmen's clubs and participated in the convention at Wyandotte
that created the Kansas Greenback-Labor party. In May, 1878, finding that neither his law practice nor his political fortunes flourished
in Council Grove, Hiram moved his family by prairie schooner to
Eureka in Greenwood County.

At the Greenback-Labor convention on July 3, 1878, Hiram was
nominated for the office of chief justice of the Kansas state supreme
court. The platform did not satisfy the Kansas voters, however. In a
banner agricultural year, they preferred the "honest" Republican
Greenback—"that shall always be worth its face in coin"—to the in-
flationary Greenback-Labor "rag baby." Hiram Vrooman received
an encouraging total of 26,503 votes, compared to 34,913 for the
Democratic aspirant and 76,752 for the successful Republican candidate.[30]

The national Greenback-Labor campaign reached its peak in the
1878 congressional elections when the party received more than one

---

[28] Wilder, *Annals of Kansas,* 771.
[29] *Ibid.,* 793.
[30] Council Grove *Democrat,* Sept. 13, 1877, p. 3, col. 2; Sept. 20, 1877, p. 3, col. 3;
Wilder, *Annals of Kansas,* 770-71, 825; [A. T. Andreas], *History of the State of
Kansas* (Chicago: A. T. Andreas, 1883), 581; conversation with Carl Vrooman,
Nov. 28, 1960.

million votes and sent fifteen members to Congress. With the return of prosperity and the restoration of specie payments on January 1, 1879, the Greenback issue became, for all practical political purposes, a dead issue. The labor unions were still too disorganized to provide the basis for long-term, large-scale political action. The businessmen of the entrepreneurial Greenback clubs, and some of the laborers, turned from Greenbackism to the single tax ideas contained in Henry George's new book, *Progress and Poverty*. The farmers returned to their land speculation and watched crop prices carefully.[31]

The decline of labor participation was only one of the problems that faced the Kansas Greenback-Labor party as it prepared for the 1880 campaign. Kansas was booming. Population had reached the impressive total of 996,000, and land was being claimed at the rate of one million acres a year. Corn and wheat prices rose toward record levels. The 1879 state legislature had extended railroad charters for seventy-nine years, had called for the abolition of the tax exemption on personal property, and had abolished the one-mill school tax. The Kansas Greenback-Labor party could only denounce these actions and renew its call for government control of the railroads. Hiram Vrooman, who had been a delegate to the national Greenback convention, was named the gubernatorial candidate for the Kansas Greenback-Labor party. His campaign against the dynamic Republican prohibitionist John P. St. John was hopeless.[32]

Why did Hiram Vrooman agree to run for governor on the Greenback-Labor ticket in 1880? Looking back over his career since 1870, he could certainly see that the Greenback cause had been doomed since the passage of the Public Credit Act in March, 1869. All the victories of the Greenbackers and moderate antiresumptionists had been temporary. He had supported Carl Schurz and Horace Greeley in the liberal Republican movement even though they both were ardent resumptionists and hard-money men. The glowing ideal of a new party system emerging from the liberal Republican campaign to sweep away the old parties and the corruption of the times had

[31] Selig Perlman, *A History of Trade Unionism in the United States* (New York: Macmillan, 1922), 61.

[32] Zornow, *Kansas,* 165–66, 190–91; Wilder, *Annals of Kansas,* 877, 884–85, 887, 908; Eureka (Kans.) *Herald,* Aug. 5, 1880, p. 2, col. 4.

not been realized. The Independent Reform, National Greenback, and Greenback-Labor parties in Kansas had all proved to be unable to draw more than 6 percent of the vote in an independent campaign.

During the 1880 Greenback-Labor convention that tendered him its nomination Hiram Vrooman remarked, perhaps with some bitterness, that he once had been wealthy. Certainly his financial collapse in 1873 had dealt him a hard blow. Historians often assume that depressions create reformers, but not all who fail in business end up as reformers. Some bounce back even more dedicated to the prevailing orthodoxy. If failure shakes a man's faith and confidence in the justice of the prevailing system, however, he then may turn to reform. Equality of rights—more accurately, equality of opportunity —was one of the great ideals that stirred nineteenth-century American life. Did equality of opportunity exist for the Gilstraps and Vroomans of America if, through government favoritism and political pressure, neither the national banks nor the Treasury would insure an adequate credit supply for the small entrepreneur? Did equality of opportunity exist when banks foreclosed mortgages to protect their liquidity, when insurance companies could be ruined by rumors, or when railroad ventures could be destroyed by speculators on Wall Street? These and a host of similar questions must have plagued Hiram. Why did he cross that vague line that marks the boundary between an out-of-luck politician and a dissatisfied reformer? "He read a pamphlet and got converted"—that is the way his son explained it eighty years later. The historian can estimate declines in status, assess probable economic motives, and trace ideological influences, but in the end he can only bow before the contingencies of history and the mystery of the human personality.[33]

Hiram Vrooman ran for governor in 1880, then, because he was a reformer. Greenbackism had long since ceased to be a viable economic or political strategy; it had become a cause. The ideal for which Hiram labored was equality of opportunity. It was the responsibility of a democratic government to provide the means, in this case credit through an adequate supply of currency, so that the citizen could by his own initiative achieve this ideal. Other threads

[33] Conversation with Carl Vrooman, Nov. 28, 1960.

were woven into his reform program, but this was the dominant motif. He wanted American society to realize the economic meaning of equality.

The fortunes of the Greenback-Labor party in Kansas clearly were waning when Hiram moved his family to Topeka in the autumn of 1881. In its search for a wider basis of support the Greenback-Labor party joined the Anti-Monopoly party in issuing a plea for cooperation to the single tax leagues, the new farmers' organizations, and the state labor assembly. The Greenback-Labor state convention at Topeka in August, 1882, included delegates from the Knights of Labor, the Farmers' Alliance, and the Socialistic Labor Club. But the gubernatorial contest between John P. St. John, the Republican prohibitionist, and George Glick, a "whisky Democrat from Atchison," overshadowed the campaign of the Greenback-Labor candidate, Charles Robinson, who received only 20,933 votes.[34]

The antimonopoly movement of the 1880's was another ill-fated attempt to unite small entrepreneurs, farmers, and trade unionists around the rallying cry of equal rights. Equality of opportunity did not mean the same thing in 1880 that it had meant fifty years earlier, however. Where the antimonopoly movement of the 1830's had tried to prevent the federal government from doing something, namely granting business privileges based on charters, the antimonopolists of the 1880's took an opposite stand in the platform of the Anti-Monopoly party:

5. That it is the duty of the Government to immediately exercise its constitutional prerogative to regulate commerce among the States. The great instruments by which this commerce is carried on are transportation, money, and the transmission of intelligence. They are now mercilessly controlled by giant monopolies, to the impoverishment of labor, and the crushing out of healthful competition, and the destruction of business security. We hold it, therefore, to be the imperative and immediate duty of Congress to pass all needful laws for the control and regulation of those great agents of commerce in accordance with the oft-repeated decisions of the Supreme Court of the United States.[35]

[34] Wilder, *Annals of Kansas*, 974, 986; Zornow, *Kansas*, 193; [Andreas], *History of Kansas*, 581; William Allen White, *The Autobiography of William Allen White* (New York: Macmillan, 1946), 82.

[35] Kirk H. Porter and Donald Bruce Johnson, *National Party Platforms, 1840–1964* (Urbana: University of Illinois Press, 1966), 64.

The antimonopoly movement of the 1880's was weak, therefore, because it departed from the previous reform tradition. While it used the language of the 1830's, it called for a fundamental change in attitudes toward the role of government that many voters were not prepared to make.

In May, 1884, Hiram Vrooman was designated to attend the Anti-Monopoly convention in Chicago as a fraternal delegate for the Greenback-Labor party. The convention nominated Benjamin F. Butler as its presidential candidate. Two weeks later the national Greenback convention at Indianapolis endorsed Butler's candidacy. The Kansas Greenback-Labor convention empowered the party leaders to seek a fusion agreement with the Anti-Monopoly forces in the state. Hiram Vrooman again allowed his name to be put forward for the position of chief justice of the state supreme court. The convention refused, however, to take a stand on the controversial issue of prohibition.[36]

In dodging the prohibition issue the Greenbackers at least avoided an internal schism. Prohibition became an issue in the presidential campaign when John P. St. John bolted the Republican party and ran for president on the National Prohibition ticket. When the "Third Party" Prohibition convention in Kansas refused to put up a state ticket, about forty members of the convention bolted and held a midnight session. They pledged their support to the National Prohibition ticket and presented their own state ticket. It endorsed Hiram Vrooman for chief justice of the state supreme court. Although he ran with the endorsement of Greenback-Labor, Anti-Monopoly, and National Prohibition tickets, Hiram received only 15,773 votes, the smallest number he had received in a decade of political activity. Henceforth, he confined himself to the duties of chairman, organizer, and journalist. In December, 1884, he served as chairman of a meeting of National Prohibition party supporters in Topeka. He continued to support the prohibition movement in Kansas but never again ran for public office.[37]

No event symbolized so acutely the status of the reform movement in the early 1880's as the death of Wendell Phillips on February 2, 1884. Many of the leaders of the reform movement, such as Hiram

[36] Wilder, *Annals of Kansas,* 1055, 1078.
[37] *Ibid.,* 1079–80, 1096, 1117.

Vrooman, had been inspired by Phillips' moral idealism. They shared his belief in the supremacy of ideas, the infallibility of "the people," and the moral necessity of agitation in a republic. Like Phillips, their ideal society was a small-town, equalitarian society based on individualism, natural rights, and small entrepreneurship tempered with social responsibility.[38] The men who operated on these assumptions continued in their reform efforts in the face of repeated failures because they felt that it was their moral duty to do so. When Hiram Vrooman ran for public office in 1884 and supported Butler for president, he knew—as Phillips had known when he ran for governor of Massachusetts in 1870 on the Labor Reform and Prohibition tickets and when he supported Butler for senator in 1871—"that his chances for election was hopeless. The canvass would be simply a protest and an education." [39] For a decade Hiram had supported various reform parties that had polled less than 10 percent of the total vote. He had run for office three times on third-party tickets and had lost. Clearly, the politics of protest paid small returns for the investment required.

[38] Oscar Sherwin, *Prophet of Liberty: The Life and Times of Wendell Phillips* (New York: Bookman Associates, 1958), 599–601.
[39] *Ibid.,* 579.

Chapter Three

An Education in Reform &
Radicalism, 1883-1890

SOCIALISM, ANARCHISM, AND
THE LABOR MOVEMENT, 1883–1886

Social scientists believe that initial political attitudes and loyalties are established during the formative years of childhood. By the age of seven or eight the child has formed an emotional identification with the political party or values of his parents or the dominant parent. Traumatic experiences of the parents' racial, ethnic, or economic group, such as persecution, discrimination, or deprivation, are translated into political loyalties that are passed on by the children to the next generation long after the initial determining events have ceased to exist. These early emotional and preferential loyalties of the child are subject to some change by rational persuasion and education between the ages of sixteen and eighteen. Thereafter the modified pattern of political loyalties will remain fairly constant unless subjected to major shock by experiences, such as war, depression, or personal misfortune.[1]

An understanding of the "politics of trauma" can help the historian to explain continuity within the reform and radical traditions. The child who identifies with his parents' values, whether reformist or radical, has taken an initial position that can be modified by his own experiences. Not all the children of reformers or radicals follow in their parents' footsteps. The pathway is made easier, however, if it has been blazed by parental love. Such was the case with the sons of Hiram Perkins Vrooman.

Hiram's reform activities may have cost him the patronage of many potential clients, but they did not antagonize his sons. They listened respectfully when he lectured to them on the necessity of fighting for ideals. His financial failure, his frequent changes of location, and his political activity provided the setting for their lives. His career created the role for their own efforts. While all the Vrooman brothers followed their father's tattered banner of protest, each marched to his own martial music.

Sarah Buffington Vrooman, Hiram's wife, added the impress of her personality to the childhood of her sons. The daughter of an ardent Republican newspaper editor from Illinois, she was no stranger to political idealism. Her contribution, however, lay in the direction of religious conviction. At one point in his career, Hiram had undergone a period of skepticism, doubt, and free thought in religion. Sarah was a devoted Calvinist who adhered to the Presbyterian and Congregational churches. Under her influence Hiram returned to religious orthodoxy and became an active churchman in the Congregational Church. When his former companions chided him about the miracle stories and other "nonscientific" elements in the Bible, he would remark, "I read my Bible like I eat fish. I pick out the bones first." Sarah's religion sustained not only her husband, but her sons as well.[2]

Frank Buffington Vrooman, the oldest son, acquired a love of learning from his father and a concern for religion from his mother. In the autumn of 1881 Frank enrolled in Washburn College, a small Congregationalist-supported school in Topeka. The rest of the Vrooman family joined him in Topeka the following year. Frank was something of a problem for the Washburn faculty. On the one hand, he was an exceptionally bright student. A classmate later recalled that "he was a tall, slim chap, remarkably smart and seemed to

---

[1] H. D. Schmidt, "Bigotry in School Children," *Commentary*, XXIX (March, 1960), 253–57. For application of these theories to current problems, see Ross Paulson, "Hate Campaigns," *Luther Life*, LXXII (Nov., 1960), 32–38; "Fringe of Hate," *Frontiers*, XIII (Jan., 1962), 17–20; "Extremism in the Classroom," *Augustana Alumni Bulletin* (Rock Island, Ill.), LXI (Winter, 1966), 16.

[2] At the time of her marriage to Hiram Vrooman, Sarah Buffington was a member of the First Presbyterian Church in Kalamazoo, Mich. See "Minutes of the First Presbyterian Church, Kalamazoo, Michigan," Dec. 26, 1860; Feb. 20, 1862. Information furnished by Mrs. J. Worst, church secretary, Aug. 25, 1965. Statements on Hiram's religious experiences based on a conversation with Carl Vrooman, Nov. 28, 1960.

possess the ability to learn without studying." [3] On the other hand, he was frequently in trouble on minor disciplinary matters. He was one of the boys caught at a secret dancing party in the women's cottage. He could not be penalized, however, because as a day student who lived in town and commuted, he was "not a member of the college family." [4] In November, 1882, he was warned about unexcused absences and admonished to "attend strictly to duty." [5]

Like most students, Frank took delight in ridiculing some of the shibboleths of the society around him. On June 14, 1883, he acted as secretary for a mass meeting in Topeka. The participants adopted resolutions stating that enforcement of the state's new prohibition amendment was impossible. A local observer retorted: "The late meeting at Topeka, which openly defied the law, was a crime against Kansas, an impudent, brazen and infamous piece of treason, and every one of the miserable and disloyal whelps and whippersnappers engaged in or aiding and abetting the same ought to be sent to the penitentiary, where they would have reason to learn that the only safety for republican institutions is obedience to law, and reverence for the constitution of our fathers." [6] Frank preferred his father's version of political wisdom: the best safeguard for democratic institutions lies in a vigorous spirit of protest and an enlightened electorate.

After three years at Washburn College Frank started working for the Topeka *Daily Capital*. In July, 1884, he left Topeka to become the editor of the Emporia *News*.[7] But journalism did not satisfy his restless spirit for long. Where his father had transformed his religion of progress and humanity into political activity, Frank

[3] Topeka (Kans.) *Journal,* Nov. 13, 1915, clipping in the Kansas State Historical Society Biographical Collections. The remark is by Robert Stone, class of 1889 at Washburn and a lawyer in Topeka for many years. On Frank Vrooman's academic record, the minutes of the Washburn faculty for May 29, 1882, note that he received highest standing in examinations with an essay on "Ideality."

[4] Faculty minutes, Washburn College, Topeka, Kans., Nov. 26, 1881.

[5] *Ibid.,* Nov. 28, 1882. The same night Frank participated in the Public Rhetoricals with a speech entitled "Desdemona." Program in the archives of Washburn University.

[6] Daniel Webster Wilder, *The Annals of Kansas,* new ed. (Topeka: T. Dwight Thacher, 1886), 1028.

[7] Topeka (Kans.) *Daily Capital,* July 22, 1884, clipping in Kansas State Historical Society Biographical Collections.

sought to combine his intellectual curiosity with a strong religious motivation in a career in the ministry. In 1885 he entered Beloit College in Wisconsin to study theology.[8]

Harry, the second eldest of the Vrooman boys, is an example of a son of the reformer who turns not to reform but to radicalism. During the crucial years between 1877 and 1884, when Harry was thirteen to twenty years of age, the country was racked with industrial strife and subjected to a barrage of radical ideas. Hiram Vrooman's participation in the Greenback-Labor party exposed Harry to the ideology of the labor movement at a time when the Knights of Labor were organizing in Kansas.[9] Then in 1883 Harry's interest was captured by a series of articles on Socialism written by Professor James H. Canfield of Kansas State University and published in the Topeka *Daily Capital*. Canfield's definition of Socialism— "that school of thought that dares to question the present condition of society, hoping to improve the common lot of humanity, particularly that of the lower classes"—appealed to Harry. He had enrolled in Washburn College in the fall of 1883, and during the winter of 1884 he helped to form the sociology club at the college for the purpose "of investigating the merits and claims of Socialism." His effort must have been successful; in March, 1885, someone reported to the Washburn College faculty that "socialistic sentiments" were being circulated among the students.[10]

Harry Vrooman's conversion to Socialism came at a crucial juncture in American history. The American labor movement faced a critical choice: should it seek an accommodation within capitalism or seek an alternative to capitalism? A host of claimants for leadership of the labor movement arose in the land: the anarchists, the Socialists, the single tax advocates, the trade unionists, and the

---

[8] "Frank Buffington Vrooman," *Who's Who in America*, VII (1912–1913), 2172; *Catalogue of the Officers and Students of Washburn College for the Academic Year, 1881–1882* (Topeka: Geo. W. Crane, 1881), 8; "Frank Buffington Vrooman," Harvard University Alumni File, Widener Library.

[9] Wilder, *The Annals of Kansas*, 986. He may have been exposed to Socialistic doctrines when a Socialistic Labor Club delegation attended the state convention of the Greenback-Labor party in Topeka on Sept. 23, 1882.

[10] Harry Vrooman, "Kansas to the Front," *Dawn*, I (June 15, 1889), p. 6, col. 3; p. 7, col. 1; *Kansas Workman* (Quenemo), May 28, 1886, p. 2, cols. 4–6; *Catalogue of the Officers and Students of Washburn College for the Academic Year, 1883–1884* (Topeka: Kansas Publishing House, 1883), 10; faculty minutes, Washburn College, March 2, 1885.

entrepreneurial reformers. The numbers involved in the struggle were small; the stakes were momentous.

To complicate the situation further, each of the contending groups was split into warring factions. Three tiny anarchists' associations constituted the American contingent of the International Working People's Association, the so-called Black International, in the 1880's —(1) the New York social revolutionaries led by Johann Most; (2) the Chicago association of social revolutionaries nominally headed by August Spies and Albert Parsons until the Haymarket incident; and (3) the West Coast remnant of the International Working-men's Association, the so-called Red International, under the leader-ship of Burnette G. Haskell.

Haskell's peculiar version of anarchism combined a native Amer-ican emphasis on natural rights with a belief in an ultimate social revolution in which the use of force by the workers might be neces-sary to achieve their goals. In the meantime Haskell discounted both political action by the workers and "propaganda by deed." He relied upon educational techniques and infiltration of labor organ-izations to help prepare for the revolution.[11]

The Socialists, represented primarily by the Socialistic Labor party, were divided roughly into the Marxists, who stressed the need for economic organization by the workers as a prelude to political action, and the Lassalleans, who believed that independent political action by Socialist groups would bring workers into the Socialist camp.[12] The single tax followers of Henry George in-cluded a radical antipoverty faction headed by the excommunicated Catholic priest, Father Edward McGlynn, and a moderate middle-class entrepreneurial faction. The trade unionists joined either the Knights of Labor, which favored a "mixed union" policy of inclusive membership, or the Federation of Organized Trades and Labor Unions, which leaned toward "simon pure" trade unionism.[13]

[11] John R. Commons and others, *History of Labour in the United States* (New York: Macmillan, 1918), II, 292–99; Chester McArthur Destler, *American Radicalism, 1865–1901,* Connecticut College Monographs No. 3 (New London: Connecticut College, 1946), 78–97.

[12] Howard H. Quint, *The Forging of American Socialism: Origins of the Modern Movement* (Columbia: University of South Carolina Press, 1953), 8.

[13] Peter Alexander Speek, *The Singletax and the Labor Movement,* Bulletin of the University of Wisconsin, Economics and Political Science Series, VIII, No. 3 (Madi-son: University of Wisconsin, 1917), 145–48.

The year 1885 proved to be an important one for the labor movement in Kansas. On March 5, 1885, a state bureau of labor was
established as the result of Knights of Labor lobbying, and on
March 15 a strike of shopmen on the Missouri Pacific Railroad was
settled on terms favorable to the strikers. This victory, coupled with
the apparent capitulation of Jay Gould in the early phases of the
Wabash strike later in the year, stimulated a rapid expansion of the
Knights of Labor in Kansas. The Knights in Topeka kindled further interest by organizing a boycott of the Topeka *Commonwealth*
newspaper.[14]

The Missouri Pacific strike and the ensuing labor unrest in Kansas
provided an ideal situation not only for the growth of the Knights
of Labor but also for the circulation of anarchistic ideas. Joseph
R. Buchanan, an organizer for the Knights of Labor and secretly
a member of Burnette Haskell's Red International, initiated striking
Missouri Pacific workers into the Knights of Labor and spread
Haskell's version of social revolutionary anarchism.[15] On July 9,
1885, Albert Parsons, the leader of the Chicago section of the "Black
International," visited Topeka. His address before an outdoor rally
sponsored by the Knights of Labor was paraphrased by the Topeka
Daily Citizen.

A social system which creates a hell on earth for the greater part of the
people; a system which degrades man by poverty; ruins women by starva-
tion, and dwarfs and stunts the minds and bodies of little children, is
what has given birth to the labor movement, and will ultimately produce
the social revolution. Socialism explains these facts, points out their analogies and teaches the operation of natural law.... Government was an in-
vasion of man's natural right to life, liberty, and the pursuit of happiness,
and only when all political forms of government were abolished, could it
be possible for men to be free and equal.[16]

After this meeting Parsons wrote to his wife, "In Topeka I found
such stalwart champions of revolutionary Socialism as Comrades

[14] Edith Walker, "Labor Problems During the First Year of Governor Martin's
Administration: Labor Legislation in 1885," *Kansas Historical Quarterly,* V (1936),
36–47.
[15] Edith Walker and Dorothy Leibengood, "Labor Organizations in Kansas in the
Early Sixties," *Kansas Historical Quarterly,* IV (Aug., 1935), 284; Joseph R. Buchanan,
The Story of a Labor Agitator (New York: Outlook Co., 1903), 103, 266–74.
[16] *Daily Citizen* (Topeka, Kans.), July 10, 1885, p. 2, cols. 3–4.

Henry, Blakesley, Whitely, Vrooman, Bradley, and others—intelligent and fearless young men who cry out against and spare not the infamies of the capitalistic system." [17]

Harry Vrooman's activities on behalf of Socialism did not go unchallenged in the press. In an editorial entitled "One of the Results" the Topeka *Commonwealth* criticized the Red International IWA and its Kansas secretary, Harry Vrooman, for spreading Socialism.[18]

ONE OF THE RESULTS

The massacre of Chinamen at Rock Springs is one natural result of the indifference with which incendiary characters are treated in this country. The principle that free speech should not be interfered with, no matter how violently it may be addressed to the prejudices and passions of the ignorant, is really a dangerous theory, and is liable at any time to be borne to fatal results in any community. In this city we are quite complacent under the influence of vicious extremists who announce in public the most extravagant of socialistic views, urging their adoption, inciting their followers to catch at their alleged rights by the most hazardous of means. That we have had no serious demonstration here since 1876 is not because the same elements that then participated in the riots have not been urged to repeat their uprising. The lower classes are led by the most intemperate and adventuresome spirits of their various leagues, and if at any time their strength may be thought sufficient for the purpose, it is to be expected there will be an outbreak to secure the "rights of labor." As a matter of fact the legitimate labor classes are not inclined to do violence to any interests, and but for firebrand leaders of socialistic and anarchistic tendencies would be quite easy to deal with in all matters relating to the adjustment of wages. Affairs like that at Rock Springs are disgraceful to the country. In social order as well as in domestic economy a little prevention is worth a great deal of cure, and if police regulations were so amended that blatherskites, wherever found preaching violence and disregard of law, might be seized and incarcerated, we would have fewer so-called labor outrages to lament over.—*Chicago Inter-Ocean.*

In this connection we desire to inform our readers that there is an office, and we presume lodges of the International Workingmen's association, or as they seem to prefer to call it, the "Red (American) International" in

---

[17] Lucy E. Parsons, *Life of Albert Parsons* (Chicago: Lucy E. Parsons, 1889), 30.
[18] Topeka (Kans.) *Commonwealth,* Sept. 11, 1885, photocopy furnished by the Kansas State Historical Society, Topeka.

Kansas, with headquarters at 114 East Seventh Street, with H. C. Vrooman as secretary for Kansas.

Harry responded with a vigorous letter in which he said:

I see in your issue of Friday last, an article entitled "One of the Results," in which myself and the worthy association which I represent, was made quite conspicuous. I desire to thank you for the valuable space in your paper, but owing to the unfair—as I think—and misleading connection with which you presented facts and names, I think it only justice that you allow me further space to explain. . . .

As you made mention of my name personally, aside from the association, I would state in this connection, that as for myself, I know no nation, race, creed, color or class; but the clanking of servile chains in any clime awakes to fraternal strains the socialist chord of my heart. Every being in whose bosom throbs a human soul is my brother. I proclaim my sincere belief in that gospel preached by St. Paul on Mars hill that God "hath made of one blood all nations." Yes, John Chinaman is my brother, and to him I extend the hand of a fellow slave, and bid him strike with me for liberty. Yes, outraged and robbed humanity, though weltering in ignorance and squalor, as long as God gives me a conscience and a tongue, will find in me an advocate, weak as it may be.

I know this is unpopular in this pleasure and wealth-chasing world. I know, as young as I am, it has already cost me many friends and much money and reputation. But I did not enter this cause blindly. I counted the cost and upon my own head I am willing to take the consequences. I am no rash enthusiast. My belief is the result of years of cool study and patient investigation in to the deep problem of life, and the cause of human ills. . . . Constitutional means are the present weapons chosen by us. If the capitalists force upon us a change of weapons they must be responsible for the wounds. Concerning your charge that we are "led by the most intemperate and adventuresome spirits of their various leagues," I would merely say that the chief officer of the Missouri Valley division uses neither alcoholic liquor or tobacco in any form, or tea or coffee. How much more temperate would you have him be?

We are simply striving to realize the principles of Moses and Christ. Plato was a much more radical socialist than the modern "Red (American) International." So also was Sir Thomas More, the statesman scholar, saint and martyr. They were communists—a much more radical school than modern socialists. Wendell Phillips and Victor Hugo, are other heroes in our cause—true socialists. . . . In conclusion I would say for the benefit of friends in Topeka, that we have just received at headquarters— No. 151, Kansas avenue, a new and large supply of the very latest improved dynamite, with which we propose to explode society. At present we have about a thousand small bombs, ready for use at from one cent each and upwards. They are in pamphlet form—ably edited, and represent the double distilled dynamite of the mind. Still for "liberty, equality and fraternity," I remain,

Respectfully, Harry C. Vrooman [19]

Harry's letter reveals the extent to which his rejection of the premises of his society had proceeded. He rejected the private ownership of the means of production, the implicit class system of the late nineteenth century, the profit motive, and the entrepreneurial dream. But he retained a belief in constitutional action while preaching an ultimate but vaguely defined social revolution.

The strikes and turmoil of 1884 and 1885 aroused the antipathy of many Midwesterners, including some within the ranks of the Knights of Labor. Far from supporting either a social revolution or Socialism, their habitual conservatism found expression in the resolution of an Iowa District Assembly to the national executive committee of the Knights of Labor: "Our people in the west will not countenance strikes in any shape unless at the ballot box." [20]

In September, 1885, the Topeka Knights of Labor entered a Workingmen's ticket in the local elections. Harry Vrooman supported the new party, but the results showed that few workingmen were prepared to strike even at the ballot box. [21] The wage earners, farmers, and petty professionals who had joined the Knights of Labor during 1885 did not join because they had been converted to a particular program of working-class action. They flocked to the Knights because the victories in the railroad strikes had fostered exaggerated reports of the strength of the movement or because they wanted to learn the secrets of the order.

The national leadership of the Knights was imbued with the

[19] *Ibid.*, Sept. 17, 1885, photocopy furnished by the Kansas State Historical Society, Topeka.

[20] Norman J. Ware, *The Labor Movement in the United States: 1860–1895: A Study in Democracy* (New York: D. Appleton, 1929), 137.

[21] Walker and Leibengood, *Kansas Historical Quarterly*, IV, 288–90.

reform philosophy of the old National Labor Union and continued to emphasize education rather than direct action in the form of strikes or political action through third parties. Basically the Knights in 1885 represented a vague sentiment of solidarity, a quasi-religious impulse that transformed the local assembly into a sanctuary, social club, and educational center. On the other hand, the anarchists, the Socialists, the trade unionists, and a few independent politicians saw in the organization a means for guiding the labor movement into more opportunistic or rigidly ideological paths.[22]

The same mixed sentiments and confused motives concerning the labor movement can be found in the Vrooman family's activities during the crucial year of 1886. Hiram Vrooman, the veteran reform politician, saw in the resurgent labor movement a chance to educate workingmen in the proper use of the ballot. In May, 1886, he became the associate editor of the *Kansas Workman,* a labor newspaper edited by Cyrus Corning of Quenemo. Hiram addressed an open letter to his reform associates in the state: "What we now most need is an educational force which shall seek to elevate the people through peaceful means, not force. The ballot is the great conservator of the people's rights and liberties and if it shall fail now, this is an end to popular liberty and free institutions. The *Workman* will endeavor in the fullest sense to be that EDUCATIONAL FORCE." [23] To carry this message directly to the workers Hiram Vrooman, Cyrus Corning, Harry Vrooman, Walter Vrooman, and the Reverend John Melvin organized the Workmen's Bureau of Information, a clearinghouse for their lecture activities. The bureau recommended such books as Laurence Gronlund's *Coöperative Commonwealth,* Henry George's *Progress and Poverty,* John Ruskin's *Crown of Wild Olives,* and selected works by Wendell Phillips.[24] But Hiram was not one to be bound by any particular theory

---

[22] Ware, *The Labor Movement,* xvi, 67, 96; Gerald N. Grob, *Workers and Utopia: A Study of Ideological Conflict in the American Labor Movement, 1865–1900,* Northwestern University Studies in History, II (Evanston: Northwestern University Press, 1961), 60–61. See T. V. Powderly's "secret circular" of March 13, 1886, reprinted in Grob, *Workers and Utopia,* 67–68.

[23] *Kansas Workman,* May 21, 1886, p. 2, cols. 1–2. The *Kansas Workman* was a weekly labor newspaper with a circulation of 800 in 1886. *The Edwin Alden Company's American Newspaper Catalogue for 1886* (Cincinnati: Edwin Alden Co., 1886), 116.

[24] *Kansas Workman,* June 18, 1886, p. 3, col. 4.

of labor organization or any strict ideology. At a prohibitionist rally in October, 1886, he spoke for two hours on the financial, anti-monopoly, labor, and other reform questions of the day. To him they all constituted the "cause of the people." [25]

Harry Vrooman, the corresponding editor of the *Kansas Work-man,* was more ideologically inclined than was his father. At the same time his version of Socialism was influenced by the religious humanitarianism of the leading exponents of liberal theology in America. In an open letter to the Osage County *Republican* in August, 1886, he invoked religious sanctions for his Socialism: "We demand that the Christian principles of brotherhood be applied to economics and industry, instead of building on a foundation of selfishness and antagonism. In short we would reconstruct by intro-ducing scientific coöperative management of production and distri-bution." [26] Throughout the summer and autumn of 1886 Harry performed various tasks within the Kansas labor movement. He corresponded with the leaders of cooperative colonies, gathered statistics on the conditions of the coal miners in Peterson, Kansas, and lectured to local assemblies of the Knights of Labor. [27]

Nowhere was the tension between the quasi-religious origins of the labor sentiment and the ideological demands of Socialism better illustrated than in the career and the rhetoric of Walter Vrooman. This sickly, semi-invalid child had found his personal childhood hero in a lyceum circuit phrenologist and health faddist named O'Leary. "This distinguished gentleman, with the theatre stage, which he used as his platform, covered over with polished skeletons, manikins, human heads in chloroform and colored pictures of the various parts of the human frame," impressed young Walter with his theories of healthful living. For several years Walter and a friend "subsisted on a diet of bread and apples" supplemented by whole wheat. [28]

In spite of his delicate health he made an itinerant sales tour through the West in 1883 and then embarked upon a new career in the summer of 1884 as a boy phrenologist. In the autumn of 1884

[25] *Ibid.,* Oct. 8, 1886, p. 1, col. 6.
[26] *Ibid.,* Sept. 3, 1886, p. 2, col. 1.
[27] *Ibid.,* Aug. 27, 1886, p. 3, col. 3.
[28] Walter Vrooman, *The New Democracy* (St. Louis: by the author, 1897), 71, 74

he followed the Vroomans' well-worn path to Washburn College Preparatory School. He soon returned to the lyceum circuit for a tour through the South as a replacement for the famous Doctor Fowler. But Walter could not remain outside the circle of interests of the Vrooman family for long.[29]

Under the influence of his brother Harry, Walter also became a radical and a Socialist. Since he was only seventeen years old, his role within the labor movement was that of the boy orator who could say in public what his adult audience only muttered in private. The themes of religion, of social revolutionary anarchism, of Socialism, and of recent developments in the Kansas labor movement were uniquely blended in his speeches. In response to criticism of his Sunday activities by fellow members of the Congregational Church, he replied:

Sunday is the proper time to hunt and search for some way or method by which you can free yourselves from those who are not only starving your bodies but murdering your souls. Today we do not want to excite our feelings or influence our passions, but we want to take a philosophic view of the situation. This is no local affair, but we are nearing a climax of a universal struggle of ages. The struggle cannot be settled in one day or by one spirit, but is something that will be hotly contested on both sides throughout the world. The question will not be solved in any little way because *the whole system is wrong.* Society is on an artificial basis. We will have to change the whole foundation, and that will not be done by a few strikes, a dynamite explosion, nor a mob. I am not much in favor of all of these little strikes, but believe in preparing for the big one which will go to the very foundations. Compromise can never settle any great questions. Arbitration is not a panacea for present evils, although arbitration would be good at the present time. [Italics added] [30]

He defended Socialism as a "just, loving, and peaceful system." He concluded one speech with a curiously mixed peroration: "the

[29] Harlan Buddington Phillips, "Walter Vrooman: Restless Child of Progress" (unpublished Ph.D. dissertation, Dept. of History, Columbia University, 1954), 8–12, 15–16; *Catalogue of the Officers and Students of Washburn College for the Academic Year, 1884–1885* (Topeka: Kansas Publishing House, 1884), 15; Topeka *Daily Capital,* July 18, 1883, clipping in Kansas State Historical Society Biographical Collections. The records at Washburn indicate that Walter Vrooman attended only the second term of the 1884–1885 academic year.
[30] Topeka *Daily Capital,* April 20, 1886.

working men of all races and all colors and all nations should unite in one common cause for one purpose under one flag of one color—the red flag—denoting what Paul said on Mars Hill that God made from one blood all nations to banish forever all forms of tyranny and depression from the world." [31]

Walter Vrooman's relationship to the labor movement was more complicated than that of his brother Harry. Harry saw the labor movement as a field for ideological battle; Walter viewed it as a holy crusade. Public opinion in Kansas and Missouri had turned violently against the Knights of Labor during the summer of 1886 in reaction to the prolonged Southwestern railway strike, to the use of troops to restore order among the strikers in Parsons, Kansas, and to the news of the Haymarket bomb incident.[32] When Walter spoke in behalf of the Knights of Labor during the summer and autumn of 1886, he frequently was treated harshly by the local authorities. In Ottawa, Kansas, the town fathers revoked his permission to speak; in Kansas City, Missouri, he was arrested. In St. Joseph, Missouri, he was again arrested in an incident that almost touched off a riot. Newspaper reporters were careful to reassure their readers that young Walter Vrooman was not an anarchist.[33]

The controversies that accompanied Walter's efforts were not caused solely by adverse public opinion. Harry was addressing similar audiences on similar themes in the same climate of opinion without creating any public disturbances. An alternative explanation is suggested by the following passage from one of Walter's letters to the *Kansas Workman:* "I began to thump the crowd over the head pretty hard with the golden rule, carve their vitals with the sword of the spirit, and depress the minds of some with weighty truths from holy writ." [34] This is not the prose of a reasonable young orator but the heavy-handed rhetoric of a young egotist striving for effect. An editor in the Atchison, Kansas, *Daily Champion* tried to explain Walter Vrooman for his readers: "The only

[31] *Ibid.*
[32] Ware, *The Labor Movement,* 149; Dorothy Leibengood, "Labor Problems in the Second Year of Governor Martin's Administration," *Kansas Historical Quarterly,* V (1936), 195–201.
[33] *Kansas Workman,* May 21, 1886, p. 2, col. 4; Oct. 29, 1886, p. 3, col. 3; Phillips, "Walter Vrooman," 28.
[34] June 11, 1886, p. 2, cols. 4–5.

trouble with him is what might be called talkomania. It is often said of a man that he had rather talk than eat. This is literally the case with young Vrooman. He is usually [willing] to suffer for food if he can only indulge in oratory. The dry goods box, the torchlight, the crowd, these are necessary to his existence." [35] Through his startling oratory the seventeen-year-old agitator sought to establish his own identity within the Vrooman family circle and within the labor movement in Kansas and Missouri. He combined the religious fervor of his brother Frank, the Socialistic rhetoric of his brother Harry, and the moral drive of his father in a unique personality that displayed its full power only when confronting a crowd in an oratorical situation.

Both Harry and Walter had entered the Socialist camp through the route of Christian humanitarianism. Socialistic economic concepts coexisted in their vocabulary with ethical precepts gleaned from the writings of Wendell Phillips, R. Herbert Newton, and Richard T. Ely. In October, 1886, Harry and Walter established the *Labor Organizer* in Kansas City, Missouri, a newspaper espousing Socialism within the labor movement.[36]

The two young Socialists were carried further into the orthodox Socialist movement by the visit of Eleanor Marx Aveling, one of Karl Marx's daughters, and her husband, Edward Bibbins Aveling, to the Kansas City area on a speaking tour sponsored by the Socialistic Labor party. Mrs. Aveling noticed "a very young and eager face" in the audience during a meeting in Kansas City on November 21, 1886. After the meeting the Avelings "were introduced to its owner, Walter Vrooman, the boy-orator." [37] The Avelings were so impressed with the enthusiasm of Walter and his twenty-two-year-old brother that they included a description of the "Vrooman boys" in their report on the labor movement in the United States: "Walter and his brother Harry were the editors of the American

[35] Oct. 16, 1886, clipping in the Kansas State Historical Society Biographical Collections.

[36] *Labor Enquirer* (Denver), May 21, 1887, p. 8, cols. 1–2. The *Labor Organizer* had a circulation of 6,000 in 1886. *The Edwin Alden Company's American Newspaper Catalogue for 1886,* 187.

[37] Edward Bibbins Aveling and Eleanor Marx Aveling, *The Working Class Movement in America,* 2nd ed. (London: Swan Sonnenschein, 1891), 210. The date of the meeting was determined from comments in Edward Bibbins Aveling, *An American Journey* (New York: John W. Lovell, 1887), 95.

labour paper of Kansas City,—the *Labour Inquirer* [*Organizer*]. Harry, nineteen years of age [*sic*] had contributed to the Bureau of Labour for Kansas state a most valuable set of facts and statistics on the Labour movement. Both boys we found frank, open-hearted, delightful; quite boys still and with a keen sense of fun, as their older brother, a Unitarian clergyman, and not yet a Social-ist, found out, for they chaffed him good-humouredly, but merci-lessly. A fourth boy, fifteen years of age, they announced as 'coming on,' and sure to work with them before long." [38] The Avelings' re-port undoubtedly helped to spread the reputation of the "Vrooman boys" in Socialistic circles throughout the country.

By the end of 1886 Frank, Harry, and Walter Vrooman had re-ceived a thorough education in the techniques of agitation—third-party politics, labor strife, journalism, preaching, and oratory. In addition, they had been exposed to a wide range of ideological positions: the Greenback theories of their father, the reform-oriented program of the Knights of Labor, the peculiar natural-rights an-archism of Burnette Haskell, the more orthodox anarchism of Albert Parsons, the "Christian" Socialism of liberal theology, and the Marxist Socialism of the Avelings. Their father's newspaper, the *Kansas Workman,* even carried articles and correspondence on communitarian and Utopian Socialist colonies in Mexico and Cali-fornia that were backed by Kansas radicals. [39] Events soon conspired to test the education that Harry and Walter had acquired in Kansas and Missouri in the larger field of national Socialist and labor politics. [40]

[38] Aveling and Aveling, *The Working Class,* 211–12. Frank, the older brother, was, in fact, a Congregational minister who was at that time occupying a Presbyterian pulpit at Oskaloosa, Kans. *Kansas Workman,* May 21, 1886, p. 3, col. 1; Sept. 17, 1886, p. 5, col. 1.

[39] See *Kansas Workman,* Aug. 13, 1886, p. 3, col. 3, for article on the Crédit Foncier of Sinaloa, a Utopian Socialist colony backed by men who later became prominent in Populist circles in Kansas. See also letter from J. H. Redstone of San Francisco to Harry Vrooman concerning a new colony in California. *Ibid.,* Oct. 8, 1886, p. 3, cols. 2–3.

[40] There is no evidence that the Vrooman brothers ever advocated the "Black International" version of anarchism or the nihilistic creed of "propaganda by deed." One of the boys, probably Walter, was known locally as "the dynamiter"; however, as Harry's letter to the Topeka *Commonwealth* shows, their ammunition was verbal and their ordnance was ideas, not incendiary bombs. Albert Parsons' letter referring to "revolutionary Socialism" cannot be taken as proof that they advocated initiating violence. The Red International version of anarchism favored by Harry stressed edu-cation more than violent action.

THE SOCIALISTIC LABOR PARTY
AND THE UNITED LABOR PARTY, 1887–1888

During the 1886 New York City mayoralty campaign a coalition of single tax, Socialist, and labor forces had been formed to support the candidacy of Henry George against Democrat Abraham Hewitt and Republican Theodore Roosevelt. After the unsuccessful George campaign, the single tax forces had established Land and Labor clubs. The single taxers also joined the Socialists to form a new party, the United Labor party. It was clearly an unstable alliance and a marriage of convenience for both groups. In January, 1887, the tension between them came to a head when the Socialists seized control of the United Labor party newspaper, the *Leader,* and named a Socialist, Serge Schevitch, editor. Henry George retaliated by founding his own newspaper, the *Standard.* The Socialists continued the struggle with pamphlet attacks upon George's ideas by their leading theoretician, Laurence Gronlund.[41]

In the spring of 1887 both the single tax and Socialist forces maneuvered to strengthen their positions within the United Labor party. In April, 1887, Walter Vrooman was invited by Redpath's Lyceum Bureau to lecture at the Cooper Union in New York City on behalf of the single tax Land and Labor clubs. He turned the editorial control of the Kansas City *Labor Organizer* newspaper over to Harry Vrooman and set out for New York City.[42]

In Pittsburgh Walter sparked a local Socialist revival during the first week of May. Oswald Kuhn, the local Socialistic Labor party representative, reported to the party leaders that he expected to organize an English-speaking section among the local workers with Walter's assistance. At an outdoor rally on May 9, 1887, Walter said that in the light of the miscarriage of justice in the trial of the Haymarket anarchists the American flag had been reduced to a mere rag on a stick. "Patriots" in the audience took violent exception to this slur on the flag, and in the ensuing melée, Walter was arrested. In the judicial inquiry into the incident it was revealed that he was a member of the Socialistic Labor party, and Walter was

[41] Commons, *History of Labour,* II, 456; Quint, *American Socialism,* 44–45.
[42] Phillips, "Walter Vrooman," 34.

fined twenty-five dollars and costs on a charge of disorderly conduct.[43]

The arrest, confinement, and unfair conviction served only to add fuel to Walter Vrooman's burning zeal for the cause of Socialism. In New York City Laurence Gronlund arranged a series of outdoor rallies for him under the auspices of the United Labor party and the Socialistic Labor party. Walter proceeded to vent his spleen before the curious crowds.

All we want is that the laborer shall receive the full value of his labor, and still there are some who come with their courts of arbitration. Courts of arbitration are nonsense. I don't want any—of what use are they, when the commissioners are paid and bribed by the capitalists to decide against us? Away with them! Do business with the devil and you'll be swindled. The nationalization of railroads and land cannot alone help us. We want the full value of our labor—that's all. Did you notice the signs of the times? Did you notice how the "republicans" and "democrats" combined against the Labor Party in this city, in Chicago, Cincinnati, Milwaukee, in order to defeat us? I am a democrat, but not a member of the "democratic" party composed of aristocrats and flunkeys, but of the real democracy who call themselves Social-Democrats.[44]

There never can be and ought never to be harmony between Capital and Labor, until all Capital is owned by Labor who produce it. The war between co-operative production and individual ownership in the means of production will continue until those who co-operate in production will receive the benefits derived from the co-operation. This can only come about by the people taking control of the land, the railroads, telegraphs, factories and commerce, and instituting integral co-operation, which is Socialism.[45]

Walter was in his element—agitation. During the summer of 1887 he conducted a vigorous propaganda tour through New York, New Jersey, and New England, lecturing to Land and Labor clubs, Central Labor unions, and outdoor rallies.[46]

[43] *Workmen's Advocate* (New Haven), May 14, 1887, p. 1, col. 4; Phillips, "Walter Vrooman," 40–44; *Labor Enquirer,* May 21, 1887, p. 8, col. 2.

[44] *Workmen's Advocate,* May 21, 1887, p. 1, col. 4.

[45] *Ibid.,* May 28, 1887, p. 1, col. 4.

[46] Walter Vrooman spoke in Elizabeth, N. J.; Hoboken, N. J.; New Haven, Conn.; Providence, R. I.; Boston, Mass.; and New York City. See *Workmen's Advocate,* June 11, 1887, p. 1, col. 3; July 2, 1887, p. 1, cols. 5–6; July 9, 1887, p. 1, col. 3; *Labor Enquirer,* July 23, 1887, p. 5, cols. 1–2.

Walter's attitude toward techniques of agitation was illustrated neatly by two letters written during the summer of 1887. In June, 1887, he defended the leaders of the Crédit Foncier of Sinaloa, a cooperative colony in Topolobampo, Mexico. In a letter published in the *Workmen's Advocate* he wrote:

I have made the personal acquaintance of the leaders in the movement and find them all to be thoroughly sincere, devoted and self-sacrificing.... The collectivity owns the land, the houses, the railroad, the ships, the stores, the hotels, and all means of production and exchange. Interest and rent do not exist in the colony, and if the enterprise is a success it will illustrate many truths and a valuable experiment to the world. I believe that complete social revolution is the only outcome of the present false social conditions, but *I believe in encouraging everything that will illustrate in any way the principles that society must someday, universally adopt.* [Italics added] [47]

In a letter dated July 28, 1887, Walter described the pioneering settlement-house efforts of Stanton Coit in New York City and stated more specifically his own conception of the role of the agitator: "In striving to be factors in the evolution of mankind we should not only be interested in agitating and promulgating our ideas, but in aiding every new development that in any way illustrates the beneficial results of co-operation and organization." [48]

These comments are highly revelatory of Walter's attitude toward techniques of agitation during this early phase of his career. As an agitator he would encourage others to experiment but would not himself submit to the discipline, the attention to detail, and the mundane pace of such cooperative or social ventures.

In August, 1887, the long-smouldering feud between the single tax advocates and the Socialists within the United Labor party flared anew. On August 5, 1887, John McMackin, general chairman of the county general committee of the United Labor party, reversed a previous ruling on dual membership. He ruled that members of the Socialistic Labor party were ineligible to serve as delegates to the United Labor party convention in Syracuse under the provisions of the United Labor party's constitution. This decision directly

---

[47] *Workmen's Advocate,* June 18, 1887, p. 1, col. 3.
[48] *Labor Enquirer,* Aug. 13, 1887, p. 5, col. 1.

affected several leading Socialists who had been elected to serve as delegates to the Syracuse convention—George Block, Hugo Vogt, Max Boehm, Laurence Gronlund, Serge Schevitch, and Walter Vrooman.[49] Henry George ostensibly remained aloof from these issues and benignly advocated allowing the Socialists to attend the Syracuse convention: "Since the relation of the United Labor Party with Socialism has been brought into such prominence and will enter into the most important part of the proceedings of the convention, it is all the better that Socialism should be represented there by its ablest exponents, and it would be a pity to rule out of the convention on technical grounds three such men as Messrs. Schevitch, Gronlund and Vrooman—the first a well-known Socialistic editor; the second a well-known Socialistic writer and the third an accredited missionary and orator of the Socialistic Labor Party."[50] For Walter Vrooman there was an additional problem. He was declared ineligible to serve as a delegate because he was a minor and a nonresident.[51]

When the Syracuse convention of the United Labor party opened on August 17, 1887, the single tax forces were firmly in control. The convention adopted the majority report of the credentials committee, which ruled against the Socialistic Labor party members. On a motion from the floor the Socialists were allowed five minutes apiece to explain their position. Walter Vrooman came quickly to the point:

Two years ago the Socialists formed the Labor Party. The Socialistic Labor Party is not for political purposes but for propaganda. The constitution says it shall act with the Labor Party whenever there is one. The hot-headed regulars here are saying: "Sit down on the Socialists." Socialists are not cushions. You will probably find that out if you sit too hard. There is no effort to make this party Socialistic. Socialism is a philosophy, a science, and it takes long and hard shakes to weaken it. We do not think people will vote for philosophy. Do not change the United Labor Party into a pocket convention.[52]

[49] Speek, *Singletax,* 106–108; *Workmen's Advocate,* July 30, 1887, p. 1, col. 3; Quint, *American Socialism,* 46.

[50] *Labor Enquirer,* Aug. 13, 1887, p. 1, col. 1.

[51] *Ibid.,* Aug. 20, 1887, p. 6, col. 1.

[52] *Ibid.,* Aug. 27, 1887, p. 1, col. 5.

The delegates were unmoved by the appeals. They proceeded to eject the Socialists and to adopt a platform based upon the single tax. Then they nominated Henry George for secretary of state in the forthcoming New York state elections.[53]

The expulsion of the Socialists from the United Labor party was a serious blow to the Socialistic Labor party. It consisted of a few thousand German-speaking Socialists and a few hundred English-speaking sympathizers organized into small sections in the major industrial centers. The native American members never accounted for more than 10 percent of the party's membership.[54] The action of the Syracuse convention tended further to isolate them from the mass of American workers. In order to recoup their losses the Socialist leaders called for a party congress to meet in Buffalo, New York, during September, 1887, to undertake a thorough examination of the status of the party. The agenda called for a consideration of a scheme put forth by Burnette Haskell to unite his Red International anarchists with the Socialists. It also called for a review of the party's attitude toward the single tax United Labor party, the agrarian-dominated Union Labor party, the Knights of Labor, and the trade unions. Revision of the organizational structure of the party, consideration of the means for consecutive agitation, and examination of the party newspapers were also listed.[55]

The Socialistic Labor party called for reinforcements in its battle with the single tax forces. From halfway across the continent Harry Vrooman responded to the call. When Walter had departed for New York City in April, 1887, Harry had taken control of their newspaper. Harry then formed a journalistic alliance with Burnette Haskell's Denver *Labor Enquirer*.

[53] Speek, *Singletax,* 122–26. Walter Vrooman and Laurence Gronlund were excluded because they were nonresidents of the state of New York.

[54] Ira Kipnis, *The American Socialist Movement, 1897–1912* (New York: Columbia University Press, 1952), 19. See Daniel Bell's essay in Stow Persons and Donald Egbert, eds., *Socialism and American Life* (Princeton: Princeton University Press, 1952), I, 237.

[55] *Workmen's Advocate,* Sept. 17, 1887, p. 1, col. 3. Haskell's attempt to bring dissident Knights of Labor into his scheme had been foiled on April 30, 1887, by the Chicago *Knights of Labor* newspaper which exposed his scheme and hinted darkly that he planned a revolution in 1889. See Destler, *American Radicalism,* 79–81, 101–103; Henry David, *The History of the Haymarket Affair* (New York: Farrar & Rinehart, 1961), 146–48.

On May 21, 1887, the Denver *Labor Enquirer* absorbed the subscription list of the Vrooman brothers' *Labor Organizer*. When Harry Vrooman joined the *Labor Enquirer* staff, Haskell warned his readers: "Mr. Vrooman has a habit of telling the truth, no matter whom it hits." [56] While he continued to serve as the official lecturer of the Missouri State Assembly of the Knights of Labor, Harry furnished a weekly column on the labor situation in the Kansas-Missouri area for the Denver paper.

Harry possessed a passionate and, at times, poetic prose style. His style occasionally was marred, however, by his vitriolic pen. With scorn he denounced the capitalistic press for misrepresenting his brother's arrest in Pittsburgh, accused college youths of intellectual prostitution, and jeered at flag-waving veterans in the GAR.[57] Some of his better journalistic items were widely published in other labor newspapers. He wrote:

Recent economic history has . . . verified the assertion that wage-earners under the present industrial regime can be nothing else but slaves, living helpless and hopeless at the mercy of their masters. They can gain only a few of the attributes of freedom by means of a relentless industrial war. The slaves must sustain a constant organized fighting front in order to even persuade their masters that it is more profitable to grant them a decent living than to fight them.[58]

The world is starving to death for sympathy and love. A cold, universal *laissez-faire*—a concentrated selfishness and hardheartedness—is congealing the finer feeling and emotions of humanity, and civilization is developing into a stagnation of soul.[59]

But the strain of continual travel, agitation rallies, and journalistic work had proved too much for Harry's health. He returned to his father's house to recuperate in July, 1887.

When Harry Vrooman was called east in August, 1887, in the interests of the Socialistic Labor party, he used the trip as a means for investigating the condition of the party. In Kansas City, he

---

[56] *Labor Enquirer*, May 21, 1887, p. 4, col. 1; p. 8, cols. 1–2.

[57] *Ibid.*, May 21, 1887, p. 8, col. 2; June 4, 1887, p. 5, col. 2; June 25, 1887, p. 3, cols. 1–2.

[58] *Ibid.*, May 28, 1887, p. 5, col. 4.

[59] *Ibid.*, June 4, 1887, p. 5, col. 3.

found support for Haskell's plan of union: "In Kansas City the sentiment runs strongly toward union and even if no basis of union can be found for Herr Most's crowd [Black International] and the Socialistic Labor Party, which union is gravely doubted, yet all agree that the International Workmen's [sic] Association—Red International—can and should be one with the Socialistic Labor Party, since their principles are identical." [60] Harry also complained of the bickering among the members, the "allowing of trifles and individualities to overrule the broader and weightier matters" of the labor movement. He concluded that the greatest drawback to the progress of the Socialistic Labor party in the United States was "the unadaptability of its members to Americans or American methods." [61]

In Dayton, Ohio, he found that the members of the local section of the Socialistic Labor party favored the union of all secret labor organizations on the basis of the Socialistic Labor party program, maintenance of separate party newspapers, and employment of a few highly skilled English-speaking agitators. They also asked Harry to represent them at the Buffalo congress of the party.[62]

As a member of the propaganda committee of the American Socialist Federation, Harry also used the trip from Kansas City to New York City to continue his lecturing and propaganda work by addressing Socialist rallies in Cincinnati, Dayton, Cleveland, Pittsburgh, and New York City. He arrived in New York City in time to witness an immense Labor Day parade on September 5, 1887.[63]

The marching ranks of laborers in the parade did not represent an actual solidarity among the workers. The New York City labor scene was seething with conflict in the wake of the ouster of the Socialists from the United Labor party. On September 8, 1887, a group of Socialists and dissident anti-George trade unionists adopted the title Progressive Labor party for their effort to organize a new party to compete with the single tax United Labor party.[64] Harry Vrooman found that his brother Walter was busily engaged in

[60] Ibid., Sept. 3, 1887, p. 4, col. 3.
[61] Ibid.
[62] Workmen's Advocate, Sept. 3, 1887, p. 1, col. 4; Labor Enquirer, Sept. 10, 1887, p. 6, cols. 1–2.
[63] Labor Enquirer, Aug. 20, 1887, p. 2, col. 1; Sept. 17, 1887, p. 6, cols. 1–2.
[64] Speek, Singletax, 135.

protesting the ouster of the Socialists from the United Labor party and in denouncing the impending execution of the Haymarket anarchists. Walter had planned an extensive agitation tour through Connecticut, Massachusetts, New Hampshire, and Rhode Island from September 4 to September 22, 1887, but, with the pressure of other duties mounting, he turned the tour over to Harry.[65]

Harry interrupted the tour to attend the opening of the Buffalo congress of the Socialistic Labor party on September 17, 1887. As the convention progressed, the strength of the Lassallean faction became evident. Harry and Laurence Gronlund were appointed to the platform committee and addressed an "English-speaking" rally called to protest the treatment of the Haymarket anarchists. Burnette Haskell's letter appealing for the admission of his International Workingmen's Association was referred to a five-man committee that included the leading Lassalleans in the Socialistic Labor party—Harry Vrooman, Haskell's journalistic associate; W. L. Rosenberg, editor of *Der Sozialist;* J. E. Busche, editor of the *Workmen's Advocate;* and Gronlund. As a result of convention action on their report, Haskell was designated Pacific Coast organizer for the Socialistic Labor party, and his group gradually was absorbed by the party.[66] The Buffalo congress did not adopt the pure Lassallean program of independent Socialist political action. However, leading members of the Socialistic Labor party, including Harry Vrooman, also served as organizers for the Progressive Labor party as a first step in that direction.[67]

Harry undertook to organize Progressive Labor party sections along the Erie Railroad route on his return from the Buffalo congress. He then journeyed to Providence, Rhode Island, where he became the editor of a Socialist newspaper, *The People.* In friendly labor newspapers he explained the rationale of the strategy behind the formation of the Progressive Labor party: "In order to more thoroughly

[65] *Workmen's Advocate,* Aug. 6, 1887, p. 1, col. 4; Aug. 27, 1887, p. 1, col. 6; Sept. 3, 1887, p. 1, col. 6; Sept. 10, 1887, p. 4, col. 1.
[66] *Ibid.,* Sept. 24, 1887, p. 1, col. 2; *Labor Enquirer,* Oct. 1, 1887, p. 2, col. 1; p. 8, col. 2; Quint, *American Socialism,* 52; Commons, *History of Labour,* II, 300, n. 88. Quint sees the acceptance of Haskell's letter as a modification of a Marxian faction maneuver by the Lassalleans. But Harry Vrooman's statements indicate that the Lassalleans favored Haskell's plea before the convention.
[67] *Labor Enquirer,* Oct. 1, 1887, p. 8, col. 2.

control the moulding influences affecting society it is now absolutely necessary that the labor reform take control of the political government. To this end we advocate independent political action." [68]

The issue, as Harry saw it, was simply one of unity among the workers:

In order to overcome the evils that surround the labor movement, we must unite. The capitalists stand together and protect themselves and should not the working people? You must organize an independent party. Neither old party intends to do anything for the laboring man. They put in catch planks and patch up their platform to catch your votes, but they never keep their promises. The record of both parties for long years back is a record of treachery to the interest of the workingmen. You must have an independent party and stand by it. The laboring class is the largest in the country, and if you will only stand together you can soon say who shall be in power and who shall walk in your halls of legislation. [69]

The performance of the Progressive Labor party in the New York state elections hardly justified Harry's enthusiasm. While the United Labor party polled approximately 72,000 votes, the Progressive Labor party tallied only about 5,000. [70]

As editor of *The People* in Providence, Rhode Island, Harry pursued two lines of endeavor: first, to promote the establishment of an independent labor party in Rhode Island; and, second, to protest against the treatment of the Haymarket anarchists. The causes were intimately related in his mind. He wrote:

Capitalistic conspiracy is organized to throttle every progressive movement. Political and industrial organizations are both under their ban. Now is the crisis. They are hanging men in the west for pushing the 8 hour agitation and insisting on the right of free speech. They will do so here if workmen do not take control of the political management of the State pretty soon. The genius of aristocracy is pushing itself forward today with a wonderful assertive power. Workmen must throttle it very soon

[68] *Ibid.*, Oct. 22, 1887, p. 4, col. 2.
[69] *Workmen's Advocate*, Oct. 1, 1887, p. 2, col. 6.
[70] Speek, *Singletax*, 140; W. D. P. Bliss, ed., *The Encyclopedia of Social Reform* (New York: Funk & Wagnalls, 1897), 1358, lists the following totals: ULP, 70,055; PLP, 7,622.

with that now mightily crippled instrument the ballot or it will be eternally too late. Rally now or never.[71]

The Central Labor Union of Rhode Island voted to hold a convention on Thanksgiving Day, 1887, to organize a labor party, and invited Harry Vrooman to deliver a "Thanksgiving address to the Proletaire." [72]

An editorial in *The People* summarized Harry's attitude toward the anarchists:

Already our capitalistic vilifiers are pointing the finger of scorn at all who either cry for justice or for mercy for the condemned in Chicago. To-day's *People,* if read cautiously, cannot fail to explain to any reasonable man why we must champion the cause of these men. The evidence of the Mayor of Chicago, Carter Harrison, proves conclusively that these men were only exercising their constitutional right of free speech and free assemblage, in upholding and encouraging the great strike for an eight hour workday, and protesting against the murder of their striking brothers by the police. Whatever a man may think of their philosophy, the fact of innocence of crime should draw out our condemnation of their butchery.... The police authorities should have been tried and sent to the penitentiary for life—not to the gallows.—There is no room in civilization for a scaffold. Retaliation, vengeance, blood to satiate justice, cannot be tolerated by either human or divine sanction in an advanced society. It is a relic of brutism, whether developed in church, or State, or newspaper ravings.[73]

But the cause of the Haymarket anarchists was hopeless. The same edition of *The People* that carried this editorial was edged in black and carried a hastily inserted note that the anarchists had been executed. Thinking back to that July in 1885 when he had heard Albert Parsons speak in Topeka, Harry undoubtedly had personal as well as political reasons to mourn the death of the Chicago social revolutionary.

The continuing emphasis on unity and political action in Harry's rhetoric reflected a basic tension between the economic determinism

[71] *The People* (Providence), Nov. 12, 1887, p. 2, col. 2.
[72] *Ibid.,* p. 2, col. 1.
[73] *Ibid.,* p. 2, col. 2.

inherent in his Socialism and the democratic assumptions of his family heritage. Economic forces within capitalism were forcing the workers into combination and cooperation in their unions and on the job, he maintained. But the workers would derive little benefit from the economies of superior social organization in this Socialism of production until Socialism in distribution was also instituted. At this point in his economic analysis he fell back upon the assumptions of his family tradition: *"Through the ballot and the labor organization lies the true solution. When the capitalists suppress these, it is time to talk of other methods. The producers organized nationally, and federated to act for each others interest must take control of the State, then recognize governmentally the heads of these trades departments as cabinet officers. This would then be the social democracy."* [Italics added] [74] Harry occasionally revealed in his speeches the extent to which his family experience had influenced his Socialism. He rejected the use of force in destroying the capitalist class and stated that the proper solution was to do away "with the necessity of the capitalistic class" by putting them to work in order to "make useful citizens out of them." [75]

The passionate rhetoric of class conflict in orthodox Socialism clashed with the peaceable yearnings that lay at the heart of Harry's Socialism. In a brilliant speech in New Haven on March 7, 1888, he spoke of Socialism as the "philosophy of fraternity."

For ages men and women have hoped and looked for that fraternity which they say will arrive here one of these days. The selfishness we hear so much about is not inherent in man but is brought about by the struggle for existence. We want the individual to forget himself in the collectivity. The man who opposes organization does a very unscientific thing. Where men have things in common, there is a fraternal sympathy and naturally greater good comes from it.

The idea of every man for himself is the most damnable thing ever thought of. Isolated individualism will never make a society. [76]

---

[74] *Workmen's Advocate,* Oct. 8, 1887, p. 2, col. 6.

[75] *Ibid.,* Sept. 8, 1887, p. 1, col. 4. Similarly, when a heckler shouted that the Socialists would kill such men as Jay Gould, Walter Vrooman replied, "We shall not do anything of the kind, but we must destroy these idlers and gamblers by setting them to work." *Ibid.,* July 2, 1887, p. 1, col. 6.

[76] *Ibid.,* March 13, 1888, p. 4, col. 2.

But the "spirit of fraternity" was not manifest in the wrangling feud between the Marxists and the Lassalleans within the Socialistic Labor party that followed the disastrous election campaign of 1887. In May, 1888, Harry announced that he was resigning from *The People* and returning to Kansas.[77] A Rhode Island Socialist confessed, "The people of this state are too indifferent to the broader humanitarian aspects of the labor agitation to accept readily the doctrine he taught, and so we could not keep him." [78] Basically, Harry was responding, as had his brother Walter a few months earlier, to the inner call of his intensely religious nature. He had decided to enter the ministry.

BELLAMY NATIONALISM

AND CHRISTIAN SOCIALISM, 1888–1890

On March 30, 1889, the following advertisement appeared in the Socialist newspaper *Workmen's Advocate:*

Walter Vrooman will lecture any place within reach of Boston upon the following subjects:
"The Object of the Labor Movement"
"The Degradation of Labor"
"The Future Society"
"Is Marriage a Failure?"
"Money and Morals"
"Shorter Hours"
"Socialism"
For further information address: Walter Vrooman, 18 Felton Hall, Cambridge, Mass.[79]

The address given in the advertisement was that of Walter's oldest brother, Frank, a graduate student at Harvard University. After a year in the West, which included five months of lay preaching at the Pilgrim Congregational Church in Kansas City, Kansas, Walter had returned to the East in September, 1888, and established his residence

---

[77] *Labor Enquirer* (Chicago), May 5, 1888, p. 1, col. 6.
[78] *Ibid.,* May 26, 1888, p. 4, col. 1.
[79] March 30, 1889, p. 3, col. 1. The same advertisement appeared in *The Nationalist,* I (May, 1889), 27.

with his brother.[80] The selection of topics in Walter's lecture card reflected the continuing tension in his thought between the ethical humanitarianism of his family tradition and the economic emphasis of orthodox Socialism.

The tensions in Walter's social thought were emblematic of the broader conflict between the Lassalleans and Marxists in the American Socialist movement. Three developments during the period from 1888 to 1890 directly affected this conflict and hastened the breach between the opposing factions: (1) the growth of the Bellamy Nationalist movement; (2) the organization of the Christian Socialists Society; and (3) the independent political campaign of the Lassallean wing of the Socialistic Labor party in 1888. But something more than doctrinal purity or control of the Socialistic Labor party was at stake in the contest. The ultimate issue was whether American society would be reformed by political action of an enlightened middle class guided by its own socially conscious leaders or whether it would be recast in a radically different social system by the economic and political action of the labor movement, guided and informed by the Socialists.

The Bellamy Nationalist movement stemmed from the publication in June, 1888, of Edward Bellamy's well-known utopian novel, *Looking Backward,* which envisioned an enlightened nation gradually and peacefully absorbing all economic activities into one giant trust owned by all and served by all in benevolent cooperation. The Socialist Labor party endorsed the novel and encouraged its members to publicize the book.[81] The Socialists were instrumental in establishing the original Nationalist clubs and in promoting the new movement. When Edward Bellamy expressed his fear that the Social-

[80] *Massachusetts Spy* (Worcester), Aug. 18, 1892, p. 1, col. 1; *The Harvard University Catalogue, 1888–1889* (Cambridge: by the University, 1888), 278. Walter was received into the First Congregational Church of Independence, Kans., in Dec., 1887, by profession of faith. Frank Vrooman was the minister at the time. Walter served in the Pilgrim Congregational Church from May to Sept. 10, 1888. When Frank announced his intention of leaving Independence to study at Harvard, the congregation voted unanimously to accept the services of Harry in his stead. Minutes of the First Congregational Church, Independence, Kans., and Pilgrim Congregational Church, Kansas City, Kans., Congregational Church Archives, Washburn University, Topeka.

[81] *Workmen's Advocate,* July 21, 1888, p. 1, col. 3. The title Socialist Labor party became common in 1888 and is adopted here for consistency.

ists were trying to take over the new movement, Cyrus Willard, one of the founders of the First Nationalist Club of Boston, wrote to Edward Bellamy on March 22, 1889: "Do not be alarmed about the Socialists capturing the Nationalist Club. I am a Socialist... but I have no desire to see the Club captured by them or anyone else.... The Socialists can get along without you but you cannot get along without the Socialists. Henry George tried it in New York when his ideas were better known than yours and after he had received 68,000 votes. He expelled the Socialists and [the] consequence was his movement as a political movement flattened out." [82] The Socialists viewed the Nationalist movement primarily as a means of spreading Socialistic ideas among the workers, but the Nationalist movement found its greatest support among middle-class professionals and liberal-minded members of the social elite. [83]

The Christian Socialists Society sprang largely from the efforts of an indefatigable agitator, the Reverend William Dwight Porter Bliss. In January, 1889, he published the following notice in the *Workmen's Advocate:*

It is proposed by some in Chicago and in Boston to start a society of Christian socialists. It is not proposed to antagonize other socialist or nationalist societies, but while agreeing with them on their economic platform... it is proposed to make this society distinctly Christian, basing our socialism on the fatherhood of God and the resultant brotherhood of man, and trying to carry it out in the spirit of Him who was the first born among many brethren.... Any who are interested in this view, and without binding themselves to enter such an organization, would like to consider it and know about it, are invited (especially clergymen), to send their names and addresses and any suggestions to Rev. W. D. P. Bliss, 100 G St., So. Boston, Mass. [84]

The Reverend W. D. P. Bliss joined the Reverend Francis Bellamy, a cousin of Edward Bellamy and pastor of the Dearborn Street Baptist Church of Roxbury, Massachusetts, in issuing the call for the first meeting of the Christian Socialists for February 18, 1889. While the

[82] Arthur E. Morgan, *Edward Bellamy,* Columbia Studies in American Culture No. 15 (New York: Columbia University Press, 1944), 373.
[83] Quint, *American Socialism,* 84–86.
[84] Jan. 26, 1889, p. 1, col. 5.

Christian Socialist movement was never as successful as the Bellamy Nationalist movement, it too helped to spread moderate Socialist ideas, particularly among the clergy in the Protestant denominations.[85]

Within the Socialist Labor party the Lassallean faction, which had begun to assert itself during the Buffalo congress, finally achieved its goal of committing the party to independent political action. In 1888 Socialist Labor party candidates were entered in local elections in New York City, Milwaukee, and New Haven, and a slate of presidential electors was offered by the New York Socialists.[86] In April, 1889, the party secretary in Boston reported enthusiastically upon the progress of the new tactics and on the prospects for the future.

> The American Section has already, in conformity with the acts of the State Convention, chosen a City Committee. The committee consists of comrades Walter Vrooman, Carl Friede and David Taylor.... What we socialists want in this city is a few active, sincere young men, to push on the work of the Party. We have a splendid chance to roll up a big vote this fall, as we have a mighty engine in our favor—the Australian system of voting, so that our ticket will be found in every precinct in the State. And between socialists, Christian socialists, and members of the Nationalist Club and the discontented generally, we ought to make a good showing at the fall elections. Socialistic propaganda is carried on at Dr. [Francis] Bellamy's church every Monday evening by such men as Walter Vrooman, Laurence Gronlund, Drs. Bellamy, Lawton, Bliss and others; the last three are Christian Socialists, but in my opinion are practically radical, revolutionary socialists and I believe they are doing good work.[87]

The appraisal of W. D. P. Bliss' Socialism may have been too enthusiastic. While he was certainly a radical Christian, his attitude toward Socialism was closer to Fabian gradualism than to revolutionary radicalism.

The impact of these moderate tendencies within the Socialist movement was evident not only in the shift of tactics by the Socialist Labor party but also in the emphasis placed upon educational tech-

[85] James Dombrowski, *The Early Days of Christian Socialism in America* (New York: Columbia University Press, 1936), 93–95, 99–101.
[86] Quint, *American Socialism*, 54–55.
[87] *Workmen's Advocate*, April 27, 1889, p. 1, col. 4.

niques by the Nationalists and the Christian Socialists. The attitude of these moderate Socialists was summed up succinctly by W. D. P. Bliss: "Socialism has only to be understood to be embraced." [88] Walter Vrooman shared this attitude even while he continued to agitate for the Socialist Labor party. In a speech before the Jewish Workingmen's Education Club in Boston on April 7, 1889, he proposed that a school be established where there would be "no prejudice or superstition, false patriotism, and hatred for members of other nationalities, religions, or sects." [89]

On June 3, 1889, he set out to capture the citadel of capitalistic education, Harvard University, for the Socialist cause. Twenty students gathered in room eleven of Stoughton Hall to hear an exposition of Nationalist and Socialist theories. The first speaker was Walter Vrooman. Here was his chance to redeem those soft-handed, soft-brained dandies whom he had so frequently scorned in front of working-class audiences. But the months of constant activity and hour-long harangues at outdoor rallies had taken their toll of his health, and, sick and exhausted, he made only a few remarks. The Nationalists took over, and, at the conclusion of the meeting, the students voted to establish a Nationalist Club at Harvard at the beginning of the next term.[90]

Socialist, Christian Socialist, Nationalist—the lines between these positions were vague, and membership frequently overlapped. Even the soft-handed sons of the "exploiters" at Harvard seemed interested in the religion of the horny-handed sons of toil. The Marxist purists within the Socialist Labor party grew increasingly restless under the dominance of the Lassalleans and their education-oriented friends. In a party meeting in Chicago "many were disposed to disparage the element known as Christian Socialists, claiming that their activity might be merely an attempt to nullify the whole movement." Thomas J. Morgan, a powerful figure in Chicago Socialist circles,

[88] *Ibid.*, Feb. 16, 1889, p. 1, col. 3.
[89] *Ibid.*, April 13, 1889, p. 4, cols. 1–2.
[90] *Daily Crimson* (Cambridge), June 3, 1889, p. 1, col. 2; *Workmen's Advocate,* June 8, 1889, p. 1, col. 4. Walter Vrooman was occasionally described as a student at Harvard University. *Workmen's Advocate,* May 25, 1889, p. 4, col. 1; *Massachusetts Spy,* Aug. 19, 1892, p. 1, col. 1. There is no evidence in the Harvard archives to substantiate this point; however, he may have attended classes with his brother or used the facilities of the university.

rose to the defense of the Christian Socialists and referred to an eminent example of a sincere Socialist and devoted churchman—Comrade Reverend Harry Vrooman.[91]

When Harry had returned to Kansas from Rhode Island in May, 1888, he had decided to enter the ministry rather than to continue his career as a labor agitator. After a year of preparation he was ordained into the ministry of the Congregational Church in Independence, Kansas, on April 30, 1889.[92] In reply to newspaper reports that he had given up his Socialism on becoming a minister Harry informed the editor of the *Workmen's Advocate*: "I am urging the philosophy of fraternity, of universal social co-operation with none the less enthusiasm and success for having changed my profession." He still believed, wrote, and preached "that Social Democracy is but the ideal of Christianity materialized." [93] But his subsequent actions showed that he had given up trying to convert the labor movement into a vehicle for a broad Socialistic movement and was casting about for a new social group to carry the burden of his radical program.

When the first issue of *The Dawn,* the official journal of the Christian Socialists Society, appeared in May, 1889, the Reverend Harry Vrooman of Independence was listed as an associate editor. In surveying the situation in Kansas Harry reported:

Christians here are feeling the spirit of *The Dawn.* There is much loose Christian Socialist sentiment here, but owing to lack of organization and any definite program it has never been crystallized. We have worked variously, as circumstances allowed. Some have thrown in their lot with the Scientific Socialists, some have carried on a personal propaganda with what there was of Christian Socialist literature. Many, seeing little encouragement for radical work, cast in their lot with the first movement in that direction, and in their respective localities were among the leaders in the Labor Party and Knights of Labor, and such popular manifestations of discontent and aspiration. Again, others have contented themselves with an occasional newspaper article or sermon on some phase of social regen-

[91] *Workmen's Advocate,* June 15, 1889, p. 1, col. 4.

[92] *The Year Book of the Congregational Christian Churches of the United States of America: Statistics for 1948* (New York: General Council of the Congregational Churches, 1948), 56.

[93] *Workmen's Advocate,* July 6, 1889, p. 1, col. 1.

eration, so that this unorganized sentiment furnishes a fine field for *The Dawn*.[94]

Harry's belief in the potential for organization of a Christian Socialists Society in Kansas reflected the educational emphasis of Christian Socialism and the mores of the middle-class professionals with whom he was associated. In July, 1889, he organized a class in Independence to study Edward Bellamy's *Looking Backward*. The Christian Socialists adopted the study class technique, probably derived from the familiar Bible study classes of the Protestant churches, and created Christian Economics classes.[95]

The Christian Economics classes were designed to show "that wealth and prosperity and happiness" would be "better stimulated and distributed when selfishness is deliberately overthrown as the god of the business world, and regard for humanity installed instead." [96] Harry's Christian Economics class in Independence, which included the principals of two schools and a leading physician, seemed to be a success. "We have," Harry reported, "the very best social elements of our city interested, and there is every evidence of a wide movement here soon." [97] But local politicians denounced the class as a secret political movement and attempted, unsuccessfully, to turn Harry's congregation against him. This attitude of suspicion stemmed in part from two incidents in the 1888 political campaign in Kansas. Union Labor party accusations that the Republicans had attempted to dynamite the Union Labor printing house at Winfield had created an atmosphere of recrimination and hostility. Furthermore, during the campaign several leaders of the Union Labor party in Kansas had been initiated into the secret, oath-bound, farmer-labor National Order of Videttes. The Republican press therefore assumed that Harry Vrooman's class was another such attempt at organizing a secret political movement.[98]

---

[94] "Kansas to the Front," *The Dawn*, I (June 15, 1889), 5.
[95] Harry Vrooman, "Independence, Kansas," *The Nationalist*, I (July, 1889), 94.
[96] "Studies on Social Christianity," *The Dawn*, I (Sept. 15, 1889), 5–6.
[97] Harry Vrooman, *The Nationalist*, I, 94.
[98] Harry Vrooman, "The West," *The Dawn*, I (Nov. 15, 1889), 6–7; Wayne Powers Harrington, "The Populist Party in Kansas," *Collections of the Kansas State Historical Society*, XVI (1923–1925), 405.

The activities of the Christian Socialists only strengthened the complaint of the Marxist purists within the Socialist Labor party that Lassalleans and middle-class elements were leading the Socialist movement astray. Their response to the situation was a typical Marxist maneuver. In September, 1889, the New York Marxists instituted an executive coup d'état and proceeded to purge the Socialist Labor party of moderate Socialists.[99] Among those cast out was Walter Vrooman, who already had begun to drift toward Fabianism.

Harry Vrooman continued to publicize Christian Socialism but confined his efforts to the Congregational Church and the Nationalist clubs in the Kansas-Missouri area. In October, 1889, he delivered a lecture on "Christianity and Socialism" before the Kansas General Association of Congregational Ministers, and in May, 1890, he spoke on "The Relation of Nationalism to the Church" to the Kansas City Central Nationalist Club.[100]

Harry was joined in this effort by his younger brother, Hiram Greeley Vrooman, a first-year student at Washburn College Preparatory School in Topeka. A skilled debater with a rapid, nervous delivery and a prolific writer with an easy, confident style, Hiram carried the campaign for Christian Socialism into the halls of Washburn and into the columns of its student publications. "Christian Socialism," he wrote, "commences at the foundation of human suffering and will establish a harmony in those things that have a more nearly direct influence on the lives of each individual. It will not change man's nature, but it will change the environment that influences man's nature for good or evil." [101] Socialism, he explained to his fellow students, meant simply "national cooperation," a system whereby through government ownership all industries would be run scientifically at cost, not for profit, for the benefit of all.[102] Such a system would seem morally right and "Christian" to men once they looked

[99] Quint, *American Socialism*, 56–58; *Workmen's Advocate*, Sept. 14, 1889, p. 3, col. 1.

[100] Harry Vrooman, *The Dawn*, I, 6–7; II, 38–39.

[101] Hiram G. Vrooman, "Christian Socialism," *Washburn Argo*, V, No. 9 (Feb. 18, 1890), 91.

[102] Hiram G. Vrooman, "Co-operation," *Washburn Reporter*, IV, No. 2 (March 12, 1890), 3.

at the Bible through the Swedenborgian "law of correspondence." Such a reading of the Bible would show "the inevitable consequence of self-love and would lead all to the higher life," where they would live happily in love and appreciation for each other.[103]

The final achievement of this educational campaign came in July, 1890, when Harry helped to organize the Kansas State Society of Christian Socialists. His father, Hiram Perkins Vrooman, served as president, while Harry acted as corresponding secretary.[104] But the dissident elements in Kansas listened neither to the accusations of the warring factions of the Socialist Labor party nor to the idealistic sermons and vague promises of the Christian Socialists and Nationalists. Instead they joined the Farmers' Alliance and the newly organized Kansas People's party. After years of falling prices coupled with high mortgage and interest rates the farmers and other dissident groups in Kansas were ready to help launch a powerful new political movement—Populism.

From 1886 to 1890, during the struggle for control of the labor movement, the contending groups succeeded largely in checking each other or in defeating their own purposes. The anarchists, suffering heavily in the reaction to the Haymarket incident, remained an isolated minority and failed in their attempts to infiltrate the Knights of Labor. Burnette Haskell's scheme of unity ended in a simple merger with the Socialist Labor party. The Socialists engineered the creation of the United Labor party in New York but lost control of the party when the single tax supporters captured the Syracuse convention in 1887. The single tax advocates nullified their previous gains through an internal split and the refusal of the radical wing to merge the United Labor party with the agrarian-dominated Union Labor party in 1888. The Socialists within the Knights of Labor engaged in a fratricidal dispute with the trade unionists that led to the formation of the American Federation of Labor. The Marxist purists purged the Lassallean elements from the Socialist

---

[103] Hiram G. Vrooman, "Science in Religion," *Washburn Argo*, VI, No. 1 (Sept. 17, 1890), 3.

[104] *The Dawn*, II (July–Aug., 1890), 164. A typographical error lists Judge H. C. Vrooman as president, but this error is corrected in the endsheets of the bound volume to read Judge H. P. Vrooman.

Labor party and succeeded, ultimately, in cutting themselves off from the mainstream of the labor movement and from the masses of Americanized workers. Thus, by 1890 the struggle for control of the labor movement had not been settled but had simply been reduced to a contest between the Socialists and trade unionists within the American Federation of Labor.

In embracing Socialism, Harry, Walter, and Hiram G. Vrooman adopted a radical intellectual attitude that led them away from the heart of their father's reform position. For Socialism committed them not simply to an alternate means of ownership in the industrial system but to radically different definitions of equality as well.

Their father, as a reformer, had sought to make the American political and economic system live up to its ideal of equality of opportunity. His definition of equality was essentially an entrepreneurial conception, including the freedom to enter business on an equal basis without undue restriction from incorporation laws, the opportunity to exploit the natural and social resources of a developing society, and the right to enjoy the fruits of risk and labor free from excessive and discriminatory taxation. This whole scheme of values rested ultimately on the worth of individual effort.

The three Vrooman boys in their Socialistic rhetoric gave a different meaning to equality. In a speech in Boston in 1887 Harry attempted to outline some of the requirements of the future society envisioned by the Socialists:

First—Organized Society will guarantee to every citizen, male and female, an opportunity to toil at some calling suited to their taste and talent.

Second—Each citizen shall receive for his work the full product of his labor, partly in personal remuneration and partly for public benefits.

Third—Every child shall be guaranteed a free complete education, physically, mentally, morally and intellectually.[105]

Equality of opportunity to labor—this was the concept that lay behind their continual references to "setting the idlers to work." That this view was not the same as the entrepreneurial conception was made clear in an article by Hiram Greeley Vrooman in 1890: "[Un-

---

[105] *Workmen's Advocate,* Oct. 8, 1887, p. 2, col. 6.

der Socialism] nine tenths of the retail merchants will not be needed and will necessarily follow some productive occupation. Real estate agents, bankers, lawyers and the whole heard [*sic*] of social parasites will then aid in production." [106] Labor had a restrictive meaning, and productive labor was a term they applied literally. Equality of opportunity to labor was more than a right; it was an obligation as well.

The second and third points in Harry's outline of requirements indicated another shift in meaning in their use of inherited terms. The Socialists of the late nineteenth century had raised the questions whether equality of opportunity implied an approximate equality of social rewards or incomes and whether government had any responsibility to see that this goal was fulfilled.

To the first question most Americans, whether conservative or reformist, would give the orthodox answer of late nineteenth-century American thought: equality of opportunity did not mean equality of results. What the reformers called for was reward proportionate to effort. When they complained of inequality in America, their complaint was that the natural and just distribution of social rewards through a free market economy had been disturbed and upset by political favoritism or by the economic cunning of speculators and lawbreakers. As entrepreneurially-minded thinkers, they wanted simply to insure an equitable return on their investment, a fair return for their labor above the subsistence level of wages, and a reasonable price for the farmer's sacrifices and risks of a year's unremitting toil on the stubborn soil.

The reformers' position implied a view of the role of government that was not shared by all their contemporaries. The Greenback platform of 1880 declared:

Civil government should guarantee the divine right of every laborer to the results of his toil, thus enabling the producers of wealth to provide themselves with the means for physical comfort, and the facilities for mental, social and moral culture....

Corporate control of the volume of money has been the means of dividing society into hostile classes, *of the unjust distribution of the products*

[106] Hiram G. Vrooman, "Co-operation," *Washburn Reporter*, IV, No. 2 (March 12, 1890), p. 3, col. 2.

of labor, and of building up monopolies of associated capital endowed with power to confiscate private property.[107] [Italics added]

The role of government was to provide the financial mechanism whereby the natural and just distribution of rewards in proportion to effort and risk might take place. They were not asking government to redistribute income to various classes in shares proportionate to their percentage of the population. They simply did not want government to take something from the one who produced and give it to another who had not earned it.

The equality envisioned by the Vrooman brothers' Socialism, on the other hand, was something more than the labor theory of value. "Full value of labor," "philosophy of fraternity," "the cooperative spirit"—they groped for words to convey their ideal. Hiram Greeley Vrooman came the closest to defining it.

Under a socialistic government, where business is operated scientifically, less than two hours labor per day from all, would produce enough, to give each individual those necessaries and luxuries of life which are now enjoyed by those who have an income of ten thousand dollars a year. The nation would furnish great libraries, theaters that would be elevating in their character, baths for swimming and such places for amusement as the public would call for; it would give each the means to furnish a home that would be more comfortable than the saloon. But above all each would know that his enjoyment helped to make others happy, his riches not the product of other's toil; his product not the riches of others.[108]

An approximate equality of enjoyment of the product of modern ingenuity and industry was the ideal for which they labored.

The Vrooman brothers' view of equality was ultimately an ethical precept. The right of sustenance, dignity, and culture was not defined solely by a man's functional role in an economic system. Honest labor was the hallmark of the good citizen, but his claim on society exceeded his contribution in labor, particularly for the disabled, the

---

[107] Kirk H. Porter and Donald Bruce Johnson, *National Party Platforms* (Urbana: University of Illinois Press, 1966), 57. The Labor Reform platform of 1872 had stipulated "that it is the duty of the Government to establish a *just standard of distribution* of capital and labor by providing a national circulating medium...." *Ibid.,* 43. [Italics added]

[108] "Christian Socialism," *Washburn Argo,* V, No. 9 (Feb. 18, 1890), 92.

enfeebled, and the young. They thus took a more extreme position than most orthodox Socialists who made social rewards proportionate to useful labor. The Vroomans logically turned to Christian Socialism after their brief term with the orthodox Socialists because they posited the moral worth of man in his being and not alone in his mode of existence.[109]

While the three Vroomans were driven into a radical intellectual position toward the social and economic assumptions of their society, they did not reject the democratic political system. They defined Socialism as a philosophy and looked upon the Socialist Labor party as a means of educating the workers in the proper use of the ballot. However, their Socialistic scorn of compromise and temporary measures, such as arbitration boards, ultimately drove a wedge between them and their potential supporters in the labor movement. The workers, moreover, were too individualistic, too inclined to the appeal of the entrepreneurial dream, and, in a word, too concerned with their own self-interest to wait for the distant social revolution. The Vrooman brothers' search for alternate bases of support, whether the middle-class professionals in Bellamy Nationalism or the clergy in Christian Socialism, involved them in slightly different techniques of agitation but did not change their basic commitment to the democratic system. Regardless of the means, tactics, or techniques they would use in the future, they would always be radicals at heart because they held a different ideal, a different concept of equality, from their society.

Frank Vrooman had not joined his three younger brothers in the Socialist cause. He stayed within the path of religion and pursued his theological education diligently. On one point, however, all the Vrooman brothers stood together. Whether a reformer, such as Frank, or a radical, such as Harry, the brothers believed that the selfishness in man was caused by his environment, the struggle for survival, or the social system. Believing, in other words, in the inherent goodness of man and in the manifest evil of society, they faced the classic liberal dilemma of change in a democratic society:

[109] For a contemporary statement of the orthodox Socialist view of equality as it relates to social rewards, see Laurence Gronlund, *The Cooperative Commonwealth*, ed. Stow Persons (Cambridge: Harvard University Press, 1965), 94–95, 100–103, 130–33.

that in order to change the social system they had somehow to change men's attitudes first. But if men's attitudes are a product of their environment, as both Socialism and reform Social Darwinism assumed, how could they break out of the cycle?

Several options were logically available to them. Religion might be able to overcome the world and convert the individual. By political action they might secure control of the state and reorder the environment. Through education they might change the attitudes of a select few. Through utopian colonies or economic experiments they might change the immediate environment for a select group and gradually spread their effect throughout the entire society. With their talent for innovation and their varied personalities and careers the Vrooman brothers tried all the options. The period from 1884 to 1890 had been their first confrontation with the urban scene and the unique demands that it presented to the radical and the reformer. Their immediate task was to create new social groupings to replace those which had proved inadequate to carry forward their aspirations.

Chapter Four

Religion, Radicalism, &
Reform, 1890-1896

UNIONS FOR CONCERTED MORAL EFFORT,
1890–1893

On two points all the Vrooman brothers were in agreement: social problems arise from selfishness in man, and selfishness is caused by an unfavorable environment. They believed that if they could change the environment and overcome that selfishness, they could overcome the evil in society. In turning to the churches after their unsuccessful attempts to utilize the labor movement, the Socialist parties, and the Christian Socialists Societies for this purpose, Harry, Walter, and Hiram Greeley Vrooman were following the trail that had been blazed by their older brother, Frank. In effect, all the Vroomans took an instrumental rather than sacramental view of the church. That is, they did not turn to the church primarily for the strength that they could draw from its worship but for the strength that it could lend as a social institution to their efforts. In so doing they had to answer two questions: first, how could the church help most effectively to change the environment, and second, why should the faithful participate in such endeavors? The first was an institutional question; the second a theological one. Their experiences in answering the first helped to shape their answer to the second.

Frank Vrooman's interest in the role of the Christian churches in social change had been sharpened by his graduate study at Harvard University in 1888. After a year at Harvard he pursued his studies in historical theology and sociology in Berlin and at Oxford University.[1] In London's teeming Whitechapel and East End he confronted the challenge that the urban slums posed for the church. He saw university men from Cambridge and Oxford lecturing to working-men. He visited Tee To Tum Clubs where tea, coffee, and low-cost meals were provided to combat the attractiveness of the pubs. When faced with a choice between becoming the pastor of the Holloway Congregational Church at Oxford or joining the Reverend Thomas K. Beecher, a brother of Henry Ward Beecher, in a joint ministry in Elmira, New York, Frank decided to return to the United States in December, 1890.[2]

In Elmira, Frank attempted to duplicate some of the experiments that he had investigated in England. He organized a Double Dozen club, a group of twenty-four young people trained to apply Christianity to meet the needs of the poor. They reached the children with music and the parents through the children. But the joint ministry did not give him enough freedom for further activity. In May, 1892, Frank accepted a call to the Salem Street Congregational Church in Worcester. He told an inquiring reporter from a local newspaper that he believed in "active Christianity and not theoretical" piety. Just what he meant by active Christianity was not clearly defined, but he did express the desire to continue his efforts to involve the church in the service of the poor.[3]

Frank's attempt to mitigate the plight of the slum dwellers by ac-tion within the Congregational Church was paralleled by Walter Vrooman's activities during the same period. As a reporter for the New York *World* in 1890, Walter had helped to organize the New York Society for Parks and Playgrounds for Children in an effort to save the slum children of New York City from the depressing effects of their overcrowded neighborhoods.[4] Despite the efforts of the society the issue of more parks for children was lost in the bureau-cratic maneuvers and political dodges by public officials. "The present

[1] New York *Tribune,* Sept. 8, 1897, p. 6, col. 5.
[2] Worcester (Mass.) *Telegram,* June 3, 1892, clipping in Vrooman scrapbook for 1892, Vrooman papers.
[3] Worcester (Mass.) *Evening Gazette,* May 9, 1892, p. 6, col. 4; May 21, 1892, p. 4, col. 6.
[4] Walter Vrooman, "Playgrounds for Children," *Harper's Weekly,* XXXV (May 9, 1891), 349–50. For a detailed account of this episode see Harlan B. Phillips, "Walter Vrooman: Agitator for Parks and Playgrounds," *New York History,* XXXIII (Jan., 1952), 25–32.

attitude of our park officials," Walter charged, "is that it is better for grass to grow green over our children's graves than yellow under their feet." [5] The society did succeed in establishing a free playground on the East Side, but the children who came to play were "wild and full of spirits. They smashed everything on the grounds, stoned Vrooman and his assistants, burned down the shelter house." [6] He had better luck in establishing the New York Old Folks' Aid Society, which sheltered 1,500 elderly people in a single year. [7]

Impatient with the procrastination of public officials, the lassitude of the general public, and the disunity of the civic improvement forces in the face of massive urban problems, Walter attempted to do something about it. In November, 1891, he published a call in the New York *World,* ostensibly signed by a number of prominent men, for the formation of a New York Union of Religious and Humanitarian Societies for Concerted Moral Effort. Unwisely, he used the names of some of the prominent men without their express permission, prompting bitter attacks by rival newspapers. "Walter has apparently put his foot in it," Dr. Josiah Strong, one of the union's backers, remarked. Undaunted, Walter continued to hold meetings in the name of the union and to pursue the park and playground issue. The adverse publicity soon had its impact, however, and the union was reduced to a handful of faithful followers by the end of the year. [8]

In their separate experiments during 1890 and 1891 Frank and Walter Vrooman were trying to find some means of applying religious conviction to three basic problems that characterized urban areas in the 1890's: (1) the lack of social services for the working masses; (2) the sporadic and uncoordinated nature of improvement efforts by charitable, civic, and reform organizations; and (3) the isolation of the individual in the urban mass. Basically, the Vrooman brothers were preaching variations of the social gospel, although they did not use that term.

[5] Walter Vrooman, "Playgrounds for Children," *The Arena,* X (July, 1894), 286.
[6] New York *Times,* Nov. 20, 1891, p. 2, col. 7.
[7] *Massachusetts Spy* (Worcester), Aug. 19, 1892, p. 1, col. 1.
[8] New York *Times,* Nov. 14, 1891, p. 8, col. 4; Nov. 20, 1891, p. 2, col. 7; Nov. 25, 1891, p. 8, col. 2; Nov. 27, 1891, p. 5, col. 1; Dec. 11, 1891, p. 8, col. 4; Dec. 23, 1891, p. 5, col. 3.

Frank wanted the church to find renewed vigor through service to the individuals caught in the urban mass. Walter believed that the churches alone could not meet the diverse problems that confronted the urban dwellers, and he favored a union of all humanitarian societies. From his varied experiences in radical activities he realized that neither the quasi-religious sentiment of the Knights of Labor lodge nor the militant solidarity of the Socialist agitation section would suffice to meet the varied needs of the inhabitants of the sprawling cities of the 1890's. A freer, more open, and more highly organized social structure would have to be created. His radical vision transcended the limits of the mundane methods that he chose to follow in this period of his career as an agitator.

On June 2, 1892, Frank and Walter startled the parishioners of the Salem Street Congregational Church by suggesting that it was the church's duty to "redeem things from surroundings which are evil and degrading and bring them up to surroundings which are help-ful and ennobling." Frank stated his position concisely: "I believe the questions of rapid transit, modern tenements, and public parks and meeting places and public education ... should be taken hold of by us as pertaining intimately to the people, and that everything that is calculated to lift up man to a higher life, we dare not let pass by." [9]

Walter suggested that work with people a few doors from the church was more valuable than missionary efforts among foreign heathens.[10] These advanced ideas—termed the Forward Movement by the press—were discussed at a meeting of the Worcester Congrega-tional Club on June 13, 1892, by Robert A. Woods, superintendent of Andover House in Boston. He explained that the Forward Move-ment in church work meant that the church must meet "men in their daily walks of life and there do them good." [11]

On June 15 Walter seized the initiative in the Forward Movement when he proposed

that there be formed an organization called the Salem Street Branch of the National Union for concerted moral effort. This organization has four

[9] Worcester *Telegram* [?], June 3, 1892, clipping in Vrooman scrapbook for 1892, Vrooman papers.
[10] Worcester *Evening Gazette,* June 3, 1892, p. 4, col. 3.
[11] *Ibid.,* June 14, 1892, p. 6, col. 2.

lines of work—educational, legislative, temperance and extension. In the educational line the plan is to go about the city giving concerts to the children in their homes or wherever they can be found. The legislative work is to look after all matters pertaining to Christianity, with the idea of securing such legislation as may be necessary to further Christian work.

The temperance work is considered very important and in this line the proposed amusements, the introduction of bowling and billiards, base-ball, etc., into the church to give it attractions such as the saloon has, are proposed. The idea is to offer a substitute to the evil surroundings of the saloon.[12]

Walter's suggestion that billiards and amusements might be brought into the church caused considerable comment among the parishioners, and Frank was constrained to calm the fears in certain quarters. Then Frank made a serious tactical error. Since he had not taken a vacation in two years, he now decided to return to England for six weeks to investigate urban reform activities. This meant that Walter would be in control of the Forward Movement during the critical early phases of the plan.[13]

Walter had learned from his experiences in New York City not to rely solely upon the endorsement of prominent men to launch an urban social movement. This time he labored carefully to make the Worcester Union for Concerted Moral Effort a true federation of religious, charitable, and labor organizations. At the opening ceremonies on August 4, 1892, he patiently expounded his theme: "No faith, no sentiment, no moral considerations divide those whose private gain is at variance with the public good. They work together. . . . If the friends of justice and humanity are to overcome the enemies of society, they also must unite and step and act together without regard to color, creed or class. . . . The first reform needed is a general breaking up of race, class and theological distinctions . . . and a coming together of all well meaning men and women."[14] The method of the union, he explained, was simply to condemn an evil, concentrate the moral force of the community on it, and abolish it.

The members of the Worcester Union for Concerted Moral Effort adopted a moving and eloquent statement of principles, reaffirming

[12] *Ibid.*, June 16, 1892, p. 4, col. 3.
[13] *Ibid.*, June 20, 1892, p. 4, col. 4; June 28, 1892, p. 4, col. 4.
[14] *Ibid.*, Aug. 5, 1892, p. 4, col. 3.

their commitment to peaceful change at a time when the Homestead strike and the Coeur d'Alene incident had raised the specter of class warfare and bloodshed. The attempted assassination of Henry Frick by Alexander Berkman, who had lived in Worcester with Emma Goldman, added to the atmosphere of concern.[15]

STATEMENT OF PRINCIPLES

WORCESTER UNION FOR CONCERTED MORAL EFFORT

Preamble: We, the representatives of the various religious and philanthropic societies, labor unions and business interests of Worcester, assembled in convention this fourth day of August, 1892, agree to unite our efforts in the common work of municipal improvement and human elevation, and we adopt the following constitution,—

Statement of Principles: Recognizing the moral law as the supreme law of the universe, we believe that its supremacy should be enforced in all of the affairs of life. We believe that man should not only harness in his service the material forces of nature but that he should also direct and control all social forces and tendencies, that all human laws, customs, and institutions should be brought into harmony with the moral laws and made to secure the highest interests of our race. We believe that this world is large enough and rich enough, and that it contains all things necessary to become the beautiful and happy home of perfected humanity. But we also believe that every individual man, woman and child, has an important part in working out his glorious destiny. We therefore call upon the sincere people of every faith and nationality to forget their differences and join with us in the making of this ideal, a fact.

We believe in "law and order" as the basis of civil life and the starting point of progress, and we shall strive always to enforce law, to cultivate a higher respect for it among all classes of people, and to see that no person, class or combination is ever allowed to defeat or to defy it. Laws framed in defence of life and health, of childhood and womanhood, we regard even more sacred than laws protecting property, and we determine upon their enforcement with equal promptness. As there can be no liberty without enlightenment, no progress without knowledge, we consider education not only the basis but the inspiration and life of civilization, the one hope of our country and its free institutions. The undoubted right of every child to an education we shall defend upon every occasion.

[15] James Joll, *The Anarchists* (Boston: Little, Brown, 1964), 144.

We shall strive for vigorous enforcement of existing factory and school laws, and for such additional legislation as will be found necessary to protect this most sacred of the divine and natural rights of man—the right to that knowledge and training which alone can make him free and self-respecting. We condemn the illiteracy and ignorance of our country and shall strive by every possible means for their extinction.

We believe that the application of intelligence and justice will eventually subdue the universal struggle between the classes characterized capital and labor, and that each man's just share of the wealth produced by the social aggregation in which he works, can be secured to him upon a basis of equality.

We believe that the masses who do the hard and disagreeable work of the world are destined to enjoy a constantly increasing share of the good things resulting from the civilization that their labor has made possible. We condemn those labor battles known as strikes, whether precipitated by employers or employees, as a brutal and barbaric method of warfare, and unbecoming the age in which we live. And we urge that the labor struggle be transferred from the open field into the legislative chamber. To those who think they are oppressed and wronged we recommend the ballot as the most effective weapon of our time, the one adequate means of defence of the otherwise poor and helpless against the rich and powerful. We therefore urge that at all times the interest of the voter and his ideas of right and justice be held superior to party name and party tradition. We believe that the giving of commercial or political patronage to men or institutions known to conduct their affairs in a manner detrimental to the public welfare is complicity with crime. We therefore ask the public to cease patronizing business enterprises that disregard common decency and common humanity, and to co-operate with us in placing their patronage only with such persons as encourage honest industry, tempered by human feeling and the love of justice.

Our method is, whenever possible, to work through existing institutions and societies, instead of building new ones. We intend to give occupations to organizations whose original functions have disappeared and whose life has become too feeble to utilize their immense framework and perfected machinery. We aim to subdue all the special and selfish interests of society and to bend them so that they shall uphold the general welfare. All the inspiration that religion gives we bring into the world of reality, substituting the strength of conviction and the power of enlightened hope for a weak and helpless piety, made impotent by its own fetters.[16]

[16] Worcester *Evening Gazette*, Aug. 5, 1892, p. 4, col. 3.

The concept of equality embedded in the statement of principles was probably closer to the precept of equality of enjoyment than to the traditional entrepreneurial dream of equality of opportunity. This fact was masked from the average reader by the ambiguity of the language and the emphasis in the statement upon moral law. "Each man's just share of the wealth produced by the social aggregation" could mean reward proportionate to effort, a safe and orthodox view. However, when the phrase, "secured to him upon a basis of equality," was considered, it could imply reward proportionate to need or, at least, the underwriting of a minimum standard of living by the state. The same phrase could also be interpreted to mean equality before the law; that is, each man's just rewards for labor would be guaranteed by law and an impartial judiciary, another favorite theme of nineteenth-century political orthodoxy. The ambiguity of the rhetoric enabled various kinds of reformers and radicals to work together but foreboded inevitable tensions within any common effort to achieve such a vaguely defined goal.

The Worcester Union for Concerted Moral Effort also represented a concerted effort by the Vrooman family. Frank served on the advisory board, and Walter sat on the executive committee as the organizer for the union. Harry and Carl Vrooman, students in Harvard College, commuted to Worcester from Cambridge to help conduct services during Frank's vacation and to aid in the work of the union. Walter established a branch of the Union for Concerted Moral Effort at Providence, and Harry explained the new movement to single tax clubs in the area. When Frank returned from England, he rented an eighteen-room house on Summer Street in Worcester as a center for the family's activities. Hiram Perkins Vrooman came from Kansas City, Missouri, to join his sons' enterprise and brought the rest of the family with him.[17]

The Worcester Union for Concerted Moral Effort moved forward on three fronts during August and September, 1892. First, the union provided legal assistance to Jews who had been assaulted by young toughs in the Quinsigamond area. One young assailant was bound

[17] *Ibid.*, Aug. 6, 1892, p. 3, col. 1; Aug. 13, 1892, p. 4, col. 3; Aug. 27, 1892, p. 5, col. 1; interview with Carl Vrooman Nov. 28, 1960; *The Harvard University Catalogue, 1892–1893* (Cambridge: by the University, 1892), 151, 175.

over to juvenile court, another fined, and a third dismissed when the complaint was found to be in error.[18] Second, an interested citizen offered to permit the union to use a large skating rink for a lecture hall, a Tee To Tum restaurant, an educational center, and a general arena for its activities. Walter furnished the recreation area with nine pool and billiard tables, which he purchased on credit for $2,300.[19] Third, Walter attempted to make the rink a neutral ground where labor and management could meet to discuss their differences. When the Coal Handlers' Union threatened to strike, the Central Labor Union invited the coal dealers to discuss the handlers' request for increased wages at a meeting of the Union for Concerted Moral Effort. The union also ran an employment bureau at the rink for the benefit of both labor and management.[20]

The reaction of the community to this energetic venture was complex and varied. On September 26, 1892, the Reverend Frank Vrooman was "blackballed" by the Worcester Congregational Club because of the club's opposition to the union. Ironically, the meeting was called to discuss the topic "the duty of the church in municipal affairs." The Women's Christian Temperance Union refused to endorse the new movement officially but referred the matter to the individual members for their consideration. The presence of the pool tables in the rink brought down the wrath of the Young Men's Christian Association upon the union and split the Salem Street Congregational Church into conflicting factions. The Central Labor Union also complained that Walter used their name without authorization in asking the Hebrew Political Clubs to endorse Central Labor Union candidates in the forthcoming municipal election.[21]

The basic difficulty with the union was that Frank and Walter Vrooman held conflicting conceptions of its purpose and nature.

[18] Worcester *Evening Gazette,* Aug. 25, 1892, p. 4, col. 5; Aug. 26, 1892, p. 4, col. 4; Sept. 2, 1892, p. 2, col. 3.

[19] *Ibid.,* Aug. 8, 1892, p. 4, col. 2; Aug. 29, 1892, p. 4, col. 4; Sept. 2, 1892, p. 2, col. 3.

[20] *Ibid.,* Aug. 11, 1892, p. 4, col. 3; Sept. 22, 1892, p. 3, col. 1; Oct. 6, 1892, p. 4, col. 5; Oct. 10, 1892, p. 4, col. 3; handbills for the Worcester Union for Concerted Moral Effort in the Vrooman scrapbook for 1892, Vrooman papers.

[21] *Ibid.,* Sept. 13, 1892, p. 3, col. 1; Sept. 27, 1892, p. 4, col. 3; Oct. 1, 1892, p. 4, col. 2; Worcester *Telegram* [?], Oct. 24, 1892, clipping in Vrooman scrapbook for 1892, Vrooman papers.

Frank saw in the union a reproduction of the successful settlement houses, workingmen's clubs, and Tee To Tum restaurants that he had visited in London. He was primarily interested in its educational features—classes in English for immigrants, classes in home economics, reading rooms, and extension lectures—and believed that the rink provided a home to which men, women, and children could come for "innocent amusement, entertaining instruction, the enjoyment of music or the study" of such popular subjects as French, English, and German.[22] Walter—now referred to in the press as the Reverend Walter Vrooman [23]—looked upon the union as a continuation of his efforts in New York City to unite all religious, charitable, and laboring groups into an effective organization for peaceful change of the social system. He defended the controversial pool tables by pointing out that the union was separate from the Salem Street Congregational Church and that the boys were not allowed to gamble, smoke, or loaf in the recreation section of the rink. He announced his intention of using the rink as a forum for lectures on various phases of the labor problem. The union, he said, "stood ready to help anybody or any class in need of help." [24] In short, Frank, as a reformer, wanted a social program auxiliary to the church; Walter, as a radical, welcomed the church as an auxiliary in a broad movement for restructuring society.

By the end of October, 1892, the Union for Concerted Moral Effort was floundering amid rumors of financial difficulties and peculation of funds. Walter denounced his critics as "gold worshipers" and threatened to leave Worcester. To bolster its financial status the

[22] Worcester *Evening Gazette,* Aug. 29, 1892, p. 4, col. 3; Oct. 12, 1892, p. 4, col. 5. While in London, Frank lived in Toynbee Hall and was introduced to General Booth of the Salvation Army, W. T. Stead, editor of the *Pall Mall Gazette* and *Review of Reviews,* and John Burns, Socialist Parliament member. *Massachusetts Spy,* Aug. 12, 1892, p. 1, cols. 7–8; Aug. 19, 1892, p. 1, col. 1.

[23] Walter and Hiram G. Vrooman were granted four-year licentiate status by the Windham Congregational Association of Dayville, Conn., on June 7, 1892. Harry Vrooman was pastor of the Dayville church at that time. He then accepted a call from the Congregational Church in East Milton, Mass., and served there while attending Harvard. *Connecticut Minutes: General Association and General Conference* (Hartford: Case, Lockwood & Brainerd, 1894), 743; *General Association of the Congregational Churches of Massachusetts* (Boston: Congregational House, 1892), 130; Allan B. Lincoln, ed., *A Modern History of Windham County* (Chicago: S. J. Clarke, 1920), 539.

[24] Worcester *Evening Gazette,* Sept. 15, 1892, p. 4, col. 6; Oct. 10, 1892, p. 4, col. 2.

Vrooman brothers voted to incorporate the union.[25] But not even the combined efforts of the Vrooman family could save it. As the venture failed, they began to drift apart. The Reverend Hiram Greeley Vrooman, who had managed the Tee To Tum restaurant for a short period, accepted a call to be the associate pastor of a large Presbyterian church in Baltimore. Frank resigned from the advisory board at the end of November.[26] A week later the Union for Concerted Moral Effort was defunct. Walter stated publicly that the cause of the failure was the refusal of prominent citizens who had promised funds to come to the aid of the manager in meeting the weekly expenses of operating the rink.[27] Frank hinted at another reason for the failure in an interview with a reporter: "If the [Union for Concerted Moral Effort] can not exist without Saturday night dancing and cheap theatricals it is better dead than alive. I resigned a week ago because I could not be longer responsible for things in which I do not believe. I did my best to keep these things out. The dancing was begun while I was in Baltimore, and the theatricals since I resigned. It is due not only to my church, but to myself, to wash my hands altogether of that." [28] Frank also defended his brother Walter against rumors of misappropriation of funds. Despite its failure the Worcester experiment set the pattern for organization and action that the Vrooman brothers followed when they left the city.

From Worcester Walter moved to Philadelphia, where he teamed up with Charles W. Caryl, a religious eccentric and settlement-house worker. On February 6, 1893, Walter addressed the Baptist Ministerial Conference in Philadelphia urging an organized attempt "not to relieve, but to abolish" the slums.[29] Out of this meeting grew the Central Conference of Moral Workers, which was officially launched on March 24, 1893. Similar to the Worcester union in structure and function, the conference secured the endorsement of numerous min-

---

[25] Worcester *Telegram* [?], Oct. 29, 1892, clipping in Vrooman scrapbook for 1892, Vrooman papers; Worcester *Evening Gazette*, Nov. 7, 1892, p. 5, col. 1; Nov. 10, 1892, p. 2, col. 3.

[26] Worcester *Evening Gazette*, Nov. 7, 1892, p. 3, col. 1; Nov. 25, 1892, p. 3, col. 1.

[27] *Massachusetts Spy*, Dec. 9, 1892, p. 7, col. 5.

[28] *Ibid*.

[29] Quoted in Diana Hirschler, "Union in Philadelphia," *The Arena*, IX (March, 1894), 548. See Harlan B. Phillips, "A War on Philadelphia's Slums: Walter Vrooman and the Conference of Moral Workers," *Pennsylvania Magazine of History and Biography*, LXXVI (1952), 47–50.

isterial associations, labor organizations, and educational groups. But the Central Conference was short-lived, too. A Model Dwelling Association backed by the conference was regarded with suspicion by certain Christians within the conference because of Jewish support for the project. Other members resented Walter's friendliness toward striking garment workers. Suspicious clergymen were antagonized by the exposure of his radical past and his propensity for using the names of prominent men without their permission. Caryl, Walter's associate, discredited the movement further by confusedly hinting that it was an anarchist plot to spread the plague from the slums to the wealthy neighborhoods. By the end of April, 1893, only a few faithful workers remained in the conference.[30]

Hiram G. Vrooman was more cautious and more successful in his attempt to transplant the Worcester union. In Baltimore he organized a young men's club and a downtown Sunday school for slum children. He also established a night school for newsboys and bootblacks, featuring classes in mechanical drawing, biographical studies, boxing, and military drill.[31] In June, 1893, he helped to launch the Baltimore Union for Public Good, which coordinated the efforts of sixty-three churches, labor unions, and civic improvement societies under the leadership of Baltimore's most prominent patrician reformer, Charles J. Bonaparte. Hiram's success in Baltimore, compared with Walter's difficulties in Philadelphia, showed that the factors for success had been present in the pattern established in Worcester in 1892.[32]

By the beginning of 1893 the Vrooman brothers had, each in his own way, come to grips with the peculiar demands of urban problems for the church. They saw that cities such as Worcester were "divided into alien camps, ignorant of each other's ways of life and

[30] Phillips, "Conference," *Pennsylvania Magazine of History and Biography,* LXXVI (1952), 50–61.

[31] This information is derived from an unidentified newspaper clipping pasted in the endpapers of a copy of Hiram Vrooman, *The Bible: Its True Nature and Its Spiritual Inerrancy* (Boston: New Church Union, 1899) deposited in the Andover Library, Harvard Divinity School.

[32] Hiram Greeley Vrooman, "Organization of Moral Forces," *The Arena,* IX (Feb., 1894), 349. Hiram took charge of a Swedenborgian church in Baltimore in Sept., 1893. *The Washburn Mid-Continent* (Topeka, Kans.), Sept. 28, 1893, p. 2, col. 3.

antagonistic to one another." Walter wished to establish a common platform on which all those who wanted to change society could unite. Frank was more interested in creating a "Peoples Palace Home" auxiliary to the church where working people could find companionship, culture, and recreation to compensate for the isolating and dehumanizing tendencies of the urban setting.[33] Hiram G. Vrooman shared much of Walter's radical social vision, but, for the time being, he was content to work within the framework of genteel reform established by the civic betterment movement. Perhaps all the Vrooman brothers were attempting to recreate, in the urban setting of the East, the same social settings and religious influences that had characterized their Kansas boyhoods.

The rock on which the Worcester Union for Concerted Moral Effort and the Philadelphia Central Conference of Moral Workers foundered was that of propriety and respectability. The older established members of the upper governing class took up the leadership of the civil service reform movement and the civic betterment drive in the absence of effective working-class efforts and in protest against the blatant unconcern of the *nouveau riche*. In his zeal Walter frequently violated the sense of decorum of those prominent members of the community who could have aided his cause. The use of the names of prominent clergymen without their express consent, the rumors of anarchism and financial irregularity that were linked with his efforts, and the intemperance of his attacks on the "gold worshipers" in the churches drove away the potential supporters of his projects. Hiram G. Vrooman worked within the ground rules of urban reform in Baltimore and succeeded in establishing a fruitful and productive relationship with the prominent men who directed the genteel reform forces in the city.[34] In the final analysis perhaps the infamous pool tables in the rink in Worcester did more to destroy the Union for Concerted Moral Effort than all the "hosts of darkness" combined.

[33] Worcester *Evening Gazette,* Aug. 5, 1892, p. 4, col. 3; handbills for the Worcester Union for Concerted Moral Effort in the Vrooman scrapbook for 1892, Vrooman papers.

[34] For a contemporary statement of the "ground rules" for urban reform efforts, see William H. Tolman, *Municipal Reform Movements in the United States* (New York: Revell, 1895), 185–86.

THE UNION FOR PRACTICAL PROGRESS, 1893–1895

The Vrooman brothers were representative of a larger group of radicals and reformers who were aroused by their religious sensitivity to the disparities that they saw about them. Yet these same zealots were often dissatisfied with the status of the churches, suspicious of religious orthodoxy, and inclined toward newer trends in secular thought. Benjamin Orange Flower, editor of *The Arena* magazine, sensed this "heart hunger for nobler attainments evinced by hundreds of young men and women throughout the land" and lamented the "inestimable waste to humanity of vital and uplifting energy through a lack of concerted action." [35] Noting that some readers of his magazine had formed clubs to discuss its provocative articles, Flower suggested in June, 1893, that similar clubs be formed in every community "where the new liberal and reformative thought" had taken hold of "earnest natures." [36] However, he was opposed to the use of the words "Arena" or "Christian" in the title because their use might alienate potential sympathizers. He concluded, "I believe the day is not far distant when societies embracing Christians, Hebrews, Buddhists, and Agnostics—in a word, societies embracing all who love mankind enough to sacrifice self in the interest of humanity—will strike hands for a common good." [37] He recommended that such a society be called the "League of Love," "Federation of Justice," or the "Order of Servants of Humanity."

The phrase "lack of concerted action" might have been lifted bodily from one of Walter Vrooman's speeches. Walter paid a personal call on Flower to discuss the editorial. The resulting conversation and the favorable response of other interested readers caused Flower to publish a call for a national Union for Practical Progress. [38] The plan represented an extension of Walter's Union for Concerted Moral Effort scheme. It called for small groups of enlightened, self-

---

[35] "Union for Practical Progress," *The Arena*, VIII (June, 1893), 78.

[36] Flower, "Notes and Announcements: Arena Club No. 2," *The Arena*, VIII (June, 1893), xxiii.

[37] *Ibid.*

[38] Harlan Buddington Phillips, "Walter Vrooman: Restless Child of Progress" (unpublished Ph.D. dissertation, Dept. of History, Columbia University, 1954), 127–28.

sacrificing lovers of humanity to direct local efforts in cooperation with the policies and plans laid down by a national advisory board. Local efforts would be supported by supplementary material published in *The Arena*.

Out of his experiences during the previous three years, Walter had developed a new theory to overcome the weaknesses of the old union. First, he distinguished between the status-conscious reformers, "those who expect to lead the masses from whom they isolate themselves," and the scientific agitators, those who remain with the poor and utilize established social institutions in the cause of progress.[39] In other words, he rejected the prominent-man approach to social change and rationalized his own alienation from polite society into a glorification of the position of the poverty-embracing agitator: "I am supposing this scarcity of cash on the part of our first three organizers [for a local Union for Practical Progress], because my experience in reform work has taught me that the most spiritual and sympathetic men and women are condemned by existing social chaos to lives of poverty, and the probabilities are that in the majority of localities, the inaugurators of the new movement will be very poor."[40] Because of his numerous tiffs with pusillanimous clergymen, Walter urged his scientific agitators to withdraw from the "gold worshiping" churches and to form wandering congregations of the socially enlightened. They should infiltrate church meetings to speak out for Jesus, the "Social Reformer."[41]

The second theory behind the Union for Practical Progress was that of the economy of moral forces. Instead of forming a new organization for every new idea, the Union for Practical Progress would direct and synchronize the efforts of existing organizations. Walter explained the theory in the New York *Voice:*

The object of the Union for Practical Progress...is to make possible simultaneous action on the part of all the religious and moral forces of society. At the present time a thousand different people are talking a

---

[39] Walter Vrooman, "The Church as a Missionary Field," *The Arena*, IX (April, 1894), 696. He used the term "scientific reformer" rather than "scientific agitator." For consistency the latter term is used throughout this book. It also appears to be closer to his meaning in its original context.

[40] "First Steps in the Union of Reform Forces," *The Arena*, IX (March, 1894), 541.

[41] *The Arena*, IX, 698.

thousand different reforms at the same time, and to the public all these reform ideas become a medley. Our idea is to have one subject brought up at a time and induce all the clergymen, labor unions, reform societies and other organizations founded upon an unselfish idea to speak out upon the same day upon the same subject. This is to be repeated by raising of a new moral issue every month.[42]

The local Union for Practical Progress would direct the reform effort in its locality in conjunction with national efforts.

Implicit in Walter's theories was a belief in the efficacy of moral power in achieving social change. During his efforts in New York City in 1891 he had proposed to a group of young followers that they invade the tenement districts with a brass band and torchlight transparencies to urge the people to amend their ways. When some-one objected that the slum dwellers would probably throw garbage and eggs at them, Walter replied that "moral suasion would be too powerful to admit such a thing." [43]

In reference to the union he assured potential members that "lethargy, stolidity, and sympathies utterly stifled by worldliness" were the only real obstacles and that these could be "melted away by the fire of enthusiasm." [44]

Despite Walter's denunciations of patrician reformers, it is doubt-ful whether the Union for Practical Progress could have succeeded on a national scale without the prestige, certification, and support provided by the national advisory board. The national advisory board included such prominent reformers as Professor John Bascom, the Reverend Minot J. Savage, Hamlin Garland, David Starr Jordan, Francis E. Willard, Carroll D. Wright, and Charles J. Bonaparte.[45] Above all, in receiving the blessing and active support of Benjamin O. Flower the movement was assured of a wide audience. Flower's personal philosophy was based on the premise that true progress must be grounded in moral idealism. With the strength of this con-

---

[42] Reprinted in *The Kingdom*, VII (April 27, 1894), 30.
[43] New York *Times*, Dec. 5, 1891, p. 6, col. 2.
[44] Walter Vrooman, *The Arena*, IX, 543.
[45] Benjamin O. Flower, *Progressive Men, Women and Movements of the Past Twenty-Five Years* (Boston: The New Arena, 1914), 128; Ella Reeve Ward, "The Union for Practical Progress," *The Reform Advocate*, VII (July 7, 1894), 376.

viction he was able to gather together an extraordinary group of writers, reformers, and schemers and to provide them with a forum for their ideas.[46]

The process of organizing the Union for Practical Progress on a national scale took some time. The national advisory board outlined a full schedule of topics for the ten months between February and November, 1894: "The Sweating System," "Tenement House Reform," "How Best to Treat the Saloon Evil," "Child Labor," "Public Parks and Playgrounds," "Prison Reforms," "Municipal Reform," "The Problem of Unemployment," and "Best Methods of Combating Political Corruption."

By July, 1894, at least forty local unions had been established across the country. Articles to back up the local efforts were appearing monthly in *The Arena,* and lecturers were making the rounds of the local unions.[47]

Three cities in particular—Boston, Philadelphia, and Baltimore—witnessed vigorous action by the local Unions for Practical Progress and Arena clubs. The Boston Union for Practical Progress experimented with a Peoples' University extension system. Thomas E. Will, secretary of the Boston Union, reported enthusiastically in *The Arena* on the efforts of Harry Vrooman and other members of the Peoples' University to institute rural propaganda campaigns in the New England area. While noting that the classes, libraries, and debating clubs favored by the Peoples' University were designed to "arouse the mind of the community," Will also stressed the need for

[46] The Union for Practical Progress project brought together a remarkable group of men who continued to work together in various enterprises for the next ten years. Thomas Elmer Will, a Harvard graduate, became secretary of the Boston Union for Practical Progress after being released by Lawrence University in Appleton, Wis., for alleged heresies in economics. Frank Parsons, a writer of legal textbooks and a lawyer, joined the Philadelphia Arena club and lectured for the national union. Walter Vrooman served as national organizer for the union, while Harry acted as national secretary-treasurer. Carl, president of the Harvard Union and of the Intercollegiate Debating Union, attempted to coordinate the activities of the debating union with those of the Union for Practical Progress. All the Vrooman brothers contributed articles to *The Arena* to support the activities of the Union for Practical Progress.

[47] Thomas E. Will, "The City Union for Practical Progress," *The Arena,* X (July, 1894), 264; "Union for Practical Progress," *The Kingdom,* VII (April 27, 1894), 30; Ware, *The Reform Advocate,* VII, 376.

a permanent general welfare club to direct the "active, executive work of social reform." [48] In Philadelphia the remaining members of the Central Conference of Moral Workers reorganized to form a local Union for Practical Progress in January, 1894. They secured lists of sweatshops from the Knights of Labor and induced state commissioners to examine them. They also conducted fashionable ministers on a tour of the sweatshops. In Baltimore the local union supported anti-sweatshop and child labor laws drafted by Charles J. Bonaparte.[49]

The Union for Practical Progress represented the most successful social experiment with which the Vrooman brothers were associated during the period from 1890 to 1895. From the Vrooman brothers' point of view the churches offered "the most promising field in the world to the social reformer" because they already possessed "the money, the buildings, the membership, the latent moral enthusiasm, that are required to make a great reform movement successful." Since, however, some of the most advanced social thinkers could no longer accept the creeds of the churches, the Vrooman brothers hoped that the Union for Practical Progress would act both as a substitute church for these free souls and as a means of exerting pressure on the orthodox churches to arouse their latent moral enthusiasm.[50]

In effect, the Vrooman brothers wanted to retain the motive power of religious conviction but to work within a nonsectarian framework. But the line between nonsectarian and secular proved to be an extremely hard one to draw. Secular civic federations, good government leagues, and civil service reform leagues could, and did, duplicate the program of the Union for Practical Progress with-

[48] "How to Organize the Union for Practical Progress in the Villages and Country Districts," *The Arena*, XII (March, 1895), 67.

[49] Hirschler, *The Arena*, IX, 551–52; Ware, *The Reform Advocate*, VII, 376.

[50] Walter Vrooman, *The Arena*, IX, 540–41. For the Vrooman view of the role of the church in reform, see Hiram G. Vrooman, "The Organization of Moral Forces," *The Arena*, IX (Feb., 1894), 354–57; Frank Vrooman, "The State and Dwellings for the Poor," *The Arena*, XII (May, 1895), 421–23. Walter resisted the efforts of the anti-Catholic American Protective Association to penetrate the Union for Practical Progress and emphasized that the union sought to unite Protestants, Catholics, Jews, and atheists in the spirit of the World Parliament of Religions. See Aaron I. Abell, *American Catholicism and Social Action: A Search for Social Justice, 1865–1950* (New York: Hanover House, 1960), 119–20.

out its religious rationale. Was a religious motive necessary for a civic improvement campaign?

A THEOLOGY FOR THE SOCIAL GOSPEL, 1894–1896

The question of religious conviction inevitably brought the Vrooman brothers back to the issue of self-interest, or selfishness as they preferred to call it. The Calvinistic tradition in which they had been reared allowed self-interest, if not selfishness, to occupy a position in its system. As part of the reformed tradition, it could safely assert that man is not saved by good works but by the grace of God through faith in Jesus Christ as Lord and Savior. If man was freed from meritorious acts of piety—good works in the theological sense —he was free, therefore, to do good work—in the practical economic sense—as an act of love for a neighbor. Surely God would reward those who were faithful in such love; thus, wealth could be regarded as evidence of God's blessing and a measure of the stewardship of the elect.

The Calvinistic separation of a transcendent God from a dependent man had, in the course of time, a paradoxical effect. The emphasis on the distance between God and man had been designed to enhance the sovereignty, and hence the authority, of God over man's action. The breach between the two was healed by the atonement or the sacrifice of Christ. The practical effect of these views, coupled with a scientific view of a mechanistic universe, had been to leave man more and more to his own devices. A transcendent God, an impersonal machinelike universe, and a distant dying Christ had all added up to a vague sanctification of the *status quo*. God's elect, increasingly identified with His financial stewards on earth, would take care of His business by diligently pursuing their own.[51]

A theological attack on the status of self-interest in the Calvinistic tradition would have to begin with a reexamination of the concept of transcendence itself. Frank Vrooman's thoughts on this theme developed slowly during the busy years of his practical ministry.

[51] Sidney E. Mead, "American Protestantism since the Civil War, Part II: From Americanism to Christianity," *The Journal of Religion*, XXXVI (April, 1956) is a useful summary of the literature on this theme.

He did not publish his ideas until 1895, but they underlay all his reform efforts in the early 1890's. Under the impact of the evolutionary doctrines of Darwin and the historical studies of the German "higher critics," he believed that theologians had ceased to think in terms of an anthropomorphic and transcendent God. Rather, they began to emphasize the immanence of God in the process of evolution as a guiding spirit. Revelation, therefore, did not refer to an absentee executive who dictated to selected scribes "a very large bundle of very small, infallible fragments called verses, each assuming pontifical dignity." Revelation really meant that God was in nature and in history progressively realizing himself, in the Hegelian sense, through the activity of the Holy Spirit. Atonement, therefore, did not refer to a once-for-all propitiatory sacrifice by Jesus to please an angry God. It meant simply a reconciliation between God and man, a willing and intelligent cooperation by man with the Spirit of God acting in history and nature.[52]

In simpler terms, the new theology implied that man would find his reconciliation with God not by pursuing his own self-interest and trusting in the merits of Jesus Christ to rescue him at Judgment Day but by subduing his self-interest and helping to achieve God's will here and now. The common good of the Kingdom of God was greater than the sum total of the good work of men, even charitable men. The common good of the Kingdom of God on earth included the establishment of real brotherhood—of true charity—and willing sacrifice by each for the good of all. But the new theology seemed to be avoiding the issue that it had been designed to confront. If there were no eternal damnation to avoid and no future heaven to seek, then why sacrifice one's self-interest for the sake of others?

Harry Vrooman attempted to answer this question by developing ethical theories to accompany the new theology. He distinguished three levels of evolutionary ethics: (1) the ethics of egoism, the demand of the ruling class for the security of the old regime based on pure selfishness and the survival of the fittest; (2) the ethics of prudentialism, the calculating "does-it-pay" approach derived from considering the balance of contending forces; and (3) the ethics

---

[52] Frank Buffington Vrooman, "The New Bible," *The Arena*, IX (March, 1894), 466–75.

of altruism, the development of the self in the service of the whole.[53] The ethics of altruism constituted a "new ideal" for the age:

The new ideal asks for the realization of brotherhood and equality instead of the doling out of life's necessities, in a manner to emphasize and make permanent the inhuman inequalities. It has studied the cause of the social unrest, of poverty and of crime, *and with the true insight born of the altruistic ideal and the scientific method it sees that these causes lie in human selfishness,* as expressed in the institutions of the political and industrial life of to-day, with their accompanying special privileges, class distinctions, pride and brutality. It would arouse the community to abolish class privileges, to remove from wealth the power of controlling the destinies of millions; to equalize opportunities in life by the establishment of the coöperative commonwealth. [Italics added] [54]

Selfishness could be overcome by striving to achieve the ethics of altruism, which would mean the development of the true self in the service of the whole community. Or, in religious terms, man, acting in cooperation with the Spirit of God in history to achieve an ethical ideal, could hasten the Second Coming, the realization of the immanent Christ.

In appealing to men to overcome their self-love or self-interest by losing themselves in the service of God's love, the Vrooman brothers had, for all the trappings of new learning, returned to one of the oldest themes of Protestant thought. As H. Richard Niebuhr has written, the theory behind Calvinism "was that human power to do good did not need to be generated but needed only to be released from the bondage to self and the idols, from the conflict in which divided loyalty involved man and in which power inhibited power, from the frustration by which the vanity of all temporal things discouraged life." [55] If men could only be taken up on the rhetorical mountain, to view the beauty and perfection of the Kingdom of God, then they would be released, set free, from their bondage to self.

Several dangers were inherent in the new theology, although they did not all become immediately apparent. The first was the

[53] Harry Vrooman, "The Ethics of Peace," *The Arena,* XI (Dec., 1894), 118–27.
[54] Harry Vrooman, "Charity, Old and New," *The Arena,* XI (Jan., 1895), 279.
[55] *The Kingdom of God in America* (New York: Harper, 1959), 118.

instrumental view of the church. As the sacramental view of the church faded, the instrumental view changed their conception of the nature of the church. To demonstrate the religious basis on which they thought civic groups should operate Walter Vrooman, Hiram G. Vrooman, pastor of the Swedenborgian Church of the New Jerusalem in Baltimore, and Carl Vrooman launched a People's Church in the Lyceum Theater in Baltimore in October, 1894. The main theme of their opening services was "dynamic religion." Hiram defined dynamic religion as the spirit of self-sacrifice and said that it was the cause of humanitarian movements and the source of the energy that could make their instruments effective. Carl, a senior on leave from Harvard College, defined dynamic religion as that spirit which served in the "aggressive advancement of human welfare." Walter's sermons before the fashionable audiences were dramatized by living examples and tableaux on the stage. But the appeal of his civic religion soon faded, and the sermons ended in February, 1895.[56]

Adherents of the new theology also ran the risk of being accused of heresy by more orthodox contemporaries. In 1896 Frank Vrooman moved from Massachusetts to Chicago, where he took a pastorate at the Kenwood Presbyterian Church. When he applied for membership in the Chicago Presbytery, he encountered considerable opposition. His critics charged that his article on the Bible in *The Arena* contained views that were contrary to Presbyterian doctrines. Specifically, he was charged with denying the doctrines of the atonement, of the propitiatory sacrifice of Jesus, of the justification of sinners by the righteousness of Jesus, and of the final state of the impenitent.[57]

A special commission of the Chicago Presbytery was convened to examine Frank's views. The text of the examination reveals dramatically the clash between the inherited Calvinism of the examiners and the liberalism of Frank's views:

[56] Baltimore *World* [?], Oct. 12, 1894, clipping in the Vrooman scrapbook for 1894, Vrooman papers; Hiram Vrooman, "Dynamic Religion," *The Washingtonian*, I (Dec., 1897), 35–38; Carl Vrooman, "Dynamic Religion," *The Washingtonian*, I (Nov., 1897), 41–48; Walter Vrooman, *Dynamic Religion: Sermons Preached before the People's Church, Baltimore, Md.* (Baltimore: Patriotic Literature Printing Press, 1895).
[57] New York *Daily Tribune*, Apr. 22, 1896, p. 2, col. 2.

Q. Do you believe in the possible eternity of sin?

A. I do not believe in the eternity of sin.

Q. Do you believe that any are ceaselessly and endlessly punished?

A. No sir, I do not.

Q. Do you believe in the future repentance and restoration of the wicked after death?

A. I cannot say that I do, sir. If there is anything which relieves my mind of the possibility of everlasting and endless torment, it would be that death is simply, death.

In reply to a question on Christ's sacrifice Frank said: "His offering was vicarious, but in no sense has he taken the punishment because we bear the punishment today and we always will, for our sins." In answering another, he came to the heart of his views:

I am free to say, brother, that so far as the idea of an angry God requiring blood to be satisfied, that whole idea I reject absolutely.

I like the word which the revised [version of the Bible] substitutes for it [atonement], reconciliation. [Having consulted several Greek dictionaries] I do not find one but what will show me that reconciliation is always reconciling man to God and not God to man.

I think Jesus is the one who comes down here to represent [the divine mind]; that He opens and shows the divine mind and heart; that He comes here to take such action or to cause such effect upon the hearts of his rebellious people who are turned from God, not from whom God has turned, that these are brought back into relationship with Him in the image of whom they are first created.[58]

The critics were not satisfied when the commission approved Frank's application, and his opponents appealed his case to the Synod of Illinois in an attempt to reverse the decision.[59]

On October 20, 1896, the Synod of Illinois convened in Danville. The Reverend W. S. P. Bryan filed a nonjudicial complaint—thereby avoiding a formal charge of heresy—asserting that the Chicago Presbytery had erred in receiving Frank Vrooman into its ministry. The complaint soon became involved in a question of polity peculiar to the Presbyterian Church: could a synod overrule a presbytery on a

[58] Topeka (Kans.) *Journal*, 1896, clipping in the Kansas State Historical Society Biographical Collections, V, I, 357.

[59] New York *Daily Tribune*, April 22, 1896, p. 2, col. 2.

matter of ministerial competence? The judicial committee returned a majority report upholding the competence of the Chicago Presbytery in such matters, but the delegates adopted the minority report upholding the right of the synod to review the matter. The adoption of the minority report touched off a prolonged controversy that was settled with a compromise plan. A special commission of twenty-five was appointed to reexamine the Vrooman case thoroughly.[60]

On the evening of October 22, 1896, the delegates at the Danville meeting heard the final report of the commission. First, they clarified the right of the synod to review the decision of the presbytery. Second, by a vote of fifteen to eight, the commission held: "Mr. Vrooman expresses his belief in language too sharply conflicting with our doctrinal standards to entitle him to our ministry, and that the Presbytery erred in receiving him. The Commission, therefore, directs the said Presbytery of Chicago to reconsider and reverse its action on the question of sustaining the examination of said Reverend Frank B. Vrooman, and to return to him his credentials." [61] From the pulpit of the Kenwood Presbyterian Church on October 25, 1896, Frank lashed back at his critics. The foundations of Presbyterianism had been securely laid by the reformers, he said, but "prejudice, bigotry and intolerance had visibly weakened the entire Christian faith." [62]

Frank's ejection from the Presbyterian ministry was another step in his progressive separation from organized religion. This process began in 1892, when the Worcester Congregational Club refused to accept him into membership, and found its completion in 1897. From the Kenwood Presbyterian Church Frank had drifted into the Unitarian People's Church of Chicago. In September, 1897, he complained publicly that he had been "frozen out" of his pastorate in the People's Church. This incident, coupled with pressure from his wife, finally led Frank to renounce the ministry. He announced that

[60] Synod of Illinois, Presbyterian Church, U.S.A., *Minutes of the Synod of Illinois, Presbyterian Church, U.S.A., Held in Danville, Illinois, October 20–22, 1896* (Danville: Illinois Printing Co., 1896) 39–42. The minutes are deposited in the Virginia Library, McCormack Theological Seminary, Chicago.

[61] *Ibid.,* 65–66. See also New York *Daily Tribune,* Oct. 24, 1896, p. 10, col. 3.

[62] New York *Daily Tribune,* Oct. 27, 1896, p. 5, col. 5.

he was leaving the ministry to head a gold prospecting expedition in the Yukon for the Klondike, Yukon, and Copper River Company.[63]

The most serious danger in the new theology espoused by the Vrooman brothers was a characteristic of any theological system that diminished the transcendence of God. They tended to overvalue the contribution of man to the religious situation and to ignore the role of their own self-interest. They simply assumed that their visions of the Kingdom of God on earth coincided with the heavenly vision. How did Harry know that God wanted a socialistic commonwealth? How did Walter know that God wanted only the worship of the socially enlightened? How did Frank know that reconciliation was always from man to God? How did Hiram know that Swedenborg's theory of correspondence provided the correct method of interpreting Scripture? Were they not trying to use the church for their own purposes as much as the "gold worshipers" that Walter criticized? Out of their desperate need for allies in their attempts to change their society they had universalized their own religious convictions.

The attempt to form an alliance between religious institutions and civic improvement forces was, in fact, pulling the Vroomans in two directions. On the one hand, their instrumental approach to the church was constantly raising intellectual issues that pushed them into theological controversies. On the other hand, their civic-unity approach to urban problems was continually pulling them toward political action. The church could not create parks, regulate health, or run the rapid-transit lines. If religious conviction was weak, or if the institutional framework of the civic improvement movement was inadequate, how could they secure the desired results? From religion they turned to politics to find the answer.

[63] *Ibid.*, Sept. 8, 1897, p. 6, col. 5; *The Washingtonian*, I (Dec., 1897), 3; interview with Carl Vrooman, Nov. 28, 1960. Frank had married Gracia M. Black, daughter of Civil Service Commissioner John Black, in 1893. They had one son, John Black Von Egmont Vrooman, born March 4, 1899.

Chapter Five

Politics, Radicalism, &
Reform, 1895-1900

THE VROOMAN BROTHERS, POPULISM,
AND THE ROLE OF THE STATE, 1895–1897

The rise of the Populist movement in the 1890's presented an enticing prospect for a wide range of radicals and reformers, such as the Vrooman brothers, who found themselves cast adrift by the turbulent events of the era. Daniel DeLeon exercised an iron control over the Socialist Labor party and expelled anyone who did not follow his line. Samuel Gompers was grimly battling the Socialists in the American Federation of Labor to hold that organization to his program of accommodation within capitalism. Eugene Debs, president of the American Railway Union, was trying to hold the remnants of his organization together in the aftermath of the disastrous Pullman strike. Between the Democratic party of Grover Cleveland and the Republican party of Mark Hanna the radicals and reformers had little choice. As a result the Vrooman brothers, along with other urban reformers, independent Socialists, utopian colonists, and direct democracy ideologues, flocked to the Populist banner in 1895. That a few tried to seize it and march off in their own direction is not surprising.

To evaluate the Vrooman brothers' relation to Populism certain questions of interpretation must be answered first. Was Populism actually Socialism in disguise? Were the Populists forward-looking heralds of Progressivism, backward-looking Jeffersonian agrarians, or the ominous forerunners of American fascism? These questions, and a host of related ones, have made Populism one of the most controversial topics in recent American history. Before calling the movement radical, reform, or even retrograde one must clarify certain of its characteristics. First, the means advocated by Populists need to be sharply distinguished from their goals. Second, their theory of the state must also be examined with reference to means and ends.[1]

Some Populists, particularly in the southern and western groups, did advocate measures usually associated with Socialism, such as government ownership of the railroads and telegraph. But does government ownership *per se* constitute the criterion of Socialism? Could any government exist if it did not own something? If government ownership of police stations, courthouses, capital buildings, arsenals, and navy yards constitutes Socialism, then all government is inherently Socialistic. Such an argument—advanced by Walter Vrooman at one point—concedes the grounds of the argument in advance to the Socialist. The only escape from Socialism, then, would be pure anarchism—no government at all. One need not be a Socialist to say that every democratic society endorses government ownership of certain types of property and defines that line as the proper limit of government action.[2]

If the advocacy of government ownership of the railroads and the telegraph does not necessarily prove that the Populists were Socialistic, does not their advocacy of government intervention in the economy at least earn them a place in the radical tradition? Did not their denunciation of laissez faire constitute a radical break with tradition? No. As a whole school of recent commentators has shown, laissez faire was a rhetorical smokescreen used to cover the reality of intimate connections between business and government. The early tradition of nineteenth-century thought sanctioned government aid to business in the form of support for internal improve-

---

[1] The controversy is summarized in C. Vann Woodward, "The Populist Heritage and the Intellectual," *American Scholar*, XXIX (Winter, 1959-1960), 55-72.

[2] Development corporations owned by municipal and state governments frequently build factories and lease them to private management. This would be an example of a Socialistic means—government ownership of productive facilities—used for a capitalistic purpose. Likewise, profit incentives instituted recently within the Russian planned economy would be an illustration of a capitalistic device used for a Socialistic purpose. The point is simply that evaluation of historical phenomena must include consideration of both ends and means.

ments, mixed public-private corporations, and protective tariffs. It also sanctioned aid to agriculture in the form of a liberal land policy. This tradition had been revived by the Republicans during the 1860's. The Populist call for government action in behalf of the farmer, laborer, and small entrepreneur was an extension of, not a departure from, the prevailing practice.[3]

Since the Populist system was based on action by the state, its theory of the state must be scrutinized with some care. Much has been made of the Populists' advocacy of the direct democracy devices: popular election of senators, initiative and referendum, and direct election of the president. Aside from the tactical necessity of securing some control over election of senators, such devices were not essential to their theory of the state. Significantly, the 1892 platform of the People's party did not endorse direct election of the president and relegated initiative and referendum and direct election of senators to the status of convention resolutions rather than platform planks. As will be shown later in this chapter, the direct legislation advocates were largely eastern ideologues who fastened themselves—and direct democracy—onto the Populists in 1896.[4]

The Populist theory of the state required only that the government be responsive to their demands. If direct democracy devices promised to do this in the future, they found support among some. The Populists were not the first to confuse their particular will with the general will, but the historian need not fall into the same confusion. To get what they wanted from the state governments the Populists used the ordinary tactics of politics: parliamentary maneuvering, fusion politics, and legislation.

[3] Robert A. Lively, "The American System: A Review Article," *Business History Review*, XXIX (March, 1955), 81–96, summarizes recent literature on this point.

[4] John D. Hicks, *The Populist Revolt: A History of the Farmers' Alliance and the People's Party* (Lincoln: University of Nebraska Press, 1961), 439–44. The demand for direct election of both senators and the president had been voiced since 1872 by various third parties and was included in all the preliminary platforms that preceded the Omaha platform of July, 1892. For some reason not mentioned by Hicks, the demand was changed to a resolution calling for a constitutional amendment limiting the president and vice-president to one term. Direct election of senators was elevated to the status of a platform plank by the Populists in 1896, but direct election of the president was not endorsed in the platform until the middle-of-the-road faction secured control in 1900. See also James C. Malin, *A Concern about Humanity, 1872–1912, at the National and Kansas Levels of Thought* (Lawrence, Kans.: by the author, 1964), 9.

For what purposes, then, would a "democratic" government exercise its powers? Why should the national government follow the People's party platform and issue currency "direct to the people," coin silver at a ratio of sixteen to one with gold, tax incomes, establish a postal savings system, own or control the railroads and the telegraph, and provide free homesteads from a reclaimed and inalienable public domain? The Populists' purpose was clearcut: to insure equality. The crucial question is, what kind of equality?

The litmus test of Populism lies, then, in its concept of equality, the end toward which its means were bent. "The fruits of toil," "our individual prosperity," "equal rights and equal privileges"—they expressed their concept in language inherited from the past. "Wealth belongs to him who creates it," the 1892 platform stated, "and every dollar taken from industry without equivalent is robbery." The Greenbackers had used the same argument in 1878 to condemn Marxian Socialism. "If any will not work, neither shall he eat," the same platform asserted. What did the Populists mean by work? Their producer psychology restricted the term to mean primarily physical labor involved in the production of commodities by farming, mining, or manufacturing, and in the rendering of services. It was used against the "idle" owners, bondholders, and speculators who manipulated artificial wealth through financial mechanisms. Since labor was the hallmark of the good citizen, it followed, conversely, that society through government ought to guarantee somehow the opportunity to labor. A man's claim on society was premised on his willingness to work.[5]

However broad and humanitarian this basic premise of their thought might seem, the proposals in their platform revealed an implicit entrepreneurialism that tended to limit the scope of their appeal. The job-conscious wage earner who had given up the dream of escaping to the farm or of getting out of the factory and into

[5] The Populist advocacy of the primacy of labor is probably closer to the Socialistic conception of the obligation to labor than are their views on equality of opportunity and of rewards. An editorial in the *Farmers' Alliance* (Lincoln, Neb.) summarized the Populist view as follows: "[The People's Party] stands upon the declaration that 'all men are created equal,' having equal right to live, labor and enjoy the fruits of their labor. It teaches that none should have power to enjoy without labor. It demands equal opportunities and exact justice *in business* [italics added] for each individual, and proposes to abolish all monopolistic privileges and power." Reprinted in Norman Pollack, ed., *The Populist Mind* (Indianapolis: Bobbs-Merrill, 1967), 21.

business for himself would have little interest in the Populist positions on an inalienable public domain reserved for settlers, cheaper freight rates through government control or operation, or inflation of commodity prices through an increase in monetary circulation. The wage earner as a consumer would hardly respond favorably to a program designed to raise living costs or to lower the purchasing power of the dollar in the midst of a depression. The Populist call for equality and justice can be translated into the call for equality of opportunity to secure honest labor or to enter business (particularly for the antimonopoly faction) with full reward for labor or risk according to the natural laws of trade unhindered by the machinations of national banks, the fluctuation of the economy, currency contraction, or any deliberate wage cuts and layoffs because of overproduction or mismanagement. The ethos of entrepreneurial capitalism colored the dreams of the Populists and linked them with the reformism of the earlier Greenbackers and antimonopolists.

Bryan sensed the power of the business creed when he said in the "Cross of Gold" speech:

> We say to you that you have made the definition of a business man too limited in its application. The man who is employed for wages is as much a business man as his employer; the attorney in a country town is as much a business man as the corporation counsel in a great metropolis; the merchant at the cross-roads store is as much a business man as the merchant of New York; the farmer who goes forth in the morning and toils all day —who begins in the spring and toils all summer—and who by the application of brain and muscle to the natural resources of the country creates wealth, is as much a business man as the man who goes upon the board of trade and bets upon the price of grain; the miners who go down a thousand feet into the earth, or climb two thousand feet upon the cliffs, and bring forth from their hiding places the precious metals to be poured into the channels of trade are as much business men as the few financial magnates who, in a back room, corner the money of the world. We come to speak for this broader class of business men.[6]

The Populist response to free silver was a natural one for the entrepreneurial segments of the party. It does not require theories based on a sellout of leadership or a stampede in fear of collectivism to

[6] William Jennings Bryan, *The First Battle* (Chicago: W. B. Conkey, 1896), 200.

account for the behavior of the Populists in 1896 in endorsing Bryan. Free silver promised a shortcut to what the small entrepreneur or would-be entrepreneur desperately needed: credit and a more flexible medium of exchange.[7]

The majority of the Populists were not radicals; they were not part of the radical tradition. They were reformers in the entrepreneurial tradition. They were calling on American society to redeem the promise of the nineteenth-century ideal, equality of opportunity. If they borrowed from past reform movements, from Socialism, and from their opponents, it was in a desperate search for ways to bring the performance of their society up to its professions. If they did not recognize the inconsistencies or foresee the consequences of some of their demands, it was because they were preoccupied with their immediate needs.[8]

The Vrooman brothers' role in Populism must be seen against the backdrop of this interpretation. Although the brothers had par-

---

[7] Howard Quint, *The Forging of American Socialism: Origins of the Modern Movement* (Columbia: University of South Carolina Press, 1953), 210–11, feels that conservative party leaders advocated a free-silver policy to counteract the strength of permeation Socialists in the Populist ranks. Robert F. Durden, *The Climax of Populism: The Election of 1896* (Lexington: University of Kentucky Press, 1965), 2–3, disagrees. He sees free silver as a logical center of Populist concern.

[8] Cf. Norman Pollack, *The Populist Response to Industrial America: Midwestern Populist Thought* (Cambridge: Harvard University Press, 1962), 11–12. He calls the Populists radicals: "While primarily an agrarian movement, Populism also contained significant support from industrial labor, social reformers, and intellectuals. ... In a word, Populism regarded itself as a class movement, reasoning that farmers and workers were assuming the same material position in society. Thus it accepted industrialism *but opposed its capitalistic form, seeking instead a more equitable distribution of wealth.* But Populism went further in its criticism: Industrial capitalism not only impoverished the individual, it alienated and degraded him. The threat was not only subsistence living, but the destruction of human faculties. According to Populism, there was an inverse relation between industrialism and freedom, because the machine was being made to exploit rather than to serve men.... Had Populism succeeded, it could have fundamentally altered American society in a *socialist direction.*" [Italics added] In my opinion Pollack reads a Socialistic meaning into key Populist terms by relying too heavily on the views of left-wing intellectuals in the party, such as Henry Demarest Lloyd. He documents the Populists' critique of the performance of their society but does not examine their proposals far enough to see their relation to ideals. He assumes his values and reads them into Populist documents. Cf. Quint, *American Socialism,* 210–11, and Chester McArthur Destler, *American Radicalism, 1865–1901,* Connecticut College Monographs, No. 3 (New London: Connecticut College, 1944), 18–20; both agree that the Populists wanted to use Socialistic means to preserve competitive capitalism. One can oppose the performance of the present system (the way it works) in order to reform it (to make it work better).

ticipated in radical and reform activities in Kansas in the 1880's, they had been associated primarily with the labor and the urban Socialist movements. The farmers' revolt that sparked the Populist protest of the early 1890's took them by surprise.[9] They were aware of the farmers' plight, but they had not participated in the early efforts of the farmers that turned the Farmers' Alliance into a political force. Indeed, after 1892 all the members of the Vrooman family resided in Massachusetts or along the East Coast. The first test of their relationship with Populism, then, must be a comparison of their conceptions of the role of the state in social change with that of the Populists. Once that is clear, their successes and failures within the People's party and the Bryan Democracy become more understandable.

Frank Vrooman, writing in *The Arena* in 1895, expressed his view of the state. He pointed out that the pressing problems of the day had been created by the "modern tendency toward the congestion of population in large centres." While the ideal home for the poor man was a suburban house where he could enjoy some of the benefits of rural life, even this salutary solution of the urban housing problem depended on the action of the state in assuring an inexpensive rapid-transit system through national ownership of the railroads.[10] From his experiences in England Frank had come to the conclusion

that the matters of sanitation and the dwellings of the poor are national problems; that they have not been solved and will not be solved by the doles of the charitably inclined; that while individual enterprises in this direction are successful as far as they go, they are altogether inadequate; *that the state is the only power competent to meet exigencies so universal;* that leaving its peremptory duty out of the question it is warranted on sound business principles by full financial value received to grapple with the problems ... because it is to the state more than to the individual that direct returns accrue from the prevention of contagion in disease and vice and crime. [Italics added]

In his view the proper question was not "has the state a right to interfere?" but "how far has the state a right to interfere?" He

---

[9] Interview with Carl Vrooman, Nov. 29, 1960.
[10] "The State and Dwellings for the Poor," *The Arena*, XII (May, 1895), 416.

adopted Arnold Toynbee's three criteria for justification of state aid
—social importance, practicality, and tendency to promote self-
reliance—in order to avoid the extremes of either laissez faire or state
Socialism.[11]

Harry and Walter Vrooman retained their belief in the importance of the Socialistic state even after they had ceased to be connected officially with the militant Socialist movement. Harry
reasoned that since the state was the only representative of the whole
people, the realization of the cooperative commonwealth would
have to be achieved through its instrumentalities.[12] While the Populists wanted to use the state to restore competition in the interests
of the farmers and other small entrepreneurs, Harry and Walter
wanted to use the state to supplant the competitive system with the
Socialist system. In a book entitled *Government Ownership in Production and Distribution,* Walter wrote: "There is no longer a
struggle between the competitive system and socialism. The competitive system has already been destroyed by its more powerful
antagonist, the principle of combination. The question now is,
whether this great mechanism of industry... shall be administered
and its results enjoyed by the few... or whether the whole people
shall secure to each a right to share in the civilization bequeathed
from our common ancestors." [13] The problem, however, was to capture the instruments of government in order to achieve the goal of
a socialized state.

In 1895 Walter returned to politics and tried to capitalize on the
Populist ground swell. In this respect he was typical of a number
of urban collectivists who sought to use the Populist movement in
spite of their disagreements with agrarian Populists on the ultimate
role of the state. In April, 1895, Walter established the so-called Party
of God in Baltimore as part of Maryland's diminutive People's
party. The main issue of the Maryland campaign concerned neither
government ownership nor free silver but focused on opposition to
the notorious Democratic machine headed by Senator Arthur Pue
Gorman. The Gorman machine was defeated by a coalition of good

[11] *Ibid.,* 416, 417-18.
[12] Harry Vrooman, "Charity, Old and New," *The Arena,* XI (Jan., 1895), 280.
[13] *Government Ownership in Production and Distribution: An Account of 337
Now Existing National and Municipal Undertakings in the 100 Principal Countries of
the World* (Baltimore: Patriotic Literature Publishing Co., 1895), 11-12.

government Republicans, under the leadership of Charles J. Bonaparte, and dissident Democrats, with the generous support of the major newspapers and the Baltimore and Ohio Railroad. The Maryland People's party, split into warring factions by a Socialist-Populist fusion ticket offered by Walter Vrooman, barely counted in the final results of the election.[14]

Hiram Vrooman had resigned his pastorate in Baltimore's Society of the Church of the New Jerusalem in April, 1895, and joined Walter's political campaign. Hiram shared his brother's belief in the ultimate necessity of collective ownership of the means of production and distribution but favored the cooperative colony approach. Successful cooperative colonies would, he hoped, demonstrate the principles of economic democracy in a miniature civilization within the competitive civilization. At the same time, he favored the adoption of direct democracy devices so that the state could be made more responsive to the groups within it who were seeking to establish the cooperative commonwealth. In 1896 he joined Frank Parsons, Benjamin Orange Flower, Henry Demarest Lloyd, and Annie L. Diggs, a Kansas Populist, in endorsing the call of the American Coöperative Union and the Brotherhood of the Coöperative Commonwealth for a national conference on cooperation to meet in St. Louis in July, 1896. He also endorsed the plans for a national direct legislation conference, which deliberately was planned to coincide with the Populist national convention. Finally, as a member of the Maryland delegation, Hiram served on the committee on permanent organization at the Populist national convention.[15]

Frank, Harry, Walter, and Hiram Vrooman thus covered the

[14] Harlan Buddington Phillips, "Walter Vrooman: Restless Child of Progress" (unpublished Ph.D. dissertation, Dept. of History, Columbia University, 1954), 140–64; Eric F. Goldman, *Charles J. Bonaparte, Patrician Reformer: His Early Career,* The Johns Hopkins University Studies in Historical and Political Science, Series LXI, No. 2 (Baltimore: Johns Hopkins Press, 1943), 26–28.

[15] General Convention of the New Jerusalem in the United States, *Journal of the Seventy-Fifth Annual Session of the General Convention of the New Jerusalem in the United States Held in the City of Philadelphia, Pa., From Saturday, June 1 to Tuesday June 4, 1895* (Boston: Massachusetts New-Church Union Press, 1895), 105; Hiram Vrooman, "Economic Democracy—A Colony Plan." *The Washingtonian,* I (Nov., 1897), 22; Imogene Fayles to Henry D. Lloyd, Aug. 4, 1896, Box 12, Lloyd papers; Eltweed Pomeroy, "Call for a Direct Legislation Conference," *Appeal to Reason,* April 11, 1896, p. 3, cols. 2–3; New York *Daily Tribune,* July 24, 1896, p. 2, col. 2.

spectrum of attitudes toward the state in their political views and actions during the Populist campaigns. Somewhere between Frank's Bismarckian welfare state, Walter and Harry's Socialistic "fraternal government," and Hiram's federation of democratized cooperative colonies, the fifth brother, Carl, was struggling to define his own position.

Carl's conception of the state was not so clearly defined as that of his brothers. He had been exposed to their arguments for many years and had participated in their urban experiments, but Carl also had another mentor—Professor Frank Taussig of Harvard. Taussig's Economics 5 class provided stiff doses of readings of Arthur Hadley, Charles Francis Adams, Jr., and E. R. A. Seligman on railroad problems, John Stuart Mill on value, and Taussig on tariffs.[16] His modified classical economics had a moderating influence on Carl over the years. Taussig took a personal liking to the young man from the West who espoused "hayseed Socialism" and spent some time conversing with Carl on economic questions.

In a debate with Yale in 1893 on the topic "Resolved that the power of railroad corporations should be further limited by national legislation" Carl traced the failure of the Interstate Commerce Act and asked rhetorically:

But what more can we expect so long as we confine ourselves to a mere prohibition of abuses and leave their causes untouched? We saw a moment ago that our most awful railroad abuses have one and the same real cause, and that cause is excessive competition. We saw that prohibition does not prohibit these abuses. Shall we still waste our energies by limiting farther the power of railway corporations, in other words, piling on restrictions and prohibitions, without removing the cause of the abuses? True statesmanship would go to the root of the matter and destroy the excessive competition in which these abuses live and move and have their being.[17]

What did Carl propose? Government ownership or government regulation? As first negative speaker, he did not have to say.

[16] Frank W. Taussig, *Topics and References in Economics 5: Railways in the United States* (Cambridge: by the University, 1892), copy in the Harvard Archives. For Taussig's economic views see Joseph Dorfman, *The Economic Mind in American Civilization*, III, *1865–1918* (New York: Viking, 1949), 264–71.

[17] Worcester *Evening Gazette*, Jan. 19, 1893, p. 4, col. 4.

Symbolic perhaps of the tensions in his inherited intellectual system, Carl was afflicted with nervous indigestion and mental exhaustion by the end of the 1893–1894 academic year. After joining Walter and Hiram in their "dynamic religion" episode in Baltimore in 1894 for a brief period, he departed for Europe to travel, study on his own, and seek comfort for his afflictions in various spiritualistic and "new thought" religious systems.[18]

Carl's trip to England and Europe in 1895 proved to be in many ways an idyllic journey. At Oxford University he was designated an honorary member of the Oxford Debating Union and represented the union in a debate with the Cambridge team. The journey through the countries of Western Europe provided an opportunity for him to study European social movements. In Paris he bravely sent his card to Georges Clemenceau and was treated to a friendly interview. While in France, he listened to a debate between Jean Jaurès, a Socialist, and Paul LaFargue, a Marxian, and later traveled in the same railway coach with LaFargue and his wife, Laura Marx LaFargue. During his travels Carl met Julia Green Scott, the daughter of Mathew T. Scott, a prominent Illinois landholder. The Scott family maintained contacts with the higher echelons of the Democratic party through Mrs. Scott's brother-in-law, Vice-President Adlai Stevenson. With the aid of his "dynamic religion" sermon and the beauty of the Grand Canal in Venice, Carl won the heart of Miss Scott, although her mother remained a bit doubtful about the idealistic reformer from Harvard.[19]

When Carl returned to the United States after eighteen months abroad, he found that his brothers already were involved in the Populist campaign. The hopes of the Vrooman brothers centered on St. Louis, where the Populists, direct legislation advocates, and co-

---

[18] "Carl Schurz Vrooman," *Harvard College, Class of 1895, Fifth Report* (Cambridge: Crimson Printing Co., 1915), 335; interview with Carl Vrooman, Nov. 29, 1960.

[19] "The Admirable Record of Regent Vrooman," *The Industrialist*, XXV (March, 1899), 157–58; "The Foremost Democratic Dirt Farmer," mimeographed document prepared for the 1924 Democratic convention, 10, Vrooman papers; interview with Carl Vrooman, Nov. 28, 1960. The debate between Jean Jaurès and Paul LaFargue probably occurred on Jan. 12, 1895. See Jean Jaurès, "Conférence contradictoire avec P. LaFargue, 12 janvier, 1895: Idéalisme et matérialisme dans la conception de l'histoire," *Oeuvres de Jean Jaurès* (Lille: Lagrange, 1901).

operative colony enthusiasts planned to hold their national conventions during the latter part of July, 1896. But events in Chicago fundamentally changed the political situation. The nomination of William Jennings Bryan by the Democrats on the free-silver platform created a serious problem for the urban reformers who had planned to use the Populist movement for their own purposes. Henry Demarest Lloyd attempted to rally the urban collectivists and independent Socialists within the Populist ranks but was unable to stop the party from nominating Bryan and concentrating on the free-silver issue.[20] While Lloyd and many urban reformers refused to follow Bryan's banner, Carl Vrooman hailed the emergence of the "peerless leader" and took to the stump for Bryan in southern Illinois, central Missouri, and southeastern Kansas.[21]

The Bryan campaign provided Carl with the opportunity to present the first full-length public statement of his reform program. By invitation of the sponsors of the National Convention of Democratic Clubs Carl shared the platform at a large labor rally in St. Louis on October 3, 1896, with William Jennings Bryan and Governor Stone of Missouri. "How will free silver benefit the wage-worker?" Carl asked rhetorically in his speech. His answer faintly echoed his father's Greenbackism. Carl argued that an increase in the volume of money would bring idle capital into circulation, since hoarded money would no longer increase in value simply because of scarcity. Once in circulation, the increased capital would stimulate enterprise and increase employment. When the wage-depressing army of unemployed had been absorbed, then the wage earners would be in a better position to raise their pay through collective bargaining.[22]

"Is not labor to participate in the blessings which flow from new inventions, the increased power which man is acquiring over nature?" Carl asked. His answer revealed the extent to which his analysis of society differed from the position that Harry and Walter Vrooman had expounded ten years earlier: "This is no campaign

[20] Quint, *American Socialism*, 234–35.

[21] "Carl Schurz Vrooman," *Harvard College, Class of 1895*, 335–36.

[22] *Carl Vrooman's Great Speech to Workingmen! Delivered to Twenty Thousand People Assembled October 3, 1896, During the National Convention of Democratic Clubs* (St. Louis: Workingmen's Bryan Club of St. Louis, 1896), 4.

of labor against capital, or of the poor against the rich, or of the West against the East. It is a campaign of all honest men, rich and poor, from East and South and West, against that predatory portion of capital which we call monopoly." [23]

Carl divided society into "those who produced the wealth of the country"—the farmers, city workers, small businessmen, and benevolent rich—and those who appropriated this wealth, including "those who are so rich and corrupt that they buy votes, and who are so poor and corrupt that they sell them." [24] When the producing classes united behind Bryan to destroy the "gold trust and its allied monopolies," then the laborer would share in all the benefits of mechanized production. Carl confidently predicted a Bryan victory "in spite of the weaklings and the bolters and all the hosts of the world, the flesh and Mark Hanna." [25]

His efforts on behalf of Bryan allayed whatever lingering doubts Mrs. Mathew T. Scott might have had about her future son-in-law. On December 28, 1896, Carl and Julia Scott were married in St. Louis. The couple settled down in Parsons, Kansas, where Carl supported the Populist-Democratic coalition.[26] In January, 1897, he announced that he would use his house in Parsons to train campaign orators in the cause of bimetallism. The idea, he explained, was "to take crude talent and drill it in public speaking, crystallize ideas on finance and turn out effective stump-speakers" by the first of April. An editorial writer for the New York *Daily Tribune,* noting that Carl had chosen an appropriate deadline, commented: "Then the keen-witted editor of 'The Emporia Gazette,' [William Allen White] whose contributions to the literature of the late campaign diffused such general delight, will have no need to ask 'What's the matter with Kansas?' for he will be able to point to the crude talent in eruption with crystallized ideas on finance from a thousand stumps, and say, 'That's what's the matter with Kansas.' " [27] The newspapers did not ask the newly-wedded Mrs. Vrooman what she

[23] *Ibid.,* 5.
[24] *Ibid.,* 8.
[25] *Ibid.,* 5.
[26] "Carl Schurz Vrooman," *Harvard College, Class of 1895,* 335–36.
[27] Jan. 10, 1897, p. 6, col. 3.

thought of her husband's plan to fill their house with shouting stump speakers.

The political experiences of the Vrooman brothers during the campaigns of 1895 and 1896 indicated that the task of using the Populist movement for their own purposes would be a difficult one. The attempt of Walter and Hiram to capture the Populist movement in Maryland failed, in part, because the eastern laborers would not desert the old parties. Carl's attempts to sell free silver to working-men simply underscored the fact that Bryan failed to attract any large-scale following among the workers.

There were deeper reasons, however, for the difficulties experienced by the brothers. These reasons became apparent only during the next few years. Early in the 1896 campaign the Socialist newspaper *Appeal to Reason* predicted: "As the Chicago convention was an epoch in the life of the democracy, so will the St. Louis convention be with the Populists. After this campaign the people's party will reorganize. One element will remain in the democratic party and give that party the place heretofore filled by the people's party, and the other element will create a socialist party on the same lines as the social-democracy [of Europe]." [28] But which elements could succeed in the Bryanized Democratic party—the radical or the reformist? Could Walter's radical goals be achieved through ordinary political channels? Or would Carl's reform program fare better in the Populist-Democratic fusion politics of Kansas?

WALTER VROOMAN IN MISSOURI POLITICS, 1897–1898

Lee Meriwether, youthful reform candidate for mayor of machine-dominated St. Louis, had entered the 1897 primary campaign confident of the support of the St. Louis Civic Federation. A few hours

[28] *Appeal to Reason* (Girard, Kans.), Aug. 1, 1896, p. 1, col. 1. On the role of labor in the 1896 campaign it is significant that in the 1895 Maryland elections the Knights of Labor supported the Gorman Democratic machine while the civil service and patrician reformers led the attack on it. See Quint, *American Socialism*, 158; Goldman, *Charles J. Bonaparte*, 26–27. Both the Populists and Socialists misread the political behavior of the workingmen during these crucial years.

before the deadline for paying the $1,400 filing fee required by law, Meriwether learned that the Civic Federation had withdrawn his name because of pressure on its leading members. In his auto-biography, *My Yesteryears,* he recalled that afternoon in March, 1897. His doorman said that a "crazy man" wanted to see him, and Meriwether dismissed him wearily:

> "Go away, Armstrong," I said wearily, "I am nearly crazy myself. I have no time for lunatics today."
>
> As I spoke the door opened and in strode the most Apollo-like youth I ever saw—six feet tall, flashing eyes, regular features, wavy, almost golden hair. This astonishing youth gave a military salute as he said:
>
> "I am here, sir, to report for duty."
>
> "What duty? Who are you?"
>
> "I am Walter Vrooman, a soldier in the war against plutocracy. I have come from Baltimore to help rescue St. Louis from corporation control. As candidate for mayor you are commander-in-chief. What are your orders?" [29]

When Meriwether explained that the Civic Federation had with-drawn its support and that he could not afford the filing fee, Walter drew out a roll of one-hundred dollar bills and gave him $2,000 to cover campaign expenses. When Meriwether protested that he was undeserving of such a gift from a stranger, Walter replied that his sole concern was "destroying Plutocracy's grip on the people." [30]

The partnership between Meriwether and Walter Vrooman, which began in such an abrupt fashion, was a natural and productive relationship. Both men were mavericks in a turbulent period of American history. Meriwether was a lawyer by trade and a vaga-bond social scientist by inclination. During 1885 and 1886 he hiked from Gilbraltar to the Bosporus to study European labor conditions. Returning to the United States, he tramped across the country as a "secret agent" for the Department of the Interior gathering data on labor conditions. As labor commissioner of Missouri from 1889 to 1891 and from 1895 to 1896, he attacked the abuses of the labor

[29] *My Yesteryears* (Webster Groves, Mo.: The International Mark Twain Society, 1942), 145–46. Meriwether notes on page 155 that all conversations recorded in his book are reconstructions and not actual quotations.

[30] *Ibid.,* 146.

contract system and established a Bureau of Justice to aid working-men. His nomination for mayor of St. Louis by the Civic Federation came after his report on street railway franchises, which pointed out that the franchise corporations were dodging taxes and supporting the corrupt political machine that ruled St. Louis.[31]

Walter Vrooman had been in St. Louis during the summer of 1896 and had helped to organize the St. Louis Civic Federation. He had served as secretary until asked to resign in a controversy with some of its members.[32]

Walter then returned to Baltimore where he announced his intention of marrying Amne L. Grafflin of that city. Miss Grafflin, a forty-seven-year-old spinster, was a woman of culture who had interested herself in social and political problems.[33] She saw in the fiery, twenty-eight-year-old agitator a chance to help humanity. As a woman of property and wealth, she was ready to use her money to aid Walter's schemes.

Miss Grafflin's wealth was derived from the estate of her father, George W. Grafflin, who at the time of his death in 1896 possessed an estate valued at between $600,000 and $1,000,000, to be divided among his three children. The estate consisted of land and shares of stock in various chemical and fertilizer companies held under a partnership agreement. Since the fertilizer business operated on long-term credit, his will provided a five-year period for liquidation of the estate to insure a profitable settlement. When Amne announced her engagement in January, 1897, to Walter Vrooman, "a clergyman and politician resident in St. Louis," her brother, William, was distressed but did not try to interfere with the plan. On the advice of her father's lawyer, Miss Grafflin signed a deed on February 13, 1897, making her brother the trustee for her share in the estate. She retained her monthly income from the business and

[31] Alexander Nicolas DeMenil, "A Century of Missouri Literature," *Missouri Historical Review*, XV (Oct., 1920), 104. Meriwether's books, *A Tramp Trip* (1887) and *The Tramp at Home* (1889), provide a valuable insight into labor conditions in Europe and the United States during the 1880's. See also Lee Meriwether, "Street Railway Franchises," *Eighteenth Annual Report of the Missouri Bureau of Labor Statistics* (St. Louis, 1896), 1–129.

[32] Phillips, "Walter Vrooman," 169.

[33] *Vrooman et al.* v. *Grafflin et al.*, 96 Fed. 278 (4th Cir., 1899); Meriwether, *My Yesteryears*, 151.

the title to some property in Baltimore. On February 25, 1897, she married Walter, and soon after they departed for St. Louis.[34] With his wife supplying the funds Walter plunged into St. Louis politics as a backer for Meriwether.

In the Democratic primary on March 19, 1897, Meriwether ran second to Edwin Harrison, the machine's candidate. But Vrooman-led delegates crowded into the local Democratic convention the next day to insure a Meriwether victory. The Harrison faction attempted to dictate the choice of convention officers but was defeated by a motion from the floor. The delegates promptly elected Sterling P. Bond, a Meriwether supporter, as chairman. The Harrison forces retaliated by calling the police. The police hauled Bond off to jail, roughed up Meriwether as he was haranguing the crowd, and, in general, attempted to oust the anti-Harrison delegates. The Meriwether forces held the hall, however, and, with the aid of other anti-Harrison delegates, promptly nominated their candidate. Walter Vrooman made the nominating speech and also drafted the platform. The platform denounced the police interference, criticized the city administration for the handling of relief activities during the 1896 tornado disaster, called for economy and more civic services, and demanded equal assessment and collection of taxes from the franchise corporations. When the Harrison forces returned with police reinforcements and authentic credentials, Walter led a strategic withdrawal from the convention hall.[35]

Two candidates, Meriwether and Harrison, contended for the right to use the party's label. Walter Vrooman claimed that the Harrisonites were Gold Democrats while the Meriwether supporters were Bryan Democrats, but the Board of Election Commissioners forbade Meriwether to use the Democratic label. To stir up enthusiasm for Meriwether's independent campaign against the tax-dodging franchise corporations, Walter staged outdoor rallies, torchlight parades, and fund-raising meetings.[36] Such leading advocates of

[34] *Vrooman et al. v. Grafflin et al.*, 96 Fed. 275–79 (4th Cir., 1899); "George W. Grafflin," *Baltimore: Its History and Its People*, III, *Biographical* (New York: Lewis Historical Publishing Co., 1912), 501–503.

[35] Phillips, "Walter Vrooman," 170–77; Meriwether, *My Yesteryears*, 148–50; Walter Vrooman, *The New Democracy* (St. Louis: Walter Vrooman, 1897) 14–15.

[36] Phillips, "Walter Vrooman," 181–82; Walter Vrooman, *The New Democracy*, 14–15.

municipal ownership of street railways as Professor Edward Bemis received rousing ovations from the throngs at the political rallies.[37] The Meriwether supporters "insisted that franchises to monopolize the public's streets ought to be sold, not given away, to private corporations."[38] Without the regular Democratic label Meriwether found the opposition of the Harrison forces too formidable to overcome. The Republican candidate won the contest with a thousand votes more than the combined total of Democratic and independent votes.[39]

On the day following the election Walter remarked to Meriwether that "the tax dodgers have won the battle, but we shall win the war." He then outlined a plan to organize volunteer workers to cover every county in Missouri to attempt to wrest control of the Democratic party from the Harrison machine. Amne Vrooman, who looked up to Walter "like you would look up at God," agreed to deposit one-half of her $2,000 monthly income into a joint account, which required the signatures of both her husband and Lee Meriwether, to finance the new venture. Walter urged Meriwether to consent to the plan and explained, "I know myself; I can arouse people against entrenched wrong, but I cannot keep money. Men can talk me out of it."[40] With Mrs. Vrooman providing the funds and Meriwether controlling the purse, Walter launched the Volunteers of Democracy.

The Volunteers of Democracy plan soon grew beyond the outlines laid down by Walter in the meeting with Meriwether. Seizing upon Carl Vrooman's proposal to train orators in the cause of bimetallism, Walter united this plan with the theory of the "scientific agitator," which he had developed while working for the Union for Practical Progress. Walter described his vision of the Volunteers of Democracy in a book entitled *The New Democracy*. The immediate purpose of the Volunteers of Democracy was to organize the Bryan and free-silver forces for the 1900 election. But his dream did not

[37] Henry D. Lloyd to Albert Shaw, April 23, 1897, Box 13, Henry Demarest Lloyd collection, State Historical Society of Wisconsin, cited hereafter as Lloyd papers.

[38] Walter Vrooman, *The New Democracy*, 15.

[39] Meriwether, *My Yesteryears*, 150.

[40] Interview with Lee Meriwether, March 24, 1961; Meriwether, *My Yesteryears*, 150–51.

stop there: "It is further hoped that the Volunteers thus organized and trained, will become a permanent force in the history of our Nation; a power in the guidance of the forces behind the nation's progress; a means of uniting the best intelligence of our race with that faith and deep religious purpose which permeate the common people, and of expediting the conscious co-operation of individuals with those giant forces that are slowly but surely destroying the old, and building up the new civilization." [41] The first step in realizing this dream was the establishment of the Volunteers' Training School for Speakers in St. Louis, where the young Volunteers of Democracy would be trained in the arts of outdoor oratory and crowd psychology. The school was scheduled to open on September 15, 1897.[42]

In *The New Democracy* Walter idealized his own career as an itinerant agitator and projected the image of the scientific agitator as the hero of civilization.

The young Volunteers who forsake home, business and personal ambition to help save our Nation from the money power, starting in the name of humanity astride bicycles, horseback, afoot and in Bryan wagons, preaching the new gospel of glad tidings without money and without price, eating whole wheat, dry bread and apples, with a square meal only now and then to remind them of the good times coming, are not impelled by any strange or new force in society. They are not disciples of a new cult or ism.... They are not a new product of civilization but on the other hand they are the real conservative [*sic*] and belong to the true nobility of the human race, that brotherhood of heroes, patriots and martyrs of all ages and nations, as old as the human family itself.[43]

The "fire of enthusiasm for humanity" would burn up any false dignity or modesty that might hinder the Volunteer's efforts. The Volunteer would ask himself only one question: "Can I get to my destination in time to deliver my message?" [44]

---

[41] *The New Democracy*, 23–24. For a similar project by Laurence Gronlund in 1891 see Dorfman, *The Economic Mind*, III, 154–55.
[42] *The New Democracy*, 228.
[43] *Ibid.*, 115–16.
[44] *Ibid.*, 65–66.

The Volunteers would carry to every city, village, and hamlet in the country the same message that Walter had been proclaiming from atop dry goods boxes, buggy seats, chairs, and makeshift platforms for ten years. This message was that "the poor people need not suffer as they do if they would but unite in behalf of their own interests and use the ballot against oppression and tyranny." [45]

This simple theme rested upon three basic assumptions.

The silver question, the question as to the power of the Supreme Court Justices, the railway question, are all merely incidental to the one great fundamental conflict that has been waged for centuries, the conflict of the general welfare resting on right against the special interests that thrive by wrong, of liberty against tyranny; [sic] the people against plutocracy....

Once convince men that their sufferings are unnecessary, that science has placed in their hands all the power and materials needed which rightly applied will give to all men the satisfaction of all their normal desires, and you at once transform the world....

[When] a monopoly becomes a government monoply, its nature changes entirely, and all that was objectionable disappears. The evil pertaining to a monopoly is its exclusiveness. When private monopoly bec[o]mes government monopoly, it is no longer exclusive, for the whole people enjoy its benefits alike. Unity of administration is not an evil if the resulting benefits are shared by all. The only possible way to destroy the great monopolies is to convert them into government functions. [46]

The Volunteers, by continually returning to these fundamental precepts, would prepare the people for the great Bryan victory in 1900. The Volunteers need not fear repeating this message, since progress in human affairs is achieved only by the "concentration of a multitude of minds on a single idea." [47]

To support the activities of the National Volunteers' Speakers Bureau Walter entered the publishing field. *The Arena* magazine had gone into receivership in 1896, and the new owners removed veteran editor Benjamin O. Flower in June, 1897. *The Arena* continued to decline despite the efforts of the new editor, John Clark

[45] *Ibid.*, 70.
[46] *Ibid.*, 143, 146, 217–18, note.
[47] *Ibid.*, 143–44. The original is printed in capitals.

Ridpath, to restore its prestige.[48] Many fly-by-night radical and reform journals were launched in 1897 in an attempt to fill the void left by the decline of *The Arena*. The Vrooman contributions were modest in scope and short-lived. The pocket-sized *Washingtonian* magazine contained reprints of "dynamic religion" sermons, news of Vrooman ventures, and romantic articles for children. *The Washingtonian* was followed by the even more ephemeral *Volunteers Quarterly,* which was published until June, 1898. The first issue of the *Volunteers Quarterly* contained a romantic novel by Lee Meriwether entitled *Miss Chunk: A Tale of the Times,* describing the exploits of a dynamic labor commissioner, who disguises himself as a workman to investigate labor conditions, and the adventures of a wealthy spinster, who gives financial aid to reform causes.[49]

By June, 1897, Walter's activities in St. Louis had fallen back into the pattern established in the Union for Practical Progress. The Volunteer represented the poverty-embracing scientific agitator who remained with the people and utilized their established institutions to spread his message. The traveling Bryan wagon would take the new gospel to the rural districts much as the Peoples' University of the union had attempted to carry out rural propaganda. *The Washingtonian* and the *Volunteers Quarterly* would help to educate the people now that *The Arena* magazine was rapidly declining. The only two elements of the standard Vrooman program that were missing—a theology for the social gospel and a theory for general welfare clubs—were soon supplied.

The quintessence of the Vroomans' theology for the social gospel appeared in a curious little book published by Walter in September, 1897, entitled *Sacred Biography for Boys and Girls: An Illustrated Story Book for Young and Old, Written to Encourage Modern Heroes as Well as to Praise Ancient Ones.* The book was based on the theory that "early ideals of character, morality and future use-

---

[48] Frank Luther Mott, *A History of American Magazines,* IV, 1885–1905 (Cambridge: Harvard University Press, 1957), 411–12.
[49] [Lee Meriwether], *Miss Chunk: A Tale of the Times* (St. Louis: Walter Vrooman, 1896). This book is erroneously attributed to Walter Vrooman by the Library of Congress because his name appears as holder of the copyright. The real author, Meriwether, did not allow his name to be published at the time but acknowledged authorship years later. See DeMenil, *Missouri Historical Review,* XV, 104.

fulness" are formed in childhood by imitation and that correct standards could be cultivated by the study of model lives.[50] The theological assumption of the book was boldly stated in the introduction: "Do you know, children, that each of you who read this book may become, if you will, a direct agent or prophet of the living God—a co-worker with God in the creation of the world, which is not yet finished, as some suppose, but is now in process of being made?"[51] The juxtaposition of Biblical prophets and modern radicals and reformers revealed Walter's panoply of heroes—Moses / Bryan, David / Lee Meriwether, Nehemiah / John Peter Altgeld, Elijah / "Sockless" Jerry Simpson, Isaiah / George D. Herron, Jeremiah / Henry D. Lloyd, Amos / Kier Hardie, Daniel / W. D. P. Bliss, and Ezekiel / Edward Bellamy. He even found Biblical precedent for the Volunteers in Samuel's description of the School of the Prophets, "a secret order going out on Evangelistic tours preaching to the people." He also found a parallel for the cooperative colony movement in the practices of the Essene sect, of which Jesus may have been a member. He predicted that one day a great revival of social righteousness and a revolt of the common people would establish the Kingdom of God on earth, or Socialism, which meant simply "applied Christianity."[52]

Walter helped to organize Bryan clubs in the St. Louis wards as part of his new campaign to win control of the Democratic party in Missouri. Harry Vrooman, pastor of the Fountain Park Congregational Church in St. Louis, aided in the effort by joining the Workingmen's Bryan Club in the twenty-eighth ward.[53] In April, 1898, Walter announced that he would run for Congress as a Bryan Democrat from the Eleventh Missouri Congressional District, thus

[50] Walter Vrooman, *Sacred Biography* (St. Louis: Walter Vrooman, 1897), 1.

[51] *Ibid.*, 7.

[52] *Ibid.*, 92–96, 97, 147, 155. Amne Vrooman prepared a series of Bible studies along similar lines to emphasize that "the principles of social righteousness as laid down in the Bible call for radical changes in the organization of society." In interpreting the Biblical stories she portrayed Joseph as a businessman with a corner on wheat and Moses as a labor agitator who organized a successful strike against the Pharaoh. The lessons were published in *The Washingtonian* magazine and later issued as a textbook. See *Silver Text Bible Lessons* (St. Louis: Walter Vrooman, 1898).

[53] "Harry Chase Vrooman," *Harvard College, Class of 1894*, Secretary's Report, No. 2 (Cambridge: Printed for use by the class, 1897), 107–108.

provoking a struggle between the Vrooman-Meriwether forces and
the politicians allied with the statehouse machine. When a gang of
rowdies tried to remove a polling booth to place it in a location
known only to the party faithful, Walter intervened to stop them.
He then hid the booth. He was subsequently arrested for stealing
public property and was put in jail when he refused to post bond.
Jail provided him with an excellent sounding board for his attacks
on the political machine. He was finally acquitted for lack of evidence, and he then stumped the state with his stolen polling booth
denouncing the fraudulent tactics of the statehouse machine. But
the political trends of the day called for unity among the Democrats
to meet the rising Republican reaction in the election of 1898.
Walter's denunciations of the bosses closed the party portals to
him.[54]

Walter's dreams always seemed to exceed the financial resources
available to him. Even his wife's monthly income did not meet his
needs. Walter and Amne filed a suit in the Maryland district court
charging that her lawyer had tricked her into making her brother,
William, the trustee for her portion of the estate. The Maryland
district court held that Amne had understood the nature of her
action and that no improper means had been used to persuade her
to sign the document. Walter appealed the case to the United States
Circuit Court of Appeals. The case rested there when Amne suggested to her husband that they take a trip to England.[55]

During three years of political activity Walter had tried, first, to
capitalize on the Populist movement and, second, to claim the title
of a Bryan Democrat. His individualistic approach to politics combined the moral enthusiasm of a preacher with the shrewd insights
of an agitator but did not produce any conclusive results at the polls.
The idealistic young Volunteers that he had envisioned in *The New
Democracy* did not spring up to answer his call. The Democratic
party in Missouri showed little enthusiasm for this self-styled Bryan
Democrat when the political necessities of the day called for party
unity. Whatever the reasons that prompted Walter to seek a seat in
Congress, he was easily distracted from this goal. Like his father,
he had discovered that the politics of protest paid small dividends

[54] Phillips, "Walter Vrooman," 185–95; Meriwether, *My Yesteryears*, 153–57.
[55] *Vrooman et al.* v. *Grafflin et al.*, 96 Fed. 275–76 (4th Cir. 1899).

on the capital invested. Walter never again entered active political life, turning instead to the paths of education and cooperative enterprise that had been blazed ahead of him by Carl and Hiram G. Vrooman. *The New Democracy* proved that, although he had put on the outward garb of a politician and a reformer in the ordinary sense, at heart he was still the radical proclaiming a new ideal for his society. Science had made possible the satisfaction of all normal desires. Government through state-owned monopolies could return to the masses all they created. The people had only to rise up and change the system.

CARL VROOMAN AND POPULISM IN KANSAS, 1897–1900

After the 1896 campaign Carl Vrooman quietly moved into a position of power within the Kansas People's party as a member of the state central committee. Soon he was involved in a controversy about the state colleges that provided an intriguing insight into the Populist theory of the state and Carl's attitude toward it. Since the state was an agent for carrying out their economic program, it is not surprising that the Populists looked to the instruments of the state for help in their efforts. The Kansas Populists had long felt that state colleges had neglected the study of economics. On April 16, 1894, the Board of Regents of Kansas State Agricultural College, under the leadership of its Populist members, had voted to institute a series of lectures on political economy. The resolution stipulated: "These lectures shall be non-partisan, but shall not ignore nor unfairly treat the positions taken by what is commonly known as the new school of political economists. The principles maintained by the advocates of land nationalization, public control of public utilities, and the reform of the financial or monetary systems shall be fairly stated and candidly examined, with a view of leading the student to grasp the principles involved in the science of production and distribution, without bias or prejudice." [56] The Board of Regents called Thomas E. Will, lecturer for the Boston Union for Practical Progress, to fill the post of professor of political economy. The

[56] Julius T. Willard, *History of the Kansas State College of Agriculture and Applied Science* (Manhattan: Kansas State College Press, 1940), 96.

Republican press in Kansas assumed that Will was an exponent of Populist views and criticized his appointment accordingly.[57]

In hiring Will to deliver the newly instituted lectures on political economy the Populist members of the Board of Regents got more than an economics professor, for they also brought to Kansas a passionate advocate of academic freedom. Will was still smarting from the treatment he had received in 1892 at Lawrence University in Appleton, Wisconsin, where he had been released for alleged radicalism in economics. In politics he could best be described as an independent. Like the Vrooman brothers, whom he had met at Harvard and worked with in the Boston Union for Practical Progress, he had spent most of his time in the East during those crucial years when the Populist party had been formed. Since 1890 he had been greatly influenced by the English Fabians, particularly by their educational methods.[58]

Will had many doubts about orthodox Socialism. In a letter to W. D. P. Bliss, the editor of the *American Fabian,* Will wrote:

I am lecturing now on Socialism and Social Reforms, and desire ... to see in its best light any plan proposed by intelligent men for promoting human progress. As to Socialism, am I right in believing that representative Socialists would not regard as satisfactory a semi-socialized state in which *industries not monopolies are not socialized ...?* I confess that after strenuous efforts to grasp the Socialist's *economic* ideal I still find myself in a fog or in the presence of adjustments so preposterous that I am unwilling to believe the better socialistic thought will sanction them.... Do you candidly believe that the objections to the *completely socialized* Society which [Richard T. Ely] brings together can be met in the present state of sociological knowledge? [59]

On the other hand, the president of Kansas State Agricultural College, George T. Fairchild, thought that Professor Will presented certain ideas "of socialistic tendency, as if they were beyond criticism." [60]

[57] George T. Fairchild, "Populism in a State Educational Institution, The Kansas State Agricultural College," *American Journal of Sociology,* III (Nov., 1897), 395–96. Will was recommended for the position by Benjamin Orange Flower, editor of *The Arena.*

[58] Will to Ely, May 20, 1897, Box 21, Ely papers.

[59] W. D. P. Bliss, "An Important Letter: From a Professor of Political Economy," *American Fabian,* I (Nov., 1895), 8.

[60] Fairchild, *American Journal of Sociology,* III (Nov., 1897), 396.

During the 1896 campaign partisan hostility toward Kansas State Agricultural College increased on both sides. The Populists "generally agreed that President Fairchild was an uncompromising Republican, an autocrat, and a man who had outlived his usefulness, that the Faculty was rusty, that the College should give more attention to economic science," and that the executive powers of the college president should be trimmed.[61] The Republicans, in turn, suspected that Professor Will was conspiring with the leaders of the Populist party and feared that the Populists intended to revolutionize the agricultural college. In the Kansas state election the Populist-Democratic fusion ticket won a sweeping victory that carried with it control of both the legislative and executive branches of the state government.[62]

When the newly elected legislature convened, the ruling coalition of Populists, Silver Republicans, and Bryan Democrats took a close look at the costs of operating the state government and its agencies. In their eagerness to cut state expenses during a period of agricultural depression they jeopardized the progress of the state's colleges. Will, acting as the chief lobbyist for Kansas State Agricultural College, called on Carl Vrooman, asking for his assistance in restoring some of the reductions made in the appropriation for the college. Carl used his political influence to help Will secure funds for a domestic science building.[63] The legislature did, however, reduce salaries and make other minor cuts in the college's budget. After a complex legislative debate the legislature passed a bill that deprived the president of Kansas State Agricultural College of his ex officio status on the Board of Regents, added an extra regent to the board, and lengthened the regents' terms to four years. Critics of the bill pointed out that it assured a Populist majority on the board for the next four years. Governor John W. Leedy promptly appointed five new regents, all of whom were either Populists or sympathetic to their educational reform program.[64]

[61] John D. Walters, *History of the Kansas State Agricultural College* (Manhattan: Kansas State Agricultural College, 1909), 111.

[62] Fairchild, *American Journal of Sociology*, III (Nov., 1897), 398.

[63] Interview with Carl Vrooman, Nov. 28, 1960.

[64] Thomas E. Will, "The College and the Legislature," *The Industrialist*, XXI (March 22, 1897), 111; Walters, *History*, 113. The new board included Populists C. B. Hoffman, Harrison Kelley, J. N. Limbocker, T. J. Hudson, and Mrs. John P. St. John, the wife of the former governor.

On April 8, 1897, the new Populist-controlled Board of Regents adopted a resolution, submitted by C. B. Hoffman, that created one of the most controversial academic freedom cases of the 1890's: "Resolved, that the term 'school year' [as employed in recent acts of the legislature] shall begin July first of each year and end June 30th of the following year, and that the term of employment of all present employees shall expire June 30th, 1897." [65] In effect, the board had discharged the entire faculty. In vain the Populist regents protested to the clamorous Republican press that the action was designed to make the school year coincide with the fiscal year used by the legislature. When President Fairchild, weary of strife, declined to consider reelection to the presidency, the board promptly elected Thomas E. Will as the new president.

This action brought another howl of protest from the Republican press. The board attempted to counter some of these accusations with a resolution that sought to clear Will of any complicity in the changes at the college. [66] By an ironic turn of events Will, the ardent advocate of academic freedom, had become the president of a college that had experienced a wholesale dismissal of its faculty.

The Board of Regents moved quickly to rehire those members of the old faculty who were satisfactory to the new president and who expressed their willingness to cooperate with the new administration. By June, 1897, eight professors had been fired and four had resigned for personal reasons. In addition, several staff members declined reemployment. Thus, of a faculty of twenty-four, one-half were replaced in the reorganization. [67] President Will attempted to secure replacements by asking Richard T. Ely of the University of Wisconsin to recommend known reformers in the fields of sociology, political economy, and domestic science who would be fitted to serve "in an institution seeking to do broad and

[65] *The Industrialist*, XXI (April 12, 1897), 123.
[66] Walters, *History*, 112.
[67] Willard, *History*, 100; "Press Misrepresentations Rectified," *The Industrialist*, XXII (Aug. 16, 1897), 171. Fairchild states that twelve were retained out of twenty-four on the faculty and that ten were retained out of sixteen on the staff. However, he does not distinguish between firings and resignations not connected with the reorganization. See Fairchild, *American Journal of Sociology*, III (Nov., 1897), 401. Willard uses the figure of fourteen dismissals and three resignations but does not provide a breakdown of cases.

progressive work." President Will confided to Ely: "We shall attempt here something in the way of a new departure."[68]

The Populist-controlled Board of Regents announced the names of the new faculty members in June, 1897. To the critics of the reorganization Will and the board appeared to be bent on turning Kansas State Agricultural College into a haven for academic freedom refugees, radicals, and urban reformers. The new faculty included Edward Bemis, an economist and sociologist who had been fired by the University of Chicago, allegedly for his views on municipal monopolies; J. Allen Smith, a political scientist who had been dismissed from Marietta College for his Populist views; Helen Campbell, a freelance lecturer in domestic science; and Frank Parsons, an expert on municipal monopoly problems. Bemis, Parsons, and Will were all members of the National League for Promoting Public Ownership of Monopolies and frequently attended private conferences sponsored by Henry Demarest Lloyd. In addition, they all had been involved in such ventures as the Union for Practical Progress, the American Fabians, and the Brotherhood of the Coöperative Commonwealth. How they would fare among the agrarian Populists of Kansas remained to be seen. But President Will, knowing that he enjoyed the support of Carl Vrooman on the Populist state committee, was optimistic.[69]

The Kansas state elections of 1898 returned the Republicans to full control of the state government. In a final attempt to secure a railway rate bill Governor Leedy called a special session of the lameduck legislature to meet on December 21, 1898. The special session also considered the situation at Kansas State Agricultural College. The death of a Populist regent in August, 1897, had reduced the Populist contingent on the board to six, including three members whose terms were to expire in April, 1899. Governor Leedy submitted Carl Vrooman's name to the Senate to fill the un-

[68] Will to Ely, April 19, May 14, 1897, Box 21, Ely papers.
[69] Walter P. Metzger, *Academic Freedom in the Age of the University* (New York: Columbia University Press, 1961), 149–50, 153–54. For the careers of Bemis, Parsons, and Campbell, see "New Appointees," *The Industrialist*, XXI (July 15, 1897), 164–65; Walters, *History,* 127–29, 133–35; Frank Parsons to Henry D. Lloyd, Dec. 8, 1897, Box 14, Lloyd papers; Lloyd to Parsons, March 17, 1897, Box 13, Lloyd papers.

expired term, and on January 6, 1899, the Senate confirmed his appointment.[70]

The Republican press of Kansas denounced Carl as an anarchist and "the most conspicuously unfit man in Kansas"[71] to serve on the board. The problem, as Edward Bemis explained it in a letter to Richard T. Ely, was that the Republican press, perhaps deliberately, had confused Carl with Walter Vrooman: "Mr. [Carl] Vrooman is a Socialist, although a mild and exceedingly able type, and a brother of Walter Vrooman, who greatly sympathized with the anarchists, and is confused with Carl in the minds of many Kansas people. The Republicans are threatening to get control of the board [of regents] in some way and to sweep away everyone connected with the teaching of economics and political science which means President Will, Parsons and myself. The storm will somewhat abate, I think, before long."[72]

Edward Bemis' use of the term "Socialist" to describe Carl's views was indicative of the lingering conflict in Carl's thought. In an article published in June, 1898, Carl had declared that "the whole trend of statesmanship of the world" was toward Populism. He defined Populism as government ownership of railroads and telegraph systems, and government-sponsored savings banks and insurance companies, municipal ownership of public utilities, and income and inheritance taxes.[73]

The first move by the new Republican administration was to challenge the legality of the extra session of the lameduck legislature that had appointed Carl to the board. When this failed, the Republicans faced a delicate situation. Edward Bemis summarized the situation in a letter to Richard T. Ely: "The Republicans will put in three more [regents], and will be unable to control the board

[70] Willard, *History*, 120–21; Walters, *History*, 119.

[71] "The Admirable Record of Regent Vrooman," *The Industrialist*, XXV (March, 1899), 157.

[72] Bemis to Ely, Jan. 19, 1899, Box 25, Ely papers. The Republican papers revived the incident of Walter's arrest in Kansas City, Mo., shortly after the Haymarket bombing of 1886 but implied that it had been Carl. See *The Industrialist*, XXV (March, 1899), 157. The Republican press also tried to confuse Frank Parsons with Albert Parsons, the Haymarket anarchist who had been hanged ten years earlier. See *American Fabian*, IX (Aug., 1898), 8.

[73] Carl Vrooman, "International Populists and Populism," *The New Time*, II (June, 1898), 372–74.

unless a death occurs, or unless the governor removes a regent on some trumped up charge of unfitness." [74]

The Republicans were too impatient to wait for nature to take its toll; they instigated an investigation of charges against C. B. Hoffman and L. N. Limbocker, Populist regents, for alleged irregularities in the management of the college. After an investigation by a legislative committee composed of four Republicans and one Populist, the Republican governor removed the two Populist regents and appointed two Republicans to take their places.[75] In May, 1899, the new Republican-controlled Board of Regents moved to reduce the amount of time devoted to economics and history in the new curriculum. A student protest meeting in the chapel was denounced in the press as a Populist trick. Finally, the board canceled a commencement address by William Jennings Bryan.[76]

On June 10, 1899, Edward Bemis' suspicions were confirmed. The Republican-dominated board dismissed Thomas E. Will, William H. Phipps, the president's secretary, Duren H. Ward, professor of English, Frank Parsons, professor of history, and Edward Bemis, professor of economics.

Carl Vrooman rose in the regents' meeting to denounce the action of the board in dismissing the four professors. He denied that the Populist reorganization in 1897 had been politically inspired, pointed out that the Populist board had rehired numerous Republican professors, and noted that the board had hired new professors, such as

[74] Bemis to Ely, undated letter, probably between Feb. 15 and Feb. 24, 1899, Box 25, Ely papers.

[75] Bemis to Ely, May 10, 1899, Box 25, Ely papers. The Populist Board of Regents had established a dining hall, bookstore, and printing office. These ventures were highly popular with the students but were equally unpopular with the local businessmen. The irregularities charged against the two Populist regents were apparently part of an attack on these economic ventures. When the Republicans regained control, they abolished the bookstore and dining hall and restricted the activities of the printing plant. The major political charge against the two regents read: "Perversion of the College to the teachings of socialism and political doctrines; use of college funds to print and disseminate socialistic and political doctrines and theories; changing [THE] INDUSTRIALIST into a monthly wherein were taught socialistic views and political doctrines and political heresies; use of college with connivance of Hoffman and Limbocker for the purpose of distributing populist pamphlets to the students." This charge was not sustained by the evidence. See Frank Parsons, "The Regents' Investigation," *The Industrialist*, XXV (June, 1898), 378–87; Walters, *History*, 121–22, 139; Willard, *History*, 122–23.

[76] Bemis to Ely, May 16, 1899, Box 25, June 3, 1899, Box 26, Ely papers.

Edward Bemis, who did not even believe in the cardinal Populist idea of free silver. In particular, Carl deplored the firing of Professor Ward, a Unitarian, simply because "a lot of little preachers" were "howling at his heels." Above all, he denounced the political motive that lay behind most of the firings: "But the mistake made at the time in canceling the Bryan engagement was nothing in comparison with the mistake now about to be made. If these professors are dismissed on the slight ground here shown, nothing will persuade the people of the country that this is not a political movement. The word will go abroad that this institution had been prostituted for political ends. Were there mitigating circumstances it might be possible to convince at least the republican party that this action is for non-political motives." [77] Carl warned that if the Republican board continued in its policy, the Populists would rise in the next election and sweep the Republicans from the scene. In calling on the Populists to rise in righteous anger, Carl was summoning a ghost. In its brief history the Kansas People's party had shown that it could achieve a major victory only in cooperation with the Democrats. But the fusion coalition had begun to break down in 1898, and the Populist strength was dwindling rapidly.[78]

The incident at Kansas State Agricultural College held a lesson for Carl: use of the instruments of the state required control of the state, and control could be achieved only by coalition. In November, 1899, he wrote: "The campaign of 1900 is upon us, and all factions are frantically exclaiming, 'The reform forces must unite!' When 'how' is asked, unanimity gives way to chaos. Each one wants every one else to 'fall in' behind him. This is clearly impossible. 'Unite on the silver issue,' suggests one. We are united on the silver issue to the extent of fusion. Further than that the silver issue cannot carry us. If we are to have any permanent, any organic union, we must have not only a common issue but a *common policy*." [79] The common

[77] "Regents on the College Changes," *The Industrialist*, XXV (July, 1899), 465–66. Ward sued the Board of Regents for breach of contract. On appeal, the Circuit Court of Appeals, Eighth Circuit, sustained the board and refused to inquire into the reasons for dismissal. See *Ward* v. *Board of Regents of Kansas State Agricultural College*, 138 Fed. 372–81 (8th Cir., 1905).

[78] Wynne Powers Harrington, "The Populist Party in Kansas," *Collections of the Kansas State Historical Society*, XVI (1925), 447.

[79] Carl Vrooman, "Twentieth Century Democracy," *The Arena*, XXII (Nov., 1899), 584.

policy of the reform forces "must be both conservative and constructive," he said; "simple enough to be easily comprehended by the masses and fundamental enough to meet the exigencies of the situation." [80]

Carl saw two "irreducible elements" in the common reform policy: "The first stands for the liberty of the individual citizen and for the inalienable and equal right with every other citizen to a voice in the affairs of government—in a word, for political democracy. The second stands for the protection of the economic rights of the individual citizen from the tyrannical aggressions of monopolistic aggregations of wealth, *by extending the sphere of popular government into the realm of business and industry.* This is commonly and somewhat vaguely known as populistic or socialistic legislation; accurately speaking, it is simply business democracy." [Italics added] [81] Government ownership of railroads, telegraphs, and telephones; government-sponsored insurance programs, postal savings banks, employment bureaus, and farms for the unemployed; legislation providing for an eight-hour working day, an inheritance tax, and a graduated land tax bearing heavily on absentee owners— these constituted some of the "Populistic reforms that lead to business democracy." The immediate task, however, was to assure the effectiveness of political democracy through the adoption of the initiative and the referendum. The next step would be to attack the two great creators of the trusts—"the railroad combine and the money power"—through government ownership of the railroads and bimetallism. [82]

By the end of 1899 Carl Vrooman had concluded that the states were powerless to cope with the problems created by the trusts. Only the national government could attack the problem; only a nationwide political coalition could exert sufficient pressure upon Congress to force it to act. [83] Rumors circulated in the press charging that he wanted the congressional nomination in the third district and that he had entered into an alliance with another Kansas State Agricul-

[80] *Ibid.,* 595.
[81] *Ibid.,* 584.
[82] *Ibid.,* 590–91, 596–97.
[83] Altamont (Kans.) *White Banner,* Nov. 3, 1899, clipping in Kansas State Historical Society Biographical Collections, V, I, 353. See also Carl Vrooman, *Taming the Trust* (Topeka: The Advocate, 1900), copy in Library of Congress.

tural College regent in a bid for support. The Topeka *Journal* noted: "Vrooman is a conspicuous figure in Populist affairs. He is writing the platforms this year; directs the policy of the state committee; selects the men who are sent on special missions.... The recent plan of fusion adopted by Democrats and Populists was devised largely by Vrooman." [84] Carl stood on the threshold of his political career, but something held him back. Populism was too slim a reed on which to lean for much support. If he wished to get ahead, he would need a broader base of support.

The confrontation with Populism had brought into sharp relief the Vrooman brothers' varied attitudes toward the role of the state in social change. Frank, as a reformer, was prepared to call upon the state to interfere in all matters involved with the early environmental surroundings of children—housing, sanitation, education, and public health. He was not prepared to go beyond this point, fearing the destruction of the self-reliance of the people. Harry and Walter, true radicals, still believed in the ultimate efficacy of the Socialist state. Hiram, also a radical, believed that a direct democracy government could foster the cooperative colonies that would lead to the cooperative commonwealth. Carl emerged in the campaign as a reformer, closer in spirit to Frank than to Walter. He favored a step-at-a-time "Populistic" program based on a gradual extension of welfare and economic activities by a thoroughly "democratized" state into the economic sphere to destroy those monopolistic aggregations of power that hindered competition and entrepreneurial effort.

The political experiences of Walter and Carl revealed the basic difference between them. Compromise is the heart of politics, and Walter, as a true radical, failed in politics because he could not compromise. He was more interested in proclaiming a new ideal than in winning the reforms that Meriwether advocated. Carl, who emerged from his Populist experiences as a reformer at heart, was more at home in politics. He trimmed and fitted the rhetoric of his brother's position and tried to tame it to fit the label of Populism. But the heart of Carl's program lay closer to the entrepreneurial reformism of his father with its attack on the money power and the

[84] Topeka (Kans.) *Journal,* March 30, 1900, clipping in Kansas State Historical Society Biographical Collections, V, I, 362.

railroad trusts. He played the game of politics according to the rules and supported the Democratic-Populist fusion policy. However, Republican victories in the 1896 and 1898 elections showed that, fusion or not, "the people" were not ready for Populism. They still had to be convinced—and that was the task of education.

Chapter Six

Education, Radicalism, &
Reform, 1899-1900

CARL VROOMAN AND THE COLLEGE
OF SOCIAL SCIENCES, 1899–1900

The incidents at Kansas State Agricultural College—the Populist reorganization of the college followed by the Republican purge—came at a time of great public controversy over the concept of academic freedom. Beginning in 1895 a number of radical and reform-minded professors, who espoused everything from free silver to municipal ownership of transportation systems, were ousted from their posts. To the men involved the reason was obvious. The plutocracy that controlled the nation also ruled the colleges through gifts, endowments, and selection of the presidents by their captive boards. The plutocracy did not want "the people" to find out the truth, and it forced its hirelings to fire the dissenters.[1]

A closer examination of the subsequent history of the Kansas State Agricultural College refugees, however, will better illuminate the nature of academic freedom and will also illustrate the difficulties facing the radicals and reformers as they tried to educate the public.

Thomas E. Will revealed the bias of the academic refugees when he wrote in April, 1899, that academic freedom was jeopardized "when governing boards declare ... that *the professor must express not the results of his investigations and the conclusions reached by his unbiased judgment,* but the 'dominant sentiment of the community'; when they declare that the professor who dissents from this 'dominant sentiment' will be 'hauled up before the board' and compelled to 'walk the plank.'" [Italics added][2] The important point here is not the literal truth of Will's contention but his conception of academic freedom as protection of the process of arriving at conclusions. Will's mistake lay in assuming that the Populist-dominated Board of Regents had shared his conception of academic freedom.

When C. B. Hoffman, a Populist regent, proposed that lectures in political economy be given at the college, he referred to specific doctrines and economic proposals. These proposals had long formed the basis of radical and reform programs. The Populist-controlled board that hired Will to deliver the lectures did not thereby ask him to undertake pure research. They wanted him to present certain programs in a fair light. When Will turned to Carl Vrooman for aid in liberalizing the college, he found a sympathetic supporter. But Carl also shared the assumptions of the Populists and held that "prejudice, false education, and self-interest" were the only enemies of Populism.[3] If these enemies could be attacked by helping Will to make Kansas State Agricultural College a "progressive" institution, then Carl was ready to use his political influence to further that end. As long as the academic personnel and the Populists faced pressure from a common opponent, they assumed that they meant the same thing when they spoke of academic freedom. But the tension between those who believed that academic freedom meant the right to present a certain doctrine and those who believed that it meant the right to pursue scientific inquiry was bound to increase once the external pressure had been removed.

[1] This theory, hallowed by Populist mythology, sanctified by the scholarship of Thorstein Veblen, and codified by the writings of Charles Beard, has been subject to recent scrutiny by Walter Metzger in his book *Academic Freedom in the Age of the University* (New York: Columbia University Press, 1961), 147 ff. Metzger offers the thesis that the Kansas State Agricultural College case disproves the Populist myth by showing that both Populists *and* Republicans violated the canons of academic freedom, but such a plague-on-both-your-houses attitude does not go far enough. The lesson to be learned from the Kansas episode is not simply that both parties transgressed against some vaguely defined standard of academic freedom, but that the participants in the events—the academic reformers, the Populists, and the Republicans—held different and ultimately conflicting conceptions of the nature of academic freedom.

[2] Thomas E. Will, "The Evolution of Education," *The Industrialist*, XXV (April, 1899), 216.

[3] Carl Vrooman, "International Populists and Populism," *The New Time*, II (June, 1898), 374.

The academic freedom refugees from Kansas State Agricultural College planned to carry their protest against the action of the Republican-dominated board to a large conference of reformers and radicals scheduled to meet in Buffalo from June 28 to July 4, 1899. Edward Bemis, who had been considering for some time the idea of a bureau of municipal investigation, wrote to Richard T. Ely on June 12, 1899: "I have arranged time to appeal to the Buffalo Conference for support of such a bureau of municipal research, and Professors [John R.] Commons and [Frank] Parsons, [Carl] Vrooman and myself, and possibly others are to have a considerable time to appeal for securing of chairs of teaching and research, either in a State University or by special endowment." [4]

On June 28, 1899, Frank Parsons called a special meeting at the Buffalo Conference of all those interested in academic freedom. Numerous proposals were tossed into the discussion. Edward Bemis described the bureau of municipal research that he had been planning for more than a year. John R. Commons, a fellow refugee from Syracuse University, spoke of a plan developed earlier in the year by George H. Shibley, a prominent Democrat, for a bureau of economic research. Thomas E. Will outlined the advantages of the correspondence school system in freeing education from the control of the plutocracy. Parsons outlined his own ideas for a "People's University or College of Liberal Thought," which would be based upon complete academic freedom. A ways-and-means committee was appointed to call a second meeting and to synthesize the suggestions. Surveying the results of the special meeting, Eltweed Pomeroy predicted that if the plans outlined at the meeting were adopted, the Buffalo Conference would be recognized in two years as "the turning point in the history of political and economic agitation." [5]

---

[4] Bemis to Ely, June 12, 1899, Box 26, Ely papers. See also Bemis to Ely, June 3, 1899, Box 26, Ely papers. Henry Demarest Lloyd had proposed in February, 1898, that Bemis and Parsons undertake an examination of municipal monopoly problems in Boston at his expense, but later had to delay the project. See Lloyd to Bemis, Feb. 17, 1898; Parsons to Lloyd, Feb. 24, 1898; Lloyd to Bemis, May 4, 1898, Box 15, Lloyd papers.

[5] Frank Parsons, "Academic Freedom and the New School of Economics," *The Coming Age,* II (Sept., 1899), 291–94; Parsons to Ely, July 26, 1899, Box 26, Ely papers; Eltweed Pomeroy, "The National Social and Political Conference," *The Social Forum,* I (Aug. 1, 1899), 82. For the Commons-Shibley proposals see John R. Commons, *Myself* (New York: Macmillan, 1934), 64–65.

The temporary committee labored to bring all the various plans into one scheme. Professors Bemis and Commons were encouraged to proceed with a research bureau. Kansas State Agricultural College refugees Frank Parsons and Duren Ward were asked to undertake teaching and extension work for the proposed correspondence school, and Will was offered its presidency. When this tentative arrangement was presented to the Buffalo Conference at a session chaired by Carl Vrooman, the delegates responded enthusiastically and pledged $15,000 for the proposed College of Social Sciences.

Carl appointed a temporary executive committee for the College of Social Sciences that included Edwin D. Mead, a Boston publisher, George F. Washburn, a Massachusetts Populist, George H. Shibley, the Democratic bimetallist, Dr. C. F. Taylor, a wealthy Philadelphian and a reform enthusiast, C. B. Hoffman, a former regent of Kansas State Agricultural College, John W. Briedenthal, a Kansas Populist, and Willis J. Abbot, a member of the Democratic National Committee and a journalist. The delegates to the Buffalo Conference had launched a school of economic and sociological research with complete academic freedom. Through the correspondence school approach it would combat plutocracy's grip on higher education—or so the delegates assumed.[6]

Bemis was suspicious of the motives of some of the backers of the college. He feared, above all, that the Kansas Populists would con-

---

[6] Willis J. Abbot, "Necessity of an Independent School of Economics," *The Arena,* XXII (Oct., 1899), 479; Will to Ely, July 20, 1899, enclosing clippings from Topeka (Kans.) *State Journal,* Box 26, Ely papers; Willis J. Abbot, "Plutocracy's Training Schools," *The Social Forum,* I (Sept. 1, 1899), 133–35. The response of the Buffalo Conference delegates to the plan for the College of Social Sciences was typical of the enthusiasm that marked all the sessions. Pomeroy described the tone of the discussions as "one of the purest altruism unmixed with any tincture of self seeking." The reaction of some academic economists to the Buffalo Conference was not so enthusiastic, however. David Kinley, an economist at the University of Illinois, noted: "The trouble with these conferences is that they are too much in the hands of the dilettantes and superficial reformers. Bemis, Parsons, and Commons, of course, are in a different class,—though perhaps I should not class Parsons with Bemis! ... But after all, most of the people who take part in the promotion of these enterprises, do not know enough about the subject they discuss. Dr. C. F. Taylor, for example, is a well-meaning, pleasant sort of man, but he knows but little about his hobby—the money question. And Mr. Pomeroy is—well, I regard him as a kind of Dogberry. He is personally bumptious and overweeningly conceited." Kinley to Ely, July 7, 1899, Box 26, Ely papers. David Kinley was dean of the College of Literature and Arts of the University of Illinois and one of Ely's former students. Kinley refused to attend the Buffalo Conference because of Pomeroy's role. See Kinley to Ely, May 21, 1899, Box 25, Ely papers.

trol the new college and use it for political propaganda. In a long letter to Carl Vrooman, proxy for John W. Briedenthal on the executive committee for the college, Bemis outlined his objections:

[1] The executive committee has as many as five or six members known chiefly for political activities instead of having two or three such men and a dozen others of liberal, and indeed more or less socialistic tendencies, but who stand high in their respective communities for business and professional capacity and success....

[2] George F. Washburn does not hold a high business or other standing in Boston, and is greatly handicapped in public estimation by being chief trustee of the Peoples' Church...although he is personally liked and respected by the few that happen to know him. He had hardly been heard of in Boston in any prominent way prior to the Buffalo Conference, save as chairman of the National Committee of the Populists....

[3] Everyone with whom I have conferred endorsed the position of Professor Parsons that the valuable work proposed by Willis J. Abbot should be entirely divorced from your executive committee, and be run in connection with an independent organization.... *There is an essential, vital difference between a college and a propagandist such as the proposed department is bound to be.* [Italics added] [7]

Bemis suggested that the executive committee abandon the high-pressure advertising campaign to establish a correspondence college and work instead to raise funds for "chairs of investigation" at state universities.

By August 11, 1899, Bemis, Shibley, and Commons had agreed to bolt the executive committee of the College of Social Sciences and to establish their own board of directors if the executive committee was not increased to twenty or twenty-five, as Shibley had suggested, to counter the influence of the Populists. The executive committee did not expand but attempted to placate the dissidents by designating the Bemis-Commons bureau the department of research of the

---

[7] Bemis to Carl Vrooman, July 26, 1899, copy enclosed in Bemis to Lloyd, July 26, 1899, Box 17, Lloyd papers. Howard Quint discussed this incident but was misled by his sources to believe that J. W. Briedenthal was a former regent of Kansas State Agricultural College. See Howard Quint, *The Forging of American Socialism: Origins of the Modern Movement* (Columbia: University of South Carolina Press, 1952), Chap. 4.

Social Reform Union that had been formed at the Buffalo Conference.[8]

By the time Carl Vrooman called on Henry Demarest Lloyd in September, 1899, the centrifugal forces of geographical dispersion and conflicting conceptions had altered the College of Social Sciences plan. Will, residing in Manhattan, Kansas, was placed in charge of the correspondence school and the preparation of leaflets and study material for the Social Reform Union. Parsons, who had returned to Boston University, headed the lecture department of the Social Reform Union. Willis J. Abbot, who had declined to serve on the executive committee of the College of Social Sciences, agreed to head the press department for the Social Reform Union from New York City. Carl's task was made even more difficult by the fact that the Bemis-Commons research bureau already had contacted Lloyd.[9]

Lloyd and Abbot were reluctant to endorse the research bureau because of Shibley's role in the project. They finally endorsed the bureau, but Abbot warned Lloyd not to become involved in the financial details of the venture. Bemis, for his part, felt that Abbot should dissociate himself with the bureau because Abbot's political activities might create misunderstandings about its scientific character.[10]

[8] Bemis to Ely, Aug. 11, 1899, Box 26, Ely papers; Abbot, *The Social Forum*, I, 135; Bliss, *The Social Forum*, I, 130; Bemis to Lloyd, July 26, 1899, Box 17, Lloyd papers. Lloyd had already received information on the Buffalo Conference plan and had written to Richard T. Ely on July 19, 1899, "How does this plan appear to you? *Do you regard it as a wise scheme of propaganda,* in the first place, and do you believe, in the second place, that it would have a fair chance of becoming self-supporting?" [Italics added] Lloyd to Ely, July 19, 1899, Box 17, Lloyd papers.

Bemis believed that both education and propaganda could play an important role in agitation, but he was, of course, anxious to promote his own research bureau. On July 26, 1899, he wrote to Henry Demarest Lloyd to suggest that he hold an immediate consultation with the latter on the plan for the College of Social Sciences. Bemis, in a delightfully mixed metaphor, expressed his fear that the plan was "on the wrong track so much as to render likely its shipwreck." Bemis stated that he was proceeding with the plans for a bureau of municipal research "at all hazards" and that he was counting on the financial support of Lloyd and other wealthy friends of municipal reform.

[9] Parsons to Lloyd, Sept. 13, 1899, Box 17, Lloyd papers; "The Social Reform Union," *The Bulletin of the Social Reform Union,* I (Sept. 15, 1899), 1, 7.

[10] Lloyd to Bemis, Oct. 15, 1899; Abbot to Lloyd, Oct. 17, Nov. 4, 1899; Bemis to Lloyd, Oct. 18, 1899, Box 18, Lloyd papers.

The conflict between the so-called impartial investigators, such as Will, Commons, Bemis, and Parsons, and the political propagandists, such as Carl Vrooman, Shibley, and Abbot, that had emerged earlier at Kansas State Agricultural College split the supporters of the new college into separate factions and threatened to destroy the bureau. It rested ultimately on divergent conceptions of the nature of truth. To the social scientists truth was something that one derived from patient research and analysis; to the political leaders truth was a program that needed to be propagated or a proposal that needed to be empowered in order to make men free. From these divergent conceptions of truth they developed slightly different conceptions of academic freedom. To the social scientists academic freedom meant the right to inquire and to express the results of this inquiry; to the politicians academic freedom meant the right to present their points of view, their program.[11]

When the social scientists and the politicians spoke of academic freedom, however, there was enough common ground for cooperation. Thus, the action of the Populist-controlled Board of Regents in firing the eight professors in 1897 did not seem to Will and Bemis to be a violation of academic freedom because the professors were nonprogressive in their work—that is, not sufficiently scientific.[12] But the action of the Republican-dominated board two years later seemed to them to be a gross violation of academic freedom because the firings admittedly were aimed at the political and religious opinions of the professors. To the professors these opinions were true because they were the result of scientific inquiry, and any at-

[11] An example of the conflict in viewpoints can be seen in an incident related by John R. Commons. In 1900 Shibley moved to Washington to act as an economic adviser for the Democratic National Committee in the Bryan campaign. Shibley paid the Bureau of Economic Research to compile an index number of prices showing the relation of prices to the gold standard. Throughout the early part of the campaign the index figures showed the average fall in prices; however, the index figures leveled off and began to rise in Sept., 1900, indicating the start of the "McKinley prosperity." George Shibley promptly canceled the contract and refused to continue publishing the figures. See Commons, *Myself,* 64–67, 88.

[12] This is the sense in which Bemis made the statement to Ely, which is criticized by Metzger, that the Kansas State Agricultural College regents "were not really violating academic freedom." See Metzger, *Academic Freedom,* 151. See Bemis to Ely, Oct. 4, 1897, Box 22, Ely papers.

tempt to suppress them constituted a breach of academic freedom.[13]

For a political leader such as Abbot, on the other hand, violation of academic freedom meant "that in most if not all of our American colleges *the truth is denied a hearing and excluded from the class room* if it seems to conflict with the selfish interests of the monied classes from whom endowments are to be expected." [Italics added] [14]

Abbot believed that the very existence of the College of Social Sciences would be "a protest against that narrowness in educational ideas which would deny to any school of economic thought a full hearing in college class rooms." [15] To Lloyd he wrote: "I have *views* about Commons. When we Bryanites carried Nebraska we elected a majority of the members of the board of regents of the State university. I think since 'academic freedom' is denied us we will take a hand at reorganizing colleges when we get control. This may not be wholly ethical, it is not the golden rule, it is surely far from Tolstoian but I am doing all I can to put Commons, and one or two other men in a college which we shall control now for some years." [16] He was even prepared to reorganize the Nebraska state universities to secure a hearing for the truth as he saw it.

The conflict between the social scientists and the political leaders on the question of academic freedom was symptomatic of the continuing struggle in reform and radical circles between those who favored partisan political action and those who favored nonpartisan educational ventures. In June, 1898, the political actionists had bolted the Social Democracy of America convention to form a new party, the Social Democratic party. This party laid plans to enter

---

[13] Will commented on the action of the Republican-controlled Board of Regents: "A distinct advance will have been made in the Agricultural College controversy, now two years old, when it is recognized that the populist board did not remove professors because they were republicans but *because they were nonprogressive* in their several lines of work, and that the republican board did not remove professors primarily because they were called populists, but because they taught economics and civics, taught them in a thought-compelling way, and stood for the enlightenment of the people on all aspects of the great economic, social and political issues of the day, hewing to the line wherever the chips might fall." [Italics added] See Thomas E. Will, "The Issue," *The Industrialist,* XXV (July, 1899), 472.

[14] Abbot, *The Social Forum,* I, 135.

[15] Abbot, *The Arena,* XXII, 480.

[16] Abbot to Lloyd, Nov. 15, 1899, Box 18, Lloyd papers.

the 1900 presidential election with a clearcut Socialist platform, including both immediate and long-range demands.

The Social Reform Union that had been established by the Buffalo Conference represented a last-ditch effort, therefore, to bring together on a nationwide level all those dedicated to the nonpartisan educational approach. In December, 1899, the national executive committee of the Social Reform Union rejected a proposal that the organization form a Union Reform party to enter the 1900 election. In effect, the executive committee voted to remain an educational association while its members waited to see whether the radical Social Democratic party or the reformist Democratic party would prove to be the better vehicle for their hopes.[17]

For Carl Vrooman the events of the period from 1899 to 1900 had shown the limitations of both independent political action and educational efforts on behalf of the people. The Kansas People's party clearly was declining, and Carl could expect to receive little benefit from pursuing third-party politics. Although he still subscribed to the principles of the People's party, he had begun to look to the Democratic party to carry out these aims under the leadership of William Jennings Bryan. He moved to Bloomington, Illinois, in 1900 and promptly became a supporter of Bryan's campaign.

The episode of the College of Social Sciences had shown Carl that dissemination of reform proposals through such educational institutions was, at best, a difficult task. He had attempted to uphold the principles of academic freedom as he understood them but had been criticized in turn by Edward Bemis for emphasizing political propaganda at the expense of pure research in the college. Nevertheless, Carl continued to support the College of Social Sciences scheme until Walter Vrooman returned from England fired with enthusiasm for his newest educational venture—the Ruskin Hall movement.[18]

---

[17] "Chicago Conference," *The Social Forum*, II (Jan., 1900), 4. Bliss had made a proposal in Sept., 1899, that the Social Reform Union adopt a few basic statements and support these proposals "in the largest party which would accept them, perhaps the Democratic Party." Carl endorsed the letter. See W. D. P. Bliss, "Reform's Political Course or After the Buffalo Conference, What?" *Publication of the Social Reform Union,* I (Sept. 22, 1899), 1–2.

[18] "Carl Schurz Vrooman," *Harvard College, Class of 1895, Fifth Report* (Cambridge: Crimson Printing Co., 1915), 335–36; Carl Vrooman, "Twentieth Century Democracy," *The Arena,* XXII (Nov., 1899), 597.

WALTER VROOMAN AND THE RUSKIN HALL
MOVEMENT IN ENGLAND, 1899–1900

Walter Vrooman's experiences in Missouri politics had not diverted him from his faith in political action. Like his brother Carl, Walter turned to educational ventures to further his political ambitions, not as a substitute for them. Arriving in England in the summer of 1898, Walter and his wife, Amne, journeyed to Oxford. There they met Charles A. Beard, an American graduate student who had a slight acquaintance with Carl Vrooman. Beard had come to England in 1898 to study European and English history. He was a self-styled follower of John Ruskin who had been influenced by the reform opinions of his mentor at DePauw College, James R. Weaver, and had spent a short session at Hull House in Chicago. Out of the conversations between Walter and Beard came the idea to establish a labor college at Oxford to train the future leaders of the working class. Beard proposed that the new institution be called Ruskin Hall.[19]

Mrs. Vrooman told Beard that she would finance the establishment of Ruskin Hall if he could win the endorsement of Charles W. Bowerman, leader of the London Society of Compositors. By December 27, 1898, Beard had secured the approval of Bowerman and, through him, the support of the Oxford Trades Union Council.

[19] Hubert Herring, "Charles A. Beard: Free Lance among the Historians," *Harper's Magazine*, CLXXVIII (May, 1939), 643; Charles A. Beard, "Ruskin and the Babble of Tongues," *New Republic*, XXXVII (Aug. 5, 1936), 372; Burleigh Taylor Wilkins, "Charles A. Beard on the Founding of Ruskin Hall," *Indiana Magazine of History*, LII (Sept., 1956), 282. I am unable to share Harlan Phillips' view that, "removed from the conservative influence of home and family, Beard made Vrooman's social ethic his own and was carried along by its passion and optimism." In the absence of a detailed reconstruction of Beard's undergraduate opinions, the inference cannot reasonably be drawn. As shall be shown, Beard was absent during some of the crucial periods of Walter Vrooman's activities at Ruskin and cannot be associated with them. See Harlan Buddington Phillips, "Charles Beard, Walter Vrooman, and the Founding of Ruskin Hall," *South Atlantic Quarterly*, I (April, 1951), 187. For alternative explanations of Beard's social thought, see Burleigh Taylor Wilkins, "Frederick York Powell and Charles A. Beard: A Study in Anglo-American Historiography and Social Thought," *American Quarterly*, XI (Spring, 1959), 21–39; Lee Benson, *Turner and Beard: American Historical Writing Reconsidered* (Glencoe, Ill.: Free Press, 1960); Harlan Buddington Phillips, "Charles Beard: The English Lectures, 1899–1901," *Journal of the History of Ideas*, XIV (June, 1953), 451–56.

Mrs. Vrooman kept her promise and immediately wrote a check to start the venture.[20] By January 1, 1899, the Ruskin Hall project was receiving favorable publicity.[21]

Several facts should be noted before embarking on an examination of Walter's conception of Ruskin Hall. First, Ruskin Hall was not the first college in England to provide educational opportunities specifically for laborers. The Working Men's College of London had been established in 1854 to provide an education for working-class students.[22] Second, the project had no official connection with either Oxford University or the University Extension System. Third, Ruskin Hall was not set up to provide workingmen with a full university education.[23] Its purpose was clearly stated by Walter in an interview in February, 1899: "We wish to instruct the young men who may one day control the English-speaking peoples here and in America—to teach them how to improve things. . . . We have no 'ism' to teach, we have no party and no creed. The men we want are the leaders who aspire to be vestrymen, county councillors, members of Parliament, trade-unionists, fellows who harangue crowds in the street and who organize clubs." This statement contained the unmistakable traces of the theory of the scientific agitator and of the

[20] Mary Ritter Beard, *The Making of Charles A. Beard: An Interpretation* (New York: Exposition Press, 1955), 17. Mary Beard's statement that the check written by Amne Vrooman amounted to $60,000 seems questionable in the light of other evidence. A correspondent who visited Ruskin Hall shortly after its establishment wrote, "The house, [14 St. Giles St.] which was taken by Mr. Vrooman on a lease from Balliol College, is rather worse for wear, and money has by no means, I found, been lavished on its furnishings. . . . For the rest, it is not—as the visitor is soon made aware—an expensive philanthropic fad." See "Ruskin Hall," *New York Tribune Illustrated Supplement,* Nov. 19, 1899, p. 7, col. 4, quoting from an unspecified article in *The Sketch.* Furthermore, Amne Vrooman probably did not have $60,000 to spend at this time, unless she had received her annual share of the profits from her father's business or had sold her property holdings in Baltimore. Finally, Mary Beard was not present at the founding of Ruskin Hall and cites no documentary evidence for this incident.

[21] Henry Demarest Lloyd to Lee Meriwether, Jan. 1, 1899, Box 17, Lloyd papers. Lloyd wrote, "You will be interested in the enclosed newspaper clippings about our friend Vrooman. I greatly lament that he has thus impulsively allowed his financial strength to go to the reinforcement of the English when it is so much more needed here."

[22] See J. F. C. Harrison, *A History of the Working Men's College, 1854–1954* (London: Routledge and Kegan Paul, 1954).

[23] L. T. Dodd and J. A. Dale, "The Ruskin Hall Movement," *Fortnightly Review,* N.S. LXXIII (Feb., 1900), 326; New York *Daily Tribune,* Feb. 12, 1899, p. 5, col. 4, quoting from the *Telegraph.*

Volunteers of Democracy. Ruskin Hall, in short, was designed to train the leaders of the labor movement, not the masses of working-men.[24]

Walter's speech at the opening ceremonies for Ruskin Hall on February 22, 1899, contained more echoes of past projects and future hopes. After Beard enrolled the seventy-two initial students and charged them to work earnestly and faithfully in the spirit of Ruskin's belief in the dignity of all labor, Walter spoke for an hour attacking the monopoly of education by the upper classes. "It was not as the opponent or critic of scholarship that Ruskin-hall began its work," he declared, "but as the representative of the masses repentant and remorseful for their long neglect."[25] Reverting to a favorite stereotype of Vrooman oratory, he contrasted the sturdy yeoman with the detached dilettante scholar. Then he shouted, "May God forbid that any student of Ruskin Hall, under the influence of the historic monuments and sacred relics of Oxford, shall ever acquire such a degree of scholarship that in viewing [a scene of misery] or an overworked woman, or a nation oppressed, his first instinct shall be to take notes upon the various aspects of the phenomenon, instead of reaching out a helping hand, or if need be, a clenched fist!"[26]

Nevertheless, he conceded that "the scholar's hand must hold the lantern" to make the way clear for the "ruder and readier" hands "to carry forward the banner of progress."[27] He observed that "the immense good that a very little scholarship did to a fortunate class of young Englishman [sic] was one basis of their hope that even a little learning would prove an inestimable blessing *to the leaders of the working class.*" [Italics added] The one thing Ruskin Hall students repudiated, Walter declared, was "the ideal that required a

[24] *Ibid.;* J. A. Dale and L. T. Dodd, "Ruskin Hall at Oxford," *St. George: Journal of the Ruskin Society of Birmingham,* II (April, 1899), 99.
[25] *The Times* (London), Feb. 23, 1899, p. 10, col. 2.
[26] "Ruskin Hall, Oxford," *The Herald* (Port Adelaide, Australia), July 1, 1899, p. 4, clipping in Box 18, Lloyd papers. Carl Vrooman also denounced the "idea of a scholar and a gentleman [as] a man who stands outside the struggle and conflict of life, calmly observing, criticising, gathering data, and perchance once in a great while going so far as to extend a helping finger." Carl Vrooman, "Dynamic Religion," *The Washingtonian,* I (Nov., 1897), 43.
[27] Dodd and Dale, *Fortnightly Review,* N.S. LXXIII, 327.

gentleman to make ignorant men his servants instead of using his position and power to educate them into wise and self-respecting citizens." [28]

In taking such a belligerent position, Walter misjudged the mood of his audience. An editorial writer for the *Oxford Magazine* offered a few criticisms of the temper of the speech because he felt that the students of Oxford possessed a genuine interest in the new venture: "There are doubtless many modes of education, and none is a perfect instrument; but though Mr. Vrooman rejected hotly and vaguely that which is given here, he did not show that he had formed any clear conception to himself of what he would give to those for whom he is working." [29] Walter had no patience for such details; all the duties of securing lecturers and establishing the residential hall fell upon the shoulders of Charles Beard. Walter considered Ruskin Hall "only as a centre" from which would emanate "an educational system fitted and prepared to spread over the whole of the English-speaking world." [30]

The themes in Walter's speech revealed the subtle change that had occurred in some of his ideas through the years. The emphasis on education, the moralized view of the labor movement, and the theory of the dedicated leader who sought to raise, not rise out of, his class were all familiar tenets in his program. But the editorial writer for the *Oxford Magazine* complained of a discordant note that Walter had sounded in his inaugural address: "Mr. Vrooman's enthusiasm may damage his cause unless he can take more comprehensive views. Even his patriotism is a little sectarian; need the fine idea of Anglo-American Alliance be rammed down with denunciations of the aggressions of 'Slavic and Asiatic despotism'?" [31]

By "Slavic despotism" Walter meant the paternalism of the Russian state, which he had denounced as early as 1895. The proposal for an Anglo-American alliance rested on the assumption, which he had first expressed in 1897, that the patriotism, religious fervor, and heroism of the common people had "saved the dominance of the

[28] *The Times* (London), Feb. 23, 1899, p. 10, col. 2.
[29] XVII (March 1, 1899), 230.
[30] Dale and Dodd, *St. George,* II, 104–105.
[31] XVII, 230.

Caucasian race and all those principles and institutions" characteristic of the advanced nations in the western world. From this premise he derived a simple conclusion: "The union of those who profit
by tyranny necessitates the union of all who believe in liberty. The
internationalism of millionaires is creating an internationalism of
the common people." [32]

He spelled out the basic premise on which these ideas rested in a
little magazine, *Young Oxford,* issued in support of Ruskin Hall.
The struggle for existence was no longer an individual matter, he
wrote. The new unit of survival was the race.

If, where we receive one of the elements of life direct through our individual hand, we receive many elements indirectly through a great multitude of hands organically connected to us by new social attachments, then
the bulk of life's interests become social. The ultimate aim of life remains
the same, to continue and to extend itself, but the plane of the chief struggle and labour is changed from the individual to the corporate realm. In
this larger realm, where the issues change from the old question of the
individual thinker getting a living, to the living and growth of the race,
knowledge is a thousand-fold more demanded.[33]

Walter planned to use Ruskin Hall, therefore, not simply to educate workingmen, but as a means to serve his plans for saving the
Caucasian race.

Walter attempted to regulate the communal life at Ruskin Hall
according to his own dietary principles and views on cooperative
living. For example, he had "bags of oatmeal and apples, loaves of
bread, pieces of cheese," and other food scattered about the house
"so that anybody could help himself when he felt inclined." The
English students did not respond favorably to this system and instituted student cooking on a rotation basis. Another dictum—"At
Ruskin Hall we have no servants because we are all servants"—
meant that housekeeping duties were shared on a rotation system
by all the students. The only exception to this rule occurred when

---

[32] For Walter's views on Russia, see Walter Vrooman, *Government Ownership in
Production and Distribution* (Baltimore: Patriotic Literature Publishing Co., 1895),
178; for his views on race and alliance, see Walter Vrooman, *The New Democracy*
(St. Louis, 1897), 117, 174–76.
[33] Walter Vrooman, "Modern Scholarship," *Young Oxford,* I (Oct., 1899), 6.

the students finally hired a professional cook. The Kansas teetotaler allowed no alcoholic beverages inside Ruskin Hall. But afternoons were free, and in matters of discipline the labor college was "nearer akin to the freedom of America than to the strictness of the older institutions of England." [34]

Whatever stability characterized the infant college for labor leaders can be attributed to its secure financial position and to the tireless efforts of Charles Beard. Walter wrote enthusiastically to Lee Meriwether that "as Aristotle's pupils followed him in an Athenian grove, so [the] students in Oxford walk up and down under Ruskin Hall's trees while listening to lectures." [35] But the task of delivering the lectures fell to Denis Hird, the principal of Ruskin Hall, and occasionally to Beard, who also ran the correspondence system associated with the school. Another important factor in its stability was the support given to the project by the trade unions, cooperative societies, and Ruskin societies. A board of trustees composed of delegates from these groups helped to administer the school. Even John Ruskin sent a letter of congratulations to the students in March, 1899. [36]

While others handled the details of administration, Walter maintained contact with the situation in the United States through correspondence with his brothers and friends. When Beard prepared to return to Cornell University in the autumn of 1899, Walter considered sending him as an emissary for the Ruskin Hall movement. Edward Bemis noted in a letter to Richard T. Ely on August 11, 1899: "It is cabled to the Chicago papers from Europe that Charles M. [sic] Beard, a young American who, with Walter Vrooman, organized the Ruskin Labor College at Oxford, is on his way to Chicago to organize one there with myself as the probable head, but I shall not wait much longer before definitely deciding on [joining the Bureau of Economic Research in] New York, and am not sure

[34] Henry Furniss, Lord Sanderson, *Memories of Sixty Years* (London: Methuen, 1931), 87; Dodd and Dale, *Fortnightly Review*, N.S. LXXIII, 327, 330–31.

[35] Meriwether, *My Yesteryears* (Webster Groves, Mo.: The International Mark Twain Society, 1942), 157.

[36] Dodd and Dale, *Fortnightly Review*, N.S. LXXIII, 326–28; *New York Tribune Illustrated Supplement*, Nov. 19, 1899, p. 7, col. 4; *The Times* (London), March 4, 1899, p. 4, col. 3.

that I would want to be head of the Ruskin Labor College, any-
way." [37] Beard did return to the United States in 1899, but not as the
ambassador of the Ruskin Hall movement. An event in Baltimore
had caused Walter to change his plans.[38]

On August 26, 1899, the United States Circuit Court of Appeals
for the Fourth Judicial Circuit refused to reverse a lower court ruling
in the case of *Vrooman* v. *Grafflin,* thereby affirming that William
H. Grafflin was the legal trustee for Amne Vrooman's share of her
father's estate. In effect, the ruling meant that the Grafflin estate
would not be terminated officially until 1901.[39] As a result of this
decision, Walter had to alter his ambitions to fit his financial resources. He remained in England but kept a watchful eye on Carl
Vrooman's efforts in Kansas. An article in an English journal in
February, 1900, reported that "the dormitory arrangements of
Ruskin Hall" had been "modelled largely after those of the Kansas
State Agricultural College at Manhattan, Kansas." [40]

On March 9, 1900, delegates representing the Trades Union Congress and the Independent Labour party joined friends of Ruskin
Hall in an important meeting. After a year of running Ruskin Hall
as a personal venture Walter was prepared to sign a trust deed turning control over to a general council. In its first year of operation
the school had had an income of approximately £794 and expenses
of more than £2,926. The Vroomans paid the deficit and guaranteed
£500 a year for four years to support it. The council expressed its
appreciation to the Vroomans for their generosity and confidence.
A trade union delegate expressed satisfaction that "the management was in the hands of the council, while the finding of the
money was left to Mr. Vrooman." [41]

Two peculiar incidents at the meeting threw a curious light on
Walter's ideas on education and radical action. One incident in-

[37] Bemis to Ely, Box 26, Ely papers. Bemis was engaged in the dispute with Carl
Vrooman over the College of Social Sciences scheme at this time.
[38] Herring, "Charles A. Beard," 643.
[39] *Vrooman et al.* v. *Grafflin et al.,* 96 Fed. 275–80. (4th Cir. 1899).
[40] Dodd and Dale, *Fortnightly Review,* 332.
[41] "The Establishment of Ruskin Hall," *Young Oxford,* I (April, 1900), 5. Beard
was appointed head of the extension department, although he was not present. Beard
married Mary Ritter in March, 1900, and returned to Oxford the following month.
Herring, "Charles Beard," 643; *Young Oxford,* I (April, 1900), 26, editorial note.

volved his proposal that certificates of achievement at Ruskin Hall be based upon a system of one hundred marks, with thirty-five for scholarship, twenty-five for personality, twenty-five for achievement, and fifteen for enthusiasm. He explained that one of his purposes in starting the movement was to aid "men of brightness and originality," not to foster mere "brain-cramming." One delegate objected, but Walter was supported by another delegate who argued, to cries of "Hear!" from the audience, that "it was for the workers through the Council to decide what they should be taught." Denis Hird papered over the disagreement with a motion that in awarding certificates the Faculty should recognize, "not only success in studies, but also personality, achievement, and enthusiasm." This incident showed that Walter confused education and agitation. Carl had been accused of confusing the two by Bemis in the College of Social Sciences, and now Walter was denounced by the editors of the *Oxford Magazine* and by some supporters of Ruskin Hall. He defined education as "man-making"; what he really meant was the training of agitators.[42]

The second incident involved a proposal that "the second anniversary of the foundation of Ruskin Hall be celebrated in the Town Hall, Oxford, by a conference to discuss the subject of the union of the English-speaking peoples for the advancement of free institutions." The resolution was passed, with the provision that Walter undertake "to pay all expenses in connection with the conference, except cost of the Hall and postage." Just what the resolution meant in detail was not explained, but the financial arrangements probably eased the way for its passage with the tight-fisted trade union delegates.[43]

Two months later an article in *Young Oxford* attempted to explain the rationale behind the resolution. The rank-and-file in the English-speaking countries were in the grip of an international plutocracy, the article stated. They had no control over declarations of war or other decisions that affected their future. While not all

---

[42] *Young Oxford,* I (April, 1900), 6–7.
[43] *Ibid.,* p. 6. The resolution was also reported in *The Times* (London), March 10, 1900, p. 8, col. 6.

the rich were in the plutocracy, thoughtful men no longer questioned the existence of such an international conspiracy. The article continued, "All the special interests are organized. Money and dividends are well protected, but where is the organization for the purpose of looking after the general welfare, for guarding human life and the interests of posterity, the peace and goodwill of peoples?" The time was ripe, it concluded, "for a real organization of the English-speaking democracy along broad lines on behalf of those vast national and social interests which include the peace and security of the living, and the lives and liberties of those who are to come." The Ruskin Hall movement had grown in Walter's mind from a simple college to educate labor leaders into the transatlantic political movement to rescue the race from the plutocracy.[44]

Walter had a specific reason for wanting to take the Ruskin Hall movement back to the United States in the summer of 1900. He had not forgotten that in 1900 the hosts of the Democracy, under Bryan's banner, would once again confront the plutocracy at the polls. In a speech before an East London audience in Stepney Meeting House on May 27, 1900, he claimed that the trade unionists of England had started a subscription fund to help finance a Ruskin Hall in the United States in appreciation for the American gift in establishing Ruskin Hall at Oxford. He expressed the hope that £4,000 would be raised by the time two representatives of English labor sailed on June 16, 1900. These representatives would carry the gift to the United States along with an invitation to the American labor organizations to send delegates to the Anglo-American convention the following year. Such a good will mission from the English working-class movement was particularly important at the moment, he declared, because "the party most closely identified with labouring interests" in the United States was "showing symptoms of renewed hostility to the British Empire."[45]

[44] "The Anglo-American Convention," *Young Oxford*, I (May, 1900), 9.
[45] *The Times* (London), May 30, 1900, p. 9, col. 5; reprinted in an edited version in the *New York Tribune Illustrated Supplement*, June 17, 1900, p. 14, col. 4. The 1900 presidential campaign had begun, and someone carefully removed all mention of the fact that the Ruskin Hall movement was coming to aid the Democratic party. For details of Walter's proposal, see "Democracy's Forward Step," *Young Oxford*, I (June, 1900), 9–10.

As far as readers of the London *Times* could tell, the Ruskin Hall representatives were given a rousing sendoff by friends of the movement at a meeting in St. Martin's Town-hall on June 15, 1900, and departed for the United States the next day "with a gift to the American democracy for the foundation of a Ruskin-hall." [46] Walter and Amne Vrooman and the two trade union representatives, C. W. Bowerman and James Sexton, sailed for the United States confident of the success of their mission.[47]

Walter was returning to the scene of his former labors after an absence of almost two years. The founding of Ruskin Hall would prove, in time, to be his greatest contribution to history and the most permanent. In a sense, Ruskin Hall succeeded in spite of Walter, not because of him. It met an important need for the English trade union movement. Significantly, the assumption of control of the school by the trade union-dominated general council coincided with the establishment of the Labour Representation Committee, the nucleus of the Labour party. Henceforth, Ruskin Hall would train some of the future leaders of the trade union movement and of the Labour party.[48]

[46] *The Times* (London), June 16, 1900, p. 12, col. 3. A similar dispatch was published in the New York *Times,* June 16, 1900, p. 6, col. 3. See also "Britain's Brotherly Gift" *Young Oxford,* I (July, 1900), 34–39.

[47] The enterprising editors of the *American Architect and Building News* magazine reported that St. Louis had been selected for the site of the American Ruskin Hall because it was the home of Walter Vrooman, the founder of Ruskin Hall at Oxford. Obviously, architects in the St. Louis area would be interested in this new reform venture. See "Two Ruskin Halls," *American Architect and Building News,* LXIX (July 7, 1900), 7–8. This story is a pasteup of a dispatch from *The Times* (London), June 5, 1900, p. 10, col. 5 (reprinted in the *New York Times Saturday Review of Books and Arts,* June 23, 1900, p. 2) and of a dispatch from London, dated June 15, 1900, printed in the New York *Times,* June 16, 1900, p. 6, col. 3.

[48] A. M. McBriar, *Fabian Socialism and English Politics, 1884–1918* (Cambridge: Cambridge University Press, 1962), 307. When Walter Vrooman returned to the United States in June, 1900, he left an unresolved conflict at Ruskin Hall. Denis Hird was "one of those curious men who like doing something different from, and something which clashes with, the work for which they are paid." Henry Furniss, Lord Sanderson, *Memories of Sixty Years* (London: Methuen, 1931), 88. Hird believed that it was his duty to convert the students at Ruskin College—as it was called after 1903—to his own brand of Socialism. In 1908 a group of students followed Hird into the Industrial Unionist movement associated with the I.W.W. In Oct., 1908, the dissident students formed the Plebs League and launched a vigorous attack on "what its members called capitalist or bourgeois education" at Ruskin College. When the council of Ruskin College called for Hird's resignation, the Plebs League called a strike against the labor college. The issue, according to the

The Ruskin Hall episode revealed two serious weaknesses in Walter Vrooman's radical efforts. The first was a tendency to lose sight of the original purpose of any venture and to attempt to expand it too rapidly. Ruskin Hall was changed into the Ruskin Hall movement and began to pick up the rag, tag and bobtail of the English eccentric fringe as well as educational efforts aimed at the workingman. In addition to trade union delegates and representatives of the Independent Labour party the Ruskin Hall movement included representatives of the Brotherhood Church, the National Home Reading Union, the Ruskin societies, and various correspondence schemes. The dreams of an international organization of English-speaking peoples had little connection with the mundane pace of Ruskin Hall.

The second weakness revealed by the Ruskin Hall venture was the financial laxity with which it was conducted. Walter financed it out of his wife's inheritance, but he pretended that the funds came from American friends of John Ruskin.[49] At one point, it seemed as if he had found the device to make Ruskin Hall self-supporting. "The Co-operative Movement is a giant in resources and influence," an article in *Young Oxford* declared; "it is abundantly able to solve

---

supporters of Ruskin College, involved the function of the college: "Shall Ruskin College remain an institution existing for the purpose of giving a broad general education on social subjects to working men, or shall it be used as a forcing house for a narrow sectionalism? Shall it be a *staff college to the labour movement or a propaganda hostel?*" [Italics added] F. W. Walker, *Ruskin College and Working-Class Education* (Oxford: Students' Committee for Ruskin College, 1909), 5. The Hird faction finally established the Central Labour College in competition with Ruskin College.

The bolt of the radical faction under Hird left Ruskin College under the control of the more moderate trade unionists and Socialists associated with the Labour party. During the times of stress and labor violence before and after World War I, Ruskin College went about its business of preparing the future leaders of the labor movement. Two members of the first Labour government of 1924 were trained at Ruskin. Of the early students, six went on to become members of Parliament. Furniss, *Memories*, 90–98.

In 1949 Ruskin College celebrated its fiftieth year of service to the British working-class and labor movements. Over the years Charles Beard had become famous, and Walter Vrooman was all but forgotten. It was not surprising, therefore, that most of the praise went to the historian from Indiana rather than to the erratic radical from Kansas who had long before passed from the scene of his labors. New York *Times*, May 22, 1949, p. 67, col. 2; *The Times* (London), May 23, 1949, p. 2, col. 1.

[49] New York *Daily Tribune*, Feb. 12, 1899, p. 5, col. 4; Feb. 24, 1899, p. 6, col. 6.

the problem of a People's University." Representatives of the Co-operative Education Committee were added to the Ruskin Hall movement, but the finances of Ruskin Hall did not improve.[50]

As Walter prepared to take the Ruskin Hall movement back to the United States, he faced an uncertain prospect. To succeed in the United States he would have to overcome the weaknesses evident in his efforts in England: the confusion of education and propaganda, the conflict of purposes, and the insufficient financial resources. With the prestige of the endorsement of the English trade union movement he planned to return in triumph to St. Louis as the founder of Ruskin Hall, the benefactor of the Bryan Democracy, and the apostle of Anglo-American unity.

[50] "A Co-operative University," I (Nov., 1899), 20; "The Ruskin Hall Movement," *Young Oxford,* I (Dec., 1899), 5.

Chapter Seven

Cooperation, Radicalism, & Reform, 1900-1903

THE CO-WORKERS FRATERNITY AND THE RUSKIN HALL MOVEMENT IN AMERICA, 1900–1901

The phrase "cooperative commonwealth" had beguiled American radicals since it had been given currency by Laurence Gronlund in 1884. Its ambiguity made it mean all things to all kinds of radicals. To the orthodox Socialist it was a synonym for the Socialist state. To the moderate Socialist it conveyed the image of an Americanized utopia, a nonviolent society of equality. To those who believed in replacing the raw Darwinian competition of capitalism with some form of fraternal cooperation, the phrase frequently was identified with the colony idea. In the chaos in reform and radical circles that characterized the turn of the century, two separate tendencies—the cooperative colony movement and the "people's" educational ventures—frequently were combined under the rubric of the cooperative ideal. This union, which should have been a strengthening experience for both movements, proved to be a disappointment. The failure of these hybrid ventures revealed the internal weaknesses of the radical cooperative movement and showed why the reform-minded Progressives rather than the radical cooperators flourished in the first decade of the new century.[1]

During the year 1899, while Walter attempted to unite education and cooperative living in the communal life at Ruskin Hall, the Reverend Hiram Greeley Vrooman of Roxbury, Massachusetts, struggled with the problems that confronted the radical cooperative movement in the United States. Surely, he reasoned, some organizational device could enable these "model civilizations in miniature" to overcome their economic disadvantages so that they could show the way out of competitive chaos into the harmony of cooperation.

Harmony seldom prevailed in cooperative colonies and experiments. According to the radical cooperative ideology, all property should be held in common and owned by the coworkers. When the seemingly inevitable withdrawal of dissident members occurred, however, a cooperative colony faced "ugly legal complications" arising from its simple joint-stock form of organization. Hiram had faced this problem first in 1897 when he had tried to establish a colony in Maryland. He had planned to overcome these difficulties by entrusting control of the colony to the "business management" for three years. The management reserved the right "for three years to discharge or eject anybody in the colony who should prove himself indolent, or morally unfit for membership, or in any way a disadvantage to the colony." But, because of the peculiarities of the Maryland incorporation laws, Hiram Vrooman had turned to the expedient of seeking incorporation for the colony under the guise of a university.[2] He did not pursue the issue, but he did continue to meditate on the advantages of the university idea.

In 1899 Hiram helped to promote the Brotherhood of the New Age, a Swedenborgian cooperative association, and to foster their plans to establish a colony in Florida. The group secured a charter of incorporation from New Jersey under the name National Production Company. The National Production Company was capitalized at $200,000, of which $50,000 was designated preferred stock paying 7 percent return on investment.[3]

During the autumn of 1899 Hiram finally worked out "the details of his long contemplated plan for creating a college organization to be the legally safe trustee of a cooperative corporation."[4] In

[1] Radical cooperatives characterized by common ownership of the means of production and, in some cases, equal distribution of rewards must be distinguished from moderate consumer or marketing cooperatives designed to enhance the competitive position of small entrepreneurs.

[2] Hiram Vrooman, "Economic Democracy—A Colony Plan," *The Washingtonian*, I (Nov., 1897), 28–29; "A Colony University," *The Washingtonian*, I (Dec., 1897), 56–57.

[3] Alexander Kent, *Coöperative Communities in the United States*, U.S. Dept. of Labor Bulletin No. 35 (Washington: Government Printing Office, 1901), 632–33.

[4] Co-operative Association of America, *Official Prospectus for 1902* (Lewiston, Me.: Co-operative Association of America, 1902), 5.

January, 1900, Hiram received a charter from Massachusetts for the Co-Workers Fraternity. The Co-Workers Fraternity, an educational corporation, purchased the preferred stock and received the deeds for all the property held by the National Production Company. Dividends on the stock held by the Co-Workers Fraternity would be set aside for educational benefits for the members of the company.[5] Hiram finally had devised an organizational scheme to overcome the legal difficulties of cooperative ventures—the holding company.

While Hiram experimented with an educational corporation as a stockholding device for cooperative colonies, another cooperator, George McAnelly Miller, attempted to unite cooperation and education in a different way. In 1899 Miller, "chancellor" of the People's University College system of Chicago, planned to establish the first People's University College in a "product-sharing," cooperative village that had been proposed by Walter Thomas Mills, an eccentric Socialist.[6] When the proposed village failed to materialize, Miller signed a ten-year agreement in June, 1900, with poverty-stricken Avalon College of Trenton, Missouri.

Throughout the summer of 1900 Miller worked to secure the services of such well-known educators as George D. Herron and Frank Parsons for the summer sessions at Avalon College. He also made plans to institute his industrial plan at Avalon. The industrial plan meant simply that a student, after making a contribution to the college equipment fund, could work his way through college in the cooperative industries and agricultural enterprises that supported the school.[7]

---

[5] Kent, *Coöperative Communities*, 632. The National Production Company established a colony in East Point, Fla., with seventeen members, mainly refugees from the Christian Commonwealth Colony in Georgia. See Ralph Albertson, "A Survey of Mutualistic Communities in America," *The Iowa Journal of History and Politics*, XXXIV (Oct., 1936), 420; Kent, *Coöperative Communities*, 632–33. Hiram Vrooman had exchanged fraternal greetings with the leaders of the Christian Commonwealth Colony and welcomed their support in the Florida venture after the Georgia colony failed. James Dombrowski, *The Early Days of Christian Socialism in America* (New York: Columbia University Press, 1936), 138; interview with Carl Vrooman, Nov. 30, 1960.

[6] *A Product-Sharing Educational Village of the People's University College System* (a pamphlet marked "ante June 20, 1899" by staff of the State Historical Society of Wisconsin), Box 26, Ely papers.

[7] Thomas E. Will, "A College for the People," *The Arena*, XXVI (July, 1901), 16; Trenton (Mo.) *Weekly Republican*, Sept. 13, 1900, p. 1, col. 1.

The event that ultimately brought together Hiram's cooperative experiments and Miller's educational innovations was Walter Vrooman's return to the United States in June as the founder and chief promoter of the Ruskin Hall movement. Much to Walter's consternation, the Ruskin Hall representatives were met in New York City by reporters armed with a cable from the London Trades Union Council denying that they had sanctioned a $20,000 fund to inaugurate the movement in America or had endorsed the Anglo-American conference. Nevertheless, Walter persisted in claiming that the money was from a subscription fund given by English workingmen and other friends of labor to aid the work in the United States. Bowerman and Sexton were shocked to learn that Walter was not the well-known philanthropist and friend of labor that he had seemed to be on the other side of the Atlantic. After a few weeks they returned to England, but Walter continued to speak and act as if the English trade union movement were solidly behind the Ruskin Hall movement. In September, 1900, he opened an office in New York City to direct the movement in the United States.[8]

A member of the staff of the New York *World* called Walter's attention to George Miller's plans for Avalon College. When Miller received an inquiry from Walter, he had "no hesitancy in inviting him to visit Trenton and Avalon College," because he knew several members of the Vrooman family through the Social Reform Union. On September 26, 1900, Walter and Miller concluded an agreement whereby Avalon College became Ruskin College. Ruskin College, in turn, would become the central institution for the Ruskin Hall movement in America and around it would be established cooperative industries designed to support the college.[9]

The executive committee of the Social Reform Union's College of Social Sciences voted to turn its instruction program over to Ruskin College. Thomas E. Will, who had struggled to keep the College of Social Sciences correspondence school going after the bolt of the Bemis-Commons research bureau, became the general

---

[8] Trenton *Weekly Republican*, Oct. 4, 1900, p. 5, col. 1; New York *Times*, June 23, 1900, p. 7, col. 6; New York *Daily Tribune*, Sept. 10, 1900, p. 9, col. 4; Sept. 16, 1900, sec. II, p. 1, col. 6.

[9] Trenton *Weekly Republican*, Oct. 4, 1900, p. 5, col. 1.

secretary of the Ruskin Hall movement in the United States and a faculty member of Ruskin College.[10]

In Boston Hiram Greeley Vrooman was deeply engrossed in a new cooperative venture but watched his brother's activities with interest. Hiram's latest project had developed from the suggestion by an unemployed architect, J. Pickering Putnam, that a loan company or group of investors finance the construction of a building by unemployed workers in the building trades. The workers would be paid in "labor checks" on a union scale of wages. The labor checks would, in turn, be redeemed from the income derived from the sale or rent of the building. The article had aroused interest in Boston, and Putnam explained his idea further to the social science department of the Twentieth Century Club of Boston.[11] During the summer and autumn of 1900 negotiations proceeded between the members of a committee from the Twentieth Century Club and representatives of the Building Trades Council of Boston. These discussions resulted in the formation of the Workers' Coöperative Association of Boston.

Hiram Vrooman, the president of the Workers' Coöperative Association, chaired an important meeting of the association on December 4, 1900, in Boston's historic Faneuil Hall.[12] The main speaker was Henry Demarest Lloyd, the millionaire radical. "The world belongs to those who can combine," he said, "and in an age of universal combination, from international to industrial, the working men and farmers and other producers must combine or perish." [13] Coming quickly to the purpose of the meeting, he praised the success of cooperative building societies and said, "This meeting of the 'Workers Coöperative Association to give Employment to the Un-

[10] New York *Daily Tribune*, Oct. 2, 1900, p. 3, col. 4; reprinted in the Trenton *Weekly Republican*, Oct. 4, 1900, p. 1, col. 6. For Will's efforts in behalf of the College of Social Sciences see *The Social Forum*, II (April, 1900), 164; Thomas E. Will, "Prostitution of Education to Wealth," *The Social Forum*, II (Aug., 1900), 270–76; "A College at Your Door—Let the Light Shine," *The Social Forum*, I (Nov., 1899), 190–91.

[11] J. Pickering Putnam, "Suggestions for a Cooperative Building Scheme to Employ the Unemployed," *American Fabian*, V (Sept., 1899), 7–9; Putnam to Lloyd, Nov. 15, 1899; Putnam to Lloyd, Nov. 25, 1899, Box 18, Lloyd papers.

[12] Co-operative Association of America, *Official Prospectus for 1902*, 6.

[13] Henry Demarest Lloyd, "Coöperation: Address delivered on December 4, 1900, at Faneuil Hall, Boston," unpublished manuscript, p. 1, Box 20, Lloyd papers.

employed' has not been called (if I understand it rightly) to put into operation a cut-and-dried plan, but to form an association of workingmen and co-operators by which the feasibility of such a plan [as Mr. J. Pickering Putnam has suggested] may be discussed and by which, if found feasible, it may then be tried." Looking beyond the specific suggestions contained in the association's plans, Lloyd pointed to the beneficial effects of cooperation. Cooperation in industry would make the people democratic, he said. When they had instituted democracy in their industrial life, they would truly be "democratic Socialists." [14]

Hiram informed the meeting that several proposals had been presented to the association. George F. Washburn, the president of the Boston Bryan Club and owner of a large department store, had offered to redeem the labor checks at his store. Several labor unions had proposed that the association build a Central Labor Temple, and Walter Vrooman had proposed that they build a Ruskin Hall in Boston. Skillfully balancing the demands of the unions, on the one hand, and Walter's suggestion, on the other, Hiram concluded the meeting with a modest statement: "I feel that I may safely say here to-night that the first building operations which this Association will undertake will be the erection of a Ruskin hall and labor temple. Both buildings can be merged into one, and the labor college and this Association can be of great mutual help." [15] Walter was not present to witness his brother's skill in compromise. He was on his way to Louisville where the American Federation of Labor was scheduled to take up the Ruskin College proposal at its annual convention.

At the A. F. of L. convention James Duncan of the Granite Cutters' National Union had been designated by the group's executive council to investigate the Ruskin College proposal when C. W. Bowerman, James Sexton, and Walter Vrooman had first told it to Samuel Gompers in June, 1900. The departure of Bowerman and Sexton, and his own investigations, led Duncan to conclude:

I find little foundation for the claim publicly made that the college is founded on money provided for that purpose by the Trade Unions of

[14] *Ibid.,* 2.
[15] Quoted by Benjamin O. Flower, "A Significant Meeting in Faneuil Hall," *The Arena,* XXV (Feb., 1901), 215.

Great Britain. Ruskin Hall, in England, was founded by Mr. Walter Vrooman, of the United States, who is financially supporting the institution [until] it is on a paying basis, and nearly all the money provided in starting Ruskin College in Trenton, [Missouri,] has been provided by Mr. Vrooman. The Parliamentary Committee of the British Trades Congress [*sic*] is represented on the governing board of Ruskin Hall, England, and Mr. Vrooman desires to have representatives of the American Federation of Labor on the Trenton College governing board.[16]

Duncan moved that the floor be granted to Walter Vrooman during the afternoon session on the third day. Walter charged "that the big colleges, as well as the magazines, and even the children's books had been warped by the power of money and that the cause of the people and a true exposition of social, economic conditions were not allowed to be presented to the younger generation." [17]

His complaint takes on additional meaning from the context of the times. Undoubtedly, he was referring to the academic freedom cases at Kansas State Agricultural College, Syracuse University, and the University of Chicago when he charged that the money power had seized the big colleges. The accusation against the magazines may have been an inference drawn from the fact that numerous reform and radical magazines had floundered and ceased publication during the year. The concern for the younger generation and the children's magazines reflected the "race-life" emphasis in Walter's thought. But these were hardly the arguments to sway an audience of practical union men.[18]

Walter's speech showed how far he had strayed from the path on which he had started in England. There he had established a school

---

[16] "Executive Council's Report," *Report of the Proceedings of Twentieth Annual Convention of the American Federation of Labor held at Louisville, Kentucky, December 6 to 15, 1900* (New York: American Federation of Labor, 1901), 70. For Gompers' attitude toward Ruskin College, see Samuel Gompers, *Seventy Years of Life and Labor* (New York: Dutton, 1925), 448–49.

[17] "Walter Vrooman, Remarks before the Convention," *Report of the Twentieth Annual Convention, A. F. of L.,* 77.

[18] It was prosperity, not the plutocracy, that killed the magazines. See the editorial note in *American Fabian,* V (Jan., 1900). The leading reform and radical journals of 1901 were *The Arena, International Socialist Review,* the *Bellamy Review,* and the *Social Crusader.* See Eltweed Pomeroy, "A Comparative View of Reform Journals," *Social Unity,* I (Jan., 1901), 9–10. The concern for the children had been evident in 1897 in Walter Vrooman's *Sacred Biography* and in *The Washingtonian* magazine.

to train labor leaders and had gradually expanded it into a working-men's educational movement. While he had entertained grandiose dreams of using Ruskin Hall to foster Anglo-American unity, Charles Beard and the British labor leaders had managed to hold Ruskin Hall to a safe, moderate program. In the United States the Ruskin Hall educational movement was turning into a diffuse, uncoordinated venture in education and cooperation. A special committee at the A. F. of L. convention recommended a "no endorsement, no agreement" policy pending further investigation of the Ruskin College proposal, and the convention adopted the recommendation.[19]

The treatment afforded Walter by the American Federation of Labor was symptomatic of the uneasy relationship between the professional agitators and the organized labor movement in the United States. For twenty years members of the Vrooman family had attempted to establish a working relationship with the labor movement. However, in the business unionism of the A. F. of L. there was little room for the paraphernalia of the professional radicals. The same A. F. of L. convention that refused to endorse Walter's Ruskin College proposal also refused, by a vote of 4,169 to 685, to endorse the Social Democratic party.[20] By necessity, self-appointed leaders of the people such as the Vrooman brothers were forced to create their own social groupings, institutions, and social movements. The Socialist Labor party long before had closed the door to them; the American Federation of Labor now did the same.

Seemingly undisturbed by the action of the A. F. of L., the Ruskin Hall movement surged forward like a spring flood picking up the debris of wornout reform, radical, and crank movements. "Professor" Jay G. Rogers' International University became the Ruskin Association, and Rogers was offered the chair of Christian Evidences at Ruskin College. The purpose of the Ruskin Association, as Judge Hiram Perkins Vrooman explained at a meeting in Trenton, Missouri, was to reach the people, particularly the poor people, who could not be reached by the churches.[21]

[19] "Report of the Committee on the Executive Council's *Report,*" *Report of the Twentieth Annual Convention, A. F. of L.,* 156.
[20] *Social Unity,* I (Jan., 1901), 14.
[21] Trenton *Weekly Republican,* Dec. 6, 1900, p. 2, col. 3; Dec. 27, 1900, p. 8, col. 1.

The success club, another project associated with the Ruskin movement, also required some explanation. As Walter Vrooman said, it was designed "to teach young people how to succeed by studying the lives of great men." In Kansas City, Missouri, three thousand singing, cheering young people gathered at a success club rally to hear the "Ruskin man," Walter Vrooman, promise a trip to England as a delegate to the English-speaking people's convention for the youngster who recruited the most members for the success club. The city council of Kansas City had already voted to send an official representative to the convention as one of the three thousand delegates expected to attend from the United States.[22]

The citizens of Trenton were bewildered by all the clubs, associations, institutes, and movements that were springing up in their midst, but they agreed that the proposed Trenton-Ruskin Manufacturing Company was a good thing. By February 7, 1901, the citizens had raised $10,895 to start the project. The management of Ruskin College retained an option to purchase the $10,000 in capital stock issued by the company at par value plus 8 percent interest compounded from the date of issue. Profits, after deductions for taxes and a 10 percent reserve fund, would be divided among the investors at a rate of 8 percent on their investments, the remainder of the money going to the college. Ruskin College, in turn, would pay the students who worked in the company canning factory. The students could earn as they learned.[23]

Having failed to secure the endorsement of the A. F. of L., the backers of Ruskin College decided to seek the support of the Social Reform Union at its national conference, which was scheduled to meet in Detroit from June 28 to July 4, 1901. By any standard, the conference was a failure. Edward Bemis complained to Henry

---

[22] *Ibid.,* Dec. 27, 1900, p. 2, col. 1; p. 3, col. 1; Jan. 17, 1901, p. 6, col. 2.

[23] *Ibid.,* Jan. 24, 1901, p. 5, col. 1; Jan. 31, 1901, p. 4, col. 2; Feb. 7, 1901, p. 3, col. 1.
In addition to the proposed canning factory the Trenton residents approved of Ruskin College. While some cast a critical eye at the Ruskin Sociological Institute, others were delighted to learn that the Missouri State Board of Education had endorsed the college's summer institute. Participants could earn credits for a teacher's certificate during the summer. The lecturer for the summer institute, Professor Frank Parsons of Boston, proved to be a fine scholar and a Christian gentleman instead of an anarchist and an agitator, as some had feared. *Ibid.,* May 2, 1901, p. 8, col. 5; May 9, 1901, p. 8, cols. 1–3; May 23, 1901, p. 2, cols. 1–3.

Demarest Lloyd that only about 230 delegates attended and that the sessions "rapidly degenerated into ridiculous effervescence by extreme radicals and cranks." [24] Thomas E. Will and George Miller managed to secure the endorsement of the Detroit conference for the Ruskin Hall movement; however, this endorsement was of dubious value as the whole conference was brought into disrepute by the antics of the doctrinaire Socialists.[25]

While Walter was encountering difficulties with the Ruskin College plan in the West, Hiram Greeley Vrooman was launching a new venture in the East. The meeting of the Workers' Coöperative Association of Boston in Faneuil Hall on December 4, 1900, had brought Hiram into contact with Bradford Peck of Lewiston, Maine. Peck, a wealthy businessman and disciple of Edward Bellamy, was the author of a utopian novel, *The World a Department Store,* and the founder of the Co-operative Association of America.[26]

Hiram Vrooman and Bradford Peck were complementary personalities. Peck was a dreamer, a health faddist, and a successful businessman who lacked the ability to express himself easily; Hiram was a theorist and an unsuccessful promoter of cooperative colonies who possessed the Vrooman eloquence in speaking and writing. He increasingly became the spokesman for Peck's ideas.

During the two weeks following the meeting in Faneuil Hall Peck and Hiram Vrooman elaborated the plans and policies necessary to unite Peck's Co-operative Association of America with Hiram's Co-Workers Fraternity and Walter Vrooman's Ruskin Hall movement.[27] The resulting organizational arrangement would have delighted a corporation lawyer or a utopian theorist.

[24] Bemis to Lloyd, July 1, 1901, Box 20, Lloyd papers.

[25] Trenton *Weekly Republican,* Aug. 22, 1901, p. 5, col. 1. The doctrinaire Socialists hammered through, one by one, a series of propositions that were tantamount to an endorsement of the Social Democratic party. Willis J. Abbot, a Bryan Democrat, charged that the adoption of the resolutions violated the rules of the conference. He finally secured the passage of a motion tabling the Socialist resolutions. See A. M. Simons, "The Detroit Conference," *International Socialist Review,* II (Aug. 1, 1901), 112–14; Abbot to Lloyd, July 16, 1901, Box 20, Lloyd papers.

[26] Peck was president of the B. Peck Company Department Store of Lewiston, Me., president of the B. Peck Real Estate Company, and vice-president of the Joliet Dry Goods Company, Joliet, Ill. He first conceived the idea for his utopian scheme in 1899. He organized the Co-operative Association of America and secured a charter from Maine in Jan., 1900. Co-operative Association of America, *Official Prospectus for 1902,* 5.

[27] *Ibid.,* 6.

Peck deposited 90 percent of the stock of the Co-operative Association of America with the Co-Workers Fraternity of Boston.[28] Walter's Ruskin Hall, which claimed to be the officially recognized educational institution of both the cooperative and labor movements of England, was regarded by the Co-operative Association of America as an affiliated organization.[29]

The association outlined an ambitious program for 1901. The plans called for the development of a colony near Lewiston to conform with the plan described in Peck's novel, the cultivation of five hundred acres of farmland in Maine, and the establishment of a workingmen's college, based on the Ruskin Hall system. In addition, the association planned to erect a four-story building in Lewiston to house its banking, manufacturing, wholesale sales, and administrative activities.[30]

For the uninitiated, those to whom the proposals of the association seemed to emulate the economic practices of the trusts, Hiram explained the theory behind this cooperative venture: "Now then, the essential difference between The Co-operative Association of America and the trust is this, that the trust gives employment to laborers but gives to laborers in return for their labor, wages barely sufficient to keep life in their bodies, while The Co-operative Association of America gives employment to laborers, and at the same time gives the laborers in return for their labor all the wealth that the laborers

---

[28] *The Co-operator,* I (Feb., 1901), 11–12. The trustees of the Co-Workers Fraternity included:

The Reverend Hiram Vrooman, pastor of the Roxbury, Mass., Church of the New Jerusalem, president of the Workers' Coöperative Association, and president of the Co-Workers Fraternity.

The Honorable Carl S. Vrooman of Parsons, Kans., former regent of the Kansas State Agricultural College.

The Reverend Harry C. Vrooman of East Point, Fla.

Professor Frank Parsons of Boston University Law School, a member of the advisory council of the Workers' Coöperative Association.

George F. Washburn of Boston, vice-president of the Workers' Coöperative Association.

Bradford Peck of Lewiston, Me., president of the Co-operative Association of America and vice-president of the Workers' Coöperative Association.

J. Pickering Putnam of Boston, vice-president of the Workers' Coöperative Association.

Charles E. Lund of Lewiston, Me., secretary of the Co-operative Association of America.

Arthur D. Ropes of Boston, secretary and treasurer of the Co-Workers Fraternity.

Arthur E. Harris of Boston, an artist.

[29] *Ibid.,* 4.

[30] "Plans of Operation," *The Co-operator,* I (Feb., 1901), 6–7, 26.

create." [31] In short, the Co-operative Association of America proposed to establish a people's trust for the exclusive benefit of its coworkers by forming an independent society.

In March, 1901, Peck, Mrs. Peck, and Hiram traveled to Florida to inspect the land held by the Co-Workers Fraternity for the defunct National Production Company. In Apalachicola they were joined by Harry Vrooman, who had been looking after Hiram's cooperative interests in Florida since 1899. The party started across Apalachicola Bay in a sailboat to visit the townsite of East Point. Suddenly, about four miles from shore, the sailboat capsized. Encumbered by the characteristic feminine attire of the day, Mrs. Peck drowned. Peck, Harry, and Hiram clung to the overturned boat for nearly two hours before they were rescued by a friend who had set out in search of them in response to a premonition. This miraculous rescue cemented the bond of friendship between the three cooperators. [32]

The prospects for the cooperative movement seemed bright to Hiram in 1901 as the Co-operative Association of America was reorganized along the lines that he had drawn with Peck. In *The Arena* magazine Hiram proposed that the federal government establish cooperative colonies in Nevada to provide jobs for the unemployed and offered the Co-operative Association of America as a model. When the association opened its first store in Lewiston, Hiram wrote a congratulatory letter to Peck in which he predicted that within two or three years the association would be able to employ in its industries all interested laborers in the Lewiston area. [33]

The association proposed to admit laborers to membership on the condition that they paid or promised to pay three hundred dollars. This requirement reflected the premise that the employees should own the capital of the enterprise and share in all profits. Hiram reasoned that "if each employee were an investor in the business to an amount equal to the cost of that part of the equipment which made his labor effective, then his wages, plus his proportionate share of the

[31] Hiram Vrooman, "The Possibilities of the Co-operative Association of America," *The Co-operator*, I (Feb., 1901), 31–32.

[32] Co-operative Association of America, *Official Prospectus for 1902*, p. 6. Harry Vrooman was appointed manager for the CAA in Florida in March, 1901. See *The Co-operator*, I (May–Aug., 1901), 14–15.

[33] Hiram Vrooman, "The Government Can Employ the Unemployed," *The Arena*, XXV (May, 1901), 533–36; *The Co-operator*, I (Nov., 1901), 16.

profits, would represent the approximate amount of wealth which his service had brought into existence." [34] In effect, this scheme meant that the laborer was required to make a deposit as a condition of employment or to "purchase" the machinery on which he worked. Similar practices had been denounced by the Vroomans in their earlier efforts.[35]

The backers of the association frankly admitted that they proposed to achieve their goals, not "by going up stream against the opposition of capitalistic legislation, but by getting into the middle of the current, and going full blast down the stream, assisted rather than hindered, by laws which monopoly has secured." [36] They hoped that the essential quality of the people's trust, namely that the ownership of the means of production resided with the coworkers, would compensate for any similarities between their methods and those of the capitalistic trusts.

The curious mixture of Socialistic purposes and capitalistic legal devices that characterized Hiram's activities was indicative of the confused state of radical and reformed forces in the summer of 1901. The constant schisms and factionalism within the Socialist Labor party, the Social Democracy of America, and the Social Democratic party had thrown independent radical groups into temporary alliances with moderate reform elements in such ventures as the Social Reform Union and the Co-operative Association of America. In November, 1900, a faction of the Social Democratic party had rallied

[34] William Alfred Hinds, *American Communities,* rev. ed. (Chicago: Charles H. Kerr, 1902), 423; Hiram Vrooman, *The Arena,* XXV, 534; Hiram Vrooman, "The Co-operative Association of America," *Twentieth Century,* III (Feb., 1911), 432.

[35] In 1892 Walter's Central Conference of Moral Workers attacked the system of requiring garment workers to purchase the machines on which they labored. The difference, of course, was that the Co-operative Association of America deducted the money from profit shares rather than wages. See Diana Hirschler, "Union in Philadelphia," *The Arena,* IX (March, 1893), 548–51. As labor commissioner of Missouri, Lee Meriwether had exposed the system of requiring laborers to post a deposit, which they lost if they joined a union or left their job for a strike or other employment. The Co-operative Association of America promised full return of the deposit if a worker withdrew. See [Lee Meriwether], *Miss Chunk: A Tale of the Times* (St. Louis: Walter Vrooman, 1897), 67; Hinds, *American Communities,* 423. One might also question whether, in principle, the labor checks, which were issued by the Workers' Coöperative Association and redeemed by George Washburn's department store, were not the same as company chits that were redeemable only at the company store.

[36] Hinds, *American Communities,* 420.

the independent Socialist groups of Chicago—the Christian Socialist League, the Federation of Social Justice, and the Social Crusade—and had formed the nucleus for a Socialist unity drive. In July, 1901, the Socialist Unity Convention at Indianapolis united the major moderate Socialist groups to form the Socialist party.[37]

By July, 1901, independent radicals and reformers faced a peculiar dilemma. The Populist party had ceased to be an effective factor in politics. The A. F. of L. had turned a deaf ear to the would-be saviors of the labor movement. The Social Reform Union had disintegrated at the Detroit conference. Therefore, the independent radicals and reformers had to make a choice. They might join a nonpartisan, direct democracy organization, make a nominal commitment to the doctrinaire Socialism of the new Socialist party, join one of the major political parties, or pursue the cooperative approach. For the present time three of the Vrooman brothers continued in the last course. Carl Vrooman joined the effort but also continued to work within the Democratic party in Illinois.

THE VROOMAN BROTHERS
AND THE MULTITUDE INCORPORATED, 1901–1903

The economic policies adopted by the Co-operative Association of America were similar to the industrial plan instituted by Ruskin College. The Ruskin College plan stipulated that for every deposit of twenty-five dollars the student would be allowed to work one hour a day at ten cents an hour in the cooperative industries connected with the college. For a deposit of $125 in the equipment fund the student would be entitled to work thirty hours a week. In this manner, the student could earn enough to cover the cost of board, lodging, and tuition. An editorial in the Chicago *Inter-Ocean* criticized the industrial plan as an attempt to exchange a "cheap education for underpaid labor."[38]

The Trenton *Weekly Republican* reprinted the editorial but

[37] Ira Kipnis, *The American Socialist Movement, 1897–1912* (New York: Columbia University Press, 1952), 102–104.
[38] Thomas E. Will, "A College for the People," *The Arena*, XXVI (June, 1901), 17; "A College for the People" (editorial), Chicago *Inter-Ocean*, July 1, 1901, p. 6, col. 3.

denied that this constituted an attack by its own editor on Ruskin College. The hasty explanation offered by the editor indicated that Ruskin College still had the sympathetic support of most Trenton citizens. But a series of minor incidents aroused their suspicions. Ruskin College students formed a Socialist club; a student advocated Socialism in a speech before the local United Mine Workers union; and a rumor circulated that a professor had expressed satisfaction when he learned that Leon Czolgosz, an anarchist, had assassinated President McKinley. Angry citizens gathered at the GAR hall to demand that the erring professor leave the school, although sworn statements appeared in the press to disprove the charges.[39]

Walter Vrooman delivered a lecture in which he condemned Czolgosz, agreed with some of the criticisms of Socialism voiced by the editor of the *Weekly Republican,* and defined Socialism in such a mild, conciliatory tone that it meant little more than studying the laws of society. Nevertheless, he boldly declared that the principles on which Ruskin College was founded were Socialistic, but not political. The editor of the *Weekly Republican* hinted that there was "something back of this special plea for social study" but did not speculate further.[40]

Walter Vrooman's strangely moderate speech on Socialism indicated that he was experiencing another lull in his efforts. The success club movement had faded; the Ruskin Hall movement was floundering in a mass of correspondence courses, unassimilated projects, and abortive efforts. He proposed establishing a Ruskin labor mission at the University of Chicago to teach "the laws of right, of honesty and of eternal justice" to its wealthy students but soon dropped the idea.[41] In October, 1901, he left Trenton and headed for the East. Two events during the following month brought him out of the doldrums and

[39] Trenton *Weekly Republican,* Aug. 1, 1901, p. 4, col. 1; July 25, 1901, p. 6, col. 1; Aug. 22, 1901, p. 2, cols. 1–2; Sept. 19, 1901, p. 2, cols. 3–4.

[40] *Ibid.,* Oct. 17, 1901, p. 4, col. 2.

[41] *Ibid.,* Sept. 12, 1901, p. 2, col. 3; "Labor's Missionary to the University of Chicago," *The Co-operator,* I (Nov., 1901), 27. Walter proposed to use the labor mission and settlement to lecture on the following subjects: 1) historical political economy as the bulwark of social injustice; 2) plans for social readjustment; 3) psychological study of decay of those who spend their formative years devoted to books and sports rather than useful labor; 4) eight centuries of warfare between the reformers and institutions of higher learning; 5) history of American university endowments.

propelled him on a new crusade. First, the long-awaited settlement of the Grafflin estate brought his wife into her inheritance of $750,000. Second, he saw the successful results of Hiram Vrooman's efforts in the cooperative movement.[42]

With the disintegration of the Social Reform Union Hiram attempted to make the Co-operative Association of America the chief spokesman for the nonpolitical, cooperative approach to change in the United States. He invited Henry Demarest Lloyd and Willis J. Abbot to become trustees of the Co-Workers Fraternity. His next move came in the spring of 1902 when Lloyd was planning to visit England. Hiram prepared credentials designating Lloyd the official representative of the Co-Workers Fraternity and the Co-operative Association of America for the international cooperative congress in Manchester, England. Emboldened by the prospect of international recognition, the Co-Workers Fraternity bought up 90 percent of the stock of the Massachusetts Cooperative Association and voted to call a National Co-operative Conference to meet at Lewiston, Maine, on June 20, 1902.[43]

Walter Vrooman borrowed the legal formula for a cooperative holding company from Hiram, and added a few of his own distinctive features. In February, 1902, he announced in New York City that he had secured a charter of incorporation, under the laws of New Jersey, for the Western Co-operative Association. He stated that an alliance had been formed between the Co-operative Association of America and the new Western Co-operative Association and that $20,000 would be deposited in a bank in Trenton, Missouri, to insure the success of the new venture. He returned to Trenton on February 22, 1902, with the president of the Western Co-operative Association, the Reverend Harry C. Vrooman, to establish the association's main office. The W.C.A. set its membership fee at ten dollars and offered

---

[42] George W. Grafflin died on Nov. 6, 1896. Thus, the end of the five-year period stipulated in his will occurred sometime after Nov. 6, 1901. The first indication of Walter's new venture was a letter to the Trenton *Weekly Republican* announcing preliminary negotiations with "Eastern interests." Trenton *Weekly Republican,* Nov. 28, 1901, p. 3, col. 2.

[43] Abbot to Lloyd, Sept. 18, 1901; Lloyd to James Rhodes, Dec. 23, 1901; Hiram Vrooman to Lloyd, March 25, 1902; March 27, 1902; Apr. 30, 1902; Abbot to Lloyd, May 10, 1902, Lloyd papers.

refunds on all purchases in its department store or allied industries. The editor of the Trenton *Weekly Republican,* a bit troubled by these events, suggested that cooperation be construed to mean cooperation with, not competition against, local merchants.[44]

By March 13, 1902, Walter had deposited $300,000 in Trenton banks, which caused considerable speculation among local businessmen as to his intentions. He showed his intentions clearly in two documents that he signed on March 15, 1902. Although the Western Co-operative Association had been incorporated in New Jersey, Walter signed an article of association with Harry C. and Hiram Perkins Vrooman, George Miller, and Thomas E. Will to form a Western Co-operative Association in Missouri. This agreement divided twenty shares of stock, at one hundred dollars a share, among the five so that they each received one share and Walter received sixteen shares. He thus assured personal control of the new venture.[45]

Walter also filed a petition in the Circuit Court of Jackson County seeking incorporation for the Multitude Incorporated. Legally, this was an educational corporation organized for the purpose of bringing "within the reach of as many young men and women as possible, the advantage of a college education of the most practical sort." In fact, it was a holding company for Walter's cooperative ventures, similar in function to Hiram's Co-Workers Fraternity. Since the Multitude Incorporated had no capital and was not organized for profit, it received all its income from tuition, gifts, bequests, real estate transactions, and dividends on the stock of the cooperative associations. On April 9, 1902, the Jackson County Circuit Court granted the petition for incorporation.[46]

The Multitude Incorporated launched its great cooperative crusade

[44] Trenton *Weekly Republican,* Feb. 20, 1902, p. 2, col. 4; March 6, 1902, p. 3, col. 5; p. 4, col. 2.

[45] *Ibid.,* March 13, 1902, p. 2, col. 1; "Articles of Association of the Western Co-operative Association," *Record of Deeds,* Book 80, p. 420, Grundy County, Mo.

[46] "Articles of Incorporation of the Multitude Incorporated," *Record of Deeds,* Book B-788, pp. 528-31, Jackson County, Mo. The petition was signed by Walter Vrooman, Hiram Perkins Vrooman, Thomas E. Will, and two representatives of the Ruskin College administration. As an educational corporation, the Multitude Incorporated could confer academic degrees through Ruskin College. An honorary Ph.D. was bestowed on Harry C. Vrooman in June, 1901. See George Miller to James A. Noyes, Oct. 23, 1902, Harvard Alumni files, Widener Library, Harvard.

with religious exercises in Trenton on March 20. Walter said that all means, including theatricals, concerts, and stereopticon lectures, should be "spiritualized" and used for this crusade, and Harry noted the need to unite all the forces of Christianity for this practical demonstration of religious principles. Copies of the *Multitude* magazine, published in New York, were distributed at the meeting.

The Western Co-operative Association represented the business aspects of the new Vrooman crusade. The American Oxford movement—the old Ruskin Hall movement with a new name—represented its educational portion.[47] Trenton merchants began to worry when the Western Co-operative Association purchased five stores and invested $100,000 in the surrounding area. The cooperators purchased space in the local newspapers for a weekly column. "The mercantile field only awaits the organizing genius of a Rockefeller or a Morgan," the cooperators warned their readers. "And then, woe unto the independent merchant!" The only hope for the independent merchant was to join the cooperative crusade.[48]

In May, 1902, Walter carried his new crusade to Kansas City, Missouri, where he repeated the pattern that he had established in Trenton. He purchased a large tract of land southeast of Kansas City for use as the site of a model village that he planned to call "Grafflin" in honor of his wife. It would be a "paradise for children," he claimed, where the best traits of the race would be developed in a permissive atmosphere.[49]

He established his headquarters in the Century Building and began exchanging Western Co-operative Association stock, which carried a 6 percent interest rate, for the inventory, equity, or real property of any interested party. To handle these financial matters he organized a bank in Kansas City, capitalized at $100,000. To recruit members for the Western Co-operative Association he sponsored a revival

---

[47] Trenton *Weekly Republican,* March 20, 1902, p. 2, col. 1; p. 3, col. 5; p. 5, col. 4.

[48] *Ibid.,* March 27, 1902, p. 3, cols. 1–2; April 3, 1902, p. 4, col. 2; April 17, 1902, p. 8, col. 6. By June, 1902, Walter owned 1,600 acres of land southeast of Trenton in a farm associated with Ruskin College. He also owned land around Ruskin College in an area designated the "College Addition." Contemporary accounts placed his investment at $50,340. See Trenton *Weekly Republican,* May 8, 1902, p. 1, col. 4.

[49] *Ibid.,* May 8, 1902, p. 5, col. 2; *Southwestern Advocate* (Winfield, Kans.), May 15, 1902, p. 3, col. 1, quoting from the Kansas City *Journal* of April 20, 1902.

complete with tent meetings, free theatricals, stereopticon lectures, and explanations of cooperation.[50]

Walter Vrooman's efforts in Kansas City invoked the wrath of some businessmen, and one clergyman criticized the environmental sociology advanced by the cooperators. "Make the individual right," he said, "then society will be right." When newspaper reporters wondered who was financing the cooperative crusade, Walter said: "[The money came] not from any one man or set of men, but from the public, the masses who are tired [of being exploited].... Thousands of such people will put all their savings into a common pool for the formation of a people's universal trust, and that is what this movement is. I put several hundred thousand dollars in cash myself, half of all I have in the world. Others are putting in from $1,000 to $12,000 each."[51] The newspapermen failed to understand that for Walter the important point was not the source of the money but the manner of its distribution.

His intentions were further revealed in a document that he filed on June 3. He transferred his controlling bloc of stock in the W.C.A. to the Multitude Incorporated and stipulated: "All of the dividends declared to said Common Stock by said Western Co-operative Association from its earnings, above all expenses, which include dividends payable on the preferred stock of said Western Co-operative Association, shall go to the American People who become members of and purchasers of the Western Co-operative Association."[52]

He directed the Multitude Incorporated to return two-thirds of the stock dividends to the members of the association as patronage re-

[50] *Southwestern Advocate*, May 15, 1902, p. 2, col. 1, quoting from the Kansas City *Star*; Trenton *Weekly Republican*, May 15, 1902, p. 5, col. 2. From incomplete information published in news dispatches, the total of such transactions by Walter in Kansas City, Independence, and Liberal, reached approximately $66,000. A feed grain business was listed as being "worth $150,000 a year," but there is no indication whether this figure represented equity or projected income.

[51] *Southwestern Advocate*, May 15, 1902, p. 2, col. 1, quoting from the Kansas City *Star*; Trenton *Weekly Republican*, May 15, 1902, p. 8, col. 3, quoting from the Kansas City *World*. Walter sued the Kansas City *Journal* for libel because it charged that his scheme would burst like a balloon. See Trenton *Weekly Republican*, June 5, 1902, p. 5, col. 1.

[52] "Certificate of Shares: Walter Vrooman to the Multitude Incorporated," *Record of Deeds*, Book 82, pp. 122-26, Grundy County, Mo. The document was signed on May 24, 1902, and filed for record on June 3, 1902.

funds and to use one-third of the dividends to finance general benefits for the members—"University Extension Courses, Lectures, Amusements, Theatre Tickets, Excursions, Picnics, Library Privileges [and] Free Scholarships in the Ruskin College at Trenton, Missouri." He also provided that on January 1, 1950, the United States government should become the trustee of the Multitude Incorporated, on the condition that a system of direct legislation was in effect at that time. Walter was invited to attend the Lewiston conference sponsored by Hiram's group in the East but he declined and remained in Kansas City.[53]

The National Co-operative Conference opened in Lewiston on June 20, 1902, on an optimistic note. In little more than a year, the Co-operative Association of America had accumulated one-quarter million dollars' worth of property. The resolution issued by the Co-Workers Fraternity before the meeting stated, "In our belief, the economic power has superseded the political power and is now the militant and ruling power of the world, and industrial coöperation is the only force capable of democratizing this economic power."[54] In keeping with the tenor of this resolution, Carl Vrooman, Benjamin O. Flower, Frank Parsons, Bradford Peck, and Hiram G. Vrooman urged the delegates to unite their separate cooperative organizations. The delegates established a committee to carry out their directives and issued the call for an American cooperative congress to meet in 1903.[55]

Before the Lewiston meeting Carl had suggested to George Washburn, the Boston merchant who headed the cooperative People's Trust of New England, that he investigate Walter's cooperative ven-

[53] *Ibid.;* Trenton *Weekly Republican,* June 12, 1902, p. 8, col. 2. The terms of the transfer to the United States government read: "It is a further condition hereof that on January 1st, A.D. 1950, the United States Government shall succeed as Trustee herein, and perform all the conditions hereof, provided there is then existing a Department of the United States Government which will accept and agree to carry out the terms of this trust, and also provided the form of Federal Legislation known as Direct Legislation is then in vogue, by means of which the people can by petition and direct vote control the making of their Federal laws, independent of or in conjunction with Congress."

[54] Hiram G. Vrooman, "A National Coöperative Conference," *The Arena,* XXVII (June, 1902), 612.

[55] "The National Co-operative Convention," *The Co-operator,* II (Aug., 1902), 6–9. Carl and George F. Washburn were appointed to the committee to plan the 1903 conference.

tures in the West.[56] In an interview for *The Arena* magazine Washburn discussed some of the technical difficulties that confronted any expanding cooperative enterprise. He concluded that

judging from the pronounced success of Mr. Walter Vrooman's Western Coöperative Association, in so rapidly acquiring valuable properties and combining them into a general coöperative plan, this phase of the question has already been tested and solved. . . . However, to give the Coöperative movement in America the impetus and momentum its vital character deserves, it will be necessary for Mr. Vrooman or some one else to demonstrate this important requisite; namely, its ability to compete with existing establishments and yet award its patrons a share of the profits, as an incentive to their practical zeal.[57]

The day after *The Arena* interview Washburn received a telegram from Walter Vrooman inviting him to examine the activities of the Western Co-operative Association. In August, 1902, Washburn, Hiram Vrooman, Carl Vrooman, and Charles W. Caryl visited Walter's cooperative enterprises in Kansas City and Trenton. Local newspapers announced that Washburn and Walter planned to unite their organizations to form a gigantic People's Trust of America.[58]

The creation of the People's Trust of America further complicated the legal structure of Walter's cooperative organization. The Multitude Incorporated alone rivaled a robber baron's system of interlocking directorates, as it controlled the stock for three subsidiary coopera-

[56] Trenton *Weekly Republican,* Aug. 14, 1902, p. 4, cols. 4–5. Carl had recently returned from a trip to Europe, where he investigated cooperative enterprises. He talked to Walter in Kansas City and advised him to merge his organization with Washburn's group in the East.

[57] George F. Washburn, "How to Meet the Trust Problem Through Co-operation," *The Arena,* XXVIII (Oct., 1902), 414–15. The Western Co-operative Association owned six establishments in Trenton and the inventories for three other stores. The Central Western Co-operative Association of Kansas City owned ten business establishments in the city area and controlled a subsidiary, the Kansas Western Co-operative Company. The Southern Co-operative Association of Apalachicola, Fla., owned three thousand acres of land in East Point.

[58] Benjamin O. Flower, "The People's Trust: A Promising Coöperative Movement," *The Arena,* XXVIII (Oct., 1902), 434; Trenton *Weekly Republican,* Aug. 14, 1902, p. 6, col. 1; Aug. 7, 1902, p. 8, col. 3, quoting the Kansas City *Times;* Trenton *Weekly Republican,* Aug. 7, 1902, p. 6, col. 4, quoting the Kansas City *Star.* Charles W. Caryl, Walter's former associate in Philadelphia in 1893, was now a wealthy Colorado miner.

tive associations. Its backers claimed that it had revolutionized the merchandising practices in Kansas and Missouri.[59] When the Western Co-operative Association opened a store in Enterprise, Kansas, in July, 1902, neighboring farmers began to refer to the town as "Vroomansville." [60]

The Multitude Incorporated also controlled the educational features of the cooperative crusade, although Walter retained personal control of Ruskin College under the terms of the 1900 agreement. In issuing the prospectus for the 1902–1903 academic year the leaders of Ruskin College stated their case boldly.

Ruskin College stands for an ideal. It realizes that the world moves. It recognizes that mechanical progress has made want unnecessary; but that poverty, like a dark shadow, follows in the wake of progress, breeding conditions that menace civilization. This condition it traces to the survival of outgrown institutions, notably the private ownership and control of the heritage of the race—the earth and the tools with which its wealth may be made available to man. This, it believes, must give place to the public ownership and operation of such of the means of production as are found socially necessary, that each may enjoy the opportunity to live a complete life.... The change must be effected by the people and, that they may make it peacefully, they must be enlightened. But the organs of enlightenment, including colleges and universities, are largely under the control of the forces opposed to the change. Ruskin College stands for peaceful progress and the cooperative commonwealth.[61]

Sensing that the citizens of Trenton had turned against them they declared: "Ruskin College is content to stand for an ideal and to pay the price." [62]

But the brave words and legal subtleties masked a precarious financial situation. In July, 1903, Walter and Amne Vrooman sold

[59] *Catalog of Ruskin College and Ruskin Business College: Prospectus for 1902–1903* (Trenton, Mo.: Appeal to Reason Press, Girard, Kans., 1902), 32–33.

[60] Enterprise (Kans.) *Star,* June 26, 1902, p. 3, col. 2; July 10, 1902, p. 2, col. 1.

[61] *Catalog of Ruskin College for 1902–1903,* p. 6.

[62] *Ibid.* The Ruskin College faculty included George McA. Miller, lecturer in ethics, Thomas E. Will, lecturer in social sciences, Frank Parsons, lecturer during the summer sessions on political science, Harry C. Vrooman, lecturer in applied Christianity and ethics in business, and Walter Vrooman, lecturer in business organization. Amne Vrooman ran the Ruskin Home for Ladies in conjunction with Ruskin College.

their real estate in Trenton, worth $50,400, to their attorneys, who in turn sold it back to Amne. This maneuver placed the land outside the reach of Walter's creditors.[63] In August, 1902, the Western Co-operative Association began to consolidate its stores in Trenton because profits had not materialized as expected. The cooperative canning factory remained idle after drought damage to local crops. Rumors were circulated that Walter had squandered his entire fortune and that floods in Kansas City had ruined his model farm. The editor of the Trenton *Weekly Republican* benignly informed his readers that the "Big Scare" was over. In his opinion the cooperative ventures had become involved in "bad politics," that is, in Socialism.[64]

On October 11, 1902, the five charter members of the Multitude Incorporated gathered in the Ruskin College office in Trenton. The first item of business concerned the control of Ruskin College: "Walter Vrooman tendered to the Multitude Incorporated his interest in the name, authority and contracts of Ruskin College, excluding all liabilities of Ruskin College already incurred by him, it being expressly understood that none of his contracts with individuals for services in connection with Ruskin College shall hold beyond January 1, 1903." [65] The most important business was a move to increase the number of trustees for the Multitude Incorporated. By a unanimous vote the charter members elected George F. Washburn, Henry D. Lloyd, C. B. Hoffman, Benjamin O. Flower, George H. Shibley, Carl Vrooman, Frank Parsons, and the Reverend Harry C. Vrooman.[66]

The union of eastern and western cooperative organizations under the name The People's Trust of America was officially consummated by the addition of the new trustees. But the move was little more than a rhetorical flourish. Several of the men invited to become trustees hesitated to become involved financially with Walter Vrooman's precarious enterprises. The linking of Ruskin College with the Mul-

[63] *Record of Deeds,* Book 81, pp. 290–93, 316–17; Book 82, pp. 147–49, 295–99, 300–303, Grundy County, Mo.
[64] Trenton *Weekly Republican,* Aug. 21, 1902, p. 2, col. 1; Oct. 2, 1902, p. 4, col. 3.
[65] "Minutes of the Multitude Incorporated for Oct. 11, 1902," certified true copy enclosed in Will to Lloyd, Oct. 13, 1902, Box 22, Lloyd papers.
[66] *Ibid.* See also the statement by George F. Washburn, reprinted in B. O. Flower, "The People's Trust: A Promising Co-operative Movement," *The Arena,* XXVIII (Oct., 1902), 434–35.

titude Incorporated also jeopardized the college. In December, 1902, Will prepared articles of incorporation for a "Senate of Ruskin College" to strengthen the position of Miller, who was seeking new funds for the college. This procedure separated the college from the Multitude Incorporated.[67]

The critics underestimated Walter's determination to maintain his cooperative empire despite financial reverses. In October, 1902, the directors of the Western Co-operative Association had requested that all members report their purchases to the cashier at store "A" in Kansas City in preparation for the payment of the first semiannual dividends.[68]

When the Western Co-operative Association sold its store in Enterprise on January 29, 1903, the editor of the Enterprise *Star* tried to maintain a brave front: "The Western Co-operative Association is not dead; it is not bankrupt, nor is it even shaky. The opposition from this place has been both unreasonable and unfair. . . . The Association felt that it could plant its money where it would benefit the Association more." [69] Walter attempted in vain to conceal that he had taken the burden of the failure of the Western Co-operative Association himself, and he bought out the stock to save the investors. But the failure of the cooperative ventures associated with the Multitude Incorporated brought all his efforts into disrepute.[70]

[67] Will to Lloyd, Dec. 8, 1902, Box 22, Lloyd papers; George Miller, "An Academic Center for the New Education," *The Arena*, XXIX (June, 1903), 605, 607.

[68] Enterprise *Star*, Oct. 9, 1902, p. 3, col. 3. Amne Vrooman received land in Kansas City worth $31,000 during Sept. and Oct., 1902. Walter Vrooman received property worth $15,285. *Record of Deeds*, Book 821, p. 479; Book 831, p. 122; Book 832, pp. 394–95; Book 837, pp. 240, 242; Book 840, p. 379, Jackson County, Mo.

[69] Jan. 29, 1903, p. 2, col. 2.

[70] New York *Daily Tribune*, May 18, 1903, p. 4, col. 4. The real tragedy of the failure of the Western Co-operative Association and the Multitude Incorporated was its effect on Walter. The repeated failures of his cooperative ventures tended to bring to the fore in his thinking those race-life theories that previously had been only secondary considerations in his program of change. He began to expound his own "Purposive Philosophy" in the *Young Oxford* magazine and in free lectures at Kansas City. Since the race is eternal while the individual is temporal, man owes a debt to the race to pass life along through his children—this was the meaning of the new doctrine in its simplest form. In May, 1903, Amne Vrooman instituted proceedings for divorce on the grounds of infidelity. Walter filed a petition of denial. When the case reached the Circuit Court of Jackson County, he dismissed his attorney and failed to appear in court. The judge heard the evidence including testimony

The balance sheet of history must also show the other side of the story. The failure of the Western Co-operative Association was partly the result of a price-cutting agreement between some of the merchants of Trenton and their wholesale suppliers.[71] Walter also can be defended against the charge that Ruskin College "was clearly the scheme of a dreamer to make money." While Ruskin College suffered from its association with the ill-fated cooperative ventures, the legal provisions under which Walter surrendered his control of the association and his interest in Ruskin College to the Multitude Incorporated clearly showed that his primary concern was to provide educational benefits for the members of the cooperative associations.[72]

The Co-operative Association of America, which survived its brief association with Walter Vrooman's ill-fated ventures, held its annual convention in January, 1904. The convention authorized the establishment of a Co-operative Exchange, a combination banking house and educational center. By November, 1906, the association listed assets

---

that Walter planned to marry one of his secretaries as soon as he legally could to have a child to carry on his name and ideals. The judge granted a decree of absolute divorce with restoration of maiden name on June 13, 1903. Sick and exhausted from years of overwork and from the public reaction to his divorce, Walter was committed to a state hospital in New York in 1904. He languished there until his death on Dec. 2, 1909, at the age of forty. "Petition for Divorce, *Vrooman* v. *Vrooman,*" *Record of Deeds,* Book 1272, pp. 363–65; "Certified Copy of Decree of Divorce, June Term, 1903, Circuit Court of Jackson County, Missouri," *Record of Deeds,* Book 933, p. 192, Jackson County, Mo. Another certified copy is filed in *Record of Deeds,* Book 387, p. 185, Wyandotte County, Kans. For details of the divorce see New York *Daily Tribune,* May 18, 1903, p. 4, col. 4; June 14, 1903, p. 7, col. 5; clippings in Kansas State Historical Society collection. See Walter Vrooman, "The Purposive Philosophy," *Young Oxford,* III (March, 1902), 217; "The Vrooman School of Philosophy," *Young Oxford,* IV (Dec., 1902), 106–109; "The Vrooman School of Philosophy, Part II," *Young Oxford,* IV (Jan., 1903), 140–42.

[71] William Ray Denslow, *Centennial History of Grundy County, Missouri, 1839–1939* (Trenton, Mo.: by the author, 1939), 60.

[72] Earle A. Collins, "The Multitude Incorporated," *Missouri Historical Review,* XXVII (July, 1933), 306. As an educational institution, Ruskin College achieved a modest success. Enrollment increased from eighty students in September, 1900, to 320 students in 1903. Famous educators of the day, including George D. Herron, Frank Parsons, and Thomas E. Will, were associated with it. The industrial plan did help a few students to secure an education. Miller and Will had worked strenuously to turn the college into a true People's University—a school for the poor that was freed from outside control by the operation of the cooperative principle. Ruskin College was moved to Glen Ellyn, Ill., in April, 1903, where it merged with Midland University to form Ruskin University. See Miller, *The Arena,* XXIX, 605–607.

of $226,182.01 and liabilities of $168,333.20. The records showed a seemingly comfortable surplus of $57,848.81. A closer examination of the balance sheet, however, showed that from a legal point of view the association was poised on the brink of bankruptcy.[73]

The Co-operative Association of America had embarked on an overly ambitious program of expansion on the strength of an under-subscribed issue of bonds. The fund of gold bonds, bearing an interest rate of 3 percent, was registered at $1,000,000, but only $139,650 had been sold by the end of 1906. When several of the undertakings failed in 1907, Bradford Peck, the original financial backer of the association, withdrew. The directors abandoned some of the more theoretical aspects of the cooperative program, such as deducting a small sum from profit-sharing dividends in order to amortize an employee's "share" of the association's capital. They also abandoned their plans for a cooperative college and adopted a modified profit-sharing plan for their store in Lewiston.[74]

Why did the Vrooman cooperative ventures fail? The ultimate answer lies in the concept of the cooperative commonwealth held by Walter, Hiram, and Harry. At first glance, their cooperative ventures look like attempts to reform capitalism by using capitalistic devices: holding companies, trusts, stocks, and dividends. Unlike present-day profit-sharing consumer cooperatives, the Vrooman cooperative ventures subordinated economic considerations to moral purposes. Their ultimate goal was still the radical one of changing the basis of society. For competition they would substitute cooperation; for individual self-interest they would inculcate an altruistic group interest; and for private ownership of productive property they would substitute collective ownership. They saw the cooperative movement as a crusade, not as a cash proposition. By becoming involved in the economic subsidy of cooperative enterprises, however, they became dependent upon the purely economic factors of profit and loss for their success.

[73] Co-operative Association of America, *Fifth Annual Report of the Co-operative Association of America* (Lewiston, Me.: Co-operative Association of America, 1906), 1; *Souvenir Pamphlet and Program, Co-operative Convention, Faneuil Hall, Boston, January 12–13, 1904* (Boston: Co-operative Association of America, 1904), 16.

[74] Hiram Vrooman, "The Co-operative Association of America," *Twentieth Century*, III (Feb., 1911), 429–33; *Fifth Annual Report of the CAA*, 1–2.

As radicals proclaiming a new ideal for their society, Walter, Hiram, and Harry Vrooman were in their element as moral exhorters and agitators; as businessmen trying to beat capitalism at its own game, they were simply lost.[75]

[75] Both Hiram and Harry Vrooman were reluctant to embrace the materialistic Socialism of the Socialist party. With the failure of the Western Co-operative Association, Harry abandoned his efforts to establish a Ruskin College of Applied Christianity in Kansas City, Missouri, and returned to the ministry. From 1906 to 1910 Harry and Hiram made another attempt to "spiritualize" the Socialists by supporting the Christian Socialist Fellowship. See *Christian Socialist,* July 1, 1906, p. 7, cols. 1-2; May 1, 1910, p. 5; March 15, 1910, p. 8, cols. 2-3.

Harry Vrooman married Louise J. Bunton on Oct. 20, 1895, in East Milton, Mass. They had one son, Lee Vrooman, born March 20, 1897. Harry served in the following Congregational parishes: Sycamore and Independence, Kans., 1888-1891; Dayville, Conn., 1891-1892; East Milton, Mass., 1892-1895; St. Louis, Mo., 1895-1899; East Point, Fla., 1899-1904 (independent ministry); Indianapolis, Ind., 1904-1908 [?] (associated with the New Church); Dover, Mass., 1908-1910; Greenville, Me., 1910-1936. He died in Apalachicola, Fla., on Aug. 29, 1948.

Hiram Greeley Vrooman married Georgina Sullivan on June 28, 1910. They had four children: Alice, born Aug. 11, 1911; Julia, born Nov. 27, 1912; Scott, born June 25, 1915; and Egmont, born Aug. 15, 1917. Hiram was one of the founders of the Swedenborgian Philosophical Center in Chicago and served the New Church in Sheridan Park, Ill., from 1931 to 1936, and in Toronto from 1936 to 1940. He retired Nov. 14, 1953, and died in Panama City, Fla., on Feb. 24, 1954.

Chapter Eight

Progressivism, 1900-1910

FRANK VROOMAN: THE PHILOSOPHER
OF NATIONALISM, 1900–1910

While the three Socialists in the Vrooman family continued to pursue the goal of the cooperative commonwealth during the first decade of the new century, the other brothers, Frank and Carl, responded to the opportunity of the new century in a different way. During the first decade the American economy entered a new stage in its move toward maturity. A number of factors identified this new trend: the apparent success of the merger movement in business, the breakdown of family capitalism and its consequent unity of ownership and management, the separation of ownership of property and control of production created by the introduction of professional management and financial reorganization in corporate finance, and the creation of national markets and consolidated marketing systems. All these factors had combined with a rising cost of living to create a widespread sense of disquiet. Frank and Carl Vrooman, representative of some of the segments of society that responded to these developments intellectually and politically, attempted to redefine their conceptions of the good society to fit the new circumstances. In so doing they revealed some of the potential powers and limitations of Progressive reform in the twentieth century.[1]

The political response to these changes in the economy, the Progressive movement in American history, was as complex as the factors that created it. At the heart of the Progressive movement lay the perennial question of the equality of opportunity. Nineteenth-century American thought had given a peculiarly economic, or entrepreneurial, meaning to the term. This economic conception of equality had been united with a particular theory of legalistic freedom to create a powerful intellectual synthesis: the entrepreneur, given the formal, legal freedom to act by public law, would create the social and economic structures within which others would be given the chance to develop their talents and to be rewarded accordingly. Entrepreneurial liberty—or freedom of contract—was at once the engine of progress and the guarantee of social mobility, hence of equality. Free competition between entrepreneurs, unhindered by government regulation, would allocate resources, set fair prices, and insure an equitable distribution of economic rewards. The doctrine of formal freedom rested on the assumption that the law acted impartially. Since all were "free" to run the race of life, a man could blame only himself if he failed.

This peculiar union of the entrepreneurial concept of equality of opportunity and the doctrine of formal freedom came under increasing attack from several quarters during the first decade of the new century. On the one hand, the merger movement in business—the trust problem in popular parlance—raised the question of whether entrepreneurial opportunity really existed or would continue to exist in its previous forms. The independent retail merchant threatened with competition by the chainstore, the would-be manufacturer with inadequate capital resources to endure competition with the industrial giants, and the member of a profession confronted with the organizational imperatives of specialization—all wondered if the possibility of entry into entrepreneurship had not been severely restricted.

At the same time the professional managers and financiers who arranged the mergers and ran the new giants of corporate enterprise discovered the limits of the doctrine of formal freedom. The freedom of entry and the right of competition by numerous entrepreneurs threatened to plunge their industries continually into economic anarchy and costly price wars. An impartial law, or neutral government, could not protect them from the relative weakness of their own eco-

---

[1] Walt W. Rostow, *The Stages of Economic Growth* (Cambridge: Cambridge University Press, 1960), 75–76; Daniel Bell, "The Breakup of Family Capitalism: On Changes in Class in America," in *The End of Ideology*, rev. ed. (New York: Collier Books, 1961), 39–45; Richard Hofstadter, *The Age of Reform: From Bryan to F.D.R.* (New York: Alfred A. Knopf, 1956), Chaps. 5, 6; Gabriel Kolko, *The Triumph of Conservatism: A Reinterpretation of American History, 1900–1916* (New York: The Free Press of Glencoe, 1963), Chaps. 1, 2, 6.

nomic weapons. Only public sanction of their private efforts at stability and rationality could preserve the new system of opportunity that they had created: the freedom to rise within newly expanded corporate structures.[2]

While the entrepreneurs argued on the one side about the meaning of equality of opportunity and the doctrine of formal freedom, the social justice advocates—social workers, labor leaders, and some intellectuals—argued on the other side about the inadequacy of these two concepts to protect the dignity, well-being, and social status of nonentrepreneurial segments of society. Freedom for the entrepreneur frequently had been translated into freedom to exploit children and women, to deny labor's right to organize for protection, or to pass on to an unsuspecting public the cost of tariff protection, wasteful competition, and inefficient management. In short, formal freedom for the entrepreneur was not effective freedom for the worker, the public, or the unprotected.

Formal freedom did not equal effective freedom in another sense. It was false, these critics argued, to talk about everyone starting out equally in the race of life. In fact, some began handicapped by a poor education, bad health, inadequate credit resources, ethnic and racial stigmas, or personality problems. How could equality of opportunity exist among contestants who lacked effective freedom? In philosophical terms effective freedom was the freedom of the agent armed with the means to achieve his goal; that is, it was a pragmatic freedom. Formal freedom, the freedom of an agent to pursue a goal without first possessing the means to achieve it, was a sham.[3]

The Progressive movement, a coalition that included entrepreneurs and social justice advocates, was inherently unstable. The Progressives shared a concern about the reality of equality and freedom in

[2] This seems to be the real meaning of the events portrayed in Kolko's controversial book, *The Triumph of Conservatism*. One need not share his New-Left social theory and radical value standards to recognize the importance of the developments that he has outlined. The term Progressive is used here in the broad, generic sense; membership in the Progressive (Bull Moose) party is differentiated by context or special indication.

[3] Morton White, *Social Thought in America: The Revolt Against Formalism,* rev. ed. (Boston: Beacon Press, 1957), 101–103. The terminology used above is mine, not White's, and has been narrowed somewhat here to give formal freedom a legal rather than a philosophical connotation.

their day, but they differed on the meaning of the terms and ultimately on the political programs to achieve them. Concisely stated,
Progressivism was an attempt to retain the motive power of entrepreneurship and at the same time to insure effective freedom for both
entrepreneurial and nonentrepreneurial segments of society. Or,
more broadly stated, it was an attempt to retain the benefits of capitalism and answer the criticisms of Socialism at the same time.

The search for answers brought the Progressives face to face with
three basic problems. First, if the free play of entrepreneurial motives
and formal freedom did not create conditions conducive to the common good, how could the common good be achieved? Stated another
way, which unit in the human community embodied the common
good? Second, once the common good had been defined or embodied, how was it to be achieved? That is, once the agent had been
isolated, how was it to be armed to insure its effective freedom?
Third, if the formal freedom of the entrepreneur infringed on the
effective freedom of the worker, how was the conflict to be resolved?
More broadly stated, once the common interest had been defined and
the agent armed, how was the individual egoism of self-interest to be
overcome? In accommodating their thoughts to Progressivism Frank
and Carl Vrooman not only had to answer these three questions, but
they had to redefine their social visions, their goals, as well.

The appeal of Progressivism for entrepreneurs is quite evident. The
reasons why Frank, a former minister, responded to it are more
obscure. After his ouster from the Presbyterian Church and his rejection by the People's Church he had turned to prospecting in the
Klondike.[4]

In October, 1897, Frank and Harry Vrooman secured a charter of
incorporation in the state of Montana for the Klondike, Yukon, and
Copper River Company. Capital stock was listed at $12,000,000. Frank
then transferred his interests in the Silver Bow quartz mine to the

---

[4] Frank's switch from preaching to prospecting is understandable in the context of
the times. The reformers and radicals of the 1890's were not immune to the lure of
get-rich-quick. The dream of quick wealth from a gold mine beguiled the cooperative
colonists in Eugene Debs' Social Democracy of America and even drew Socialist Jack
London to the Klondike. Ira Kipnis, *American Socialist Movement, 1897–1912* (New
York: Columbia University Press, 1952), 55; Richard O'Conner, *Jack London: A
Biography* (Boston: Little, Brown, 1964).

new company in exchange for 51 percent of the capital stock. He did not own the Silver Bow mine; he had purchased control of it for one dollar. He then appointed three trustees to administer the affairs of the company—Frank Vrooman, Harry Vrooman, and Frank W. Davis of Minneapolis, their uncle.[5]

The first expedition of the Klondike, Yukon, and Copper River Company was scheduled for March, 1898, but trouble soon developed. The board of directors discovered that the financial affairs of the company were entangled. Frank had transferred some dredging equipment to the company in exchange for more stock and had taken out $6,000 in promissory notes to reimburse himself for the purchase of cigars, a bill that he claimed to have paid out of his own pocket. The board met in July and directed Frank to straighten out the books.[6]

Finally in January of 1899 some of the investors filed a petition for receivership in the Circuit Court of Cook County, Illinois. They charged that the company was insolvent because Frank had "squandered, used, and misused" $40,000 that had been paid into the company for stock. The petition listed Harry, Carl, and Hiram G. Vrooman and Frank Davis as defendants. The case was never tried; a stipulation was filed on March 17, 1900, dismissing the case at the cost of the complainants. Whatever the terms of the out-of-court settlement were, the whole incident was a severe blow to Frank's prospecting plans.[7]

Having renounced the pulpit and endangered his status as an entrepreneur, Frank cast about for a more favorable career. After a brief association with Walter's success club movement in 1901 as

[5] Topeka (Kans.) *Daily Capital,* Jan. 13, 1899, clipping in the Kansas State Historical Society Biographical Collections, V, I, 361.

[6] *Ibid.* The expedition was announced in an advertisement in *The Washingtonian,* I (Dec., 1897).

[7] *Wallace* v. *Klondike, Yukon, and Copper River Company et al.,* Circuit Court of Cook County, Ill., G. No. 19124 (information furnished by the Clerk of Circuit Court, Dec. 28, 1964). Nevertheless, Frank persisted in his prospecting efforts. In May, 1900, he set out for the Blue Mountains as head of the Vrooman Gold Mining and Prospecting Company to develop a mica deposit. See unidentified clipping, May 17, 1900, Kansas State Historical Society Biographical Collections, V, I, 363. Hiram Vrooman went to the Klondike in the spring of 1903. He claimed to have found gold dust deposits worth $100,000 in the Hootalinqua River region. Kansas City *Star,* Nov. 4, 1900, clipping in the Kansas State Historical Society Biographical Collections, V, II, 235.

organizer for the San Francisco area, he returned to journalism.[8] He combined the rigorous outdoor life of the prospector-promoter with the freedom of the freelance writer to become the unofficial philosopher, indeed the embodiment, of the strenuous life.

In 1905 he took up the task of reconciling certain elements of the Vrooman vision of the ideal commonwealth with the political theories of the Progressive movement. With a passing sneer at laissez faire economics, states' rights doctrines, and atheism he stated his political thesis boldly in the first of a series of essays in *The Arena* magazine: "The fact stands that the present tendency of all intelligent politics is away from anarchy and toward nationality. The public interest as an idea and an aim, is becoming crystalized in the laboratory of public opinion and the public is beginning to look out for itself."[9] By anarchy he meant competition. What he meant by nationality was not clear. A decade earlier he assumed that the state was the only power competent to deal with social welfare problems, but he had been reluctant to go beyond Toynbee's three criteria for state action. Now he seemed to be offering a new criterion to define the extent of the state's powers.

The next two essays provided further clues to the meaning of the term nationality. In a description of the work of the Reclamation Service, he noted: "The building and control of irrigation-plants as a national enterprise is another silver-plated screw in the lead coffin of *laissez-faire*. It is revolutionary and epoch-making. The success of the nation is so overwhelmingly brilliant in its whole conception and prosecution of the enterprise that it will certainly lead to the building and control of other public utilities and benefits, and what is as inexorable as logic and as inevitable as death, *the eventual federal control of all human necessities*." [Italics added] [10] In an essay on the work of the Forest Service he wrote, "No one who has read the history of the Forest Service, and, as well, that of the 'land-skinner,' can hesitate long as to whether 'state interference,' or *laissez-faire* . . . is the better politics, and as to whether competitive anarchy or patri-

[8] Trenton (Mo.) *Weekly Republican*, March 14, 1901, p. 8, col. 5.
[9] "Uncle Sam's Romance with Science and the Soil: Part I. The Field," *The Arena*, XXXIV (Dec., 1905), 561.
[10] *Ibid.*, Part II, "The Stream," *The Arena*, XXXV (Jan., 1906), 44.

otic nationality *is the better guiding principle in public affairs."* [Italics added] [11] He spent the next five years developing the concept of nationality as a guiding principle for the Progressive movement.

The root of the problem, as Frank saw it, was that Americans were so overwhelmingly absorbed in the pursuit of money that they interpreted politics from the point of view of personal aggrandizement. As a result, they lacked an adequate theory of the state. "In other words, our politics is economics. If we believe here and there in political morality, our ideas of it are confined to questions of the suppression of graft, the purification of elections, the elimination of spoils, and kindred phases of a much deeper question.... Is it not time to go further? There is a world-wide difference between political morality and political ethics. The crying need in America is an intelligent statement of the moral mission of the state and the ethical foundations of government from the standpoint of modern democracy." [12] Politics, in his system, meant removing issues from the market place to the area of principles.

In 1907 Frank turned from political theorizing to geographical exploration. He joined a team trekking through the Canadian Northwest. The journey by pack train through the Athabasca, Peace, and Finley river areas of the Mackenzie River basin covered three thousand miles. From Fort Grahame, British Columbia, the party floated downstream on the Finley and Peace rivers through the Rocky Mountains. Four times the party was shipwrecked on the rocks and rapids. When food ran low, the men maintained sentry duty to protect themselves from their hunger-stricken dogs. When Indians showed too much interest in the party's gear, Frank restored their respect for private property with a demonstration of sharpshooting. For his contributions to the exploration of northwest Canada he was designated a Fellow of the Royal Geographical Society of London. [13]

An invitation from the Oxford University School of Geography to deliver a series of lectures on the economic geography of northwest Canada provided an opportunity for Frank to sum up his

---

[11] *Ibid.*, Part III, "The Forest," *The Arena*, XXXV (Feb., 1906), 163.

[12] Frank Vrooman, "Spoils and the Civil Service: Part I. A Retrospect," *The Arena*, XXXVII (Feb., 1907), 156.

[13] *The Times* (London), Jan. 7, 1909, p. 4, col. 4; interview with Carl Vrooman, Nov. 27, 1960; Royal Geographical Society, *Year-Book and Record,* 1909, p. 199.

ideas on politics. He found the perfect embodiment of his theories in Theodore Roosevelt. He called Roosevelt a "dynamic geographer" and explained that "the dynamic geographer is the efficient geographer ... the man who studies the land and water with an ethical purpose in the back of his mind, with reference to getting from them, for mankind, the highest possible amount of use. The dynamic geographer is the strenuous geographer." [14] Roosevelt had "laid his big stick on the doctrine of laissez faire" and had established the foundations of a national economic policy on the firm ground of scientific geography.[15]

Roosevelt saw clearly, according to Frank, that the United States had been developing "the wrong kind of democracy."

[Roosevelt] has worked out a new constructive ethical idea on scientific foundations. He has realized that idea, not only in stemming the tide of individualism rampant, but he has shown the path which will avoid the evils of socialism. He has been the first man in a position of peculiar power or influence since Hamilton to see clearly and draw distinctly the natural line of cleavage ... between the democracy of individualism which threatens the very existence of democracy upon the earth, and the *democracy of nationalism* which offers the only rational and ethical alternative for socialism or individualism. [Italics added] [16]

He complained that no one had yet coined a phrase for Roosevelt's political philosophy and offered the term nationalism. Had he added the adjective "new," Frank would be remembered today, along with Herbert Croly, as an official philosopher of the New Nationalism. Indeed, Frank had arrived at a similar conception of the Hamiltonian state without the benefit of Croly's Comtian philosophy.[17]

The officials of Oxford University were sufficiently impressed with Frank's lectures to offer him a bachelor of science degree for a dissertation on the economic geography of northwest Canada. To meet the deadline he dictated the dissertation (which weighed ten pounds)

[14] Frank Vrooman, *Theodore Roosevelt: Dynamic Geographer* (Oxford: Oxford University Press, 1909), 9–10.

[15] *Ibid.*, 7.

[16] *Ibid.*, 17.

[17] *Ibid.*, 99–100. Herbert Croly's *The Promise of American Life* and Frank Vrooman's *Theodore Roosevelt: Dynamic Geographer* were both published in 1909.

in eighteen days, two hours, and fifteen minutes. The university granted the degree in June, 1909. The following spring Carl Vrooman joined his brother at Oxford to hear Theodore Roosevelt deliver the Romanes Lecture on the topic "Biological Analogies in History." The English audience marked the lecture "beta minus," but the lecturer "alpha plus." Even the English shared Frank's admiration for Roosevelt on this occasion.[18]

Frank presented the final version of his theory of nationalism in a book entitled *The New Politics*. He coined the phrase "Philosophy of Ishmael" to denote the laissez faire philosophy of nineteenth-century liberalism: "Its motive is self-interest. Its point of view is self. This is individualism. This is the philosophy of Ishmael. This is the philosophy of life of the Anglo-Saxon world today."[19] This egotistical theory of life, which made the basis of politics interests rather than principles, created a false foundation for political life. Progress was left to fortuitous events, the social organism was allowed to degenerate into atomism, and the very survival of the race was endangered by this faulty rationale of life.[20]

Frank maintained, on the other hand, that the whole trend of thought and progress in the nineteenth century had been "toward coordination, combination, organization, socialization."[21] There was a danger that this tendency would go too far and foster Socialism. It had, however, provided the basis for a new theory of life and a new theory of politics. The expression of the organic unity of the nation was the state. "Corporate self-government for the corporate good as opposed to political *laissez-faire* is something like the Democracy of Nationalism. . . . But the state must not stop here. It is quite impossible for one to say off-hand what are the 'duties' of a state, but that the state is founded on principles which make duties necessary is unquestioned, for the state has obligations as well as rights. The state is the *institutionalization* of the *common good*."[22] The "cohesive prin-

[18] W. H. Dean, "Two Remarkable Brothers," *American Magazine*, LXXX (Nov., 1915), 28–29; Henry F. Pringle, *Theodore Roosevelt* (New York: Harcourt, Brace, 1931), 366.
[19] *The New Politics* (New York: Oxford University Press, 1911), 42.
[20] *Ibid.*, 22–23, 30–31, 185.
[21] *Ibid.*, 20.
[22] *Ibid.*, 186.

ciple which alone makes a state possible," he asserted, was "the nexus of good will in a framework of the common good." [23]

He summed up his theory of nationalism in a discussion of the issues of antitrust legislation and conservation policy. Events in these two fields had shown that there was "a vast area of crime" over which there was no law—"the interstices, as it were, between the states." He believed that the fate of the Progressive movement would be determined by the contest over this issue: "Shall the nation then or shall it not under the Constitution annex those areas of anarchy between state and state, and between state and nation over which there is now no sovereignty at all?" [24] He called on the generation that had been born after the Civil War "to state its case" for nationality. Either the national government was sovereign, and therefore supreme, or it was not. The time had come when "the American people must choose between government ownership, the confusions of individualism, and *government control*—in other words, between socialism, anarchy, and *Nationalism*." [Italics added] [25]

After a decade of intellectual wandering Frank had settled squarely in the Progressive camp. The Progressive theory of politics provided the key to solving the tensions in his own system. He had advocated a state powerful enough to meet modern problems, had armed it with the right of government ownership in conservation matters, and had empowered it ultimately to control all human necessities. But what principle could prevent such a state from rushing on to Socialism and extinguishing the margin of entrepreneurship? Frank's activities as a prospector-promoter had placed him in the entrepreneurial tradition. Did he advocate the abolition of his own fields of endeavor?

The Progressive theory of politics rescued him from this dilemma. The state could be trusted with such power because a moral elite would restrain it. Individualism and laissez faire appealed to man's self-interest and assumed that out of antagonistic competition would arise the achievement of the common good. Nationalism and government control would appeal to man's common interests and would

---

[23] *Ibid.*, 174.
[24] *Ibid.*, 192.
[25] *Ibid.*, 279.

achieve the common good by intelligent cooperation. Those who realized this fact were fit to rule the new state. A truly democratic state would reflect their desires.

In a moving and eloquent passage in *The New Politics* Frank summed up the heart of his ideal: "What we ought to have and what we might have is an ethical democracy in which the tenderer sentiments of the human heart may not wither and die, where a man may be honest and fair and still do business, and where men will not mangle and crush their brethren to acquire their property without fair return, and where the acquisitive instinct has not gone stark mad." [26] A fair reward for effort, the right of acquisition of property restrained only by the needs of the common good, a democratic determination of the content of the common good—these were the ideals that Frank wanted his society to achieve.

CARL VROOMAN: A PROGRESSIVE
IN SEARCH OF A LEADER, 1900–1910

In December, 1902, Willis J. Abbot, the Bryan Democratic leader, wrote to Henry Demarest Lloyd to suggest that Lloyd write a column for *Boyce's Weekly,* a midwestern protest newspaper. Abbot noted:

> It has just occurred to me that I know a man living in Boston or rather in Cambridge, who could take the burden of that matter for Boyce's paper, off your shoulders and do it I think very well. You know him, or know his family. He is Karl [*sic*] Vrooman, I think the *sanest* of the whole crowd. He has sent me two very good articles of European travel, from which it appears that he particularly studied there people's banks and labor copartnerships. He writes well and is tremendously eager to get a start in journalism. I believe he would welcome a place of this sort and we would very gladly add enough to the amount you agreed to accept to enable you to pay him. That is to say I think you could arrange with him for $20.00 a week to fill out the half page we want from you.[27]

Abbot recognized in Carl Vrooman the type of young intellectual who was rapidly coming to the fore in reform circles. Harvard-

[26] *Ibid.,* p. 272.
[27] Abbot to Lloyd, Dec. 11, 1902, Box 22, Lloyd papers.

educated, politically active, and impressively equipped as a speaker and a writer, Carl attempted his own synthesis of his family heritage and Progressivism. While Frank elaborated a theoretical justification for action by the nation as the embodiment of the common good, Carl took up the questions of how the national government was to act to insure equality of opportunity and of how the reformers were to curb the egoism of self-interest.

Firmly established as a large-scale, scientific farmer in Bloomington, Illinois, and possessing a sufficient income, Carl could pursue his interests in reform and politics at his leisure. He translated his Kansas Populism into Bryan Democracy and loyally supported Bryan in the 1900 campaign. In 1902 the Illinois Democratic State Central Committee fell under the control of a conservative Democratic coalition headed by Roger Sullivan of Chicago. Sullivan's heavy hand acted as a powerful restraint on the political aspirations of Bryan Democrats in Illinois.[28]

European travel offered Carl a chance to escape from the limitations of the Illinois political situation, and from 1900 to 1910 he spent about one-half of his time abroad. Travel brought him into contact with European social movements and leaders; it also provided an opportunity for him to establish an independent reform reputation on the basis of his intellectual achievements. Accompanied by his wife, Julia, he returned to Europe periodically to investigate social and political problems, to reflect upon the weaknesses of the American reform movement, and to survey the future of the Progressive program.[29]

In Italy Carl brooded over the future of reform in the western world. In an article published in 1903 he spelled out his tentative conclusions.

Some people are amazed at the rapid growth of socialism all over the world. The reason is plain. Social and economic conditions which are be-

---

[28] "Carl Schurz Vrooman," *Harvard College Class of 1895, Secretary's Report No. 5* (Cambridge: printed for use by the class, 1915), 335–36; Carter H. Harrison, *Stormy Years: The Autobiography of Carter H. Harrison* (Indianapolis: Bobbs-Merrill, 1935), 324.

[29] For a detailed account, see Carl and Julia Scott Vrooman, *The Lure and Lore of Travel* (Boston: Sherman, French, 1914).

coming alarming in America have long been intolerable in Europe. The socialists have come before the people with two definite programs, a maximum and a minimum. The maximum is for the unknown and perhaps distant future, and promises to the poor and downtrodden peasant and working man the reign of justice on earth.... The minimum is a practical program for the immediate present.... Progress cannot be held in check. *Socialism or a saner, safer, but equally efficacious, constructive statesmanship will control the future.* [Italics added] [30]

How would this alternative to Socialism arise? Carl was somewhat vague in his answer. "In this materialistic age when we worship at the throne of the great commercial trinity of money, cunning, and mechanism," he wrote, "a reaction, or rather, a new spiritual impulse is necessary if civilization is to progress or even to endure." [31]

How would this new spiritual impulse arise? How could it be inculcated in the masses? Religion, he felt, had failed to do this: "The failure of the church to reach the masses, of which we hear so much complaint, is because teachers and spiritual leaders today have so largely lost connection with the Infinite Dynamo of Altruistic Purpose and Power which sways the planets. When preachers, priests and prophets become live wires, with direct connection, such as St. Francis had, 'with the power behind the evolution,' the masses will flock to them, drawn by irresistable attraction." [32] When he returned to the United States, Carl joined his brothers' efforts in the cooperative movement but continued to hope for political progress within the Democratic party. [33]

The nomination of Alton B. Parker by the conservative wing of the Democratic party in the 1904 presidential election filled Carl with disgust. He refused to support the party ticket. He also found Theodore Roosevelt too conservative for his tastes, but grudgingly recognized his efforts for reform. Basically, Carl was still a Bryan Democrat. The railroad problem was the key issue before the country in his mind and on that issue Roosevelt was not up to Bryan's standard.

[30] "Cycling Through Tuscany and Umbria," *The Pilgrim,* VII (Aug., 1903), 9.
[31] *Ibid.,* 10.
[32] *Ibid.* See also Carl Vrooman, "Uses and Abuses of Italian Travel," *The Arena,* XXXIV (Oct., 1905), 354–63.
[33] For Carl's relation to the cooperative movement, see Chap. 7 above.

Carl began to use his European travels to document this opinion, making an extensive investigation of European railway regulations and state ownership plans.[34]

Carl searched in Europe for clues to the riddle of how to achieve genuine reform in the United States. The one European statesman who seemed to provide the conception that he needed was Georges Clemenceau. In a conversation with Clemenceau in 1905 concerning the Radical party's call for nationalization of the railroads Carl raised the question whether Clemenceau's Radicals were serious about this "socialistic" plank. "The difference between our attitude and that of the Socialists," Clemenceau replied, "is that while they pretend to know all the minutest details concerning a future so far distant that nothing definite can be known about it, we demand reforms that seem to us realizable by this generation and about the desirability of which this generation therefore would seem to be a competent judge." [35]

The sovereignty of each generation was a concept that fitted the Progressive theory of direct democracy. The Progressive reformer need not be shackled by the past, as the conservative maintained, or bound to a future blueprint, as the Socialist claimed. Carl gradually saw that direct democracy devices, such as initiative, referendum, and recall, could not guarantee genuine change unless each generation knew exactly what it wanted and why.[36]

What did Carl's generation want? With the prospect that Bryan would again lead the Democratic party in the 1908 elections Carl was optimistic that his generation would state its case. The real issue, he wrote, was clearcut: "In the great work of social reconstruction that lies before us, the first practical step to be taken does not consist of that great task for the accomplishment of which 1900 years have

---

[34] Carl Vrooman, "Politique aux États-Unis," *Courrier Européen* (Paris), Jan. 12, 1906, copy in Vrooman papers.

[35] Carl Vrooman, *American Railway Problems in the Light of European Experience* (London: Oxford University Press, 1910), 88.

[36] In 1903 Carl regarded referendum and initiative primarily as devices to circumvent the Supreme Court. By 1908 he was warning against the misuse of these devices by scheming politicians and reactionary elements. See Carl Vrooman, "Tyranny of Servants," *The Arena*, XXIX (Feb., 1903), 186–89; "A Political Pilgrimage," *The Arena*, XL (Nov., 1908), 156–63; "England in Revolution," *Twentieth Century*, IV (Oct., 1911), 584.

proved all too short—the spiritual regeneration of the individual members of society—but rather of the more modest work of raising our corporate morality from the level of the hyena and the tiger up to the pitifully unsatisfactory but distinctly higher standard already attained by us as individuals." [37]

In short, business should be conducted with something more important in mind than the creation of excess profits and dividends on a large quantity of watered stock. Carl contributed heavily to Bryan's campaign in Massachusetts, where he maintained a summer home at Cotuit, in the hope of achieving a decisive political victory for reform. The results of the election were hardly encouraging. [38]

The failure of the third Bryan campaign in 1908 emphasized again to Carl the problem that belief in direct democracy devices posed for the reformer. "The great mass of the American people are conservative by nature," he wrote in 1909. "They are suspicious of a radical and instinctively antagonistic toward a reactionary." The Socialists, despite their positive aspects, could not hope to vote into being their industrial brotherhood. Reactionary commercialism reduced everything to monetary values and could not appeal to the better nature in men. What the country needed was "constructive conservatism," which was simply doing the right thing at the right time. "The most conservative government," he concluded, "is the government which most successfully and most constantly adjusts its policies and institutions to the ever-changing conditions of its environment." [39]

In September, 1909, Carl finished the manuscript of his book on railway problems. After discussing it with his former Harvard mentor, Frank Taussig, he sent a copy to Professor Richard Ely at the

[37] "The Ultimate Issue Involved in Railroad Accidents," *The Arena*, XXXIX (Jan., 1908), 15. In the same article he expressed the opinion that "a reorganization of our commercial and industrial life along saner and more ethical lines is certain to be brought about *in the near future.*" [Italics added] See p. 19. This passage was omitted when the article was incorporated into his book in 1910; *American Railway Problems*, 217.

[38] Boston *Herald*, Aug. 20, 1914, clipping in Harvard College Alumni files, Widener Library, Harvard.

[39] Carl Vrooman, "Constructive Conservatism: Practical Reform Is the Sanest Means of Attaining to Economic and Social Ideals," *La Follette's Magazine*, I (March 13, 1909), 7–8.

University of Wisconsin for criticism and editorial handling.[40] The classic problem of Progressivism—how to mitigate the defects of capitalism without embracing Socialism—underlay Carl's attempt to wrestle with the issues of railway regulation and nationalization. One reviewer noted, "Mr. Vrooman, though a strong believer in government ownership, holds that we will safely reach this goal only after state and government regulation has been tried; and he inclines to believe that this will prove in every way beneficial, as it will not only make it much easier for the government to efficiently inaugurate public ownership, but will also prevent hasty and ill-considered action on the part of the people." [41] Basically, Carl was attempting to document Bryan's position on the railroad question. The conclusion that government ownership could best be achieved through government regulation was a reasonable attempt to bridge the inconsistencies in Bryan's public statements.

Carl's desire to follow Bryan's politically motivated logic created problems that complicated his analysis of railway affairs. On the one hand, Carl held that the fundamental cause of America's transportation difficulties lay in "the unintelligent and inexcusable delay of the American people about inaugurating an adequate and effective system of railway regulation"; on the other hand, he claimed that "no such satisfactory system of railway regulation ever has been worked out by any nation in the world." [42]

The primary conclusion of Carl's book was a trenchant justification of government ownership:

By the foregoing studies in comparative efficiency and all round satisfactoriness, it has been clearly demonstrated that *in Continental Europe,* State railways as a rule furnish better transportation facilities and charge

[40] Carl Vrooman to Ely, Sept. 15; Nov. 5, 1909, Box 73; Ely to Carl Vrooman, Nov. 8, 1909, Box 74, Ely papers. The Mann-Elkins Act was passed June 18, 1910. Carl noted the passage of the bill but regretted that he could not discuss its effects. See Carl Vrooman, *American Railway Problems,* p. 33, n. 1. For a review and rejoinder, see Ernest R. Dewsnup, rev. of Carl Vrooman, *American Railway Problems,* in *American Economic Review,* I (March, 1911), 95–98; Carl Vrooman, "A Communication," *American Economic Review,* I (Dec., 1911), 823–26.

[41] Unsigned rev. of Carl Vrooman, *American Railway Problems,* in *Twentieth Century,* III (Dec., 1910), 254.

[42] Carl Vrooman, *American Railway Problems,* 34, 90.

lower rates than do private companies; that in connection with the State railway managements examined there exists practically nothing in the nature of a "spoils system" to prevent them from securing efficient officials and employees; that graft and corruption are much *less* frequent in connection with State railways than with private ones; that travel is much safer on Government roads than on private lines; and lastly, that State railways...in a large majority of cases, have made an entirely satisfactory financial showing.[43]

He was concerned, however, that the "widespread and deep-seated sentiment in favour of public ownership" in the United States might cause the people to insist prematurely on nationalization of the railroads.[44]

Carl had presented a strong case, in economic terms, for government ownership and operation of the railroads, but the political and moral premises of his argument intruded into his economic analysis. The real culprit in the American railway situation, he believed, was the American "corporate morality." He believed that no matter how "intelligent and humane railroad officials may be personally," in their official capacity they too often became "only so many cogs in a complicated and conscienceless mechanism" designed to create profit at the public's expense.[45]

He concluded that "the *supreme* advantage" of government ownership "would seem to consist not so much in the lowering of rates, the amelioration of the conditions of labour, improvements in service," or similar economic benefits, "but in the emancipation of the People" from their "economic subjection to the irresponsible power of railway magnates." [46] In short, government ownership was not an end in itself but a means to a more desirable end—a moral capitalism.

After a decade of intellectual effort both Frank and Carl Vrooman had achieved an accommodation between Progressivism and their family tradition. If their answers to the three questions posed by Progressivism were not entirely satisfactory, it was because they had confronted the issues only at the level of theory, not at the practical

[43] *Ibid.*, 293–94.
[44] *Ibid.*, 2, compare with p. 64.
[45] *Ibid.*, 207.
[46] *Ibid.*, 297.

level of policy formation. They believed that the state was the embodiment of the common good, and through the democratic process it could define the content of the common good. Once the common good had been defined, the state should be armed with the power to control essential areas of economic activity, they believed. Carl's formula that government regulation was a necessary and desirable stage before government ownership of limited segments of the economy could be attempted was an effort to define the proper limits of state action. To preserve the benefits of entrepreneurship the enlightened businessman would have to overcome his self-interest by pursuing the ideal of the common interest. Those who transcended their own interest were capable of leading the people and of controlling the state.

There was a neatness and balance to their intellectual system, but it rested on untested assumptions. Would men, in fact, act this way if they possessed the power of the state? The Vrooman brothers never had faced the issue squarely. No one in the family had possessed political power since Hiram resigned his judgeship in the 1870's. Carl had come the closest to possessing power in Kansas as a leader of the Populists and as a regent of the state college. Only if he could achieve political office, and power, could he test his theories in practice. In 1909 Carl lamented the fact that the statesman who could unite the religious fervor, the idealism, and the political unrest of his generation into a moral and political crusade had not yet appeared. But Woodrow Wilson was waiting in the wings.[47]

---

[47] *La Follette's Magazine,* 7. Carl noted in *The Lure and Lore of Travel* that Wilson, Bryan, Roosevelt, and La Follette represented a new type of "boss" who served the interests of the people and built efficient political machines only to achieve this goal. This comment was first published in an *Arena* article in 1908. See *The Lure and Lore of Travel,* p. 261; Carl Vrooman, "A Political Pilgrimage," *The Arena,* XL (Nov., 1908), 156–63.

Chapter Nine

Wilsonian Progressivism,
1910-1916

THE NEW FREEDOM, 1910-1914

Woodrow Wilson combined the idealism, religious conviction, and conservative instincts that the Progressive generation demanded. He saw clearly that the Progressive cause could not be confined to the nonpartisan approach, and he realized that nonpartisan tactics and direct democracy techniques were only devices by which respectable citizens sought to play politics without soiling their hands.[1]

During the first decade of the twentieth century the accommodation of the Progressive movement to the mores of a highly organized society became readily apparent. The day of Walter Vrooman's poverty-embracing scientific agitator, the man who shared the life of the common man in order to lead him, seemed to have passed; the day of the prominent reformer had long since arrived. The honorary vice-presidency of a civic organization, the letterhead endorsement of a "worthy" cause, the salaried executive-directorship of a nonpartisan reform league—these had become the signs of success in the Progressive movement. The prominent reformer jealously guarded his endorsement, his vested interest in a particular organization, and his reputation for Progressive but safe opinions.[2]

The practical politicians of the Progressive era, the men who had participated in the civic federations of the 1890's and the "insurgency" campaigns of the 1900's, shared these attitudes. Their preference for experts in government, which seemed to contradict their belief in direct democracy devices, simply reflected the prevalence of the prominent reformer syndrome in the organizational life of the Progressive movement itself. Robert La Follette once remarked,

"Get and keep a dozen or more of the *leading men* in a community interested in and well-informed upon any public question and you have laid firmly the foundations of democratic government." [Italics added] [3] The proliferation of bipartisan and nonpartisan reform organizations gave expression to this view.

The Progressive theory of politics rested on the assumption that leadership for reform would come from the men of good will who had transcended their own particular interests. In short, the new Progressive politician could be trusted to lead the people because of his moral discipline and altruism.[4] The implicit tension in the Progressive theory of politics between the desires of the self-appointed leaders of the people and the expressed will of the people through direct democracy devices was never adequately faced.

Wilson's attitude toward these features of the Progressive movement was displayed vividly in an incident in 1911. Ray Stannard Baker invited Wilson to address a nonpartisan gathering of Progressive leaders. When he politely refused, Baker "called Governor Wilson on the telephone, urging him to reconsider his decision, arguing that the movement was non-partisan, that [the group was] working for publicity of ideas and principles. Wilson responded with the real reason which was holding him back. 'I am heartily in sympathy with the movement,' he said, 'but I am convinced that I must make my fight within the Democratic party. It must be a party movement.' " [5] Wilson did not deny the usefulness of the nonpartisan approach; he simply saw that procedural, direct democracy

[1] Woodrow Wilson, "Hide-and-Seek Politics," *North American Review*, CXLI (May, 1910), 592–93, 600–601; Arthur Link, *Woodrow Wilson, I: The Road to the White House* (Princeton: Princeton University Press, 1947), 321.

[2] The nonpartisan, single-issue reform leagues had become such a prominent feature of American political life that they received the scholarly attention of foreign political observers. See Moisei Ostrogorskii, *Democracy and the Organization of Political Parties,* trans. Frederick Clarke (New York: Macmillan, 1902), II, 454–55, 658–63.

[3] Quoted by Russel Nye, *Midwestern Progressive Politics: A History of Its Origins and Developments, 1870–1958* (East Lansing: Michigan State University Press, 1959), 205. For a recent assessment of the role of reform organizations in the Progressive era, see Robert H. Wiebe, *Businessmen and Reform* (Cambridge: Harvard University Press, 1962), Chap. 2.

[4] John C. Burnham, "Psychiatry, Psychology and the Progressive Movement," *American Quarterly,* XII (Winter, 1960), 438; Richard Hofstadter, *The Age of Reform: From Bryan to F.D.R.* (New York: Alfred A. Knopf, 1956), 257–59.

[5] Ray Stannard Baker, *Woodrow Wilson: Life and Letters, III: Governor, 1910–1913* (Garden City, N.Y.: Doubleday, Doran, 1931), 185.

reforms favored by the Progressives would only change the ground rules of politics. The Progressives still had to act, he believed, in the political arena to realize the full benefit of their labors.

Three incidents in the political history of Illinois during the period from 1910 to 1914 determined the context in which Carl Vrooman responded to Wilson's leadership. These incidents—the William Lorimer case of 1910–1912, the 1912 presidential primary campaigns, and the Illinois senatorial elections of 1913 and 1914—illustrated the problems that accompanied the attempts of Progressives to translate their reform proposals into political programs. They also raised questions about whether the assumptions underlying the Progressive theory of politics were adequate for the realities of their situation.

The Lorimer case began officially in June, 1910, when the United States Senate passed a resolution authorizing the Committee on Privileges and Elections to inquire into charges that Senator William Lorimer of Illinois, a Republican, had been elected by fraudulent means. After an investigation the committee returned a majority report upholding Lorimer's election. On March 1, 1911, the Senate rejected a minority report submitted by Senator Albert Beveridge and endorsed the majority report.[6]

The Lorimer case, which came at a time when the agitation for the direct election of senators was nearing its peak, provided ample material for the proponents of this measure. The evidence—that a wealthy lumberman had set up a $100,000 jackpot to elect Lorimer because he would "stand pat" on lumber duties, that party leaders had ignored popular candidates who had secured substantial support in the preferential primaries, and that the bipartisan coalition required to elect Lorimer had been secured through bribery—spurred Progressives to action. On April 6, 1911, Senator La Follette introduced a resolution calling for a new investigation of the case. The Senate renewed the investigation, but a year passed before the committee returned its report.[7]

[6] U.S., Congress, Senate, Committee on Privileges and Elections, *Compilation of Senate Election Cases from 1789 to 1913,* 62d Cong., 3d Sess., 1913, Senate Doc. 1036, pp. 1002–1003. Cited hereafter as *Senate Election Cases.* For the majority report, see 1003–16; for the minority report, 1016–25.

[7] James Langland, ed., *The Chicago Daily News Almanac and Year-Book for 1912* (Chicago: Chicago Daily News Co., 1911), 410–11; *Senate Election Cases,* 1026–30.

During the intervening year supporters of Governor Wilson started their campaign to win the Democratic presidential nomination for him. In Illinois the Wilson managers faced a hopeless situation. The supporters of Theodore Roosevelt had rushed a law establishing a presidential preference primary through a special session of the Illinois General Assembly on March 30, 1912, in a desperate attempt to circumvent the Taft faction that controlled the Republican party machinery. With only ten days remaining before the primary the Wilson managers decided to launch a barnstorming tour in Illinois. The results of the primary in April, 1912, were disastrous for the Wilson campaign. Champ Clark carried the Illinois primary with a plurality of 142,966 votes, and Wilson received only 75,527 votes.[8]

The Illinois elections were characterized by vicious internecine warfare in the Democratic party between a conservative faction headed by Roger Sullivan and a moderate faction headed by Carter Harrison of Chicago. When moderates won a substantial number of precinct committee contests in strategic Cook County, the Sullivan faction refused to attend the regular Cook County Democratic convention and sought recognition from the state convention. The Sullivan-controlled state convention at Peoria recognized the pro-Sullivan Cook County delegation. The Harrison delegates thereupon bolted the convention and held a rival session the following day. The anti-Sullivan convention voted to send delegates to the Democratic National Convention at Baltimore and they instructed these delegates to stand by Clark as long as his name was before the convention.[9]

The contest between the rival delegations was carried to the Credentials Committee of the Baltimore convention. Harrison denounced the Sullivan-controlled Cook County delegation as a band of "plug-uglies, pickpockets, holdup-men and hangers-on of dis-

[8] James Langland, ed., *The Chicago Daily News Almanac and Year-Book for 1913* (Chicago: Chicago Daily News Co., 1912), 527; U.S., Congress, Senate, Committee on Privileges and Elections, *Campaign Contributions,* 62d Cong., 3d Sess., 1913, I, 881, 886. Cited hereafter as *Campaign Contributions.* Link, *Wilson,* I, 409–11; Langland, *Chicago Almanac for 1913,* 483.

[9] Carter H. Harrison, *Stormy Years: The Autobiography of Carter H. Harrison* (Indianapolis: Bobbs-Merrill, 1935), 323–25; *Campaign Contributions,* I, 918–25.

reputable saloons and bawdy-houses." [10] When approached by a Wilson man with a deal for support, Harrison had to admit that his hands were tied by the resolutions of the bolting convention in favor of Clark. Luke Lea, a Wilson lieutenant, made the necessary bargain with Sullivan. The Wilson forces supported the Sullivan delegation in the Credentials Committee, and the Sullivan forces aided the Wilson faction in a floor fight over seating the South Dakota delegation. This bargain added ten votes to the total number of Wilson delegates and assured Sullivan's control of the Illinois delegation. [11]

The crucial moment in the convention arrived on July 1, 1912. Wilson needed the support of either John H. Bankhead of Alabama or Roger Sullivan of Illinois to win the nomination. Weighing all the political factors, Sullivan promised to come to Wilson's aid at the proper moment. [12] The Illinois delegation caucused on July 2, 1912. On the next ballot Sullivan announced: " 'Illinois casts 18 votes for Clark and 40 for Wilson. Under the rule adopted by the delegation, therefore, all 58 Illinois votes are cast for Wilson!' ... Surlily, Clark men shouted: 'What did you get for it, Roger?' 'The choice of this convention, that's all!' was the retort." [13] Wilson was later quoted as saying, "I can never forget Illinois." Wilson need have had no fear on that point; Roger Sullivan never allowed anyone, friend or foe, to forget a favor. [14]

By the end of the national conventions Illinois Progressives must have had some sobering second thoughts about the course of Progressivism in politics. They had watched Wilson suffer an ignominious defeat in the Illinois preferential primary and then go on to win the nomination through the machinations of their arch rival, Roger Sullivan. They saw Theodore Roosevelt win a smashing victory in the same primary and then lose the Republican nomination in the Credentials Committee sessions in Chicago. Now they had to choose

[10] Harrison, *Stormy Years*, 326.

[11] *Ibid.*, 327–28; Link, *Wilson*, I, 441.

[12] Link, *Wilson*, I, 458–59; Joseph P. Tumulty, *Woodrow Wilson As I Knew Him* (Garden City, N.Y.: Doubleday, Page, 1921), 99.

[13] William F. McCombs, *Making Woodrow Wilson President*, ed. Louis Jay Lang (New York: Fairview Publishing Co., 1921), 173–74.

[14] Link, *Wilson*, I, 470.

whether to remain loyal to the Republican party, to follow Roosevelt to Armageddon, or to follow Wilson in spite of his reliance on the Sullivan machine.

A further cause for soul searching arose in the aftermath of the Lorimer investigations. The Senate Committee on Privileges and Elections presented a majority report that exonerated Lorimer personally and dismissed as inconclusive the evidence of corruption exposed by the investigation. A minority report, submitted by Senator Luke Lea, held that the election was invalid because corrupt means had been used. On July 13, 1912, the Senate adopted the Lea resolution by a vote of fifty-five to twenty-eight. Illinois needed a new senator.[15]

The Forty-Eighth General Assembly of Illinois, which convened in January, 1913, faced the dual tasks of selecting a successor to fill Lorimer's unexpired term and of electing a full-term senator to replace retiring Senator Shelby Cullom at the end of his regular term. The composition of the General Assembly reflected the political upheavals of the autumn elections.

	Senate	House	Joint Ballot [16]
Democrats	24	73	97
Republicans	26	51	77
Progressives (Bull Moose)	1	25	26
Socialists	0	3	3

With party lines shattered by the Bull Moose split and with factionalism rampant in the Democratic ranks the possibilities for bargains and alliances were numerous.

Political observers and leaders in Illinois were in a quandary. Some regarded the regular Republican candidate, Lawrence Y. Sherman, as "a second rate reactionary politician of erratic disposition." [17] The Chicago Democrats supported the candidacy of Colonel James Hamilton Lewis, a former stevedore who had worked his way up to

[15] Senate Election Cases, 1113. For the majority report, see 1031–97; for the minority report, see 1098–1113.

[16] Langland, Chicago Almanac for 1914, 458.

[17] Walter S. Rogers, "The Embarrassing Mr. Sullivan," Harper's Weekly, LIX (Oct. 24, 1914), 395.

become a great trial lawyer and a congressman. He was chiefly known in the press for "his red beard, his matched rings, cuff links and scarf pins, his punctilious selection of hats, ties, vests and socks." [18] The Democrats hoped to ride the crest of the Wilson wave and to capture both Senate seats. Republican leaders feared that any move to defeat Lewis' bid for the full-term vacancy would lead to an alliance between reform-minded Democrats and Bull Moose Progressives. The result was a complete deadlock in the legislature. [19]

When Wilson was inaugurated on March 4, 1913, Illinois presented the bizarre spectacle of a state without representation in the United States Senate. Carter Harrison and Governor E. F. Dunne of Illinois sought administration support for Lewis' candidacy. But the two former Clark supporters met with little success. Ten days after the inauguration Secretary of State Bryan announced that he would address the Illinois legislature as a private citizen. Lewis supporters claimed that Bryan was bringing secret instructions from Wilson that would break the deadlock. [20]

During the balloting in the Illinois General Assembly on February 20, 1913, Carl Vrooman received one vote for the short-term position. Throughout the balloting the total number of votes cast for Vrooman varied from ten to thirty-five. [21] He was well known among downstate Democrats as a Bryan-Wilson Progressive, and his reputation had been enhanced when Louis Brandeis called him to Boston to aid in the investigation of the New England railway situation. If either Brandeis or Bryan could secure Wilson's endorsement for Carl's candidacy, insurgent Democrats in Illinois might rally to his support. [22]

Bryan addressed the Illinois legislature on March 18, 1913, and

---

[18] "A Glance at the Real J. Hamilton Lewis," *The Commoner*, XIV (June, 1914), 19.
[19] New York *Times*, Feb. 2, 1913, p. 2, col. 5.
[20] *Ibid.*, March 5, 1913, p. 4, col. 7; March 16, 1913, p. 2, col. 2.
[21] State of Illinois, *Journal of the Senate of the Forty-Eighth General Assembly of the State of Illinois* (Springfield: 1914), 510–11 (5th ballot: 1 vote), 524–25 (6th ballot: 10 votes), 541–43 (7th ballot: 20 votes), 558–59 (8th ballot: 10 votes), 574–75 (9th ballot: 14 votes), 601–602 (10th ballot: 11 votes), 622–23 (11th ballot: 34 votes), and 642–43 (12th ballot: 35 votes).
[22] Carl Vrooman, "The Present Railway Situation in the United States: Regulation versus Public Ownership," *Twentieth Century*, VII (March, 1913), 99; *Illinois State Register* (Springfield), Jan. 30, 1913, reprinted in "Vrooman for Senator" handbill, Vrooman papers.

pontificated upon the glories of the direct election of senators; however, he carried no secret message from Wilson. Although Bryan
refused officially to take a hand in the senatorial deadlock, he did
confer privately with the Roosevelt men to secure their support for
Lewis. On March 25, 1913, after the thirteenth joint ballot, four
major candidates were locked in an inconclusive struggle for the
short-term vacancy.

Total number of votes cast	184
Total number of votes needed	93
Lawrence Y. Sherman (R)	62
Charles Boeschenstein (D)	43
Carl Vrooman (D)	24
Frank H. Funk (P)	24

The Republican leaders finally reached an agreement with the Democratic leaders, and sufficient votes were exchanged to insure the
election of Sherman for the short-term position and of Lewis for
the full six-year term.[23]

Once again the Progressive forces in Illinois had to swallow a
bitter pill. By their divisions and political wranglings they had
weakened their own cause. Wilson's silence and Bryan's hesitant
role had secured Lewis' election at the price of giving the reactionary
Sherman a temporary berth in the Senate. Ironically, on May 31,
1913, President Wilson announced the adoption of the seventeenth
amendment. They could at least hope that a Progressive-minded
candidate would win the first direct election for a United States
senator from Illinois when Sherman's term expired. Their optimism
was rudely shaken in September, 1913, when Roger Sullivan intimated that he would seek the Democratic senatorial nomination
in the spring primary.[24]

Carl Vrooman decided that the time had arrived to make a stand
against Sullivanism. As one of the outspoken Progressive intellectuals in the country, he had joined the Committee of Fifty, which

[23] New York *Times,* March 19, 1913, p. 7, col. 3; March 27, 1913, p. 8, col. 4;
Langland, *Chicago Almanac for 1914,* 458; State of Illinois, *Journal of the Senate,*
662–63.
[24] New York *Times,* Sept. 7, 1913, sec. II, p. 9, col. 2; Oct. 4, 1913, p. 22, col. 4.

sponsored the First National Conference on Popular Government at Washington, D.C., on December 6, 1913. It resulted in the formation of the National Popular Government League. Carl served on the finance committee of the newly formed league. Knowing that he enjoyed the respect and support of the leading Progressives in the league, he announced his candidacy for the United States Senate in opposition to Sullivan.[25]

Carl launched a vigorous primary campaign with the slogan "Down with Sullivanism! Let the People Rule!" An editorial in the *Wisconsin State Journal* commented favorably on his platform: "In his platform he declares that he believes in 'regulated competition' as advocated by President Wilson and other exponents of the new freedom. He approves of voluntary co-operation in business and industry whenever possible. He believes in the gradual adoption of public ownership and operation of natural monopolies. 'I believe,' he declares, 'in the recall, the short ballot, the full right of suffrage for women and in the right of labor to organize. And I pledge myself to work unremittingly for the abolition of human exploitation in all its forms.'"[26] La Follette supporters praised his stand against "sodden commercialized politics." Senator Robert Owen joined the chorus of praise in a special interview for the Chicago *Daily News*. As Carl's campaign progressed, rumors were circulated in the press that Secretary of State Bryan would soon endorse his candidacy.[27]

Bryan was deeply concerned by the Sullivan candidacy. When Sullivan announced that he was in full accord with Wilson's policies, Bryan denounced Sullivan as the Lorimer of the Democratic party. Sullivan supporters tried to disparage Bryan's opposition as personal

[25] "The Committee of Fifty Proposing the National Popular Government League," undated letter in the Christian Sorensen papers, Nebraska State Historical Society, Lincoln; New York *Times,* Dec. 7, 1913, sec. IV, p. 10, col. 1; [Norman Hapgood], "The Senator from Illinois," *Harper's Weekly,* LVIII (Jan. 3, 1914), 3. Senator Robert Owen presented a copy of an article by Carl Vrooman to the Senate on Dec. 3, 1913. U.S., Congress, Senate, *Journal of the United States Senate,* 63d Cong., 2d Sess., 1913–1914, p. 10; Carl Schurz Vrooman, *Initiative and Referendum in Switzerland,* 63d Cong., 2d Sess., 1913–1914, Senate Doc. 253, *Senate Documents,* XXVI.

[26] Richard Lloyd Jones, "A Clear Solution," *Wisconsin State Journal* (Madison), Jan. 6, 1914, reprinted in a handbill, "Vrooman for Senator," Vrooman papers.

[27] "Vrooman for Senator" handbill, Vrooman papers, quoting: *La Follette's Weekly,* Feb. 14, 1914; special correspondence for the Chicago *Daily News,* dated Washington, March 18, 1914; and Mattoon (Ill.) *Commercial-Star,* March 22, 1914.

rather than official, and they pictured Sullivan as a moderate who was simply moving with the times. Since the Illinois primary law allowed plurality nominations, Bryan feared that divisions among the Progressives would aid Sullivan. He decided to intervene personally in the contest to unite support for Democrat Lawrence B. Stringer.[28]

In reviewing Bryan's decision later, the Washington correspondent for *Harper's Weekly* noted: "It was most unfortunate, as all progressives see now, that when Secretary Bryan interfered in the Illinois campaign he was not better informed as to the real situation. Carl Vrooman had made a most aggressive campaign against Sullivan and all that he stood for. In the event of his nomination he would have had the support of Raymond Robins, and all the National Progressive strength he could have thrown to Vrooman. But Bryan, following the counsels of Dunne and Harrison, was persuaded that Stringer would be the best candidate to oppose Sullivan." [29] Carl withdrew from the race at the personal request of Bryan and supported Stringer's candidacy. Shortly after his withdrawal, he was appointed assistant secretary of agriculture in the Wilson administration.[30]

The results of the Illinois primary on September 9, 1914, were discouraging. Roger Sullivan defeated Lawrence Stringer by a plurality of 31,000 votes. Raymond Robins, the Bull Moose candidate, made a poor showing, and Lawrence Sherman won the Republican race by a wide margin. Senator Norris submitted a resolution in the Senate calling for an investigation of the expenses of the candidates involved in the Illinois and Pennsylvania senatorial primaries. The move was regarded as an attack by the Progressives on Roger Sullivan and Senator Boies Penrose of Pennsylvania. Carl Vrooman, who

[28] New York *Times,* Jan. 18, 1914, p. 4, col. 8; [William Jennings Bryan], "Sullivan, Senator: No!" *The Commoner,* XIV (Feb., 1914), 2; Peter Clark Macfarlane, "Is Roger Sullivan a Boss?" *Colliers,* LIII (Aug. 8, 1914), 5–6, 29–30; William Jennings Bryan, "Get Together," *The Commoner,* XIV (March, 1914), 4; "Shall Illinois Democracy Commit Suicide?" *The Commoner,* XIV (June, 1914), 2.

[29] McGregor(pseud.), "Around the Capitol," *Harper's Weekly,* LIX (Oct. 17, 1914), 377–78.

[30] Interview with Carl Vrooman on Nov. 28, 1960. He joined the Wilson administration on Aug. 12, 1914. See U.S. Dept. of Agriculture, *Program of Work of the United States Department of Agriculture for Fiscal Year 1915* (Washington: Government Printing Office, 1914), 27, n. 1.

had financed his own campaign, testified on the high cost of campaigning against Sullivan, but the investigation was stymied by a lack of facts to back up the allegations of corrupt practices leveled against Sullivan and Penrose.[31]

The nomination of Sullivan brought Carl face to face with the problem of party loyalty. If anyone thought that his silence had been purchased by his appointment to a post in the administration, they might well have pondered the statement that Carl issued shortly after the Illinois primary:

I am told that certain editorial writers in Illinois profess a feeling of uncertainty as to how I shall vote and how my influence will be thrown in the coming campaign. It has even been suggested that my silence has been arranged for by the simple process of stopping my mouth with pie. While it is manifest that a man who even in a moderate capacity has become a part of the federal administration must so far as possible refrain from doing or saying anything that could involve or embarrass the administration [sic].

At the same time a federal officeholder does not become an automaton or a political eunuch.[32]

Shortly thereafter, he "sent word to the President that he was leaving Washington to stump the state of Illinois for Raymond Robins, the Bull Moose candidate, on the ground that Roger Sullivan was not a genuine Democrat, and that his resignation was ready at any time if he wished to accept it." [33]

The National Progressive party candidate, Raymond Robins, was a former coal miner, lawyer, gold prospector, Alaskan settler, settle-

[31] U.S., Congress, Senate, *Journal of the United States Senate*, 63d Cong., 2d Sess., 1913–1914, pp. 512–13; New York *Times,* Sept. 17, 1914, p. 8, col. 8; Sept. 19, 1914, p. 10, col. 2; Chicago *Journal,* Sept. 25, 1914; Chicago *Record-Herald,* Sept. 27, 1914; clippings in Vrooman scrapbook for 1914, Vrooman papers. For the final report, see U.S., Congress, Senate, *Expenditure of Money by Candidates for United States Senate,* Report No. 979, 63d Cong., 3d Sess., 1915, *Senate Reports,* B, 6765.

[32] *Daily Bulletin* (Bloomington, Ill.), Sept. 13, 1914, clipping in Vrooman scrapbook for 1914, Vrooman papers.

[33] "The Foremost Democratic Dirt Farmer," a mimeographed document prepared for the 1924 Democratic National Convention to boost Carl Vrooman for vice-president, 6, Vrooman papers; Washington *Post,* Oct. 23, 1914, clipping in the Vrooman scrapbook for 1914, Vrooman papers.

ment worker, and labor sympathizer. The National Popular Government League supported the Robins campaign to oppose both Sullivan and Senator Sherman. Downstate Wilsonian Democrats, who had favored Stringer in the primaries, and the Bryan-Wilson Democratic League, which had supported Carl Vrooman, joined the Robins movement.[34]

The question of party loyalty plagued the insurgent Democrats who supported Robins. In a speech at Effingham, Illinois, Carl said, "I am frequently asked by Sullivan henchmen why I do not support the 'straight ticket.' ... I make reply that I am supporting all the ticket that is straight." [35] Senator Owen, in a letter to Raymond Robins, accused Sullivan of commercialized politics. Even Carter Harrison, the old-line Democratic regular, refused to campaign for Sullivan. Secretary of the Navy Josephus Daniels reluctantly refused to speak in Illinois on behalf of Sullivan.[36]

Party loyalty was only one of the complicating factors in the campaign. Sullivan, the "wet" candidate, was endorsed by the brewery interests, while Sherman had the support of the "dry" forces. Both Sherman and Robins were Protestants; Sullivan was a Catholic. The nativist Guardians of Liberty, on the one side, and the Roman Catholic Vereins Bund, on the other, tried to secure pledges from the candidates to support their respective positions. Robins had the endorsement of Theodore Roosevelt and of insurgent Wilson Democrats. He could not either be for or wholly against the Wilson administration. Sullivan, on the other hand, received the Wilson administration's blessing when Joseph Tumulty telephoned Democratic National Committeeman Charles Boeschenstein to assure him that the administration desired Sullivan's election.[37] The totals tell the tale:

[34] George Fitch, "Politics in Illinois," *Colliers*, LIV (Oct. 24, 1914), 22; Judson King, *The First Year and a Look Ahead* (Washington, D.C.: National Popular Government League, 1915), 12; McGregor, *Harper's Weekly*, LIX, 377-78.

[35] Effingham (Ill.) *Record*, Oct. 31, 1914; clipping in Vrooman scrapbook for 1914, Vrooman papers.

[36] New York *Times*, Oct. 9, 1914, p. 6, col. 6; Harrison, *Stormy Years*, 330; Josephus Daniels, *The Wilson Era*, I: *Years of Peace: 1910–1917* (Chapel Hill: University of North Carolina Press, 1944), 426.

[37] Fitch, *Colliers*, LIV, 22; Rogers, *Harper's Weekly*, LIX, 522; New York *Times*, Nov. 1, 1914, sec. III, p. 3, col. 4.

Raymond Robins (P)	203,027
Roger Sullivan (D)	373,403
Lawrence Sherman (R)	390,661

An editorial writer for the New York *Times* observed that direct election of senators had "resulted precisely as the old indirect elections would have resulted." [38]

Carl's brief foray into politics illustrated the difficulties of achieving power by espousing Progressive proposals, on the one hand, and of acting on the basis of the Progressive theory of politics, on the other. He adapted his program of reform to fit the requirements of Wilson's New Freedom. The acceptance of regulated competition, the approval of voluntary cooperation, the advocacy of public ownership of natural monopolies, and the belief in the efficacy of procedural reforms—these planks in Carl's platform all represented slight modifications of his previous beliefs.

Carl's vigorous primary campaign against Sullivanism was a model of Progressive politics in action. In withdrawing from the primary race at Bryan's request he heeded the age-old political maxim of loyalty to the best interests of the cause. In offering to sacrifice his newly acquired position in the Wilson administration to support the Robins campaign he acted according to the highest dictates of the Progressive theory of politics. He risked his personal career to fight for the principles that he supported. His ability to win votes was never tested, but his ability to lead the reform faction of his party was tried—and was not found wanting. His experiences during the period from 1910 to 1914 showed that the achievement of Progressive goals was a difficult task. With the public power that had been given to him by proxy through an appointment to the Department of Agriculture he set out to accomplish whatever was possible in translating his reform program into reality.

THE NEW AGRICULTURE, 1914–1916

In his capacity as assistant secretary of agriculture Carl Vrooman attempted to translate his belief in equality of opportunity into

[38] Langland, *Chicago Almanac for 1915*, 477; New York *Times*, Nov. 4, 1914, p. 6, col. 2.

practical programs for agricultural interests. A number of changes had taken place in American agriculture since the heyday of the Grangers and the Populists. During the golden age of agricultural prosperity in the first decade of the twentieth century new business-oriented farm organizations adopted pressure-group tactics to replace the majoritarian democracy of the earlier periods. The leaders of these new agricultural groups sought to raise prices by decreasing and controlling the volume of crop production and to increase profits by reducing the cost of marketing through cooperative associations. In effect, the new tactics implied a shift in the concept of entrepreneurship from the individual farmer to the corporate unit, the producers' or marketing cooperative, and a restriction of agrarian agitation to the needs of the more successful, highly capitalized, and efficient producers.[39]

In Carl's view the new tactics did not mean that the agricultural groups had abandoned their reform positions. In a speech in Chicago on November 29, 1915, he said: "We are engaged in no small pursuit. *The gospel of the New Agriculture* means something more than a few more dollars in your pocket or mine. It means the building up on this continent of a new civilization based upon the spirit of co-operation—for you can no more realize the possibilities of the New Agriculture as individualists and Ishmaelites than you can realize the possibilities of self-government unless you have within yourselves the spirit of democracy." [Italics added][40] He announced that the Department of Agriculture intended "to work not only *for* the farmer, but *with* the farmer" and with all business enterprises closely connected with agriculture. These three ideas—that agriculture was the foundation of civilization, that cooperation was the hope of the future, and that the government should foster both—were, of course, familiar themes. But Carl intended to give them a new relevance by associating them with the changes in agrarian tactics.[41]

"What farmers need most to know," he asserted, "is how to make

[39] Hofstadter, *The Age of Reform*, 109–12; Carl Vrooman, "Small Returns from Big Crops; Big Returns from Small Crops," draft of article for *Corn Belt Farmer* (Des Moines), Jan. 24, 1915, Vrooman papers.

[40] U.S. Dept. of Agriculture, *Proceedings of a Conference to Consider Means for Combating Foot-and-Mouth Disease, Chicago, Illinois, November 29–30, 1915* (Washington: Government Printing Office, 1916), 8.

[41] *Ibid.*, 4.

the *science* of agriculture boost the *business* of farming." Before the Wilson administration, he charged, the Department of Agriculture had regarded itself primarily as an organization for scientific research. Even its publications had the characteristics of scientific reports. Carl designed a new type of farmers' bulletin that was written to serve the needs of specific geographic or crop-growing regions. The new bulletins treated the farm as an economic unit and summarized all pertinent information into practical business suggestions.[42]

He considered the county agent system established by the Smith-Lever Act of 1914 to be the answer to the demands of earlier reformers: "This is the greatest university extension campaign the world has ever seen. It is learning democratized, learning brought out of the laboratories and the libraries, out of the experiment fields and the bulletins, adapted to local conditions, mixed with horse-sense and business gumption, and explained to the individual farmer by a man who lives in his community and understands intimately the needs both of its soil and of its people."[43] The New Agriculture would show the farmer how to increase his crop yields and, at the same time, how to increase his profits.

In reply to the criticism that the Department of Agriculture was fostering "paternalistic state Socialism" Carl said that the department's new policy was simply belated recognition by the government of the historic demands of agricultural groups. Many of the demands voiced by the Grangers, the Greenbackers, and the Populists were embodied in such New Freedom farm acts as the Farm Loan Act, the Federal Aid Road Act, and the Cotton Futures Act. These measures were designed to assure national prosperity by insuring a permanently prosperous agricultural community.[44]

Carl continually reaffirmed the belief that prosperity for the farmer would contribute to "national efficiency" and that such pros-

[42] Carl Vrooman, *Grain Farming in the Corn Belt with Live Stock as a Side Line,* U.S. Dept. of Agriculture, Farmers' Bulletin No. 704 (Washington: Government Printing Office, 1916), 2.

[43] Carl Vrooman, "The Agricultural Revolution," *Century,* N.S. LXXI (Nov., 1916), 115.

[44] Carl Vrooman, "Meeting the Farmer Halfway," *Yearbook of the United States Department of Agriculture for 1916* (Washington: Government Printing Office, 1917), 63–75.

perity could best be achieved through cooperative organizations. For him such organizations represented something more than economic pressure groups: "This is agrarian democracy of a high type, simple, effective community organization for buying and selling. Everybody involved is personally concerned in the conduct of the business. Every division of profits saved is an object-lesson in economics; every meeting of stock-holders is an object-lesson in sociology. There is hope for democratic civilization in such organization." [45] At the same time he knew from bitter personal experience that the progress of cooperation in America was slow. Therefore, he urged the farmers to form a great national federation, similar in function to the American Federation of Labor and the Chamber of Commerce, to protect the farmers' interests until the Department of Agriculture could secure effective laws to place cooperative organizations on a sound business basis. [46]

As an official spokesman for the Department of Agriculture and for the Wilson administration, Carl attempted to clarify the relationship between the government and business. On the one hand, he praised the Wilson administration for daring to "make common cause with the farmer against the usurer, the transportation shark, the fake middleman, and the other human pests" who had plagued farmers in the past. [47] On the other hand, he assured business leaders that the regulatory activities of the Department of Agriculture were designed to bring business practices up to a higher standard.

The truth of the matter is that at present the vast and mighty machinery of government is being utilized not only to redress the wrongs of the weak, ... but it is being employed to encourage and help our commercial and industrial leaders as well so long as their methods are legitimate,

[45] Carl Vrooman, *Century*, N.S. LXXI, 120. In a speech before the Thirty-Third Annual Convention of the Association of Official Agricultural Chemists on Nov. 21, 1916, Carl said, "Before we can develop in this country an invincible national efficiency, we must develop just such a national consciousness, an ideal of nationality, a conception of the whole of which we are only a part." Compare with Frank Vrooman's views, Chapter 8, above.

[46] Carl Vrooman, "Speech before the National Conference on Marketing and Farm Credit, Dec. 9, 1916," Vrooman papers; Carl Vrooman, "Help for the Farmer," *Outlook*, CXIII (July 12, 1916), 624.

[47] Carl Vrooman, "Putting the Farmer on the Map" (speech delivered at Pontiac, Illinois, Aug. 3, 1916), 1, copy in Vrooman papers.

honest and not contrary to public welfare. It believes that the strong can be strong permanently only on condition that their strength is founded upon right and justice, and that the strong are sources of national power and prosperity, and of social and economic advancement, provided they are imbued with the social rather than the anti-social spirit.[48]

But he advised businessmen not to resist the inevitable trend toward cooperative marketing and purchasing associations and warned them not to attempt to seize control of the farmers' movement.[49]

In defending the policies of the Wilson administration, Carl had to make the case for its Progressivism in the face of frequent changes of front by Wilson. Wilson's hostility toward long-range agricultural credit in 1914 and 1915 almost ended in a veto of agricultural-credit legislation. With preelection pressure mounting in 1916, however, he switched his position and supported the bill.

Throughout all the vicissitudes of politics and administration Carl held fast to the conviction that the Wilson administration was helping to achieve the Progressive goal of making success dependent upon "intelligence, determination, and industry" rather than upon the "Machiavellian ability to outwit and spoil" a competitor.[50]

In late 1916 under the title "The Agricultural Revolution" Carl spelled out his vision for the future based on the accomplishments of the Wilson administration.

In the light of what already has been undertaken we may dimly project a vision of a new civilization, a more natural and clement civilization than this, a civilization admittedly agrarian and which glories in the fact that its roots are in the soil, a civilization in which the essentiality and dignity of agriculture are realized by those who follow it, and recognized and respected by those who follow subsidiary vocations—as, indeed, all other vocations are,—a civilization in which the wholesome strength of the soil will avail to heal the canker of unbridled industrialism.[51]

[48] Carl Vrooman, "Address at Omaha, Neb., April 21, 1916, on the Attitude of the Department of Agriculture toward Business," p. 4, Vrooman papers. A similar address, entitled "The Department of Agriculture and the Business Man," was delivered before the Arkansas State Bankers' Association at Little Rock on April 25, 1916. Copy in Vrooman papers.

[49] Carl Vrooman, Century, N.S. LXXI, 121–22.

[50] Arthur S. Link, Woodrow Wilson and the Progressive Era, 1910–1917 (New York: Harper, 1954), 56–59, 225–26; Carl Vrooman, Century, N.S. LXXI, 123. "He who produces more than he acquires is a public benefactor, but . . . he who acquires more than he produces is an economic parasite."

[51] Carl Vrooman, Century, N.S. LXXXI, 119.

But the outbreak of war in Europe in late 1914 had begun to cast a pall over such Progressive dreams. The existence of western civilization itself seemed to be at stake. Increasingly, the United States was forced to confront the issues of preparedness and the prospects of peace.

Carl tried to remain loyal to Wilson's position on preparedness. He supported the administration's plan for an effective army reserve, advocated the maintenance of a small highly trained officer corps, and called for legislation to take the profits out of preparedness. To support the administration's merchant shipping bill he prepared an incisive analysis of it for the Department of Agriculture. He pointed out that agricultural prosperity depended upon the maintenance of expanded foreign markets after the war ended. He feared that once peace was restored private maritime combines would cut off these markets by diverting ships to other cargoes, or that they would deprive American farmers of the benefits of increased prices by raising shipping rates exorbitantly. He therefore proposed that the government own and operate a merchant fleet to insure an adequate supply of ships and to exert pressure on the shipping-rate structure.[52]

The issue of government ownership and preparedness arose again in March, 1916, when Senator Ellison D. Smith of South Carolina introduced a bill calling for the construction and operation by the government of a combined hydroelectric and nitrate fertilizer plant at Muscle Shoals, Alabama. In testimony before the Committee on Agriculture and Forestry Senator Smith said that before launching his plan he had "consulted the Assistant Secretary of Agriculture, Carl S. Vrooman, a pronounced liberal who strongly approved the idea. At Vrooman's direction, Francis G. Caffey, solicitor for the Department of Agriculture, had drafted the bill." [53] Senator Smith's proposal was designed to insure an adequate supply of fertilizer for agriculture in the face of disrupted shipping schedules. It ultimately

---

[52] Carl Vrooman, "Military Education and National Preparedness, A Speech Delivered at the University of Illinois, Jan. 21, 1916," Vrooman papers. See also draft marked "Address by the Assistant Secretary of Agriculture at . . . before the . . . Military Battalion, Jan. . . . , 1916," p. 4, Vrooman papers; Carl Vrooman, *The Farmer and the Shipping Bill,* Senate Doc. No. 395, 64th Cong., 1st Sess., 1916, *Senate Documents,* 42, Part II.

[53] Judson King, *The Conservation Fight: From T.R. to T.V.A.* (Washington: Public Affairs Press, 1959), 63.

became section 124 of the National Defense Act under which President Wilson ordered the construction of the combined hydroelectric and nitrate project to provide nitrates for defense needs and fertilizer for agriculture.[54]

The issue of preparedness went deeper than the question of what means the national government should use to insure an adequate defense and protect its agricultural interests. It was a question of America's role in the modern world. Frank Vrooman saw this more readily than did Carl. For several years, as a promoter of Canadian interests, he had been urging on the British government a policy of deterrent imperial defense.[55]

The outbreak of hostilities in Europe in 1914 seemed to confirm Frank's fears of a contest of empires. In the United States he advocated a program of protective militarism during the early phases of the European conflict. On March 4, 1916, he debated the question of military preparedness with William Jennings Bryan before the National Economic League. Bryan maintained that the United States should set the example for peace by denouncing jingoism and munitions making.[56] Frank was equally emphatic.

There is one thing and one thing only that can save democracy in the United States, and that is a forward movement with a moral mission. We have lost sight of both in our overwhelming prosperity, and we have been content to wax fat and near-sighted. We have come to the point where we must face the questions of duty.... We are confronted not only with an opportunity, but with a mission; and this is why I propose a forward movement of democracy, an alliance of the democracies of the world in the interest of democracy in the world.[57]

[54] *Ibid.*, 62.

[55] See Frank Vrooman, "Some Thoughts on Imperial Organization," *United Empire,* I (March, 1910), 198; *British Columbia and Her Imperial Outlook* (London: Royal Colonial Institute, 1912); "Juijutsu and the Anglo-Japanese Alliance," *British Columbia,* VIII (1912), 59; "Menace of the Anglo-Japanese Alliance," *Britannic Review,* I (1914), 72; "The Imperial Idea: From the Point of View of Vancouver," *Nineteenth Century and After,* LXXIII (March, 1913), 516.

[56] New York *Times,* March 5, 1916, p. 3, col. 7.

[57] Frank Vrooman, "Our Next Step," *Century,* N.S. LXX (June, 1916), 192b. In the debate with Bryan, Frank spoke extemporaneously. No transcript was made. This article is an expanded version of his remarks on that occasion, published at a later date and inserted between pages 192 and 193 of the June, 1916, issue of *Century.* For convenience the pages are here designated by letter.

In short, the United States should arm itself and join an alliance with England, France, Italy, and, perhaps, China to counter the power of Germany and Japan.

Frank was not suggesting preparedness for armed intervention in Europe; he was advocating preparedness for defense of the western hemisphere. He predicted a postwar coalition between Germany and Japan to break the Monroe Doctrine once and for all.[58] His speech contained several solid points offset by hysterical suspicions of "hyphenated Americans," fears of secret Japanese armies in Mexico, and accusations that German military groups were operating in South America. He rejected Bryan's Christian example theory as an attempt at "stamping a Chautauqua civilization willy-nilly upon the rest of the world." He rejected arbitration treaties as scraps of paper and belittled disarmament "so long as there is one aggressive, mad-dog militarist nation left in the world." He also rejected the idea of a league to enforce the peace as a dangerous game of bluff.[59]

In May, 1916, Carl Vrooman also faced the question of the compatibility of his position on preparedness with his Progressive assumptions. The League to Enforce Peace was holding its first convention in Washington. For the session on May 26, 1916, the league invited R. G. Rhett, president of the United States Chamber of Commerce, Samuel Gompers, president of the American Federation of Labor, and Oliver Wilson, president of the National Grange, to speak on the theme "American Interests Affected by the League Program." The main speaker for the evening was Newton D. Baker, secretary of war.[60]

When at the last minute Oliver Wilson could not attend the session, William Howard Taft, president of the League to Enforce Peace, hastily summoned Carl Vrooman to represent the agricultural interests. With only a short time to gather his thoughts Carl delivered

[58] *Ibid.*, 192d.

[59] *Ibid.*, 192b. A number of preparedness advocates rallied to Frank's banner and formed the Federation for Democracy with offices in Washington and New York. Frank was designated president of the Board of Trustees. When a Wilson critic voiced his opinions in the New York City Harvard Club in 1918, Frank threw him out and pursued him up the street. New York *Times*, Jan. 27, 1918, sec. I, p. 6, col. 3. Frank Vrooman died in Bloomington, Ill., on Sept. 22, 1951.

[60] *Tentative Program, First Annual Assemblage, League to Enforce Peace, May 26–27, 1916,* pamphlet, Harvard University collection on International Organizations, Widener Library, Harvard.

an eloquent address in which he sounded some of the same themes that Frank had evoked in his debate with Bryan a few months before: "If the nations of the world that stand for peace, international law, justice and responsible self-government adopt a negative, sentimental policy of disarmament, national self-sufficiency and isolation, it seems not only probable but inevitable that the protagonists of the cult of the superman will keep the world in a tumult of Machiavellian intrigue and carnage, until they either achieve the conquest of the world, or teach the sentimental, sloppy-minded nations *to arm and unite for self-defence* and the preservation of peace and civilization." [Italics added] [61] Carl's call for armed strength reflected the view he had been expressing in preparedness speeches across the country. "Might never makes right," he granted, "but not infrequently it is essential to the maintenance of right." To have a successful preparedness program and to prevent the misuse of its new power the United States would have to take steps to democratize the military establishment, put it on a sound and efficient financial base, and eliminate profits from preparedness by appropriate legislation.[62]

Looking beyond the confines of the United States, Carl proposed an organization of the "peace-and-justice loving nations of the world" to launch a "winning peace crusade." This crusade could eventually lead to a federation of the world, he prophesied. Like Frank, Carl had united the idea of preparedness with the idea of an alliance of nations. The difference between Frank's "alliance of the democracies of the world in the interest of democracy in the world" and Carl's "winning peace crusade" lay in the conception of the peace for which they were willing to use force. Where Frank sought to preserve Anglo-Saxon supremacy, Carl wanted "a peace with a purpose" founded on "the principles of political equality, intellectual liberty and social justice." [63]

President Wilson appeared before a session of the League to Enforce Peace on the day after Carl's address and delivered a major

[61] "Address before the League to Enforce Peace, Washington, D.C., May 26, 1916," p. 2, copy in Vrooman papers.
[62] *Ibid.*, 3–5.
[63] *Ibid.*, 9–11.

statement on American foreign policy. A few days before the address he had agreed in a conference with Colonel House to tone down the language of his address so as not to antagonize the Allies at a crucial moment in diplomacy. Peace, not preparedness, was uppermost in Wilson's mind. He only hinted at unilateral peace moves by the United States. Even his call for a postwar League of Nations was disguised under the ambiguous term, a "universal association of the nations." Such an association could help to maintain freedom of the seas, the integrity of treaties, and the political independence of all nations.[64]

In keeping with Wilson's new mood Carl submitted a milder version of his address for the printed proceedings of the meeting. The new version said that just as the farmers were learning to cooperate, so the nations of the world must cooperate in an "international syndicate of nations to underwrite the peace." To insure a permanent peace a "dominant public consciousness in favor of peace" would have to be built up by encouraging the "sentiment of mankind in favor of the productive type" of individual rather than the "predatory type." [65]

By the end of 1916 Carl could look back with satisfaction upon two years of loyal service to the Wilson administration. He had worked to turn his vision of a civilization resting on a firm agricultural base into a program for government action. He had confronted politics as the "science of the possible" and had operated within the ground rules of practical politics. But he was also a Progressive and had brought all of the assumptions, methods, and values of the Progressive mind with him.

The Progressive theory of politics rested ultimately on certain religious and psychological beliefs. The question that confronted

[64] Arthur S. Link, *Woodrow Wilson*, IV: *Campaigns for Progressivism and Peace* (Princeton: Princeton University Press, 1965), 24–26. For background of the House draft of the speech, see pp. 18–23.

[65] Carl Vrooman, "American Agriculture and the League to Enforce Peace," *Enforced Peace: Proceedings of the First Annual National Assemblage of the League to Enforce Peace, Washington, May 26–27, 1916* (New York: League to Enforce Peace, 1916), 115–22. A copy of this address marked "Original of Mr. Vrooman's Speech before the League to Enforce Peace" is in the Vrooman papers. The content of the speech actually given was verified by a conversation with Carl Vrooman on Nov. 29, 1960.

the Progressive-turned-politician was simply this: how could he reconcile the demands of principle and expediency in the struggle for the political power with which to realize his program of reform? Carl's wife vividly portrayed the Progressive's attitude toward this question in a romantic novel, *The High Road to Honor*. The heroine, Mathilde, counsels a freshman senator who faces this problem: "If it is a question of power, is it not wiser and surer in the end, to depend on power which comes as a result of adherence to what we know is right, than on the kind that comes from any lower source —which must, in the very nature of things, be a lower form of power. It's one sort of power that can keep one a senator, but sometimes quite another that can keep one a *man*." [66]

Principle above party; duty above expediency. This was the essence of the Progressive creed. According to the Progressive theory of politics, social direction "was to come from the Man of Good Will who had transcended his own interests; he governed by right of his moral superiority." [67] Carl had demonstrated his devotion to principle when he jeopardized his position in the Wilson administration to campaign against Roger Sullivan. He had shown his appreciation of the necessity of compromise when he supported Wilson's program of preparedness legislation. He rested his case for Progressive legislation in other areas on the premise that, with appropriate encouragement from the government, men of good will would overcome their self-interest by a combination of cooperation and idealism. But would men, in fact, hold on to idealism when their interests were challenged by extraordinary events?

Senator David Brandon, the fictional hero of *The High Road to Honor*, confronted this limitation and, in a moment of inspiration, saw beyond the Progressive concept of leadership to the heart of the psychological problem that confronted American civilization. The people had put their faith in an erroneous conception of equality. "This keynote idea of our American political and economic faith unfortunately has become distorted, until to-day in the minds of millions of our citizens, both rich and poor, a feeling has developed

[66] Julia Scott Vrooman, *The High Road to Honor* (New York: Minton, Balch, 1925), 209, 212.
[67] Burnham, *American Quarterly*, XII, 458.

that America owes every citizen an opportunity to exploit not only the natural resources of the country, but his fellow countrymen as well." [68] Brandon pointed out to a friend that "standards of corporation morality and honor are conspicuously lower" than the personal standards of morality of businessmen. He also saw that neither the ballot nor the legislative process could save the people until they had broken the mental shackles that bound them to their self-centered greed. Only by losing themselves in the pursuit of the ideal could the people find the true democracy, which was "organized righteousness in government." [69]

The similarity between David Brandon's political creed and Carl Vrooman's conception of Progressivism was not, of course, purely coincidental. In the end Carl had to offer only what Brandon had seen in his moment of insight—the faith that men would act as the Progressive theory assumed they would act. As political action proved an unrewarding means toward what he regarded as desirable and "possible," Carl was driven to relying completely on the religious and psychological beliefs that underlay his Progressive theory of politics. With the chaos of the First World War spread before him he returned to these themes constantly. Whether his views could survive the acid test of war remained to be seen.

[68] J. S. Vrooman, *The High Road to Honor*, 82.
[69] *Ibid.*, 151, 284–88.

Chapter Ten

Equality for Agriculture, 1917-1937

THE NEW PATRIOTISM, 1917-1918

The entry of the United States into the European war in April of 1917 did not, as some recent historians have maintained, mark the end of the Progressive movement in reform. By defining reform as an antibusiness sentiment rather than as an expression of the entrepreneurial sentiment of one segment of the total "business" community against another—an expression of resentment at restrictions on their ability to do business—these historians have ignored important continuities in the wartime period.[1] True, civil liberties were suppressed, particularly for Socialists, German-Americans, and conscientious objectors; on the other hand, social justice gains were protected by the representatives of organized labor who served on the wartime boards and agencies. The drive for rationality in industry, pushed by professional managers and corporate financiers, had official sanction under the War Industries Board. Even the operation of the railroads under a unified government administration seemed but an extension of the arguments advanced by reformers during the previous decades.[2]

The protracted debate over wartime policies was, in its essential arguments, an extension of the prewar controversy over the proper role of government in social change. Increased government activity during the war provided a dramatic confirmation of the tenets of the New Nationalism and established the precedents for later reform agitation. Carl recognized the significance of the increased wartime activity by the Department of Agriculture in an article published shortly after the declaration of war: "For the first time in our history we are now thinking, planning, and purposing agriculturally in the terms of the nation.... A country-wide agricultural program is now demanded in which nothing shall be overlooked and everything shall be dealt with in its right proportion with the common good as the primary consideration." [3] The task of translating policy into performance had created new problems that taxed the assumptions of the Progressives and involved them in an extended debate over the problems of administration, organization, and methods of social control. This debate had emerged gradually in the early months of 1917 from the conflicting attempts by government departments and legislative committees to cope with the problems created by the European war. The immediate concern of the Department of Agriculture was to increase food production. Crops already had been planted in some areas of the country, and seasonal conditions threatened to reduce production in others. Long-range questions of policy and procedure were thrust aside temporarily in a frantic effort to meet this emergency.

[1] Eric F. Goldman, *Rendezvous with Destiny: A History of Modern American Reform,* rev. ed. (New York: Vintage Books, 1958), 195–96: "America was scarcely in the war before it was taxing the conscience of Weyl and thousands of the progressives. All the dismal predictions Wilson had made to Frank Cobb rapidly came true. Reform stopped dead, large-scale business swiftly increased its profits and its power, inflation began its ravaging. Civil liberties were twisted, narrowed, virtually abolished in the traditional American meaning of the phrase." It is obvious from the context and implication of this passage that Goldman is using primarily a social justice definition of reform. The entrepreneurial tradition in reform with its emphasis on stabilizing the profits of industry and on artificially inducing inflation is ignored. Compare with Richard Hofstadter, *The Age of Reform: Bryan to F.D.R.* (New York: Alfred A. Knopf, 1956), 273–74, 279.

[2] An example of the success of a social justice group in maintaining prewar Progressive gains is found in the history of the Women's Trade Union League. Organized in 1903 by women trade union leaders and wealthy suffragettes, the WTUL helped secure state legislation for shorter hours and equal pay for women. When the National Council of Defense was established, representatives of the WTUL were included on a committee on women in industry, although the trade unions accounted for less than 10 percent of the working women in industry. When munition manufacturers proposed a ten-hour day for war workers, the WTUL representatives successfully defeated it by appealing to studies of decreased efficiency in British industry under a similar plan. Samuel Gompers secured similar gains for organized labor through the War Labor Board and War Labor Policies Board. See article on Mary McDowell in Edward T. James, ed., *Notable American Women, 1607–1957: A Biographical Dictionary* (Cambridge: Belknap Press, 1968).

[3] Carl Vrooman, "The Present Agricultural Situation," *Review of Reviews, American Edition,* LV (May, 1917), 503.

Carl Vrooman assumed the leadership of this task. He issued a statement on March 25, 1917, urging citizens to transform their yards and vacant lots into war gardens and asking the farmers to diversify their crops. A week later he advocated putting the nation on a "war bread" basis.[4] While Secretary of Agriculture Houston held an important policy-making meeting in St. Louis on April 9, 1917, Carl embarked on a whirlwind tour of the South. His task was to convince southern farmers of the need for crop diversification and regional self-sufficiency. The response was overwhelming, and southern farmers plowed up part of their cotton crops and planted food crops. The goal of this regional self-sufficiency program was to free for export the three-quarters of a billion dollars' worth of food normally shipped from the Midwest and North to the South during the winter.[5]

There were broader issues at stake than the percentage of milled wheat turned into usable flour or the regional self-sufficiency of the South. The New Freedom legislation aiding farmers, consumers, businessmen, and labor unions had implied a rough standard of equality among functional economic groups in the society. This relative equality was to be maintained by a shifting pattern of legally sanctioned privileges, government supports, and tax preferments. Whether this standard of functional equality could be maintained in the face of wartime conditions was a question that the Progressives had to face immediately.

Carl saw part of the problem; however, his Progressive premises and his own interest in agriculture kept him from seeing the entire problem in perspective. In March, 1917, a month before the declaration of war, he had written, "If national policy decrees that there

[4] New York *Times*, March 25, 1917, p. 2, col. 5; April 1, 1917, sec. I, p. 15, col. 7. The war garden idea was reminiscent of the scheme promoted by Mayor Pingree of Detroit during the 1893 depression whereby unemployed workers were encouraged to grow potatoes in vacant lots in the city. With the encouragement of Carl Vrooman in the Department of Agriculture a National Emergency Food Garden Commission was established to promote this voluntary project.
[5] Carl Vrooman, "What American Farmers Have Done This Year," *Review of Reviews, American Edition*, LVI (Nov., 1917), 500–501; New York *Times*, April 30, 1917, p. 14, col. 3; Carl Vrooman to Jules Jusserand, July 25, 1929, Vrooman papers. See also Carl Vrooman, "Address Before the Georgia Chamber of Commerce, April 6, 1917," Vrooman papers.

should be a big increase in our acreage and yields per acre of food crops, then *the nation as a whole, and not the farmers as a class, should and must assume the major part of the risk involved.*" [Italics added] [6] Increasing production would be only half the battle, however. The traditional policies of the Department of Agriculture were not designed to cope with the inflation that would accompany agricultural mobilization. Also, since no one knew how long the war would last or to what extent American farmers would be called upon to feed defeated nations, a government commitment to underwrite agricultural expansion implied a permanent policy of government aid to agriculture. Government action to insure equality of opportunity for agricultural entrepreneurs was one thing; government action to protect them from the risks of entrepreneurship was another.

There were other voices in the debate over a comprehensive agricultural policy. In February, 1917, Herbert Hoover, chairman of the Commission for Relief in Belgium, had submitted a memorandum to Colonel House outlining his approach to the food problem. Hoover's experience with relief problems in Europe convinced him that the solution of the problem required the centralization of authority for efficient administration. "The Allied parliaments were not only fearful of delegating [adequate] powers, but they were even more fearful of anything that looked like centralization of such powers. The result of this attitude was a multitude of boards, commissions, and committees among which power was to be divided. And in this departure from centuries of experience in the administration of private enterprise, there was no single individual in administrative command." [7] The "law of supply and demand" would be obsolete in a wartime economy. Hoover believed that a government food administration, to prevent profiteering and hoarding, would have to "buy the major commodities as near to the farm-market level as possible" and resell them to Allied, military, and domestic purchasers "under regulations covering markups, profits, and conservation measures." [8]

---

[6] New York *Times,* March 25, 1917, p. 2, col. 5.

[7] Herbert Hoover, *An American Epic,* II: *Famine in Forty-Five Nations and Organization Behind the Front, 1914–1923* (Chicago: Henry Regnery, 1960), 7.

[8] *Ibid.,* 12–13.

Secretary of Agriculture Houston transmitted the administration's plan for agricultural mobilization to the Senate on April 20, 1917. The administration plan called for a Food Administration armed with the power to establish prices on basic commodities. The bill soon became bogged down in a prolonged debate. Carl jumped into the foray with sensational charges that a lobby of "food speculators, food cornerers, and food gamblers" was seeking to prevent effective legislation. When grain futures on the Chicago Exchange took a sharp rise, he solemnly warned that the crisis had been joined. "It is an issue between food control by the Government," he asserted, "and food control by the speculators." [9]

Business interests were not the only forces delaying legislation, however. Some farm leaders felt that price controls would deprive them of income as Allied and speculative buyers bid against each other in the market. Above all, "the idea of economic control was objectionable to farmers as it involved their freedom to do business when, as, and how they pleased; but they were willing to receive guaranteed prices." [10] As Congress delayed action on agricultural legislation during the summer of 1917, President Wilson instructed Hoover to launch a voluntary food conservation program. Congress finally overcame the objections of contending parties and passed the Lever Food and Fuel Control Act in August, 1917. A rough division of responsibility was established between the Department of Agriculture, which concentrated on production problems, and the new Food Administration, which handled the problems of distribution control and price supports. [11]

Carl's oratorical attacks on those who opposed the policies of the Wilson administration did not go unnoticed. When he remarked that the United States would have to put five million men in the trenches if Russia withdrew from the war, Senator James R. Mann of Illinois replied, "I do not know whether [the Russians] will [withdraw] or not, ... but it was not wise for the Assistant Secretary of Agriculture to make such a statement which at this time is foolish

[9] New York *Times,* May 12, 1917, p. 20, col. 1; May 13, 1917, p. 5, cols. 2–3.

[10] James H. Shideler, *Farm Crisis, 1919–1923* (Berkeley: University of California Press, 1957), 13.

[11] *Ibid.,* 12–14. The Wilson administration dropped the request for maximum price controls on Hoover's recommendation. See New York *Times,* June 8, 1919, p. 4, col. 5.

beyond belief. I do not wonder that some gentlemen here hesitate to grant to under officials of the Secretary of Agriculture discretion which certainly would not be wisely exercised if possessed by this foolish Assistant Secretary." [12] An editorial in the *Bellman* magazine criticized Carl for allegedly using his speeches to "belittle, misrepresent and grossly insult American businessmen." The writer suggested that if he had no real work to perform in the Department of Agriculture "apart from that of working the jawbone of an ass," he might at least be "turned loose in some departmental thistle field" where his "brays" would not disturb anyone. [13]

Recent historians have criticized the way in which conservatives sought to utilize wartime "hysteria" to silence reform agitation. But patriotism was a two-edged sword. Carl's pleas for an aroused public opinion to "club into submission" the profiteers and food speculators showed that the Progressives could use wartime patriotism and enthusiasm for their own purposes. [14] On another occasion Professor Richard T. Ely sent confidential information to Carl concerning allegedly pro-German statements on land policy that had been made by Frederic Howe. He urged Carl publicly to criticize Howe's position. Carl attempted, unsuccessfully, to give the material to George Creel of the Committee on Public Information. [15]

During the months of feverish activity in 1917 and 1918 Carl increasingly assumed the role of spokesman not only for the agricultural policies of the Department of Agriculture but also for the wartime aims of the Wilson administration. His fiery rhetoric was popular with patriotic groups, and he was in constant demand for

[12] New York *Times,* May 26, 1917, p. 4, col. 3. For the text of Carl's remarks on Russia, see *State Conference on Conservation of Foods, Omaha, Nebraska, May 22–25, 1917,* pamphlet, p. 10, Nebraska State Historical Society, Lincoln.

[13] "Call Him In," *Bellman,* XXIII (Aug. 4, 1917), 119. The passage quoted in the *Bellman* editorial occurred frequently in Carl's speeches for 1917 but was always accompanied by generous praise for the loyalty of the majority of businessmen. See Marguerite Edith Jenison, ed., *War Documents and Addresses,* vol. VI of *Illinois in the World War* (Springfield: Illinois State Historical Library, 1923), 139; New York *Times,* May 12, 1917, p. 20, col. 1; Carl Vrooman, "Address before the War Conference of Michigan Businessmen, Detroit, Michigan, November 10, 1917," p. 4, Vrooman papers.

[14] Goldman, *Rendezvous with Destiny,* 195–97; New York *Times,* June 2, 1917, p. 11, col. 3.

[15] See Ely to Vrooman, March 13, 1918; Carl Vrooman to Ely, March 21, 1918, Box 113, Ely papers.

rallies and assemblies.[16] He coined the phrase "The New Patriotism" to describe the wartime version of the New Freedom: "Every hundred per cent American will see to it, not only that he does no disloyal or disreputable act himself,... but that he also enlists for active war service, either in the army, that is fighting the Huns in the trenches, or in the civilian army, that, in the business and political worlds, is fighting the equally dangerous economic and political enemies within the gates—(1) the grafter, (2) the partisan, and (3) the profiteer."[17] The New Patriotism rested on loyalty to the Wilson administration and wholehearted participation in the war effort. He continually denounced the "impractical theorists" who opposed any extension of government authority, the "fanatical pacifists" who opposed military preparations, the "sordid, unscrupulous denizens of the business jungle" who sought to profiteer in food and war supplies, and the "disloyal American citizens" who questioned defense legislation on trifling grounds.[18] He regarded his denunciation of war profiteering as a logical extension of his prewar criticism of business mores.

Carl asked all economic groups to support the Wilson administration's wartime program and to achieve an equality of sacrifice in the war effort. He pointed out that England had secured a united effort by guaranteeing "to capital a fair profit and no more, to labor a living wage and no more, and to the farmer a reasonable price for his products and no more."[19] Of course, "the sons of farmers engaged in the gigantic task of feeding the world" should be exempt from the draft, he believed, but the sons of men engaged in other pursuits should be drafted and trained immediately. To help the farmers to increase production he suggested that either the banks

[16] James R. Mock and Cedric Larson, *Words That Won the War: The Story of the Committee on Public Information, 1917–1919* (Princeton: Princeton University Press, 1939), 63.

[17] Carl Vrooman, *The New Patriotism*, Monthly Bulletin of the Missouri State Board of Agriculture, XVI, 8 (Jefferson City: Missouri State Board of Agriculture, 1918), 10. This version of the speech is a combination of two separate addresses delivered in Jan., 1918, in Columbia, Mo. Missouri State Board of Agriculture, *Missouri Yearbook of Agriculture* (Jefferson City: Missouri State Board of Agriculture, 1918), 28.

[18] New York *Times*, June 10, 1917, p. 4, cols. 6–7.

[19] Jenison, *War Documents and Addresses*, 144–45. See also Carl Vrooman, "Mobilizing for War," undated manuscript, 18, Vrooman papers.

or the government should extend additional credit to them on liberal terms. He recommended that the loans be based on crops stored in government-financed warehouses and that the money "loaned" to the Allies be paid directly to the farmers to pay for the foodstuffs allocated for overseas shipment.[20]

In a sense, Carl relished the tensions created by the war effort. He believed that the war had revealed the inadequacy of the precepts that underlay American civilization: "[This war] brings to light something vastly more significant even than the complete refutation of the fantastic theory that a permanent peace can be maintained in a world half Prussianized and half Bryanized. Our boasted 'Christian civilization,' built upon materialism veneered with hypocrisy, reason supplemented by superstition and self-interest tempered with sentimentality, has collapsed. This is the supreme revelation of the war."[21] This collapse had finally broken the hypnotic spell of material achievements and had shown that there was a psychological factor in building a permanent peace and a better civilization. "The predatory spirit is the war spirit, and until a dominant majority of the citizens of a dominant majority of the nations are willing to put national as well as internal relations on a basis of right rather than might, are willing to make productive efficiency rather than predatory efficiency the 'open sesame' to wealth and power there is no rational hope for anything even remotely resembling a permanent world peace."[22] He firmly believed that by joining the peace crusade Americans could subdue the spirit of exploitation in their hearts. The fervor of patriotism would burn out the dross of partisanship and profiteering and would raise business mores to a higher plane. America would "never again be as smug, as materialistic, as self-satisfied as she was before" the people embarked on this "great crusade for Democracy."[23]

[20] New York *Times*, May 29, 1917, p. 4, col. 1; April 30, 1917, p. 14, col. 3; Carl Vrooman, "Speech before the Commonwealth Club, San Francisco, July 16, 1917," pp. 6–8, Vrooman papers.

[21] Carl Vrooman, "The Decisive Factors of the War," 1, Vrooman papers. The manuscript is undated, but a similar address was delivered before the American Bankers' Convention at Atlantic City, N.J., on Sept. 28, 1917.

[22] *Ibid.*, 7.

[23] Carl Vrooman, "Speech at the New National Museum School for Leaders, August 28, 1917," p. 2, Vrooman papers.

But the crusade could not be won with words alone. In the spring of 1918 French agricultural officials informed the Department of Agriculture that France faced an imminent shortage of wheat and the possibility of widespread famine by winter.[24] Secretary of Agriculture Houston asked Carl to join a special agricultural commission that had been appointed in August, 1918, to survey Allied food needs in Europe for another possible year of war. The commission, headed by W. O. Thompson, president of Ohio State University, landed in England on September 9. The object of the journey, Carl told an English audience, was to bring about unity of purpose within the Allied agricultural effort.[25]

The task of serving with the commission brought Carl into contact with leading figures of the war and provided him with firsthand information on European conditions. While in France he held a "private conference with Marshal Foch at the Marshal's field headquarters; had lunch with General Pershing and his staff at the front; and he conferred privately with Clemenceau 'The Tiger,' then Premier of France." [26] Members of l'Académie d'Agriculture de France cheered enthusiastically when Carl conveyed the greeting of the commission to them in French and praised the efforts of French civilians in helping to meet the food shortage.[27]

When the commission returned to the United States in November, 1918, Carl elected to remain in Europe. The group had gathered information indicating that European demands for American agricultural products would continue at wartime levels, but Herbert Hoover apparently was not satisfied with their findings. On No-

[24] "Transcript of a Conference with Messrs. Tardieu and Monot, French Commissioners, with Reference to the Wheat Situation in France, March 20, 1918," Vrooman papers; New York *Times,* March 19, 1918, p. 7, col. 4; March 25, 1918, p. 20, col. 4.

[25] U.S.D.A. press release, Sept. 9, 1918 (copy), Vrooman papers. The records of the agricultural commission are in the general files of the Office of the Secretary of Agriculture for 1918–1919 in the National Archives. See *Handbook of Federal World War Agencies and Their Records, 1917–1921,* Records of the National Archives, Publication No. 24 (Washington: U.S. Government Printing Office, 1943), 9.

[26] "The Foremost Democratic Dirt Farmer," 5, Vrooman papers.

[27] "M. Carl Vrooman, Sous-Sécretaire d'État au Département de l'Agriculture," *Comptes rendus des séances de l'Académie d'Agriculture de France,* IV (Oct. 16, 1918), 857–60; New York *Times,* Oct. 21, 1918, p. 3, col. 4.

vember 16, 1918, he departed for Europe to survey the situation first-hand.[28] On the same day Carl wrote to Colonel House at the American Embassy in London: "Very wisely, Mr. Hoover and a staff of experts is being sent abroad to determine the immediate food requirements of the famine-menaced people of Europe. It is not only one degree less imperative that a representative of the United States, with a staff of food *production* experts, be commissioned to find out what in the way of seed, farm implements, breeding stock, temporary shelter etc. these same countries will require to enable them to produce, during this coming season, the food they will require for the following winter? [*sic*]"[29] When no commission was forthcoming from either Colonel House or Secretary Hoover, Carl resigned his position as assistant secretary of agriculture, effective January 1, 1919, and stayed in Europe. He spent the next several months studying agricultural and economic conditions in Europe and watching the Paris Peace Conference from the sidelines.[30]

While Carl lingered in Europe, agricultural prices in the United States declined irregularly in the aftermath of the armistice. The War Trade Board lifted import restrictions on corn, and corn prices broke and declined further. In Washington, Herbert Hoover of the Food Administration, Julius Barnes of the Grain Corporation, and Eugene Meyer, Jr., of the War Finance Corporation testified on the need for continued government aid to agriculture. Congress responded with legislation expanding the powers of the WFC to lend to agricultural exporters and with a plan underwriting the 1920 wheat crop. How long such support would continue in peacetime would depend not only on the wartime experiences but also on the ideological climate in the postwar period.[31]

In Carl Vrooman's view the Department of Agriculture had been laying the foundation for a new civilization based on cooperation and government-enforced equality. Also, the inauguration of the New Freedom program of regulated competition had helped to

---

[28] Shideler, *Farm Crisis*, 21.

[29] Carl Vrooman to Colonel House, Nov. 16, 1918, House papers, Yale.

[30] "Carl Schurz Vrooman," *Harvard College Class of 1895, Twenty-Fifth Anniversary Report* (Cambridge: Harvard University Press, 1930), 501.

[31] Shideler, *Farm Crisis*, 21–23.

purify prewar business practices. He had supported the principle of government ownership and operation for natural monopolies and had aided Senator Smith in drafting his bill for a combined hydroelectric and nitrates project. He had also favored the principle of government ownership of a merchant fleet to protect the farmers' interest in maintaining foreign markets. When industry and business had been reformed by government regulation, he believed that they would be valuable assets to the nation and to its position in the world. He maintained that only if America's might was based on "right" could it command respect in the world.

The wartime debate over the proper way to organize the nation's agricultural strength was, in his opinion, a continuation of the prewar controversy over the proper role of the government in guaranteeing equality for agriculture. He believed that the nation should underwrite the risks of agricultural expansion through a comprehensive program of credit incentives, price controls, and antiprofiteering restrictions. During the first year of agricultural mobilization, he had helped the Department of Agriculture to add a billion dollars' worth of food to the war effort while Herbert Hoover was organizing his Food Administration.

Hoover and Carl had agreed on the basic aims of the food program; they had differed primarily in their methods of operation. Carl, the orator, called for a militant public opinion to support vigorous government action in policing the food program in the spirit of the Progressive era. Hoover, the administrator, relied upon organization, economic controls, and voluntary participation to supervise a program of conservation, efficient allocation of resources, and price stabilization.

Above all, Carl had looked upon the wartime effort as a crusade to bring about a new level of morality in business and a new spirit of cooperation in agriculture. A new civilization would emerge from the New Patriotism. Herbert Hoover was more circumspect in his pronouncements and saw the need to "rationalize" American agriculture, bringing system and efficiency to its chaotic methods of competition. These differences in attitude became important in the postwar years when the farmers turned to the government for assistance in meeting the agricultural crisis of the 1920's.

THE NEW ERA, 1920–1926

In July, 1920, agricultural price levels, which had reached record highs during the previous month, began a long, disastrous decline. This collapse of the agricultural price structure threatened to carry down with it Carl Vrooman's hopes for the future of American agriculture.

The farmers' first reaction to the price break was one of consternation and anger. Farm leaders operated on the assumption that the price break was a temporary interruption in an otherwise sound market and that, given enough time, credit, and protection, farmers could weather the crisis by holding their crops until prices improved. Events seemed to turn against them, however. The Federal Reserve Board refused to grant emergency credit to finance crop-withholding actions, the Interstate Commerce Commission granted 25- to 40-percent increases in freight rates at harvest time, and President Wilson vetoed two bills designed to renew the War Finance Corporation and to establish an emergency agricultural tariff. Farm leaders angrily charged the Wilson administration with a plot to deflate agricultural prices.[32]

The change of administrations in March, 1921, brought into sharp contrast the policies and personalities that became involved in the prolonged search for a postwar agricultural policy. The seeds of conflict had been sown during the wartime debates over the food control program, price controls, and government ownership of the nitrates project and the merchant marine fleet. The Progressive leaders who attempted to invoke the same principles in the postwar debates reaped a harvest of discord.

In 1916 and 1917 Carl had pointed out that American agricultural prosperity depended upon the maintenance of foreign markets. His work with the 1918 agricultural commission contributed to a survey of the potential European markets for American agricultural products. When the price break occurred in 1920, he was better prepared than most observers to see the relationship between Eu-

---

[32] *Ibid.*, 52–55, 71–75; Gerald D. Nash, "Herbert Hoover and the Origins of the Reconstruction Finance Corporation," *Mississippi Valley Historical Review,* XLVI (Dec., 1959), 457–59. The WFC renewal bill was passed over the veto.

ropean markets and American prices. While serving as director of the American Farm Bureau Federation's Gift Corn Project in 1921, he talked with European officials who assured him that their countries could furnish sound security in Europe for long-term credit. The 700,000 bushels of corn donated by American farmers for the relief work in Eastern Europe fell far short of the need. Carl realized that while Europeans were suffering from want of food, American farmers labored under the burden of overproduction. He also saw that no financial mechanisms existed to bridge the gap between the two groups.[33]

Determined to aid American agriculture in its search for a solution to the crisis, Carl contacted other farm and financial leaders who had been working on the export problem. In conversations with Secretary of Agriculture Henry C. Wallace, Secretary of Commerce Herbert Hoover, and Eugene Meyer, Jr., chairman of the War Finance Corporation, Carl proposed remedial legislation to prolong the life and to enlarge the powers of the War Finance Corporation so that it could extend long-term credits directly to those foreign purchasers of American surplus crops who could offer good European securities. Meyer rejected the idea and indicated that he would use the financial powers of the WFC to aid the orderly marketing schemes of cooperative marketing associations.[34]

Carl found a more sympathetic supporter for his ideas in Senator George W. Norris of Nebraska, chairman of the Senate Committee on Agriculture and Forestry. On May 31, 1921, Norris introduced a bill, based upon a draft written by Carl, calling for the establishment of a Farmers' Export Financing Corporation. The corporation would be capitalized by the government at $100,000,000, and its powers were carefully delineated.

Section 9. That the corporation shall be empowered and authorized (1) to buy agricultural products from any person within the United States and sell such products to any person or government or subdivision of government without the United States; (2) to act as agent of any

[33] Carl Vrooman, "The Embattled Farmer," *Democracy at the Crossroads,* ed. Ellis Meredith (New York: Brewer, Warren and Putnam, 1932), 211; *The Present Republican Opportunity* (Chenoa, Ill.: by the author, 1936), 79.
[34] Carl Vrooman to Dr. R. H. Pearson, Aug. 12, 1921, draft copy, Vrooman papers.

person producing or dealing in agricultural products within the United States; and (3) to make advances for the purpose of assisting in financing the exportation of agricultural products ... to any person producing such products within the United States, or to any person, government, or subdivision of government without the United States purchasing such products, but in no case shall any moneys so advanced be expended without the United States.[35]

The Vrooman-Norris plan for a government-financed corporation —that would purchase surplus agricultural products, ship them abroad on idle ships owned by the United States Shipping Board, and sell them on credit to foreign purchasers—appealed to many Senate Progressives and members of the newly organized Farm Bloc.[36]

Although the Norris bill bore certain resemblances to the wartime Food Administration, Herbert Hoover was circumspect in his public statements about the proposal because of the position of the Harding administration. Hoover criticized the bill as an attempt to put the government into the business of marketing and suggested that more credit for orderly marketing schemes would enable American farmers to carry their crops over until the export market adjusted to the situation.[37] When Hoover intimated during testimony before the Senate Committee on Agriculture and Forestry that he would favor the Norris plan if the WFC administered the program, Carl attempted to persuade Senator Norris to agree to the change. Norris refused because he felt that it was unwise to turn the administration of the plan over to a potentially unsympathetic agency. The Norris bill received the unanimous approval of the Committee

[35] U.S., Congress, Senate, *A Bill to Provide for the Purchase of Farm Products in the United States, to Sell the Same in Foreign Countries, and for Other Purposes,* 67th Cong., 1st Sess., 1921, Senate Bill No. 1915, pp. 4–5. See also New York *Times,* May 16, 1921, p. 26, col. 4.

[36] Alfred Lief, *Democracy's Norris: The Biography of a Lonely Crusade* (New York: Stackpole Sons, 1939), 230.

[37] Shideler, *Farm Crisis,* 160–61; see also, Lief, *Democracy's Norris,* 230: "Norris was given to understand ... by someone close to Hoover—an aide in the Department, named Louis Grossette—that the Secretary would be favorable but did not want to take a position on it in conflict with President Harding's ideas." Louis Grossette was also an assistant to Carl Vrooman in the private "legislative bureau" that he set up to support the Norris bill. See Vrooman to Pearson, Aug. 12, 1921, Vrooman papers.

on Agriculture and Forestry in the official report on June 30, 1921.[38]

The Vrooman-Norris plan was not acceptable to the Harding administration, the WFC, and the American Farm Bureau Federation. The AFBF leaders were interested primarily in credit-relief legislation for marketing operations and opposed the "government in business" features of the Vrooman-Norris plan. John R. Howard, president of the AFBF, called on Senator Frank B. Kellogg of Minnesota, a supporter of the Harding administration, and discussed the AFBF's demands for credit relief. Senator Kellogg arranged a conference with Hoover and Meyer to discuss the AFBF proposal.[39]

Senators Furnifold Simmons of North Carolina and Irvine Lenroot of Wisconsin also held conferences with Hoover and Meyer to help draft a substitute for the Norris bill after Norris refused to consider abandoning its export-corporation features. By July 20, 1921, Meyer was busily engaged in drafting a substitute that entrusted administration of the credit features of the program to the WFC. Senator Walter Edge of New Jersey, an opponent of the Norris bill, urged Meyer to make the substitute bill "fairly liberal" to draw supporters away from the Norris proposal. Senator Kellogg introduced the substitute bill on July 26.[40]

At first glance the Norris bill and the Kellogg substitute seemed similar. But "the Norris bill would improve prices of farm products by extending credit to European purchasers of American surpluses; the WFC extension would provide credits in the United States to exporters and cooperative associations engaged in sales abroad, and to credit institutions holding farm paper. The first was a surplus-disposal and price-support scheme; the second was primarily a credit-relief and orderly marketing proposal."[41] The former sought to raise prices by expediting the sale of the surplus crops that were

---

[38] Vrooman to Pearson, Aug. 12, 1921, Vrooman papers; U.S., Senate, Committee on Agriculture and Forestry, *Farmers' Export Financing Corporation Act, 1921,* Senate Report No. 192, 67th Cong., 1st Sess., 1921; U.S., Congress, Senate, *Journal of the Senate of the United States of America,* 67th Cong., 1st Sess., 1921, p. 178.

[39] J. R. Howard to Carl Vrooman, Aug. 9, 1921, Vrooman papers.

[40] Lief, *Democracy's Norris,* 232; W. E. Edge to Eugene Meyer, Jr., July 20, 1921, Hoover Archives, quoted by Shideler, *Farm Crisis,* 161–62; U.S., *Congressional Record,* 67th Cong., 1st Sess., 1921, LXI, part 5, 4288–89.

[41] Shideler, *Farm Crisis,* 159–60.

depressing the market; the latter sought to raise prices by restricting and controlling the entry of crops into a self-adjusting market. The two proposals were not necessarily incompatible, but the Harding administration made them seem so when it raised the cry of "government in business" in attacking the Norris bill.

During the debate on the Kellogg bill Carl Vrooman and Herbert Hoover discussed its terms. Carl found the domestic-credit features of the bill acceptable but suggested that the foreign-credit provisions of the Norris bill be added to the Kellogg proposal, thus forming a true compromise bill. Angered by the administration's manhandling of his bill, Senator Norris refused to consider the idea. Instead, he launched into a blistering tirade on the floor of the Senate, charging that Hoover and Meyer were but the agents in a conspiracy planned by someone "higher up," presumably Secretary of the Treasury Andrew W. Mellon. At times Norris seemed more concerned with establishing the principle that the government could enter into business in behalf of the farmer than with seeking a workable solution to the urgent farm problem. The jeremiad ended on July 28 when Norris collapsed at his desk and had to be carried from the chamber.[42]

Senator Norris' intransigency complicated Carl's task of securing support for the compromise plan. Supporters of the compromise finally outvoted Norris in the Senate Committee on Agriculture and Forestry. Senator Charles McNary presented the compromise plan in the form of an amendment to the Norris bill. On August 4 the Senate passed the compromise bill, which entrusted the administration of the agricultural relief program to the WFC, and sent it to the House under a bipartisan "gentleman's agreement" assuring swift passage. Thinking that the battle had been won, the Farm Bloc leader, Senator William S. Kenyon, left Washington.[43]

Howard, president of the AFBF, wrote to Carl to assure him of the AFBF's endorsement of the compromise and to congratulate

[42] Vrooman to Pearson, Aug. 12, 1921, Vrooman papers; Carl Vrooman, *The Present Republican Opportunity*, 81–82; U.S., *Congressional Record*, 67th Cong., 1st Sess., 1921, LXI, part 5, 4375–92; Lief, *Democracy's Norris*, 233–34.

[43] *Journal of the Senate*, 67th Cong., 1st Sess., 1921, pp. 212, 217; Carl Vrooman, *Democracy at the Crossroads*, 213. Senator Kenyon stated that the McNary substitute was a compromise plan, U.S., *Congressional Record*, 67th Cong., 1st Sess., 1921, LXI, part 5, 4576.

him on a splendid job of lobbying. But opponents of the plan referred the compromise bill to the hostile House Committee on Banking and Currency. On August 11 the committee returned a report that struck down the provisions of the Senate bill authorizing credit for foreign purchasers who could show European security for their loans.[44]

Carl attempted to rally farm leaders to the support of this important provision of the compromise bill. On August 12 he drafted a letter to his wartime associate, Dr. R. A. Pearson, in which he reviewed the history of the Senate bill. He acknowledged Norris' objections to the compromise bill and restated his own conviction that the compromise plan would work.

[Senator Norris] felt that it would be a comparatively easy matter to nullify the part of the bill extending credits to foreign purchasers of farm products by simply refraining from making any effort to put it into effective operation. This unquestionably is true. If, after the law is passed, Mr. Meyer continues to take the attitude that it is a lesser evil to have the farmers go bankrupt by the million, than to have them saved by direct Government intervention—the law can be made a dead letter. There are plenty of pretexts on which he can refuse to extend credits even to such foreign purchasers of farm products as have the best *European securities* to hypothecate. I do not believe that Mr. Meyer will take any such unfair attitude, nor do I believe that the farmers of the West would long permit him to do so even if he were disposed to make the attempt. So flagrant a case of malpractice could result in nothing less than a political revolution. [Italics added] [45]

[44] Howard to Vrooman, Aug. 9, 1921, Vrooman papers; U.S., Congress, House, Committee on Banking and Currency, *Amendment to War Finance Corporation Act, April 5, 1918*, Report No. 340, 67th Cong., 1st Sess., 1921, p. 3.
[45] Vrooman to Pearson, Aug. 12, 1921, Vrooman papers. This passage was later redrafted to read as follows: "[Senator Norris] felt that it would be a comparatively easy matter to nullify the part of the bill extending credits to foreign purchasers of farm products, by simply refraining from putting it into effective operation. This unquestionably was true. If the law had been passed and Mr. Meyer had continued to take the attitude that it was a lesser evil to have the farmers go bankrupt by the million rather than to have them saved by direct Government intervention—the law could have been made a dead letter. There would have been plenty of pretexts on which he could have refused to extend credits even to such foreign purchasers of farm products as had the best European securities to hypothecate. I do not believe that the farmers of the West would long have permitted so flagrant a case of administrative malpractice."

After an extensive debate the House voted to restore the foreign-loan provision to the bill. The friends of the compromise bill rejoiced. But on August 20 the House restricted the ability of foreign purchasers to secure credit by passing an amendment requiring all loans to foreign purchasers to be secured by collateral or guarantees in the United States. The House passed the amended version of the bill on August 22.[46]

When the bill reached the conference committee, a new difficulty emerged. Representative Louis T. McFadden, chairman of the House Committee on Banking and Currency, and Representative Porter H. Dale, a Republican conferee, threatened to kill the compromise farm-relief bill in the committee unless the Senate agreed to the House restrictions on foreign credit. The Senate conferees—William S. Kenyon, Charles McNary, and E. D. Smith—were "forced to yield, and accept a bill which gave the farmer temporary relief in the shape of domestic credit while depriving him of the one thing he needed more than any and all other things combined, namely: foreign markets for his surplus crops." [47]

The emasculation of the foreign-credit provisions of the compromise bill in the conference committee seemed to Carl to be a serious blow to American agriculture. In a speech before the Illinois Farmers' Institute on February 23, 1922, he asked:

Can you tell me why Mr. Meyer and Mr. McFadden stabbed that bill in the back when it was too late to have another vote of Congress on it? ...I have asked myself a hundred times, "Why has this man done this awful thing?"...But one day I picked up a paper in which was a statement that a syndicate of international investment bankers were planning to loan a billion dollars to Europe. Suddenly the whole thing seemed to flash through my mind. Yes, these syndicates they had been loaning money to Europe ever since the signing of the Armistice and loaning it to them not only at a high rate of interest, but for big commissions as well.

[46] U.S., *Congressional Record*, 67th Cong., 1st Sess., 1921, LXI, part 5, 5084–89, part 6, 5365–66, 5376; U.S., Congress, House, *Journal of the House of Representatives of the United States of America*, 67th Cong., 1st Sess., 1921, p. 444.

[47] Carl Vrooman, *Democracy at the Crossroads*, 214; see also, Carl Vrooman, *The Present Republican Opportunity*, 82–83. McFadden was a Republican from Pennsylvania, and Dale was a Republican from Vermont.

If we loaned—as this bill in Washington provided—if we extended to them credit to the amount of five hundred million dollars with which to buy our agricultural surpluses, nobody would make any commissions.... Now do you see any reason why they wanted to stop this law? [48]

Over the years he came to believe that "the secret and sinister influence of the International Loan Brokers of Wall Street" lay behind the defeat of his bill.[49]

This conspiratorial explanation ignored many of the factors in the complex agricultural situation during the summer of 1921. Basically, the leaders of the farm organizations were not convinced that the price break was anything more than a temporary dislocation of the market. The economic nationalism of their position conflicted with the basic premises of the foreign-credit proposals and the export-corporation ideas behind the Vrooman-Norris plan. In seeking to fashion a workable compromise Carl had to work at cross purposes with Norris, whose intransigency and intemperate tactics only complicated the situation. Significantly, although the AFBF endorsed Carl's efforts, they refused to give him financial aid. The Kellogg bill split the Farm Bloc by offering easier credit for cotton farmers and cooperatives and by raising the specter of "government in business." The Vrooman-Norris plan failed, in short, because it ran counter to the prevailing state of opinion in the agricultural community.[50]

The deepest point of the agricultural price crisis was reached during the winter of 1921–1922 when credit stringencies created a wave of rural bankruptcies and when bumper crops, added to the surplus

[48] "Feeding the World; An Address before the Illinois Farmers' Institute at Monmouth, Illinois, February 23, 1922," 8–9, Vrooman papers. McFadden had offered the amendment restricting foreign purchasers and explained that it would protect the WFC. But a foreign purchaser who could post such security in the United States probably would not need credit from the WFC. McFadden admitted in the Senate that Eugene Meyer opposed the foreign-credit provisions of the Senate bill. See U.S., *Congressional Record,* 67th Cong., 1st Sess., 1921, LXI, part 5, 5085. For the original text of the McFadden amendment, see U.S., *Congressional Record,* 67th Cong., 1st Sess., 1921, LXI, part 6, 5365.

[49] Carl Vrooman, *Democracy at the Crossroads,* 215.

[50] Vrooman to Pearson, Aug. 12, 1921, Vrooman papers; see also Shideler, *Farm Crisis,* 164. For the temper of farm leadership in this period, see Theodore Saloutos and John D. Hicks, *Agricultural Discontent in the Middle West, 1900–1939* (Madison: University of Wisconsin Press, 1951), Chaps. 9, 10.

held over from the 1920 season, caused a further depression in prices. The events of 1922 finally convinced a number of farmers of the importance of exporting the swollen surpluses that adversely influenced the market. Yet when the Vrooman-Norris plan was reintroduced in the Senate in November, 1922, it again failed because of the opposition of southern cotton farmers and the AFBF to Norris' "Socialism." Not until the second half of 1923 did a substantial number of farm organizations rally behind an export-corporation plan. Even then the farm leaders adapted the plan to fit the requirements of their economic nationalism. The resulting plan, the McNary-Haugen bill, proposed to create a government-financed export corporation that would raise the prices of basic agricultural commodities to parity levels by subsidizing the dumping of agricultural surpluses over tariff walls. But the endorsement of the McNary-Haugen bill came too late. The Hoover-Meyer program of credit-relief for cooperative marketing associations secured the approval of President Coolidge, and the McNary-Haugen bill was defeated in the House on the eve of the 1924 nominating conventions.[51]

The issue of farm relief was thus thrown into the national political arena at a strategic moment. Carl had accurately forecast in 1921 that the failure of the Harding administration to relieve the distressed agricultural regions would cause a political revolution. With this situation in mind he and former Secretary of Agriculture E. T. Meredith formed a farm bloc at the 1924 Democratic National Convention and tried to wean the insurgent farmers away from the Republican party and from the La Follette third-party movement by inserting a strong agricultural-relief plank into the Democratic platform.[52]

The campaign managers for William G. McAdoo also had their eye on the La Follette supporters. They hoped to nominate a vice-presidential candidate who would be acceptable to the La Follette backers and thus secure their aid. One of the candidates suggested for this role was Carl Vrooman. His friends at the convention circulated a mimeographed document entitled "The Foremost

[51] Shideler, *Farm Crisis,* 191, 197, 241, 275–79.
[52] New York *Times,* June 22, 1924, p. 1, col. 4; Carl Vrooman to Colonel House, Jan. 18, 1924, House papers, Yale.

Democratic Dirt Farmer," which stressed his role in the fight for agricultural-relief legislation.[53]

When the convention became hopelessly deadlocked between McAdoo and Smith, Franklin Delano Roosevelt jokingly suggested to Carl that they run together and flip a coin to determine who would head the ticket. Supporters of John W. Davis finally approached Carl and asked him to run on the ticket with Davis. Although he felt that Davis was "a corporation lawyer who sold his services but not his soul to the corporations," Carl knew that he could not convince the farmers that Davis was their friend. In addition, the agricultural plank in the Democratic platform reflected primarily the views of Bernard Baruch, not those of the Vrooman-Meredith farm bloc. With his old enemy Roger Sullivan in control of the Illinois delegation Carl knew that he could expect little support from his home state. Consequently, he declined the offer from the Davis supporters.[54]

The events of 1924 marked the apogee of Carl's career as a Progressive reformer and spokesman for American agriculture. Ten years earlier he had confidently proclaimed the gospel of the New Agriculture based on the spirit of cooperation, a business-minded approach to agriculture, and government assistance for the orderly marketing of crops. In 1916 he had encouraged the farmers to form a great national federation similar to the American Federation of Labor to protect their interests. In the postwar years American farmers did adopt some of these ideas. The formation of the American Farm Bureau Federation in November, 1919, indicated that the conservative proposals of commercial agriculture finally had replaced the majoritarian agrarianism of the Populist period. The influence exercised in agricultural matters during the 1920's by such businessmen as Herbert Hoover, Eugene Meyer, Jr., and Bernard Baruch reflected the extent to which the business aspects of farming had come to the fore during the war. The cooperative marketing movement, stimulated by the price depression and encouraged by the Harding and Coolidge administrations, reached its peak between

[53] New York *Times,* June 22, 1924, p. 2, col. 2; "The Foremost Democratic Dirt Farmer," Vrooman papers.
[54] Interview with Carl Vrooman, Nov. 29, 1960.

1921 and 1925. What Carl had prescribed in prosperity the farmers had adopted in adversity.[55]

But Carl saw little reason to rejoice in the belated adoption of many of his ideas by the American farmers. The new farm organizations followed the counsel of conservativism and proved to be one of the major obstacles to his legislative proposals. In an interview shortly after the defeat of the foreign-credit provisions of the compromise bill in 1921, he complained:

I have just wired the Secretary of Agriculture that if the people who are trying to fasten on him responsibility for the beggarly price of corn had spent one half that effort and money helping to pass the Farmers' Relief bill,... that bill would have been enacted into law two or three months sooner, and would not have had its most valuable provision treacherously cut out at the last moment by chairman McFadden of the House Banking and Currency Committee, on the threat of Eugene Meyer, Director of the War Finance Corporation, that he would not put into operation that provision even if it were enacted into law.[56]

From 1921 to 1924 Carl had attempted to formulate a compromise farm-relief program that would unite southern Democrats, midwestern Republican farmers, and urban Progressives, but he could neither unite the farmers, convince the Republican administrations, nor sway his own party.

A FAREWELL TO REFORM, 1927–1937

The paralysis of the Democratic party in the 1920's created a perplexing situation for Carl. For one-quarter of a century he had looked upon the Democratic party as the chosen instrument for reform. But the coalition of southern and western farmers, labor groups, social-justice advocates, moderate Socialists, and urban Progressives that had supported Wilson in 1912 and 1916 had begun

[55] Compare with Grant McConnell, *The Decline of Agrarian Democracy* (Berkeley: University of California Press, 1959), 1, 55–56, 59.
[56] "Interview with Carl Vrooman, Former Assistant Secretary of Agriculture, who initiated ... the 'Farmers' Relief Bill' " (undated draft copy, probably late 1921), Vrooman papers.

to fall apart during the war.[57] In 1920 the national Democratic ticket polled only 34.5 percent of the total vote, "which was the poorest showing of any major party ticket since the Civil War era. This disaster, followed by the bitter wrangling and the interminable balloting of the 1924 convention, all but finished the Democrats as a serious opposition." [58] The most serious consequence of this rural-urban split within the Democratic party, in Carl's view, was the failure of the party to come to grips with the farm crisis and to offer a workable farm-relief program.

In the absence of a clearcut party program Carl attempted to use his export-credit plan, which was introduced in 1926 as the Robinson-Oldfield bill, as the basis for an alternative program to the nominally Republican McNary-Haugen bill. In testimony before the House Committee on Agriculture in March, 1926, Carl warned, "If the Coolidge administration continues to show itself unwilling to enact legislation placing agriculture on an equality with the manufacturer then the next inevitable step for those representatives of the farmer who are unwilling to sacrifice the farmer on the altar of partisanship, is to go straight to the minority party with the same offer of legislative cooperation that has been ignored and spurned by the party in power." [59]

By July he had changed his tune. Only a nonpartisan farmers' movement, he claimed, could help the farmer.[60] Events in 1928 showed that neither major party was ready to listen seriously to the farm representatives. The leading Republican farm spokesman, Frank Lowden of Illinois, withdrew his presidential candidacy in the face of the Hoover onslaught and denounced his party's failure

[57] Arthur S. Link, "What Happened to the Progressive Movement in the 1920's?" *American Historical Review*, LXIV (July, 1959), 838–39.

[58] Hofstadter, *The Age of Reform*, 295–96.

[59] U.S., Congress, House, Committee on Agriculture, *Hearings, Agricultural Relief*, 69th Cong., 1st Sess., 1926, series C, part 10, p. 362 (testimony of Carl Vrooman on March 15, 1926). Carl accused the Republican party of "assassinating" his 1921 farm-relief bill by a "partisan knife thrust in the back." Representative Tincher of Iowa, a Republican, criticized Carl's testimony as "the most partisan explosion ever brought before this committee." See New York *Times,* March 16, 1926, p. 44, col. 2. For additional testimony by Carl Vrooman, see U.S., Congress, House, Committee on Agriculture, *Hearings, Agricultural Relief,* 69th Cong., 1st Sess., 1926, series C, part 2, pp. 78–94; part 10, pp. 317–36.

[60] Carl Vrooman, "The Embattled Farmer," *The Woman Citizen,* XI (July, 1926), 11–12.

to go beyond Coolidge's farm policies. In the Democratic party the urban forces backing Alfred E. Smith were firmly in control, but they sagaciously welcomed a few disgruntled McNary-Haugenites in an effort to entice western farmers away from Hoover.[61]

Carl Vrooman, who had supported McAdoo in the Democratic primaries and Lowden in the Republican party, found the nomination of Alfred E. Smith so untenable that he departed for Europe to avoid campaigning for the party ticket. When pressed for an endorsement, he cabled back his decision: he would support Hoover in the campaign.[62] Three factors probably influenced Carl's decision. These were the role of Bernard Baruch in shaping Democratic farm policy, the Democratic party's flirtation with George Peek's dissident McNary-Haugenites, and the urban orientation of the Smith forces. Carl also agreed with the sentiment expressed by another McAdoo supporter: "If it is a choice between government by big business and government by the underworld, I'll take big business." [63]

To Carl the nomination of Smith indicated not only that the Democratic party had turned its back on the farmer, but also that it had forsaken the Wilsonian principles for which he had labored so long. But in supporting Hoover in 1928 Carl had forfeited his right to be heard in Democratic party circles. His fight against McNary-Haugenism had also jeopardized his standing with Republicans as a farm spokesman. Glumly, he could only watch from the sidelines as Hoover's Farm Board attempted to reorganize the marketing system through cooperative stabilization corporations. It was a case, Carl felt, of too little, too late, and too slow to help the farmer. In truth Carl was a captive of his own ideas. He could see no other way out of the agricultural crisis than the plan he had proposed in 1921—credit for foreign sales. In 1931 he urged publicly that Hoover link the moratorium on war-debt payments by European nations with the surplus disposal scheme. If the deferred payment could be treated as credit for the purchase of American

---

[61] William T. Hutchinson, *Lowden of Illinois: The Life of Frank O. Lowden*, II: *Nation and Countryside* (Chicago: University of Chicago Press, 1957), 600–601; Gilbert C. Fite, *George N. Peek and the Fight for Farm Parity* (Norman: University of Oklahoma Press, 1954), 203–20.

[62] New York *Times*, Aug. 10, 1928, p. 2, col. 5.

[63] Interview with Carl Vrooman, Nov. 29, 1960.

agricultural surpluses by the European nations, Carl argued, both countries would benefit.[64]

In 1932 Carl joined other veterans of the Wilson era—Brand Whitlock, Newton D. Baker, Thomas J. Walsh, and Ellis Meredith —in preparing a symposium on the future of the Democratic party. The resulting work, a compilation of essays entitled *Democracy at the Crossroads,* was designed "to restate some of the fundamental principles of the Democratic party, and to recall some of its achievements under the leadership of Woodrow Wilson." [65] When it came to suggestions for farm policies in 1932, Carl had little more to offer than what he had been proposing for ten years: more credit, better conservation to reduce overproduction, and disposal of surplus crops by credit sales abroad. "What the farmer must have before he can hope to get a 'square deal,'" he asserted, "is a Federal Administration that is not hopelessly urban minded, that can see and feel and understand the farmer's legitimate needs." [66]

For twenty years Carl had been working to achieve equality for agriculture. Franklin Delano Roosevelt invoked this standard in a major campaign speech on agriculture in 1932, when he said, "Agriculture has at no time sought, and does not now seek, such accessions to the public treasury as was provided by the futile and costly attempts at price stabilization by the Federal Farm Board. It seeks only *equality of opportunity with tariff produced industry.*" [Italics added] Yet Roosevelt's call for an agricultural tariff probably grated on Carl's nerves as being too close to an endorsement of McNary-Haugenism. The role of professional agricultural economists and social scientists in shaping Roosevelt's farm policy statements also clashed with his belief that "dirt farmers" should provide agrarian leadership.[67]

[64] Carl Vrooman, *The Present Republican Opportunity,* Appendix B, speech before the Institute of Public Affairs, June 29, 1931, on "Markets for Moratoriums."

[65] Ellis Meredith, ed., *Democracy at the Crossroads* (New York: Brewer, Warren and Putnam, 1932), 1.

[66] *Ibid.,* 229. See pages 225–29 for proposals. During the Crisis of 1933 he contacted Colonel House in an effort to influence farm-relief legislation. Carl Vrooman to Colonel House (telegram), March 27, 1933, House papers, Yale.

[67] Speech at Topeka, Kans., quoted in John A. Lapp, *The First Chapter of the New Deal* (Chicago: John A. Prescott & Son, 1933), 59. For the role of economists and social scientists in shaping the Topeka speech, see Richard S. Kirkendall, *Social Scientists and Farm Politics in the Age of Roosevelt* (Columbia: University of Missouri Press, 1966), 46–48, 51.

When the AAA was established in 1933 to deal with the agricultural crisis, Carl refused to accept a position in it. Probably he felt that the program reflected too much the conservative views of the American Farm Bureau Federation and of such former McNary-Haugenites as Peek. During the next four years Carl became increasingly critical of the entire New Deal program. As the 1936 election approached, he issued a pamphlet entitled *The Present Republican Opportunity*. He maintained that he was still a loyal administration Democrat, but that a new coalition party was needed to overcome the mistakes and fallacies of the New Dealers. He outlined a program based upon the creation of a stable dollar, maintenance of farm prices, reduction in "confiscatory local taxes," assessment of a national consumption tax, and attempts at balancing the federal budget.[68] His friends wondered whether, in turning his back on the New Deal, Carl had bid his farewell to reform.

In part, Carl's rejection of the New Deal agricultural policies was related to his experiences in the 1920's and early 1930's. The events of this period had showed him that government action to insure equality for agriculture did not necessarily guarantee equality of opportunity for each individual farmer. In other words, formal freedom for agriculture as a whole did not mean effective freedom for every farmer. The early New Deal farm legislation, reflecting the ideas and needs of the highly organized commercial farmers associated with the Farm Bureau, left the unorganized general farmers, the tenant farmer, and the sharecropper to bear the brunt of crop reductions and acreage limitations.[69] Lacking an effective voice in either the Farm Bureau or the AAA, Carl probably felt victimized by these laws. As late as 1938 he was writing personal letters to President Roosevelt in a vain attempt to influence acreage allotments in his area.[70]

In another sense Carl had not so much bid farewell to reform as he had returned to the basis of all of his reform activity—religion. In 1936 he confessed: "For many years I sought eagerly not only in

---

[68] *The Present Republican Opportunity*, 6–7, 19–20; interview with Carl Vrooman, Nov. 29, 1960.

[69] Howard Zinn, ed., *New Deal Thought* (Indianapolis: Bobbs-Merrill, 1966), xv–xxxvi.

[70] Edgar B. Nixon, ed., *Franklin D. Roosevelt and Conservation, 1911–1945* (Washington: General Services Administration, 1957), II, 779.

America but throughout Europe for a political party, a reform movement, a labor union, a church or any other organization that was able to make good men and women get up as early, stay up as late, work or fight as hard and get as much kick out of life as do the denizens of the underworld, the crafty, cohorts of grafting politicians, the fanatical apostles of Communism or the no less fanatical soldiers of fortune in the world of high finance." [71] The Oxford Group, he believed, provided such a spiritually dynamic movement. Fortunately, the nation did not have to wait until a majority of the voters had been transformed spiritually to combat the effects of the depression. A "few thousand financially successful Americans," in the Christian spirit of stewardship, could launch the new crusade.[72]

In a speech before an Oxford Group meeting in 1938, Carl declared that businessmen could save America if they would only overcome their personal greed and fear and embrace a "God-directed life." [73] After forty-six years of activity in social reform causes and politics Carl's "chief interest and hope for the world" had turned from "politics, 'the science of the possible'—the humanly possible—to religion, 'the science of the infinite possibilities of the life of the Spirit at work in human beings and in human institutions.' " [74]

[71] Vrooman, *Present Republican Opportunity*, 67.
[72] *Ibid.*, 71–74.
[73] New York *Times*, June 6, 1938, p. 19, col. 7.
[74] "Carl Schurz Vrooman," *Harvard College, Class of 1895, Fiftieth Anniversary Report* (Cambridge: Harvard University Press, 1945), 658.

Chapter Eleven

Conclusion

The Vroomans were not in that top rank of public figures whose lives traditionally have attracted the attention of American historians. Their significance lies, rather, in the uniqueness and the representativeness of their case. Primarily, the Vroomans are important because they were representative of the reformer and the radical as intellectual types.[1]

The life of Hiram Perkins Vrooman revealed some of the steps in the making of the reformer. His ascent from rural poverty and obscurity to relative affluence and prominence in Michigan and Missouri during the period from 1850 to 1870 followed the classic outlines of social mobility in the nineteenth century. The postwar credit controversies, the political realignments that accompanied restoration in Missouri, and the Panic of 1873 combined to cast him down once again into the ranks of the obscure. Given this break in expectations, the temporary dislocation of values, and the critical assessment of the performance of his society, he became a reformer. In the Greenback, Greenback-Labor, Prohibition, and Anti-Monopoly parties of Kansas in the turbulent 1870's and 1880's he found a new orientation toward his society, a renewed sense of mission, and a refurbished ideology. He called on America, through various reform proposals, to once again redeem the entrepreneurial dream.

The lives of Hiram's sons further illustrated the impact of personal and group trauma on political attitudes and values. Harry, Walter, and Hiram Greeley Vrooman could not live with the tension between their society's professions and its performance, with the ambiguity of intellectual imprecision inherent in any partial acceptance of the status quo, and with the indefiniteness of their own roles. They took the leap of negation to embrace a radical alternative to their society's values. This intellectual position provided an ideology, which gave them a sense of intellectual precision and emotional completeness, and defined specific roles and goals for their lives. Frank and Carl Vrooman, on the other hand, felt the tension of the conflicting values between their father's beliefs and their brothers' ideologies. In the social gospel movement and in Populism they tried to define their own values, resolving their uncertainties in their confrontation with Progressivism. As reformers rather than radicals, they salvaged what they could from their father's belief in positive government action and their brothers' conceptions of the cooperative commonwealth and tried to blend them into a program to achieve their own entrepreneurially defined goals.

Not only were the Vroomans representative of the reformer and radical as intellectual types, but they were also representative thinkers within their respective traditions of social thought. They have special significance for the intellectual historian who is interested in continuity because they absorbed, reflected, and synthesized the thought of their own day with startling fidelity. They were not seminal thinkers who broke with or reformulated their traditions. Rather, they displayed a sensitivity to new ideas, to strategic social movements, and to changing political conditions, which made them indicators for changes in intellectual trends in American

---

[1] The term "significance" can be used in two primary ways in the making of historical evaluations: the significance of a casual agent and the significance of a case. In determining the significance of a case study, two uses of the case must be distinguished for clarity. The case study can be used to present evidence that has been overlooked in forming previous generalizations (the *exception* that overturns the rule). It can also be used to present an examination of a case that is similar to all others in a generalization (the *example* that illustrates the rule). The first usage concentrates on the uniqueness of the case; the second on its representativeness. An example of this dual usage of the case study method is found in Lee Benson, *The Concept of Jacksonian Democracy: New York as a Test Case* (Princeton: Princeton University Press, 1961). Benson argues that New York is an exception to the prevalent generalizations about Jacksonian Democracy and, at the same time, is representative of similar cases that lead to a new generalization; see pp. xii–xiii and Chap. 15.

No attempt was made in this book to argue that the Vroomans were "typical" reformers or radicals in any statistical or sociological sense. Profiles of selected groups are useful for social or political history but are singularly inappropriate for intellectual history because they deal in statistical abstractions or fictional realities and because they implicitly assume that ideas are but reflections of social class or status.

social history. Hiram Perkins Vrooman, for example, had entered politics as a Democrat in the 1850's at a time when the concept of the negative liberal state was challenged seriously by the Republican revival of the theory of centralized government. The Democratic dogma of the 1850's held that the goal of equality of opportunity could best be achieved by reducing the functions of government to the minimum necessary to guarantee the maintenance of law and order. Once men had been released from the corrupting influence of social institutions and set free to realize their own best natures, they would overcome the evil inherited from the past. Individualism would be at once the engine of progress and the mark of righteousness. Equal rights would be the hallmark of the good republic; majority rule, its guiding light.

Hiram tried to make these ideas fit the new social conditions that emerged from the Civil War. The "equal rights" Republicans in Missouri invoked these standards to support their entrepreneurial Greenbackism, their flirtation with government support of enterprise at the local and county levels, and their attack on the Reconstruction issues of disenfranchisement and minority rule. In its attack on Grant's administration the liberal Republican movement of 1872 revived the old Democratic critique of centralized power. The Panic of 1873, the labor strife of 1877, and the failure of Greenbackism raised broad economic and political questions that could not be answered with the dogmas of the past. Gradually the reformers' insistence on the extension of national government activity on behalf of the small entrepreneur outweighed their lingering emphasis on restricting the scope of government activity. Unlike the antimonopolyism of the 1830's, the new antimonopoly campaign of the 1880's was designed to force the government to act for them as it had already acted for others.

Social Darwinism, the union of the scientific concept of evolution with the philosophical concept of progress, increasingly became the intellectual medium in which the public debate on social policy was conducted in the 1880's and 1890's. Reformers, radicals, and conservatives all tried to show in the language of Social Darwinism that their ideas were likely to increase rather than decrease the flow of material goods, to step up the pace of technological innovation, and to foster organic growth for the entire society.

Radicals such as Harry, Walter, and Hiram G. Vrooman attacked the conservative argument that social evolution would automatically bring progress if the intricate alliance of government favoritism and private endeavor was left undisturbed. They argued that current developments were bringing misery, degradation, and exploitation rather than progress to the masses. They attacked the basic principles of their day and proposed alternative values. In place of individualism they sought to foster a collective consciousness; in place of competition, cooperation; in place of the profit motive, a service motive; and in place of social antagonism, fraternal harmony. They denounced the belief that out of the free play of individual desires and profit motives would emerge a natural harmony of interests that would equal the common good. In its place they offered a view of society as an organism, a collective whole greater than the sum of its parts, and they tried to make government coterminous with society.

While they rejected the individualism of conservative Social Darwinism, they did not reject the idea of social evolution *per se*. As Socialists they believed that social evolution was inevitably bringing about a socialized economy. This rescued them from a sense of hopelessness. The role of the agitator was to help other men in the recognizing of these new forces and to work with them in the easing of the transition from one era of history to the next. Similarly, they did not reject the notion that progress meant material advancement; they simply maintained that such progress would be better stimulated and its rewards more equitably distributed through a planned Socialist system than through laissez-faire. They went even further and argued that progress should also bring culture, comfort, and leisure to the masses.

They held up the ideal of an approximate equality of enjoyment of the benefits of modern technology to be achieved through an equal obligation to labor; reward proportionate to, but not limited by, useful effort; and nationalization of the means of production, distribution, exchange, and culture.

Reformers such as Frank and Carl Vrooman also challenged their conservative opponents with the tools of Social Darwinism and tried to defeat them with their own arguments. If competition were the law of nature, then why did society's law allow monopolies and oligopolies to restrict competition through pooling, stock manipulation, and secret agreements? If natural selection were the means of social evolution, then why not allow the natural mechanism of the marketplace rather than the artificial devices of political favoritism, banker control of credit, and railway rate manipulation determine which firm survived. If survival of the fittest were the result of evolution, then why could not the moral, the honest, or the socially responsible survive in the business world instead of the immoral, the dishonest, or the inordinately selfish?

They also believed that social evolution had increased the interdependence of men and had created a social organism with an overriding common good. Their dream was that of an America in which the pursuit of the common good would be the primary goal of men, in which the agricultural base and human resources of society would be protected by public policy, and in which the efficiency of entrepreneurship would promote cooperative endeavors.

Their ideal was that of entrepreneurial equality of opportunity with rewards proportionate to risk and effort, to be assured by a strengthened national government and a heightened sense of personal social responsibility.

The Vrooman brothers were also representative of a small group of thinkers who believed that evolutionary thought did not necessarily lead to warfare between science and religion. Frank used as the basis for his social gospel theology the concept of an immanent God progressively realizing Himself in nature and human history. Harry applied this theology to ethics in order to provide a rationale for disinterested social action. Hiram utilized Swedenborg's methodology to reconcile science and religion. Walter added a slightly Manichean twist to his brothers' ideas: man was a partner with God in the ongoing evolution of the race. Carl eventually subsumed the family views on religion into the Progressive theory of politics as the psychological basis for human actions.

While the Vroomans were representative of powerful trends in American intellectual development, their case is, nevertheless, an exception to certain current historical generalizations and methodological assumptions.

Several of the instances in which features of the Vrooman case challenge current historical interpretations have been noted throughout the book and need only to be summarized briefly here. Hiram Perkins Vrooman's role in politics indicates that entrepreneurial issues may have played a larger role in reshaping postwar political alliances than did Reconstruction issues. The relation of the three Vrooman brothers to Socialism indicates that personal factors may be as important as immigration factors in explaining the course of American Socialism in the nineteenth century. The Vroomans' experiences in the social gospel movement provide a warning against excessive instrumentalism in contemporary social action theology and ecclesiology.

The Vroomans' response to Populism reemphasizes the nonagrarian origins of much of the movement's leadership, the opportunistic character of much of its support, and the entrepreneurialism of its proposals. Carl's relation to the academic freedom controversies and educational innovations of the late 1890's and early 1900's reveal the dual, rather than unitary, nature of academic freedom. The failure of radical cooperative schemes in the same period raises the intriguing question of whether or not the appeal of Progressivism was enhanced by the failure of nonpolitical alternatives to social change. The success of Ruskin Hall in England and the failure of Ruskin College in the United States calls attention to the differences in strategy between the English and the American labor movements.

Carl's service in the Wilson administration belies the view that Progressive reform ended with the declaration of war. His attempt to secure postwar agricultural relief legislation reveals some of the lines of continuity from prewar Progressivism and casts some doubts on the significance of the contributions of Senator George Norris to postwar progress. Carl's break with the Democratic party and with the New Deal suggests that the liberalism of the 1930's was something more than a revitalized Progressivism.[2] His discovery that government action to insure the formal equality of

[2] While this book was in preparation, Professor Otis L. Graham provided preliminary documentation of this last point in his book, *An Encore for Reform: The Old Progressives and the New Deal* (New York: Oxford University Press, 1967). He included Carl Vrooman in his sample and found him to be representative of a large group of Progressives who turned against the New Deal. Further work is needed on this point to separate the intellectual tendencies that differentiate the old Progressivism from the new liberalism.

agriculture in the economy did not achieve effective freedom of action for the unorganized individual farmer illuminates a characteristic dilemma of modern life.

The perspective that emerges from these various considerations of the Vrooman case allows for some tentative conclusions on the issues raised in the introduction. The premise established there—that the reformer is trying to achieve the ideals of his society and the radical is trying to change them—left one major question unexplored. Are the ideals of American society static principles that were established once for all time in the creation of the United States as an independent political entity? If so, then, the historian need only measure the accuracy of the reformer's perception of this given reality in order to determine his validity, and he can dismiss the radical as "un-American." That men have acted in the past as if ideals were such fixed values does not resolve the issue.[3]

A more dynamic view of ideals seems to be involved in the Vrooman story. Three broad concepts—conflict, compromise, and consensus—can be used to explain the role of the reformer and radical in relation to a society's ideals.

First, an ideal is born in a cry of despair. Conflict arises in society from a number of sources associated with economic, political, ideological, and racial factors. What is important for the historian is not just the origin of the conflict but the way in which individuals respond to the situation. When a man or a group cries out, "this ought not to be," then they have begun the process of defining an ideal. The Vroomans cried out against the social costs of a maturing industrial society and raised their ideals against it.

Second, ideals must be institutionalized in order to become effective in a society. The Vroomans expressed their ideals in language borrowed from Social Darwinism and attempted to embody them

[3] Another unexplored question arises from the fact that the radical Vrooman brothers retained a belief in a democratic exercise of power. This could be used to argue that they did not reject *all* the ideals of their society and, hence, were not radical by the definition offered in the introduction of this book. Rather than use modifying phrases such as "social and economic radicals" or introduce a "degrees of radicalism" concept, I have allowed the issue to pass unmentioned in the text for the sake of analytical sharpness and clarity. Recognition of this fact simply means that the Vroomans were nineteenth-century evolutionary radicals rather than revolutionary radicals.

in the developing social institutions of their day, such as labor unions and civic leagues. In one respect Social Darwinism would seem to be admirably suited for this task. Its preoccupation with the ecology rather than the teleology of social evolution focused attention on the institutional means used rather than on the social goals of the innovators. This book has demonstrated, however, that the goals ultimately influence the pragmatic viability of the means in a democratic society. In religious experiments, cooperative ventures, educational innovations, and political campaigns the radical Vrooman brothers failed, even when they used the same social instruments as their reform brothers, because their projected radical goals were not the logical, evolutionary developments of contemporary ideas and institutions but their rhetorical opposites.

Methodologically, therefore, the relationship of radicalism and reform should be viewed not as a matter of degree on a continuum but as a matter of opposition on diverging vectors. Schematically, it is a cross rather than a straight line. Radicals and reformers, representing contrary intellectual tendencies, can cooperate in temporary political alliances or social institutions. But the lines of tension related to ultimate goals eventually pull such coalitions apart and nullify attempts to use moderate social means to achieve radical social purposes. This is why the Vroomans had the propensity for failure. Frozen out of the organizations that could have served as vehicles for their programs, they had to create their own social organizations and search for quick solutions. Every venture, however modest in origin, became the bearer of their hopes for humanity. They tried to do too much with too little. They viewed the importance of institutions as the link between the individual and society, but they were too individualistic to be bound by institutional discipline.

Third, the political arena is the place in which conflicts are resolved in a democratic society. The cathartic function of politics is to focus and channel social hostilities. The symbolic function of political rhetoric is to provide the unifying myths that hold groups together. The pragmatic function of political power is to resolve tensions by bargain, partial victories, and concessions. Compromise is the spirit of American political institutions. That is why a reformer, such as Carl, could survive in politics while a radical, such as Walter, could not.

What, then, are the respective roles of the reformer and the radical in achieving the social consensus that contains both the conflict and the compromise within tacitly assumed bounds?

The reformer reads new meaning into older ideals and helps to reformulate them in each generation. The reformer fares better than the radical because his ideals are already partially institutionalized in the society. The very ambiguity of the concepts of equality and general welfare in the Declaration of Independence and the Constitution have enabled reformers throughout American history to argue that they are trying to achieve what the Founding Fathers had intended. The fact that legal and institutional precedents exist for their claims aids their cause.

There is, therefore, a hidden conservative strain in the reformer that makes him uniquely fitted for the task of reformulating ideals. Since he is trying to heal the breach between the performance and the professions of his society, he has an instinctually conservative bias toward part of the status quo. Frank and Carl Vrooman, for example, adhered to the entrepreneurial understanding of equality of opportunity from their father's day and attempted to preserve it in their own. Once the reformer is satisfied that his society has narrowed the gap between profession and practice, he acquires a vested interest in maintaining the new institutional status quo and may elaborate a rationale for doing so in the name of the slogans of his youth. His instinctual conservatism turns into ideological conservatism. Frank's preparedness program in 1916 and Carl's support of Hoover in 1928 may mark the points at which they crossed this line.

The radical proclaims new ideals that may or may not be useful in meeting current problems. Since the radical's values are largely a negation of current ones, their utility is dependent upon the presence or absence of a revolutionary situation.[4] Apart from a revolu-

[4] R. R. Palmer, *The Age of the Democratic Revolution: A Political History of Europe and America, 1760–1800* (Princeton: Princeton University Press, 1959), I, 21. "By a revolutionary situation is here meant one in which confidence in the justice or reasonableness of existing authority is undermined; where old loyalties fade, obligations are felt as impositions, law seems arbitrary, and respect for supe-

tionary seizure of power and a forceful restructuring of social institutions, the radical stands little chance of realizing his ideals.

Walter Vrooman was thus something more than a "restless child of progress"; he was a radical proclaiming a new ideal for his society. Harry and Hiram Greeley Vrooman were equally as radical as Walter in their social visions but were more successful in their radical roles. They realized that the radical in a democratic society is primarily an educator. As preachers, publicists, and professors of Socialism and social Christianity, Harry and Hiram probably made a more important contribution to American intellectual history than was made by Walter's erratic attempts at turning institutional innovations into mass movements. That their message went unheeded may indicate a greater adaptive vitality in American society than their analysis would have warranted.

If the radical is a prophet crying in the wilderness, it is because in rejecting the ideals of his society he has become a stranger in his own land. His analysis of the ills of society, therefore, tends to harden into the fixed categories of his ideology. The reformer may be driven to greater perception of his own ideas by his confrontation with radicalism and may even borrow and adapt ideas from it. The radical, on the other hand, learns little from the reformer, save confirmation of his own beliefs. The unwillingness to compromise, the dogmatic rigidity, and the clinging to the radical vision characterize a maturing radical. Hiram and Harry found the philosophy of fraternity of nineteenth-century Socialism too precious to be traded for the bread-and-baths Socialism of the new Socialist party of the twentieth century. For the radical his vision is a necessity for his self-identity.

---

riors is felt as a form of humiliation; where existing sources of prestige seem undeserved, hitherto accepted forms of wealth and income seem ill-gained, and government is sensed as distant, apart from the governed and not really 'representing' them. In such a situation the sense of community is lost, and the bond between social classes turns to jealousy and frustration. . . .

"No community can flourish if such negative attitudes are widespread or long-lasting. The crisis is a crisis of community itself, political, economic, sociological, personal, psychological, and moral at the same time. Actual revolution need not follow, but it is in such situations that actual revolution does arise. Something must happen, if continuing deterioration is to be avoided; some new kind or basis of community must be formed." It is in such situations that radicals' ideals may become the rallying cries of groups.

One final question needs to be asked. What sustained the Vroomans in the face of innumerable failures? Religion. Whether mani-
fested as a vague religion of humanity, as the spirit of Christian
stewardship, as the social gospel, or as militant idealism, their
religious aspirations served as the motivation for their continued
efforts. For, as they never tired of pointing out, is it not faith that
makes all things—even the impossible—seem possible?

Works by the Vrooman Family

BOOKS

Vrooman, Carl Schurz. *American Railway Problems in the Light of European Experience.* London: Oxford University Press, 1910.

————. *Carl Vrooman's Great Speech to Workingmen! Delivered to Twenty Thousand People Assembled October 3, 1896, During the National Convention of Democratic Clubs.* St. Louis: Workingmen's Bryan Club of St. Louis, 1896.

————. *The Farmer and the Shipping Bill.* Senate Doc. No. 395, 64th Cong., 1st Sess., 1916. Washington: Government Printing Office, 1916.

————. *Grain Farming in the Corn Belt with Live Stock as a Side Line.* U.S. Dept. of Agriculture Farmers' Bulletin No. 704. Washington: Government Printing Office, 1916.

————. *Initiative and Referendum in Switzerland.* Senate Doc. No. 253, 63d Cong., 2d Sess., 1913–1914. Washington: Government Printing Office, 1913.

————. *The Present Republican Opportunity: By a Democrat.* Chenoa, Ill.: by the author, 1936.

Vrooman, Carl S., and Vrooman, Julia (Scott). *The Lure and Lore of Travel.* Boston: Sherman, French & Co., 1914.

Vrooman, Frank Buffington. *British Columbia and Her Imperial Outlook.* London: Royal Colonial Institute, 1912.

————. *The New Politics.* New York: Oxford University Press, 1911.

————. *Theodore Roosevelt: Dynamic Geographer.* London: Oxford University Press, 1909.

————. *Vancouver: The Pacific Port of the Empire.* Vancouver: printed privately, 1913.

Vrooman, Hiram Greeley. *The Bible: Its True Nature and Divinity.* Boston: Massachusetts New-Church Union, 1899.

————. *The Divinity of Jesus Christ Scientifically Stated.* Chenoa, Ill.: by the author, 1936.

————. *Emanuel Swedenborg: Theologian.* Chicago: Swedenborgian Philosophical Center, 1950.

————. *The Federation of Religions.* Philadelphia: Nunc Licet Press, 1903.

_____. *Life After Death* (Thirty-Five Radio Talks Delivered Over Radio Station WMAQ). Chicago: Western New-Church Union, 1931.

_____. *Religion Rationalized*. Philadelphia: Nunc Licet Press, 1910.

_____. *Science and Theology: Their Co-ordination and Their Differences*. Chicago: Western New-Church Union, 1947.

_____. *A Skyline Sketch of Emanuel Swedenborg's "True Christian Religion."* Chenoa, Ill.: by the author, 1943.

Vrooman, Julia (Scott). *The High Road to Honor*. New York: Minton, Balch and Co., 1925.

Vrooman, Walter Watkins. *Government Ownership in Production and Distribution: An Account of 337 Now Existing National and Municipal Undertakings in the 100 Principal Countries of the World*. Baltimore: Patriotic Literature Publishing Co., 1895.

PAMPHLETS

Vrooman, Amne. "Silver Text Bible Lessons: A Sociological Interpretation of the Bible from Genesis to Joshua." *The Volunteer's Quarterly*, II (5). St. Louis: Walter Vrooman, publisher, 1897.

Vrooman, Carl Schurz. "The New Patriotism." *Monthly Bulletin of the Missouri State Board of Agriculture*, XVI (8). Jefferson City: Missouri State Board of Agriculture, 1918.

_____. "Taming the Trusts." *The Advocate Quarterly*, I. Topeka: The Advocate, 1900.

Vrooman, Walter Watkins. "The New Democracy." *The Volunteer's Quarterly*, I (1). St. Louis: by the author, 1897.

ARTICLES

Vrooman, Amne (Grafflin). "The Servant Question in Social Evolution." *The Arena*, XXV (June, 1901), 643–52.

Vrooman, Carl Schurz. "The Agricultural Revolution." *Century*, N.S. LXXI (Nov., 1916), 111–23.

_____. "American Agriculture and the League to Enforce Peace." In *Enforced Peace: Proceedings of the First Annual Assemblage of the League to Enforce Peace, Washington, May 26–27, 1916*. New York: League to Enforce Peace, 1916. Pp. 115–22.

_____. "An Apostle of Light." *The Arena*, XLI (July, 1909), 425–32.

—————. "The Best Side of Paris." *Outlook*, LXXIII (Jan., 1903), 209-12.

—————. "Boys' and Girls' Food Army." *St. Nicholas*, XLIV (Oct., 1917), 1067-71.

—————. "Can Americans Afford Safety in Railroad Travel?" *McClures*, XXIX (Aug., 1907), 421-27.

—————. "College Debating." *The Arena*, X (Oct., 1894), 677-83.

—————. "A Communication." *American Economic Review*, I (Dec., 1911), 823-26.

—————. "Constructive Conservatism: Practical Reform Is the Sanest Means of Attaining to Economic and Social Ideals." *La Follette's Magazine*, I (March 13, 1909), 7-8.

—————. "Cycling Through Tuscany and Umbria." *The Pilgrim*, VII (Aug., 1903), 9-10, 12.

—————. "Dynamic Religion." *The Washingtonian*, I (Nov., 1897), 41-48.

—————. "The Embattled Farmer." In *Democracy at the Crossroads*, ed. Ellis Meredith. New York: Warren and Putnam, 1932. Pp. 205-29.

—————. "Embattled Farmers." *The Woman Citizen*, N.S. XI (July, 1926), 11-12.

—————. "England in Revolution." *Twentieth Century*, IV (Oct., 1911), 579-85.

—————. "Fabricating Farmers." *Review of Reviews*, American Edition, LVIII (Sept., 1918), 265-68.

—————. "Family Balanced Ration." *Journal of Home Economics*, IX (Sept., 1917), 421-22.

—————. "Grand Old Man: Charles W. Eliot." *La Follette's Magazine*, I (June 5, 1909), 9, 12.

—————. "Help for the Farmer." *Outlook*, CXIII (July 12, 1916), 622-25.

—————. "A Highly Efficient State Railway Administration." *The Arena*, XLI (Jan., 1909), 20-29.

—————. "International Populists and Populism." *The New Time*, II (June, 1898), 372-74.

—————. "Jean Jaurés: A Prophet of Social Regeneration." *Twentieth Century*, III (Dec., 1910), 220-22.

—————. "Meeting the Farmer Halfway." In *Yearbook of the United States Department of Agriculture for 1916*. Washington: Government Printing Office, 1917. Pp. 63-75.

—————. "National Solidarity and the Food Supply." *Good Housekeeping*, LXV (Aug., 1917), 35.

————. "Our Railroad Riddle." *The Arena*, XL (Dec., 1908), 553–60.

————. "A Political Pilgrimage." *The Arena*, XL (Nov., 1908), 411–20.

————. "The Present Agricultural Situation." *Review of Reviews*, American Edition, LV (May, 1917), 503–505.

————. "The Present Railway Situation in the United States: Regulation Versus Public Ownership." *Twentieth Century*, VII (March, 1913), 97–106.

————. "Railway Corruption: Part I." *Twentieth Century*, I (Nov., 1909), 118–25.

————. "Railway Corruption: Part II." *Twentieth Century*, I (Dec., 1909), 221–28.

————. "Railway Nationalization in France." *The Arena*, XL (Sept., 1908), 156–63.

————. "Railway Nationalization Not Confiscatory." *The Arena*, XLI (Feb., 1909), 160–70.

————. "Rambles in Switzerland." *The Arena*, XXXVI (July, 1906), 26–34.

————. "Remarks before l'Académie d'Agriculture de France." *Comptes rendus des séances de l'Académie d'Agriculture de France*, IV (Oct. 16, 1918), 857–60.

————. "A 'Square Deal' for the Railroads." *The Arena*, XL (Oct., 1908), 273–82.

————. "Touring Tuscany à la Bohême." *Twentieth Century*, IV (Sept., 1911), 508–15.

————. "The Tyranny of Servants." *The Arena*, XXIX (Feb., 1903), 186–91.

————. "Twentieth Century Democracy." *The Arena*, XXII (Nov., 1899), 584–97.

————. "The Ultimate Issue in Railroad Accidents." *The Arena*, XXXIX (Jan., 1908), 14–19.

————. "Uses and Abuses of Italian Travel." *The Arena*, XXXIV (Oct., 1905), 354–63.

————. "We're All in the Same Boat." *Journal of Home Economics*, IX (Aug., 1917), 367–68.

————. "What American Farmers Have Done This Year." *Review of Reviews*, American Edition, LVI (Nov., 1917), 500–501.

Vrooman, Frank Buffington. "The All Canadian Falls Question." *The Arena*, XL (Sept., 1908), 129–36.

————. "British Columbia and Her Imperial Outlook." *United Empire*, III (Dec., 1912), 453–74.

————. "Child Life and the Kindergarten." *The Arena*, XIII (July, 1895), 292–99.

————. "Comments on the Panama Canal." *The Geographical Journal*, XLIV (Aug., 1914), 202.

————. "Future of Vancouver." *Dominion of Canada*, I (Dec., 1913), 6–9.

————. "The Imperial Idea: From the Point of View of Vancouver." *The Nineteenth Century and After*, LXXIII (March, 1913), 500–16.

————. "Juijutsu and the Anglo-Japanese Alliance." *British Columbia*, VIII (Jan., 1912), 57–65.

————. "Menace of the Anglo-Japanese Alliance." *Britannic Review*, I (June, 1914), 63–75.

————. "The New Bible." *The Arena*, IX (March, 1894), 466–75.

————. "Our National Library." *The Arena*, XXXVI (Sept., 1906), 277–85.

————. "Our Next Step." *Century*, N.S. LXX (June, 1916), [an insert after p. 192].

————. "The Peopling of Canada." *The Arena*, XXXIX (Feb., 1908), 186–92.

————. "Public Health and National Defence." *The Arena*, XIII (Aug., 1895), 425–35.

————. "Some Thoughts on Imperial Organization." *United Empire*, I (March, 1910), 197–203.

————. "Spoils and the Civil Service: Part I. A Retrospect." *The Arena*, XXXVII (Feb., 1907), 155–58.

————. "Spoils and the Civil Service: Part II. The Present Status of Our Civil Service." *The Arena*, XXXVII (March, 1907), 275–81.

————. "The State and Dwellings for the Poor." *The Arena*, XII (May, 1895), 415–28.

————. "Uncle Sam's Romance with Science and the Soil: Part I. The Field." *The Arena*, XXXIV (Dec., 1905), 561–68.

————. "Uncle Sam's Romance with Science and the Soil: Part II. The Stream." *The Arena*, XXXV (Jan., 1906), 36–46.

————. "Uncle Sam's Romance with Science and the Soil: Part III. The Forest." *The Arena*, XXXV (Feb., 1906), 159–63.

Vrooman, Harry Chase. "Charity, Old and New." *The Arena*, XI (Jan., 1895), 274–81.

————. "The Christian's Christmas." *The Coming Age*, I (Jan., 1899), 25–30.

————. "Crime and Enforcement of Law." *The Arena*, XII (April, 1895), 263–74.

_____. "The Ethics of Peace." *The Arena,* XI (Dec., 1894), 118–27.

_____. "Gambling." *The Arena,* XI (Feb., 1895), 416–26.

_____. "Kansas to the Front." *The Dawn,* I (June 15, 1889), 6–7.

_____. "The West." *The Dawn,* I (Nov. 15, 1889), 6–7.

Vrooman, Hiram Greeley. "A Colony University." *The Washingtonian,* I (Dec., 1897), 56–57.

_____. "Co-operation." *The Washburn Reporter,* IV (March, 1890), 3.

_____. "The Co-operative Association of America." *The Arena,* XXVIII (Dec., 1902), 602–609.

_____. "The Co-operative Association of America." *Twentieth Century,* III (Feb., 1911), 429–33.

_____. "Christian Socialism." *The Washburn Argo,* V (Feb. 18, 1890), 91–93.

_____. "Dynamic Religion." *The Washingtonian,* I (Dec., 1897), 35–38.

_____. "Economic Democracy—A Colony Plan." *The Washingtonian,* I (Nov., 1897), 22–30.

_____. "The Government Can Employ the Unemployed." *The Arena,* XXV (May, 1901), 530–36.

_____. "A National Cooperative Conference." *The Arena,* XXVII (June, 1902), 611–14.

_____. "Organization of Moral Forces." *The Arena,* IX (Feb., 1894), 348–58.

_____. "The Possibilities of the Co-operative Association of America." *The Co-operator,* I (Feb., 1901), 28–35.

_____. "The Question of Interest or Usury." *The Christian Socialist* (March 15, 1910), 8.

_____. "Science in Religion." *The Washburn Argo,* VI (Sept. 17, 1890), 3.

Vrooman, Julia (Scott). "The Assisi of St. Francis and Sabatier." *Twentieth Century,* III (Oct., 1910), 10–19.

_____. "An Awakening." *The Arena,* XL (Nov., 1908), 460–66.

_____. "Charles Wagner: Social Mystic." *Twentieth Century,* II (April, 1910), 20–26.

_____. "Revised Version of Venice." *The Arena,* XL (Dec., 1908), 527–36.

_____. "Stevenson in San Francisco." *The Arena,* XXXVIII (Nov., 1907), 526–29.

_____. "The Strange Case of Robert Louis Stevenson and Jules Simoneau." *Century,* LXXII (July, 1906), 343–50.

Vrooman, Walter Watkins. "The Church as a Missionary Field." *The Arena,* IX (April, 1894), 696–99.

————. "First Steps in the Union of Reform Forces." *The Arena,* IX (March, 1894), 540–47.

————. "Playgrounds for Children." *Harper's Weekly,* XXV (May 9, 1891), 349–50.

————. "Playgrounds for Children." *The Arena,* X (July, 1894), 284–87.

————. "South Carolina Experiment—How to Handle the Saloon Evil." *The Arena,* IX (May, 1894), 836–37.

Bibliographical Note

The primary sources for the Vrooman family activities and the secondary works on the topic of radicalism and reform are so extensive that only a limited number can be discussed in any detail in this essay. Scholars who are interested in pursuing further the many facets of this subject will find ample aid in the footnotes in the main body of this book and in the twenty-four-page formal bibliography appended to my doctoral dissertation on deposit at Harvard University.

MANUSCRIPTS

The most important manuscript collection bearing on the Vrooman family is that of Mr. and Mrs. Carl Schurz Vrooman, Bloomington, Illinois. It includes scrapbooks, incomplete correspondence files, manuscript copies of speeches and articles, diaries, and other personal memorabilia, in addition to a large collection of books dealing with economics, history, reform, religion, and agriculture. Photographs and literary items (Edwin Markham, Sarah Teasdale, Vachel Lindsay, and Henri Bergson) complete the collection. Mr. Vrooman's death in 1966 has robbed the future researcher of the rare opportunity of being guided through this mass of material by a man with a phenomenal memory and an unfailing sense of helpfulness.[1]

The Richard T. Ely papers in the manuscript collections of the State Historical Society of Wisconsin contain the correspondence among Edward Bemis, Thomas E. Will, and Frank Parsons concerning the academic freedom cases at Kansas State Agricultural College, the Buffalo Social Reform Conference, and the College of Social Sciences. The Ely papers include the correspondence between Carl Vrooman and Ely on the subjects of railway regulation, farm legislation, and postwar land policies. Also included in the collection is a letter from Walter Vrooman to Ely (June 4, 1897) acknowledging Ely's influence on his career.

The Henry Demarest Lloyd collection, also found in the manuscript collections of the State Historical Society of Wisconsin, is an invaluable source for any study of nineteenth-century radicalism and reform. The Lloyd papers include correspondence between Hiram Vrooman and Lloyd concerning the affairs of the Workers' Coöperative Association, the Co-Workers Fraternity, and the Co-operative Association of America. The papers also supply additional information on the Social Reform Union, the College of Social Sciences, Ruskin Hall, the Detroit Social and Political Conference, and the Lewiston Co-operative Conference. Particularly important is the correspondence between Lloyd and Thomas E. Will concerning the Multitude Incorporated.

The Christian Abraham Sorensen papers in the collections of the Nebraska State Historical Society, Lincoln, contain materials relative to the Committee of Fifty Proposing the National Popular Government League, the National Public Ownership League, and other Progressive groups with which Carl Vrooman was associated.

LEGAL RECORDS

Legal documents and local records in the following county courthouses, courts, and public libraries proved to be important source materials, particularly on the life of John A. Vrooman and the early career of Hiram Perkins Vrooman. The Lucas County (Ohio) Courthouse contains most of the land deeds, mortgages, and tax records covering Sylvania, Ohio, where John A. Vrooman settled in 1837. The census records of 1840 and 1850 for Lucas County are available in the local history room of the Toledo Public Library. Monroe County and St. Clair County records in Michigan cover the Vrooman activities in Monroe and Port Huron. The minutes of the Port Huron Common Council are available in the Port Huron City Hall. For Hiram's activities in Missouri from 1865 to 1875 the Macon County records proved invaluable, since the city records (including Carl Vrooman's birth certificate) were destroyed by fire

---

[1] During my visit in Nov., 1960, Carl Vrooman consented to tape-record an hour interview to supplement my extensive notes on our conversations. This tape is now in my possession.

in 1900. Hiram's brief stay in Decatur, Illinois, from 1875 to 1876 can be traced in the Macon County Courthouse.

Newspaper coverage for Hiram Perkins Vrooman's career in Kansas, 1876–1892, was so extensive that legal records did not have to be consulted. In untangling Walter Vrooman's activities in Ruskin College, the Western Cooperative Association, and the Multitude Incorporated, the records in the Grundy County (Missouri) Courthouse were significant. Additional information on Walter's activities in Kansas City and on his divorce can be found in the Jackson County, Missouri, and Wyandotte County, Kansas, records. Legal records for *Vrooman et al.* v. *Grafflin et al.,* 96 Fed. 278 (4th Cir. 1899) can be found in the standard federal reports, but the papers for *Wallace* v. *Klondike, Yukon, and Copper River Company et al.* are in the records of the Circuit Court in Cook County, Illinois.

The archives of Washburn University in Topeka contain the admission and grade records of the Vrooman brothers for 1881 through 1892, faculty minute books, and programs of public ceremonies, in addition to valuable printed sources. The existence of an undergraduate Socialist Club at Washburn in 1884–1885 can be documented by these sources, and the intellectual climate at Washburn can be reconstructed from the minutes of the undergraduate debating clubs. The archives of the Congregational Church, also housed at Washburn, contain the congregational minute books for the First Congregational Church of Independence, Kansas, and the Pilgrim Congregational Church of Kansas City, Kansas, with which the Vroomans were associated in the late 1880's. The record of Frank Vrooman's "heresy" trial by the Synod of Illinois of the Presbyterian Church U.S.A. are deposited in the Virginia Library, McCormack Theological Seminary, Chicago.

NEWSPAPERS AND PERIODICALS

A number of newspapers and periodicals deserve special mention because of the richness of the material contained in them. They are arranged here chronologically in order to relate them to special topics.

For Hiram Perkins Vrooman's activities in Michigan from 1850 to 1865 the best sources are the microfilms of the Monroe *Commercial* in the Monroe Evening News building in Monroe, Michigan, and the files of the Port Huron *Press* in the Carnegie Public Library, Port Huron, Michigan. Unfortunately, the files of the St. Clair County newspaper for this period were burned in 1948.

For Hiram's activities in Missouri from 1865 to 1875 the microfilm copies of the Macon *Argus,* the Macon *Journal,* the Macon *Republican,* and the Missouri *Granger* in the Missouri State Historical Society collection at Columbia are extremely valuable. His brief stay in Decatur, Illinois, can be traced through the files of the Decatur newspapers.

The newspaper sources in the Kansas Historical Society collection in Topeka are so numerous that they merit individual comment. Hiram's role in the Greenback-Labor, Prohibition, and Anti-Monopoly parties can be followed in the Council Grove *Democrat,* 1876–1878, and the Eureka *Herald,* 1879–1880. The activities of the Vrooman boys at Washburn and in Topeka can be traced in files of the *Washburn Reporter,* the Topeka *Daily Citizen,* and the Topeka *Commonwealth* for 1881–1886. The last is particularly important for information about Harry Vrooman's role in Burnett Haskell's "Red International" anarchist movement. The *Kansas Workman,* published in Quenemo, was a clearinghouse for Vrooman family activities in 1886. The file is complete and very important. Unfortunately, I have been unable to locate any copies of the *Labor Organizer,* published by Walter and Harry in Kansas City, Missouri, as a pioneering Socialist newspaper. The Kansas Historical Society collection also includes a collection of biographical clippings that are spotty in coverage but useful.

Walter, Harry, and Hiram Greeley Vrooman's relationships to Socialism between 1887 and 1890 can be traced through the *Workman's Advocate* (New Haven), which is available in the New England Deposit Library, Cambridge, Massachusetts, and in the microfilm copies of the *Labor Enquirer* (Denver and Chicago) in the State Historical Society of Wisconsin collection. Harry edited the Socialist newspaper *The People* in Providence from October, 1887, to May, 1888. A complete set is held by the Rhode Island Historical Society for future microfilming and is not available for use at this time. Fortunately, the Brown University Library has a few copies. The primary material on the Vroomans in the Christian Socialist and Bellamy Nationalist movements can be followed through *The Dawn* (Boston), *The Nationalist* (Boston), and *The Washburn Argo*. The first two periodicals are available in the major libraries in the Boston area; the latter is in the Washburn archives.

The social gospel and civic improvement activities of the Vrooman brothers can best be followed by tracing the actions of the individual brothers. For Walter's activities in New York City, see the New York *Times* for November and December, 1891, and Harlan Phillips' dissertation at the Columbia Teachers College Library. For Frank's activities in Worcester, Massachusetts, the Worcester *Evening Gazette* and the *Massachusetts Spy* files are the most rewarding. For Harry, Hiram G., and Carl's roles in these ventures and in the Union for Practical Progress the best source is *The Arena* magazine, edited by Benjamin Orange Flower. The Boston Public Library set contains important supplements not usually found in bound copies of *The Arena*. Frank's articles on religion and Walter's articles on the organizing of reform and radical forces also appear in *The Arena.*

Since the Vroomans came late to Populism, the standard western and southern sources are of little value for their story. Their theoretical debate over the role of the state can be followed in their *Arena* articles, 1895–1899. Walter Vrooman's role in Missouri politics can be traced through Phillips' dissertation, Lee Meriwether's autobiography, and Walter's writings. As far as I know, the St. Louis Public Library has the only available copy of Walter's *Sacred Biography for Boys and Girls*. Carl Vrooman's relation to Populism in Kansas was so intimately bound up with the academic freedom controversy at Kansas State Agricultural College that the best source for this phase of his career is *The Industrialist* magazine for July, 1897, through July, 1899. The *New Time* magazine, in which he published his important article on Populism in 1898, is available in the Widener Library, Harvard. Clippings in the Kansas Historical Society collection are also important for tracing Carl's relation to Populism.

Carl's role in the College of Social Sciences scheme is found mainly in the Ely and Lloyd papers, but important information is contained in several small reform journals available in the Widener Library. These are *The Coming Age* (Boston and St. Louis, January–September, 1899), *The Social Forum* (Chicago, 1899–1900), and *The Publications of the Social Reform Union* (Alhambra, California, 1899–1901). Walter's activities at Ruskin Hall in England and his writings for this period can be found in the *Young Oxford* magazine in Sterling Memorial Library, Yale University. Hiram Greeley Vrooman's role in the cooperative movement is found in his articles in *The Washingtonian* magazine for 1897, available only in the Widener Library; in *The American Fabian* for 1899, available in the Boston Public Library; in *The Co-operator* (Lewiston, Maine) for 1901–1902, available in the State Historical Society of Wisconsin collections; and in his *Arena* articles. Only one set of *The Multitude* magazine for 1902–1903 exists, to my knowledge. This is listed in the catalog of the Kansas City, Missouri, Public Library. However, it was lost in 1961 when the library moved its collections to a new building.

Frank and Carl's intellectual responses to Progressivism can be followed in their magazine articles and books listed in the bibliography of their writings, and I will make only a few comments here. Carl contributed to three ephemeral magazines edited by former associates—*The Pilgrim* (Battle Creek, Michigan), edited by Willis J. Abbot, *La Follette's Magazine* (Madison, Wisconsin), edited by Robert La Follette, and *The Twentieth Century* (Boston), edited by B. O. Flower after the demise of *The Arena*. Incomplete sets of these magazines are in the Harvard collections. Frank Vrooman's extensive activities in British Columbia are evident in the bibliography of his writings. He edited the magazine *British Columbia* at one point, but copies are not available in this country.

Carl's political campaigns and his service in the Wilson administration from 1914 to 1919 and his role in the agricultural relief legislation in the 1920's can best be traced through the New York *Times* and the relevant public documents. A few magazines are particularly important, however. *The Commoner* reveals Bryan's reactions to the situation in Illinois in 1914, although *Harper's Weekly* and *Colliers* provide more objective accounts of the same events. Carl's wartime articles in *Outlook, Review of Reviews, Good Housekeeping,* and *Century* are important for capturing the flavor of the wartime debate on conservation and food regulation and probably represent the widest audience that he reached in his career. By contrast, his magazine articles in the 1920's were placed in *The Woman Citizen,* a journal of the League of Women Voters, *The Farm Journal,* and other specialized, low-circulation journals. By the 1930's he was issuing his own works privately from a local press in Chenoa, Illinois.

SECONDARY SOURCES

The specialized secondary studies used in the preparation of this book are indicated in the footnotes. A few works are so pertinent to the interpretation established in this book that they require some additional comment.

Irwin Unger's prize-winning book, *The Greenback Era: A Social and Political History of American Finance, 1865–1879* (Princeton: Princeton University Press, 1964) places the financial issues of this period in their ideological setting and helps to establish an entrepreneurial perspective to the Reconstruction era that breaks the confines of traditional approaches to this period. He slights the important western Greenback movement, however, to concentrate on developments elsewhere. My findings on Missouri and Kansas Greenbackism tend to support his conclusions and supplement them on one point. He interprets the Independent (Greenback) vote in Kansas in 1876 as largely rural, basing this on the work of Clyde O. Ruggles, who analyzed the economic basis of Greenbackism in Iowa and Wisconsin. My evidence would emphasize the role of small-town entrepreneurs instead of the isolated, single-crop farmers emphasized by Ruggles and accepted by Unger. See Unger, *Greenback Era,* p. 319, n. 81. W. R. Brock, *An American Crisis: Congress and Reconstruction, 1865–1867* (London: Macmillan, 1963), 73–94, provides an excellent summary on Republican entrepreneurialism among the radicals that could equally apply to such men as Hiram Perkins Vrooman.

The literature on reform and radical movements in Kansas in the

1870's and 1880's is sparse and suffers from the prevailing preoccupation with explaining the agrarian roots of Populism. The findings of this study indicate that a small-town entrepreneurial tradition of reform existed in this period and may have helped to provide leadership for the Populists later. Richard Hofstadter, *The Age of Reform: From Bryan to F.D.R.* (New York: Alfred A. Knopf, 1956), 73 and 101–102, called attention to this feature of the Populist leadership but did not explore it except to note the role of the veterans of earlier antimonopoly campaigns. James C. Malin, *A Concern About Humanity: Notes on Reform, 1872–1912, at the National and Kansas Levels of Thought* (Lawrence, Kans.: by the author, 1964) approaches the problems of continuity in reform traditions from an analysis of third-party platforms. He opens up a number of interesting lines of investigation but ultimately fails to satisfy either himself or his readers because of his doubts about the definition of reform. By making reform equivalent to structural change in society he is caught in the methodological problem of saying that all change is inherently reformist, whether intentionally willed or not. By trying to avoid making value judgments for the sake of "objectivity" he is unable to evaluate the contribution of third-party ideas to the process of social change. The opposite problem plagues Chester McArthur Destler's important essay, "Western Radicalism, 1865–1901: Concepts and Origins," *Mississippi Valley Historical Review,* XXXI (Dec., 1944). He passionately asserts the existence of a native American radicalism based on antimonopoly, economic collectivism, and direct democracy. By not defining radicalism operationally, he is hard-pressed to deny that his radicalism is little more than New Deal reformism read back into the earlier period.

The literature on Socialism in the 1870's and 1880's also suffers from the methodological assumption that Socialism is wholly a foreign importation and that its adaptation to American conditions must be explained. Howard Quint, *The Forging of American Socialism: Origins of the Modern Movement* (Columbia: University of South Carolina Press, 1953) overcomes this limitation by incorporating native American, non-Marxian influences into his study. As the story of the Vrooman brothers indicates, there were non-Marxian sources of American Socialism in the liberal theology of the period. These influences interacted with the imported Marxian ideas and then flowed into the Christian Socialist movement. James Dombrowski, *The Early Days of Christian Socialism in America* (New York: Columbia University Press, 1936) emphasizes the indigenous influences in Christian Socialism but ends his survey with 1900. Some material on the relation of Hiram G. and Harry Vrooman to the Christian Socialist Fellowship of 1906–1910 was included in my doctoral dissertation, but the twentieth-century movement has been neglected by historians who have been more concerned with the fate of the Socialist party or the origins of Communism.

Two works were helpful in establishing the perspective of the labor movement utilized in this book. Norman Ware, *The Labor Movement in the United States, 1860–1895: A Study in Democracy* (New York: D. Appleton, 1929) has a humane understanding of the quasi-religious sources of reform unionism that has been lost from more recent institutional studies of the same period. Gerald N. Grob, *Workers and Utopia: A Study of Ideological Conflict in the American Labor Movement 1865–1900* (Evanston: Northwestern University Press, 1961) clarified the conflict between reform and trade unionism without distorting either.

On the question of Populism, Richard Hofstadter performed a service for all American historians in his *Age of Reform* when he laid to rest the ghosts of the frontier theory that still haunted the discussion of Populism. He then opened up new lines of analysis by stressing ideological, psychological, and institutional factors in Populist rhetoric and agrarian agitation in the early twentieth century. While I have indicated in the introduction that I do not share all of Hofstadter's methodological assumptions, I have found some of his suggestions useful in the context of the Vrooman story. In addition to his recognition of the nonagrarian origins of Populist leadership, I also found his concept of a shift in agrarian tactics in the early twentieth century to be useful in examining the career of Carl Vrooman. I am unable to agree with Norman Pollack, *The Populist Response to Industrial America: Midwestern Populist Thought* (Cambridge: Harvard University Press, 1962) and *The Populist Mind* (Indianapolis: Bobbs-Merrill, 1967) on both methodological and substantive grounds. By concentrating on the Populist critique and failing to ask searching questions about their platform he conveys the impression that the rank-and-file Populists were more radical than some of their leaders. At best, we could agree that there were radical individuals and intellectuals in the Populist ranks, such as Henry Demarest Lloyd or even Hiram Greeley Vrooman, who intended to use the movement for their own ideological purposes. Whether they were *representative* of Populist thought at large is a matter of interpretation resting on how one uses voting statistics and public documents, such as party platforms. In short, Pollack slights the Populists' means and assumes that their goals were similar to his. But, if the Populists were as radical as Pollack indicates, why were their platform proposals so moderate? Their suggestions were extreme only on the railroad question and the subtreasury plan, and even these were hedged with qualifications. I tend to agree with Quint and Destler that the Populists' means were designed to achieve entrepreneurially defined ends and that their critique stands in a similar tradition. Furthermore, an analysis of the concepts of equality embodied in the most representative Populist documents puts the majority of Populists in the entrepreneurial tradition of reform.

On the question of Progressivism I have found Hofstadter's *Age of Reform* unacceptable in some of its broader theoretical conclusions but useful in specific conceptions. Neither Frank nor Carl Vrooman would fit the Status Revolution theory of the origins of Progressive leadership, but their concern for institutional issues in solving specific problems does fit the pattern described by Hofstadter. Arthur S. Link's studies of Woodrow Wilson provided important background information, but I do not share his views on the relation of radicalism and reform. Link is primarily concerned with the emergence of a welfare state in the 1930's and tends to judge all groups in the Progressive era in reference to this. Thus, radicals and reformers are seen as taking advanced, moderate, or conservative stands as their programs approximate this goal, and all other considerations are secondary. He also favors a social justice definition of Progressivism, similar to Eric Goldman's in *Rendezvous with Destiny,* which slights the entrepreneurial or efficiency side of Progressivism.

In interpreting the agricultural crisis of the 1920's James H. Shideler, *Farm Crisis, 1919–1923* (Berkeley: University of California Press, 1957) establishes a broad and fundamentally sound perspective for the critical period involved in Carl Vrooman's postwar efforts. Shideler's analysis is free of the regionalism and special pleading that mar some of the more specialized works on the same period. The role of such independent farm spokesmen as Carl Vrooman in the late 1920's and early 1930's has not received much attention, because historians have been more concerned with the McNary-Haugen movement, Hoover's Farm Board, and the Farm Bureau's role in the establishment of the Agricultural Adjustment Administration. As a result, the presence of an old-line Progressive group which was dissatisfied with the New Deal has been slighted. Otis L. Graham's *An Encore for Reform: The Old Progressives and the New Deal* (New York: Oxford University Press, 1967), which appeared while this book was in preparation, does much to overcome this deficiency but concentrates mainly on urban Progressives.

Finally, three secondary works were helpful in establishing the Vrooman story. Grace Vrooman Wickersham and Ernest B. Comstock, *The Vrooman Family in America: The Descendants of Hendrick Meese Vrooman, Who Came from Holland to America in 1664* (Dallas: privately printed, 1949) is important in clarifying family relationships but is unreliable in biographical details. Harlan Buddington Phillips, "Walter Vrooman: Restless Child of Progress" (unpublished Ph.D. dissertation, Dept. of History, Columbia University, 1954), is very reliable on biographical details, although I disagree with the writer's final assessment of Walter's role in American history. Selected chapters have been published separately in *South Atlantic Quarterly* (April, 1951), *New York History* (Jan., 1952), and *Pennsylvania Magazine of History and Biography* (1952). My own dissertation, "The Vrooman Brothers and the American Reform Tradition" (Dept. of History, Harvard University, 1962) is available at the Widener Library, Harvard.

Index